Eisenstein, Cinema, and History

Eisenstein, Cinema, and History

James Goodwin

University of Illinois Press   Urbana and Chicago

Library of Congress Cataloging-in-Publication Data

Goodwin, James, 1945–
    Eisenstein, cinema, and history / James Goodwin.
        p.   cm.
    Includes bibliographical references and index.
    ISBN 0-252-01964-4 (cloth : acid-free). —ISBN 0-252-06269-8 (pbk.)
    1. Eisenstein, Sergei, 1898–1948—Criticism and interpretation.
2. Historical films—Soviet Union—History and criticism.   3. Motion
pictures—Political aspects—Soviet Union.   4. Marxism.   I. Title.
PN1998.3.E34G66   1993
791.43'0233'092—dc20   92–24035
                                                          CIP

For my mother,
and my family—present and future

Contents

Preface   ix

A Note on Abbreviations, Translations, and
    Transliterations   xi

Introduction   1

1   Revolutionary Beginnings: From
      Theater to Cinema   16

2   *Strike:* The Beginnings of Revolution   37

3   *Battleship Potemkin:* Pathos and Politics   57

4   *October:* History and Genesis   79

5   *Old and New:* History and Utopia   98

6   Dislocation: Projects, 1929–32   120

7   Disjunction: Projects, 1932–37   139

8   *Alexander Nevsky:* The Great Man in
      History   156

9   *Ivan the Terrible:* An Inversion of History   179

Conclusion   210

Notes   221

Filmography   237

Bibliography   243

Index   257

Illustrations follow page 138

Preface

Russian history is being remade for the third time in this century. After the 1917 Bolshevik Revolution and Stalin's "revolution from above," the process of restructuring, or *perestroika*, has brought the Soviet era to an end. Though the Soviet Union is now dissolved, much Soviet history remains to be written on the basis of old materials recently made public. The films of Sergei Eisenstein are important to our understanding of the Soviet versions and visions of history that resulted from the Bolshevik Revolution and the period of Stalin. Eisenstein's cinema profoundly addresses issues of the cultural meaning and historical fate of modern communism.

Apart from my assessment of the most important secondary works on Eisenstein, which can be found in the Introduction, I do not discuss extensively in the present book the critical positions on Eisenstein within film theory, a subject that would require another book altogether. Nor for the most part do I pursue the counterparts and counterpoints to my findings among the many books and articles published on Eisenstein, a project that would become encyclopedic. The bibliography provided indicates the scope of the scholarship I have consulted in my research.

The exchange of ideas with colleagues in conversation, in correspondence, and at conferences over the years has nurtured my understanding of matters pursued in this book. Foremost among these colleagues is Ronald Gottesman, who tutored and tirelessly encouraged my first work in film studies and who remains a greatly valued critic and friend. At its early stages, my study of Eisenstein and Marxism benefited from the insights and opinions of Dudley Andrew, Terry Castle, Raymond Durgnat, Steven Hill, Robert Maniquis, and many associates at the *Quarterly Review of Film Studies* (now *Quarterly Review of Film and Video*): Nick Browne, Regina Fadiman, Albert LaValley, Stephen Mamber, Michael Renov, Richard Whitehall, and two colleagues deeply missed, Beverle Huston and Katherine Kovacs. I am indebted to Vance Kepley, Jr., for expert advice and key editorial suggestions during the final revision of my manuscript for this book. Invaluable personal support and motivation has come from my wife, Andrea, and my daughter, Lonnie.

My knowledge of Soviet cinema owes much not only to the publications cited in the Introduction, but also to the work of the film historians, translators, and critics Marco Carynnyk, Ian Christie, Harry Geduld, Ronald Gottesman, Steven Hill, Vance and Betty Kepley, Nikita Lary, Alma Law, Ronald Levaco, Jay Leyda, Herbert Marshall, Judith Mayne, Annette Michelson, Ivor Montagu, Vlada Petric, Roberta Reeder, Luda and Jean Schnitzer, Richard Taylor, Yuri Tsivian, Alan Upchurch, Nick Worrall, and Denise Youngblood. My understanding of Soviet history, politics, and culture has benefited from the work of scholars who are independent of the Cold War ideology that has limited other Soviet studies in the West, scholars such as John Barber, John Bowlt, Katerina Clark, Stephen Cohen, Sheila Fitzpatrick, Mel Gordon, Peter Kenez, Moshe Lewin, Herbert Marcuse, Richard Stites, and Robert Tucker.

I am grateful for research support and a travel grant from the Committee on Research of the Academic Senate, University of California at Los Angeles. My research was facilitated by librarians and staff at the UCLA Theater Arts Library, the Academy of Motion Picture Arts and Sciences Library, the University of Southern California Cinema Library, the New York Public Library of Performing Arts, and the Museum of Modern Art Library. My work with film materials was aided by Audio-Brandon, Inc., Murray Glass of Em Gee Film Library, Charles Silver and Jon Gartenberg of the Museum of Modern Art Film Library, Carol Prescot and Patricia O'Donnell of the UCLA Instructional Media Library, and the UCLA Film and Television Archives. The Museum of Modern Art has granted permission for the use of photographic illustrations from its Film Stills Archive.

For assistance in the preparation of early typescript drafts of the manuscript I am grateful to Jeanette Gilkison of UCLA. For translation from German sources I wish to thank Charles de Bedts. I am indebted to Corinne Blackmer for research assistance, translation of material in Russian, and insights into Russian language and culture. All translations from French sources are my own. Ann Lowry and Carol Bolton Betts of the University of Illinois Press have provided expert guidance during the editing process.

A Note on Abbreviations, Translations, and Transliterations

After a first citation in endnotes for the major collections in English of Eisenstein's writings, this book cites them in the text using the following abbreviations:

FE *Film Essays*. Ed. and trans. Jay Leyda. New York: Praeger, 1970.
FF *Film Form: Essays in Film Theory*. Ed. and trans. Jay Leyda. New York: Harcourt, 1949.
FS *The Film Sense*. Ed. and trans. Jay Leyda. New York: Harcourt, 1947.
IM *Immoral Memories*. Trans. Herbert Marshall. Boston: Houghton, 1983.
N   *Notes of a Film Director*. Trans. X. Danko. New York: Dover, 1970.
NN *Nonindifferent Nature*. Trans. Herbert Marshall. New York: Cambridge University Press, 1987.
W   *Selected Works*. Vol. 1. Ed. and trans. Richard Taylor. Bloomington: Indiana University Press, 1988.

With Eisenstein's writings in the period 1922–34 where there is a choice in English translations between editions by Jay Leyda and that by Richard Taylor, I have generally selected the latter. In certain cases, however, as in that of the 1929 essay "Methods of Montage," I have followed the Leyda translation. "Methods of Montage" was not published in Russian in Eisenstein's lifetime. It appeared first in English translation in 1930 and then in a new translation for the 1949 *Film Form* volume. Taylor's translation of the essay, based on the first Russian publication in *Izbrannye proizvedeniya* 2 (1964), lacks an allusion central to Eisenstein's thought at the time, his analogy between the cream separator in *Old and New* and the Holy Grail.

For Russian names, titles, and familiar words I have followed the accepted transliterations generally used in English-language publications. For the unfamiliar Russian words included in this book, I have applied the Library of Congress system of transliteration.

Introduction

The importance of Sergei Eisenstein within cinema and the theory of film is unquestionably great. One commonly held belief, however, is that Eisenstein is an important director irrespective of the specific politics in his films and the immediate historical contexts of his art and theory. The present study takes the position that the relationships of Eisenstein's work to revolutionary history and to Marxist thought are formative and fundamental. Eisenstein is preeminently an artist of historical subjects and themes. And Marxism is essential, not circumstantial, to Eisenstein's imagination and to the representation of history in his cinema. His film works in the 1920s represent history within the trajectory of modern mass revolution while the works of the 1930s and 1940s weigh the meaning of a history anterior to both mass politics and modern revolution.

The extremely fertile years prior to Eisenstein's career in film, 1917 to 1923, were a period of broad debate and open experimentation about the connections between art and radical politics in the Soviet Union. As a theater designer and director, Eisenstein took a prominent role in these controversies and experiments, continued to do so in creating his silent films, and publicly defended some of his earlier, now unorthodox positions during the Stalin era. Over his career, in both films and writings, he made extensive efforts to analyze society and culture as historical and ideological formations. The contexts for these analyses in his writings and imagination are usually multiform and can entail such diverse components as art history, perceptual psychology, literary criticism, linguistics, cross-cultural study, political history, anthropology, sociology, and philosophy. Their philosophical context and analytic method often draw upon the work of Hegel, Marx, Engels, and Lenin for postulates to Eisenstein's own speculations.

Historical subject matter was common in Soviet cinema during Eisenstein's career, particularly in the silent period. In the period 1925 through 1929, for example, fully one-third of new Soviet feature releases concerned the history of the revolutionary movement in some form. Eisenstein's completed films and the major unfinished projects are all representations of history, but the historical depth and complexity of his imagination has remained largely unexplored in critical books on his life-work. In subject matter and treatment his perspective on history and its dynamics changes significantly between the silent films and the sound ones. The silent features vary in historical setting from the Bolshevik Revolution's formative period to its utopian projection into a near future. Their temporality is one of immediacy and constant change. Their conception of history's momentum is developed in terms of individual alienation and collective emancipation. The completed sound features are set in the medieval and Renaissance periods, which are recreated as eras of heroic individuality and stateliness. Russia's movement toward modern history is represented in terms of an autocratic seizure of power and national unification.

Eisenstein's lifework was itself subject to history, as he was acutely aware while nine years passed between his last silent film and the release of his first sound film. This differential between the silent and sound periods in Eisenstein's career is marked by the divergent political circumstances under which his film productions were suppressed. In Hollywood, Paramount refused the *Sutter's Gold* and *An American Tragedy* projects for reasons of commercial censorship. The *Que Viva Mexico!* footage was withheld after explicit warnings from Stalin and the breakdown of Eisenstein's agreement with the socialist author Upton Sinclair. After Eisenstein's return to the Soviet Union, the Party condemned *Bezhin Meadow* for its ideological offenses.

The differential is also contemporary with the rewriting of Party history that begins under Stalin's directives in 1931 and is followed by the purge trials of Old Bolsheviks and the Party liquidations. Over the twenty-five years of Eisenstein's film work the meaning of Marxism in Soviet politics and culture changed dramatically. The period of his career opens, in effect, with Trotsky's call for permanent revolution and Lenin's vision of international workers' unity, two essential policies from the inception of Marx's activism in the 1840s. The period closes with Stalin's statist program of socialism in one country, Soviet imperialism, and the enforcement of dialectical materialism as intellectual orthodoxy.

In the finished films there are two primary kinds of historiography, which roughly correspond to the two periods of Eisenstein's career. In his films of the 1920s, history is a process depicted in progress at the intersection of policy and chance, of plan and circumstance. Its properties are related to qualities of discourse, aleatory action, spontaneity of form, and the revolutionary outbreak. In *Alexander Nevsky* and *Ivan the Terrible*, on the other hand, history is an account of a completed past contextualized by the present, with properties corresponding to qualities of narration, closure, conventional form, and myths of individual destiny.

In considering Eisenstein's imagination and art as essentially historiographic, I have pursued a perception made by Hayden White in his extensive comparisons of historical writing to genres of fictional and dramatic literature. White has observed that in all historical writing "our desire for the imaginary, the possible, must contest with the imperatives of the real, the actual."[1] Marc Ferro, another historian, insists that the fiction film is a significant document for the study of society. Ferro seeks to reverse assumptions within the discipline of history whereby "the fiction film is despised because it dispenses only a dream, as if the dream formed no part of reality, as though the imaginary were not one of the driving forces of human activity."[2] Accordingly, in his own studies of film Ferro grants the imaginary central status as a mode of history and as a subject of historical inquiry.

Narrative and discourse, which linguists and critics like Emile Benveniste and Gerard Genette place as opposite poles of language use, are combined in the historical imagination to provide real events both a plot structure and a paradigm of explanation. Narration and narrativity are the functions through which the disparate claims of the past and the imaginary are mediated into a discourse. Discourse is the plane where events and interpretations are interrelated to give a specific structure of meaning. To write history is to constitute a meaning, to have events figure forth their significance. Every historical account conducts interpretation at two levels: one in which a story is derived from the chronicle of past events and another in which the significance of that story is progressively disclosed.

For Marx, historical knowledge was equivalent to the matter of consciousness, which had been largely examined prior to Hegel within the confines of philosophical categories. To explain historical change required development of a new mode of consciousness. With this purpose, history ceases to be a *reflection* of the past and becomes a *reflexive* instrument in comprehending present society's forms and structures. Furthermore, Marx's method promises equally to explain the historical process and to disclose the method's own procedures of explanation. The paradigms of perception and knowledge in Eisenstein's cinema share similar intentions with such a historiography.

In significant ways the core categories of Marxist thought—history, materialism, and dialectics—have functions within Eisenstein's films and his theories about them. While these three constituents do not automatically combine to form the historical materialism of Marx or the dialectical materialism of Engels, as on occasion Eisenstein would enthusiastically claim, these formulations were the dominant ideas within the society in which Eisenstein lived and worked. Across political history there is, of course, a plurality of Marxisms. To cite just those relevant in the present context, there are the formation of Marx's historical materialism in the nineteenth century; its completion and explication through Engels; Engels's own elaboration of dialectical materialism and its application to fields like anthropology and the natural sciences; the historical reformulation of Marx and Engels's ideas in revolutionary Russia during Lenin's time; and the institutionalization of dialectical materialism in the Stalin period. In these circumstances, no unified Marxist theory developed historically in the Soviet Union, but one was imposed politically by the Party and state under Stalin. This official Marxism in some important instances dictated Eisenstein's artistic life in the 1930s and 1940s. The Marxism of his art and thought, however, was never a matter of conformity to official orthodoxy. His work has a distinct and in places adversarial relationship to the Soviet Union's political lines and cultural policies.

That the categories history, materialism, and dialectics have a functional role in Eisenstein's work is apparent in even a superficial survey of his career. He published the first theoretical statement on his methods of film production—"The Problem of the Materialist Approach to Form"— in 1925 in connection with *Strike*, whose form is claimed to embody revolutionary reality. His development of intellectual cinema in the late 1920s through *October* and *Old and New* and the essays on a dialectical method of montage culminate with a film project based on Marx's *Capital*. The emphasis in the project was on capital accumulation, the fetishism of commodities, and the labor theory of value. At the end of his career, *Ivan the Terrible* provides a tragicomic representation of Russia's autocratic past that accords with Marx's dialectical interpretation of historical recurrence in *The 18th Brumaire of Louis Bonaparte*.

Marx's Historiography

The materialist conception of history is Marx's most pervasive contribution to modern thought. In an early delineation of the materialist conception as opposed to Hegel's idealism, Marx and Engels write in *The Holy Family* (1845): "*History* does *nothing*, it 'possesses *no* immense wealth,' it 'wages *no* battles.' It is *man*, real, living man who does all that, who possesses and fights; 'history' is not, as it were, a person apart, using man as a means to achieve *its own* aims; history is *nothing but* the activity of man pursuing his aims."[3] In its later exposition, the materialist conception advances the principle that economic structure, comprised of the material means and social relations of production, is the real foundation of all society from which arises a superstructure comprised of politics, law, morality, religion, metaphysics, culture—in short, all aspects of social consciousness. Within the economic base, historical development of the material forces of production determines changes in the social relations of production. Through such a process, the "mode of production of material life conditions the social, political and intellectual life process in general."[4]

Dialectics has been variously defined and applied within Marxism, as will become evident in my discussion of the Soviet contexts. For our introductory purposes here, it is to be understood as a method for Marx, a process of reason necessary to differentiate appearances and false theories from the material bases of reality. This epistemology, in the words of *Capital,* "regards every historically developed social form as in fluid movement and therefore takes into account its transient nature not less than its momentary existence; because it lets nothing impose upon it, and is in its essence critical and revolutionary."[5] What began in early Greek philosophy as a rhetorical form, designed to expose the paradoxes and logical inconsistencies in an adversary's reasoning, became for Marx a scientific approach that identifies the contradictions in thought and in social institutions (its critical function) by locating the contradictions in economic reality (its revolutionary function).

Dialectical materialism, a term Marx himself did not use, derives from Engels's extension of dialectics to natural science in positing dialectics as universal law. Developed as a natural philosophy after the Bolshevik Revolution, dialectical materialism has as its fundamental properties the transformation of quantity into quality, the unity of opposites, and the negation of the negation. These properties are claimed to be present equally in nature, society, and thought. With the policy of "revolution from above" as the state's rationale under Stalin, dialectical materialism became orthodoxy under the exclusive authority of Party interpretation.

The key connectives in Marx's thought are *critique* and *ideology,* two parameters also fundamental to any comprehensive understanding of Eisenstein's imagination. Marx, who used the term *critique* in titling all his major theoretical inquiries, employed it to designate a radical negation of existing bourgeois order and the dominant complex of theories by philosophers and social scientists in support of that order. A Marxist critique of the categories and modes of bourgeois thought exposes the material and historical basis of social reality and of its expressions as religion, philosophy, politics, and other forms of social consciousness. Parallel to this critical project is the concurrent social project undertaken through class struggle. The proletariat is the social force necessary to carry out in history the materialist critique of political economy. Thus critique functions simultaneously as an instrument of thought and as a weapon of class struggle. Marx's call for a *"ruthless criticism of everything existing,"* a remark published in 1843 that has long been treated as his motto, implies that criticism must not be afraid of its own intellectual conclusions, nor of its political conflict with the ruling powers.[6]

The term *ideology* has a complex evolution within twentieth-century

Marxism and is now widely applied in film studies. Given this situation, it is useful to restore the term to its original contexts in Marx and Engels. Its first full exposition comes in *The German Ideology* (1846), where it describes thought abstracted from the real processes of history. Such thought exists in a realm of ideas segregated from material considerations. Ideology can present a worldview coherent and sufficient unto itself, but the view is illusory and ultimately false since it is derived from consciousness alone. Though ideology is false consciousness, it yields truth value when recontextualized in the material conditions of its historical origins. In a well-known comparison, Marx defines ideology as a seemingly clear and complete—yet actually projected and inverted—image of real relations in the world: "If in all ideology men and their circumstances appear upside-down as in a *camera obscura*, this phenomenon arises just as much from their historical life-process as the inversion of objects on the retina does from their physical life-process."[7] Philosophers have formulated absolutes starting from ideas instead of material conditions because ruling social powers have placed idealizations—God, King, State—above humanity. Ideology's inversions correspond to inversions within history.

In elaborating this definition, Marx indicates that overturning the inversion is a matter of "setting out from real, active men, and on the basis of their real life-process demonstrating the development of the ideological reflexes and echoes of this life-process."[8] Where the *camera obscura* analogy suggests a paradigm of reflection, with connotations of passive and static replication, *reflex* is a more complex analogy. While retaining the sense of a reflected or copied image, it adds at least two dynamics: a process of reception, transmission, and reaction from one level to another and a habitual, predictable way of thinking or behaving. In this sense ideology is a relay from economic reality to social consciousness and its cultural forms.

For the most part, Marx and Engels presented these dynamics as unilateral, moving from base to superstructure. As the years of editing the third volume of *Capital* drew to a close, however, Engels pointed to an omission in their work regarding ideology that adversaries use to misrepresent historical materialism: "We all laid, and *were bound* to lay, the main emphasis, in the first place, on the *derivation* of political, juridical and other ideological notions, and of actions arising through the medium of these notions, from basic economic facts. But in doing so we neglected the formal side—the ways and means by which these notions, etc., come about—for the sake of content." While Engels denies ideology a history all its own, independent of material productive forces (which remain in the final instance the determining factors of historical content), he refuses to disclaim its effect upon history. Such disclaimers arise from "the common undialectical conception of cause and effect as rigidly opposite poles, the total disregarding of interaction. . . . Once a historic element has been brought into the world by other,ultimately economic causes, it reacts, can react on its environment and even on the causes that have given rise to it."[9] Thus the relationship between base and superstructure is now seen as bilateral and reflexive. Ideology, produced by the material forces of history, can subsequently help form the historical course of social conflict. As the early chapters that follow make clear, Eisenstein correlates the understanding of ideology as a reflex with his concepts of montage in the 1920s.

In the midst of social revolution, another aspect of ideology is asserted. Commenting in his preface to A Contribution to the Critique of Political Economy, Marx indicates that the superstructure is massively transformed when radical conflict between material conditions and social relations takes place in the economic foundation, thus determining the "ideological forms in which men become conscious of this conflict and fight it out."[10] This association of ideology with class struggle is developed by Lenin, whose orientation toward revolutionary practice makes for a functional definition in the Bolshevik context. Lenin applies the term *ideology* in describing the final battle between systems of thought and political practice that are based on irreconcilably opposed economic structures (the two great, hostile camps bourgeoisie and proletariat identified in the Communist Manifesto). The period of their greatest conflict is, according to Lenin, after the socialist revolution. Thus, following 1917 Lenin could write without any sense of contradiction that Marxism itself is an ideology: "Marxism has won its historic significance as the ideology of the revolutionary proletariat."[11]

It is in the context, then, of these five key components—history, materialism, dialectics, critique, and ideology—that the relationships of Eisenstein's art and theory to Marxism will be clarified. In its approach to Marxist thought, the present study adopts an insight advanced by Fredric Jameson: "Marxism, owing to the peculiar reality of its object of study, has at its disposal two alternate languages (or codes, to use the structuralist term) in which any given phenomenon can be described. Thus history can be written either subjectively, as the history of class struggle, or objectively, as the development of the economic modes of production and their evolution from their own internal contradictions."[12] In Marx's own work the alternation of codes corresponds to the Communist Manifesto's emphasis on class conflict at a time of revolutionary activity (1848) and Capital's concentration on capitalist production in a period of conservative reaction (the 1860s).

Within the objective sphere, the technical and material forces of production determine the social relationships of production. In this sphere, Marxist critique is concerned with the general category political economy and specific considerations like the technology of production, capital accumulation, and the infrastructure of productive relations. Division of labor in the production processes divides general society into classes and thus yields class struggle as a producer of history. Within the subjective sphere, Marxist critique is concerned with the general matter of ideological formations (religion, philosophy, politics, culture) and with specific issues like social class, commodity fetishism, and alienation. The mediating term between the objective and subjective codes is social class, and the interactions of social class in both instances is dialectical. These two codes of Marxism are apparent across the full span of Eisenstein's cinema and theory in degree and proportions that vary significantly over the course of his career.

Given the incomplete, undeveloped status of Marx's views on art and general culture, it was to be expected that diverse, often contentious, theories and schools in these areas should emerge across Europe. It is in the company of prominent Marxist artists and cultural analysts of his time that Eisenstein is best understood. Through a complementary and secondary line of inquiry, my study articulates important intersections between the Soviet director's work and aspects of the thought of Walter Benjamin, Georg Lukács, Ernst Bloch, and Bertolt Brecht. Within this context, the Marxist dimensions of Eisenstein's work can be fully measured. The principal contacts with these thinkers examined in the chapters that follow are the emphases on shock effect and art production found in Benjamin, on typicality and the epic in Lukács, on the principle of hope and the utopian projection in Bloch, and on the social gest and distantiation in Brecht.

Over Eisenstein's long career there are points of convergence and divergence with these concepts. The shifts mark changes in the circumstances and orientation of Eisenstein's work, and they chart some central issues in Marxist art and criticism, including those of avant-gardism, formalism, and socialist realism. It should be stressed that the Marx of Eisenstein's generation is distinct from the Marx reinterpreted by present-day theoreticians like Louis Althusser, Etienne Balibar, and Jean-François Lyotard. The texts and contexts of Marxism utilized here will remain primarily the same that surrounded Eisenstein.

Eisenstein shares with Brecht a unique importance to modern culture as a Marxist artist. Each man had begun an artistic career early in life, before discovering Marx. For both, however, initial study in Marxism (which came for Eisenstein at age twenty-four, for Brecht at twenty-eight) soon led to materialist and dialectical inquiries into their own cultural practices. These investigations in turn generated changes in the subject matter and form of their work. In the course of long careers, Eisenstein and Brecht created bodies of art and theory that constitute critiques of the material, historical structure of culture and modern ideologies. In recognition of their common aims, Brecht invited Eisenstein during the 1930s to join an organization of radical artists whose goal was to be the development of "a newer, antimetaphysical and social art."[13]

The Canons of Eisenstein Criticism

In the areas of biography, film history, criticism, and theory it is no surprise that there coexist several Eisensteins. The seven completed feature films, the numerous unfilmed projects, the body of theoretical, analytical, didactic, and autobiographical writings, the volumes of drawings ranging from free-associational expression to production designs, and the memoirs of colleagues and students constitute a vast field in which commentators have diversely marked off the foundations of his work. On these foundations criticism and theory have variously constructed and reconstructed Eisenstein over the past forty years. That process of construction and reconstruction began with Eisenstein himself, polemically in starting his film career, publicly in self-defense against Party censure during the 1930s, and intimately in the autobiographical writings during the last years of his life.

Eisenstein's available writings contain a vast resource of material and still more of his manuscripts and notebooks await publication by the Soviet archives. There is no effort here to study systematically the director's theory independently of the films. I have concentrated on those writings immediately contemporary to each film work in the examination of structure, imagery, and questions of history. The importance of the formulations most widely discussed in Eisenstein studies rests finally, in my opinion, in the unique characteristics of the films themselves. With his development of new filmmaking practices, Eisenstein evolved new theoretical concepts. In the periods of his greatest artistic activity, practice nearly always preceded theory.

Any new book on Eisenstein, preliminary to its own placement of the subject, requires as initial groundwork a survey of the prominent constructs made of him in film criticism and theory. Biographers and critics have proposed an array of principles to unify his long and diverse career. In light of the great variety of his artistic activities and the complex development of his theories, sharp disagreement over Eisenstein is inevitable. He has been constructed as an unsystematic autodidact, a modern Leonardo da Vinci, a materialist in the grip of mysticism and conversely a mystic in the grip of materialism, a neoformalist, a semiotician, a compliant propagandist, and as an artist driven by an unresolved Oedipal complex. Surprisingly, among critics in the West there has been no comprehensive study of contemporary Marxist cultural thought or of issues of revolutionary history as definitive factors in his art and theory. The extensive secondary literature could lead in itself to a book-length commentary, so some principles of selection must be set down. The condensed survey here will concern dominant critical perspectives that have defined Eisenstein studies available in English and those from France, where the theoretical approaches have been most far-reaching. These treatments are surveyed with an eye specifically toward their positions on the matter of a relationship between Eisenstein's cinema and materialist historiography and between his imagination and Marxist thought.

The first generation of Eisenstein criticism is largely auteurist in approach. The early biography by Marie Seton offers a psychological portrait deriving from meetings and correspondence with Eisenstein.[14] Seton's direct contact with Eisenstein took place in the years 1932–35 and her book contains much valuable information about this politically difficult period. She amplifies details from their conversations, particularly about his family life, into a case history. Seton's application of psychoanalysis, however, is limited to a notion of sublimation in only its most literal form. Eisenstein's creative energy is attributed to repressed homosexuality and unreformed mysticism. Having assigned these psychodynamics to its subject, the biography gives over to reductive reasoning and a melodramatic account. While granting the sincerity in Eisenstein's public support of the Soviet revolution, Seton contends that the new society intensified his personal anxieties. With the exceptions of the *Capital* project and his courses at the State Cinema Institute, the place of Marxist thought in the director's work is treated as accessory and tangential. Seton interprets the last ten years of Eisenstein's life as a period of reversion to childhood and adolescent impulses.

A subsequent biography by Yon Barna is similar in purpose in tracing from childhood Eisenstein's personality and artistic identity.[15] While Barna's interpretative direction is not Freudian, it relies heavily on the late autobiographical writings in which Eisenstein pursues his earliest impressions and engages in improvisatory self-analysis. The book's "ontogenetic" approach discovers emotional sources for characteristics found throughout the film work. These characteristics are, stylistically, the prominence of close-up and composition in depth and, thematically, impersonal cruelty and an inevitable fate. Barna's method, as in auteurist criticism generally, is synchronic in its major premises and passes over the diachronic marks within Eisenstein's career, the instances that constitute major differences from previous practices and theory. In Barna's construct of the artist, Marxism and socialist revolution are environmental factors incorporated into a consciousness with its own unique vision of life, determined by early personal fantasies and trauma.

The novelist and critic Dominique Fernandez has written a psychobiography that also proposes to reveal the director's original, secret self.[16] It presents a "third Eisenstein" that is the latent substructure to the conscious levels of Eisenstein as a formalist and a Marxist. The film works are considered as transpositions of conflicts deriving from the Oedipal complex and the family romance. The biography correlates montage to Eisenstein's repression of certain childhood experiences. Based on the assumption that social revolution and sexual power are closely associated, Fernandez concludes that Eisenstein is not a Marxist artist and that his interest in politics was a sublimation of homosexuality.

One cogent, early auteur study of Eisenstein's films is Jean Mitry's monograph.[17] Its underlying assumption is that the film works reflect a continued effort to apply a specific set of methods and ideas embodied in the montage form. While Mitry does not deny a role to chronological development, he largely sets aside such factors in favor of a synchronic treatment of montage in the contexts of linguistics and perceptual psychology. A major premise in the present study, by contrast, is that within the twenty-five years of Eisenstein's thinking on cinema—and on aesthetics, culture, and history more generally—change and disjunction, as much as elaboration and continuity, are essential to any understanding.

The volume prepared by Léon Moussinac contains valuable biographical material in the account of discussions and letters between the French critic and Eisenstein, but it provides no analytical overview of the cinema and theory.[18] Barthélemy Amengual has published two works on Eisenstein. The earlier one is a monograph that lacks the methodological clarity and reasoned argument found in Mitry's study.[19] The more recent *Que Viva Eisenstein!* is encyclopedic in its scope and length.[20] This book contains a wealth of material and insights, including suggestive analogies to Marx, Brecht, and Lukács, along with sections on the relations of the cinema and theory to Artaud, Vertov, the ideogram, Russian Formalism, Byzantine art, expressionism, and the sacred. Amengual's book shares with the present study interests in Marxist aesthetics and in the films as renderings of history, yet its finally multiple, heterogeneous approaches blur the distinctness of these issues in relation to Eisenstein's cinema.

Over the past twenty-five years considerable critical attention has been paid to Eisenstein's theoretical work, treated essentially apart from the films. Dudley Andrew employs a comparative method based on a fixed set of categories to analyze him in the company of other major theorists.[21] Eisenstein, however, stands alone among these figures as a major filmmaker. Andrew comments on a few significant alterations within his aesthetics over a long career, but the study's comparative format is static and not developmental. Correlations with Marxist concepts are acknowledged but not investigated. The reciprocal influence between Eisenstein's

changing directorial practices and his theoretical investigations falls outside the book's scope.

A comparative approach clearly outlines differences between formative
theory and realist theory, differences Brian Henderson has investigated
as a "debate" between Eisenstein and André Bazin.[22] The doctrine of
montage, Henderson believes, narrowly defines film's relation to reality
in terms of the shot and the brief montage unit, thus neglecting concerns
like associations among sequences and the narrative whole. He represents
Eisenstein's aesthetics primarily through theory formulated in the silent
period, and his account disregards the intentional predominance of discursive structure over narrative in those films. For the purposes of maintaining the profile of a debate, Henderson has limited the Eisenstein side
to synchronic elements and ignored the expansion of montage to encompass issues of unifying form.

The diachronic dimension to Eisenstein's theoretical work has received
attention from David Bordwell, who detects an epistemological shift in
the writings (dated at 1930) that leaves us with two Eisensteins.[23] The first
period of theory is grounded in physiology and dialectical materialism,
the second in associational psychology and empiricism. The major discon-
tinuities in Eisenstein's film work traced by the present book are identified much differently. François Albera, in a study of Eisenstein's aesthetics, offers a suggestive formulation of a differential within the body of
theory.[24] Albera makes a distinction between the director's theoretic discourse, which proposes ideas of unity and synthesis, and his theoretic
practice, which comprises a transformative approach. In philosophical
terms, the difference is one between a monism inherited from Hegel and
a dialectic acquired from Marx. Albera's monograph does not undertake
a systematic application of this differential to the body of film works.

Eisenstein's frequent discussions of visual language and of montage as
a producer of meaning has led contemporary criticism to account for the
theory from linguistic and semiological perspectives. Peter Wollen and
Vyacheslav Ivanov are among the first to have introduced these approaches. In providing a valuable contextualization of Eisenstein's theory,
Wollen surveys the influences of Russia's avant-gardes in art and criticism,
including the Russian Formalist movement.[25] Ivanov draws comparisons
between the theory and structural anthropology in the adaptation of linguistic categories.[26] In Christian Metz's field theory of cinema according
to a model of structural linguistics, montage is one code among a plurality
of codes within cinema's five major systems of signification.[27] His methodological focus on issues of *langage* (or linguistic potential) and textuality
does not aim to clarify the structure of montage as implemented within
specific film works. The context of linguistics will be taken up in my dis-

cussion of Eisenstein's ideas on cinema speech and that of anthropology in the analysis of myth in his last three films.

Jacques Aumont in *Montage Eisenstein* does not seek to provide the systematization of theory that Eisenstein failed to achieve in his lifetime.[28] Aumont argues that montage, the definitive conception in Eisenstein studies, is not truly a concept in the sense of a strictly logical, fixed, and constant idea. Prior to direct examination of montage and its transformations, the book presents reflections on biographical materials, a catalogue of concepts that play into montage theory, and an analysis of montage functions in *Old and New* and *Ivan the Terrible*. Aumont argues in contradiction to some of Eisenstein's most quoted assertions in concluding that the structure of meaning advanced through montage cannot be understood in terms of Marxism. While he does not doubt the sincerity of Eisenstein's initial adherence to the Bolshevik Revolution, Aumont considers it to be primarily sentimental. He judges the director's thinking on materialism, dialectics, class struggle, and history to be essentially captive to Stalinist dogma. My indirect responses to Aumont in chapters that follow are addressed to his contentions that historical events—from the generic treatment of an industrial strike or the takeover of the Winter Palace to the coronation of Tsar Ivan IV—constitute a lifeless teleology and are simply exploited in the films as acceptable story lines.

To date, the most detailed semiotic analysis of Eisenstein's montage practices has been conducted by an advanced seminar in the Centre de Recherche at the University of Paris, Vincennes. Two of a projected four volumes on the film *October* have appeared.[29] In the first, the principal collaborators Marie-Claire Ropars-Wuilleumier and Pierre Sorlin extract two montage units from *October* and explore in minute detail sequential and nonsequential correlations within each one. The second volume examines associations among the film's major segments and presents comprehensive analyses of its systems of meaning, including an excellent contribution by Michèle Lagny on its narrative and discursive temporalities of revolution.

In these two volumes *October* becomes an occasion for elaboration of theories of textuality and reading. History and revolution, the film's manifest content, are treated as textual activities and forms of writing. Their dynamics are considered an equivalent to processes of fragmentation, displacement, repression, and figuration within a text. The supposition that montage produces the film's signifiers of revolution leads seminar members to disregard its profilmic relationships to Bolshevik avant-gardism and to similar representations, like the mass spectacle. With discussion of the film in the political and cultural contexts of 1927 left to subsequent studies, there is a tendency in the two published volumes to read *over* the film's ideological form and obvious historical meanings. In that period there still remain in Eisenstein's cinema certain techniques of reduction and literalism that date back to his work in Proletkult agitational-propaganda theater.

Fundamental to the Vincennes seminar's deconstructionist findings is the function of figuration, which is considered an autonomous and antithetical process of semiotic activity that subverts conventional symbolization. Figural operations cannot be subsumed into codes of diegesis, rhetoric, referential temporality, or causal logic. They disrupt the text, put signification into flux, throw into question literal interpretation, and raise issues of intelligibility and causality. In reading the film's signification as primarily one of figuration, the seminar considers *October* to have written over the dominant cultural and historical contexts of the mid-1920s. Those contexts in my view, however, serve Eisenstein as a differential between the tsarist era and a Bolshevik seizure of history.

Another methodology of film reading is developed in Kristin Thompson's study of *Ivan the Terrible*.[30] Adapted largely from Russian Formalist linguistics and criticism, Thompson's approach concentrates on matters of form with great insight into spatial and narrative relations, acting style, and audiovisual montage. Though Thompson asserts that Russian Formalism incorporates history at all levels of analysis, her neoformalist treatment of this issue is exclusively in comparisons of *Ivan* to the historical epic as defined by classical Hollywood narrative cinema and specifically to *Mary of Scotland* (1936) and *Sergeant York* (1940), two films irrelevant to the historical meaning of tsarist politics and the Stalin period. In Thompson's subsequent exposition of neoformalism, *Breaking the Glass Armor*, the method is again confined in its historical context to "norms and deviations" measured against a paradigm of the spectator's "prior experience *backgrounds*" within conventions of the Hollywood fiction film.[31]

Eisenstein was the first theorist to consider the ideological aspects of film form, an issue revitalized with the radicalization of cinema study in the late 1960s, initially in the pages of *Cahiers du Cinéma, Cinéthique*, and *Screen*.[32] Two general critiques of cinema from Marxist viewpoints derive directly from this revitalization. Guido Aristarco shapes a critical approach largely by adapting Lukács's ideas on historical realism and Gramsci's on cultural hegemony.[33] With its main interest in the mystifications of reality by Western cinema, Aristarco's book gives Eisenstein only brief attention. Jean-Patrick Lebel, echoing the slogans of May 1968, calls for a materialist interpretation and practice of cinema in which semiology would serve as a general science on the formation and circulation of ideology.[34] His book's trajectory is not toward a critique of film history but toward a potential future for filmmaking.

As advanced by people like Jean-Louis Baudry, Stephen Heath, Laura

Mulvey, Bill Nichols, and Linda Williams, contemporary theory has invaluably interrogated the film text as a locus of ideology. At present, identification of the text's functions of ideological positioning is typically anchored to a tutor method or theory elaborated by a thinker like Althusser, Barthes, Derrida, Foucault, Kristeva, Lacan, or Sartre. To this list can now be added Gilles Deleuze, who has amalgamated the semiotics of Peirce with the philosophy of Bergson in a consideration of films as forms of inquiry into movement and time through images.[35]

Given Eisenstein's pivotal position within world cinema, it is understandable that critics have founded tenets and, in some cases, systems of interpretation in the process of analyzing his films and theory. The resultant formulations on Eisenstein's theory have served valuable ends in the advancement of understanding cinema generally. The present book does not propose, however, a new idiom for film criticism based on Eisenstein's work. I believe it will be useful now to reground Eisenstein in the Soviet contexts, historical issues, and Marxist thought of his times. The objective and subjective codes within revolutionary historiography, through which material dislocations and society's ideological formations are recognized to restructure one another, are central in Eisenstein's cinema.

CHAPTER ONE

Revolutionary Beginnings: From Theater to Cinema

The revolutionary outbreak is the epitome of history from a Marxist viewpoint. In doing violence to the established order, the outbreak is living proof that class conflict—and not a uniform evolution of society—underlies the course of civilization. The outbreak is both an objective and a subjective manifestation of the materiality of history. Its evidence that productive and class forces are the motor of history supplants old rationales that ruling power descends from divine right or ascends from a kernel of individual destiny. The outbreak asserts a new temporality against the old one of regularity and succession by interrupting continuities that have been institutionalized in cultural boundaries, social hierarchies, the cycles of work and leisure, and in urban geography. It marks a loss in the convictions of guaranteed permanence and a natural order to social life. While revolutionary outbreak is an uprising against established power, it is also a restructuring of the forms of experience.

By the start of the twentieth century, Russia was beset by contradictions. A great power among the nations of Europe, it was the last one to emerge from feudalism and also the last to industrialize. Though St. Petersburg, the Romanov capital, had drawn on Western Europe during two centuries for much of its culture and trade, Tsar Nicholas II refused to modernize the Russian bureaucracy or to allow representative institutions until events forced him to make reforms. The autocracy was rapidly destabilized by the debacle of war with Japan in 1904 and uprisings in the cities and in the countryside in 1905. With a resurgence of peasant riots in 1906, Nicholas imposed martial law. An urban working class did not emerge in significant numbers until Russia's rapid industrialization during the 1890s, but it proved remarkably organized and militant. Lenin observed in *What Is to Be Done?* (1902) that "the working masses are roused to a high pitch of excitement by the social evils in Russian life," but they had yet to consolidate into "a *single* gigantic torrent" of revolution.[1]

For over the first decade of Sergei Eisenstein's artistic development— as a graphic artist, a stage designer and director, and as a young filmmaker—his concerns were with the inception of revolution. His first published work as an artist was in response to revolutionary street actions in 1917. From the outset of his work in theater, he undertook to overthrow bourgeois story, character, and staging forms through parody and eccentric improvisations. The first film works treat strikes and mutinous activities as outbreaks anticipatory of full-scale rebellion. With *October* the events of 1917 are presented as an inauguration of modern revolution in world history. *Old and New* represents initiation into the countryside of the originally urban, industrial revolution as the initiation of a communist future.

As a boy growing up in Riga, where he was born in 1898, Eisenstein was aware of the divisions among classes and nationalities that separated Russian bureaucrats like his father, a civil engineer who held the rank of Privy Councillor, from the local Latvian and German populations. The region's German-speaking people represented a legacy from the first foreign conquest of Latvia. In the aftermath of the defeated 1905 Revolution, the Romanov monarchy appointed as governor-general over the region A. N. Meller-Zakomelsky, a reactionary notorious for his punitive policies. Political tensions that year forced the Eisenstein family to cancel the annual summer holiday at their Baltic cottage in favor of a trip to Paris.

Eisenstein's earliest responses to contemporary history are recorded in numerous line drawings and caricatures. The power of graphic art fully enchanted him by age ten, when he acquired a monograph on Honoré Daumier. An engineer colleague of his father had demonstrated to him the unique qualities of line drawing by quickly sketching animal forms with chalk on the dark cover of a card table. By adolescence Eisenstein had developed an "irresistible need to draw," typically as an outlet for a play of whimsy, youthful rebelliousness, and parody.[2] In subject matter his early drawings range from a cartoon series of animal figures in human dress enacting a bourgeois couple's daily routine to sketched street incidents and imagined scenes of war. Their style is generally slight and abbreviated, with the image built of rapid, curling—and at times rococo— lines. Evident in this style are the influences of operatic costume and gesture and popular entertainments like music hall performances and the circus. As his initial models, Eisenstein admired the contemporary Olaf Gulbransson and the nineteenth-century French caricaturists Grandville, Charles Philipon, André Gill, and, above all others, Daumier.

A 1913 notebook entitled "In the World of Animals" registers the social types familiar to him in Riga through animal equivalents for each niche in the bureaucratic and urban spheres. Eisenstein's later theater and film practices of associative transposition and conceptual representation are already suggested in these drawings. The genre of animal fable serves the young caricaturist as a resource for simplification, intensification, and comparison. He is also obviously engaged in an effort to render the telling shape, posture, and mannerism within the human scene. In theme, these early works commonly reflect the class nature of social difference and of private life. Stylistically, they anticipate subsequent theater and film work in their metamorphic comparisons, juxtaposed imagery, and qualities of fable.

After completing his secondary education in 1915, Eisenstein relocated in order to study at the Institute for Civil Engineering in Petrograd, as St. Petersburg had been renamed since the onset of war with Germany. A visit to a military hospital in this period prompted him to prepare a series of sketches of the war wounded. The war's deprivations to civilians are captured in his panoramic drawing of a food line that contains over one hundred individuals and provides a full cross section of Petrograd's inhabitants. Nineteen years old at the time of the February Revolution of 1917, which brought a Provisional Government headed by Alexander Kerensky to power, Eisenstein responded initially to the political upheaval through sketches and caricatures. Some of the drawings appeared in the Petrograd *Gazette* under the pseudonym Sir Gay, in a humorous echo of his own name and perhaps in mockery of the newspaper's political orientation. In July he became caught up in the massive demonstrations on Nevsky Prospect, which he later recreated for *October*. In August Eisenstein joined in the defense of Petrograd against a rightist coup led by General Lavr Kornilov.

In one February Revolution cartoon series Eisenstein portrays the reactions of a man from the provinces to radical activities in Petrograd. After the initial shock of seeing a red flag waving from an imperial building, this portly bourgeois wanders the streets with suitcase still in hand, gawking at demonstrators who tear down the old regime's insignia. Dumbfounded by it all, the man forgets entirely the business that brought him to the city and takes the first train home. Street fighting is depicted in another sequence of four sketches, the last showing a citizen struck in the back by one of the militia's bullets, fired indiscriminately to disperse demonstrators. In materials not accepted for publication, Eisenstein lampoons Kerensky and imagines the political fate of Nicholas II by placing the guillotined head of Louis XVI above the tsar's bed. A series entitled "Life of the Prince" presents scenes of decadent leisure and sexual corruption in the genre of antiroyalist broadsheets.

Emerging within these youthful graphic commentaries on contemporary events are an iconography, irony, historical perspective, and thematics that Eisenstein develops over his entire artistic career. Characteristics of social class and symbols of power largely define context and drama. Class identity is shown to determine the understanding of contemporary experience, which is relative and discontinuous. Politics are presented as a process of opposition and disruption, history as one of effacement and reinscription. The confluence of these elements contributes to Eisenstein's thematic treatments through an expansive, synonymic chain of meanings. In the final stages of his career, through an awareness of the reversals in Russian history within his lifetime, Eisenstein develops these thematics as an antonymic chain.

Graphic form remains essential to Eisenstein as he progresses from drawing to theater and cinema as his media. Stark linearity functions as the dominant within his graphic expression. There is a dormant period in Eisenstein's drawing activity from 1923 to 1930 that finally ends with the "paradise regained" of graphic art he experienced in Mexico. In the cultural environment of pre-Columbian artefacts, woodcut illustrations by José Guadalupe Posada, and the contemporary muralists, his style went through "a stage of inner purification in its striving for a mathematically abstract and pure line" (*IM* 44). Once renewed, Eisenstein's passion for drawing continued uninterrupted for the remainder of his life. During the period of inactivity in drawing itself, Eisenstein extensively develops cinema as a graphic art.

From Revolution to Art

During the first weeks of the February Revolution, Eisenstein saw the famed Vsevolod Meyerhold productions at the Alexandrinsky Theater in Petrograd. These included the verse drama *Masquerade* by Mikhail Lermontov, which depicted the corruption among Russia's aristocracy of the 1830s. Meyerhold staged it in a grotesque and nightmarish style. The premiere of this spectacle, designed in a lavish, baroque manner by Alexander Golovin, ironically marked an end to the imperial era in Russian life.

Over the next three years Eisenstein read widely in dramatic literature, devised set and costume designs based on his study of theater history, and helped organize amateur theatrical companies. His notebooks from this period contain sketches that range across the full repertory, from classical comedy (Aristophanes, Plautus, Terence), medieval mystery and miracle plays, commedia dell'arte and the English Rennaissance (Jonson, Shakespeare) to seventeenth- and eighteenth-century comedy (Molière, Gozzi, Sheridan, Goldoni), Naturalism (Zola, Ibsen), Symbolism (Maeterlinck, Strindberg), and the Russian masters (Gogol, Tolstoy, Ostrovsky). The notebooks also contain ideas for original propaganda pieces, pantomimes, and farces. Parody and burlesque are freely deployed in these sketches and in his subsequent stage work as designer and director. These two comic modes are essential to Eisenstein's process of artistic self-definition. They exemplify his emphasis on performance principles and on form as a dialogic response to literary and theatrical conventions.

Eisenstein transferred to the Ensigns' School of Engineering and entered military service in March 1917. While his academic field remained the applied sciences, his passions were painting and theater and he spent much of his off-duty hours studying these subjects. With civil war spreading in 1918, he volunteered for the Red Army, which assigned him as a technician in the construction of transport routes and defense fortifications along the northeastern and western fronts protecting Petrograd and Moscow. In July 1920 Eisenstein was transferred to serve as production designer for a theater company with the Red Army front lines. His responsibilities extended to the decoration of Red troop trains with posters and political slogans.

It is important to specify that the formation of Eisenstein's identity as an artist occurred in a revolutionary climate and under wartime conditions. Still vivid twenty-five years later, when he writes his autobiography, are impressions of the abandoned battleground at Dvinsk, strewn with corpses and skeletons from an offensive against German positions ordered by Kerensky in 1917, and the troop train yards at Smolensk in 1920, noisy and chaotic with the activities of mobilization for the civil war. During this period of social disruption and historical dislocation, Eisenstein took the biographically dialectical step from being a technical student with an amateur appreciation of art to making the decision to become an artist.

Upon demobilization in September 1920, Eisenstein enrolled in the Japanese language program in the General Staff Academy of Moscow. At the same time he accepted an offer to join the Proletkult Theater as head of scenic design. Within two months he had left language study and the Academy to work full-time in the theater. Eisenstein quickly advanced from design to stage direction at Proletkult and he formed there a theater workshop whose students included his future film collaborator Grigori Alexandrov. In September 1921 he entered a director's course instructed by Meyerhold. Eisenstein later summarized the politically and personally decisive years 1917–21 as a period that took him first "through the Revolution to art" in breaking away from a career in engineering and subsequently took him "through art to the Revolution" with his experiences in the new Bolshevik culture.[3]

During the first years of the Bolshevik Revolution, Russia's many avant-garde movements continued their marginal existence while old cultural institutions remained in place. On the first anniversary of October in Petrograd, Meyerhold was able to stage Vladimir Mayakovsky's Futurist allegory *Mystery-Bouffe* for only three performances with a cast of students (and the author in three roles) because the production had been boycotted by the city's theater professionals. Eisenstein first met Mayakovsky and Meyerhold in April 1921. In his *Memoirs* he identifies Meyerhold as his "second father" (*IM* 75) and to a colleague from the period he confided that without this genius of theater there would be no Eisenstein.[4] In joining the Bolshevik party in 1918, Meyerhold was nearly alone among colleagues in the theater establishment. Eisenstein's decision to enroll in Meyerhold's new director workshop is another indication of his early commitment to the political and cultural avant-garde. As yet ungoverned by centralized Soviet authority in the arts, modernism expanded beyond the horizons of symbolism, naturalism, cubism, and futurism.

The 1922 Meyerhold production of *The Death of Tarelkin*, on which Eisenstein served as an assistant director, performed the nineteenth-century satire on tsarist police corruption and violence as a circus of cruelty. The stage properties, designed by Varvara Stepanova, were rigged to make noises, spring out of reach, or completely collapse whenever performers made contact with them. Her costumes were oversized and geometrically shaped to make the actors' movements ungainly. Meyerhold had been experimenting with masked drama for nearly a decade. By this period he was substituting for each character an appropriate "social mask" to designate each niche within the class system that motivated behavior.

The generalized expression of a common social type is a technique of caricature that was already habitual in Eisenstein's graphic work. Eisenstein studied and collaborated in the winter months of 1921/22 at a theater workshop headed by Nikolai Foregger, a historian and director interested in the earliest forms of popular European drama. Foregger's initial productions were revivals of medieval French farces and commedia dell'arte pieces and through these he developed ideas for a modern theater of masks. Inherent to dramatic masks and types are factors of culturally determined cognition, which Eisenstein will elaborate into concepts of typage and attractions.

In 1922 Eisenstein also attended the design preparations and rehearsals for Meyerhold's adaptation of *The Magnificent Cuckold*, a lyric farce authored by the Belgian dramatist Fernand Crommelynck.[5] The production abandoned representational settings in favor of an installation for acting designed by Lyubov Popova. There were no canvas flats, naturalist stage properties, or illusion of place. Instead, the performance arena consisted of platforms and scaffolds connected by steps, ramps, and ladders. Blank, hinged panels served as passageways or barriers as the action required. Dominating the construction were an open wheel, a huge disk on which CR ML NCK was painted, and the frames of wind vanes (Crommelynck's play is set on the property of a grain farmer). These contraptions operated at variable speeds to accompany changes in characters' emotions. To fit the mechanized stage environment, the action entailed simultaneous forms of staging and a collective, nonpsychological style of acting. The actor's posture would be bent geometrically to match angles in the set construction. In this machine for acting, all character costumes followed a standardized design and were virtually a uniform for performance in accordance with Popova's concept of interchangeable parts.

Evident in these two Meyerhold productions are strong influences of the avant-garde movements Eccentrism and Constructivism. *Eccentric* is a word specific to Russian circus terminology, where it is another expression for "trick." Connections between Soviet theater and the circus date from Yuri Annenkov's 1919 production *The First Distiller*, in which one scene involved a flying trapeze act. In 1920 Mayakovsky prepared *The Championship of the Universal Class Struggle* for the famous clown Vitali Lazarenko, who performed it with Moscow's Second State Circus. Through such eccentricity, Soviet avant-garde theater meant to dislodge the power of tradition and decorum over cultural life.

Three future film directors—Grigori Kozintsev, Sergei Yutkevitch, and Leonid Trauberg—published manifestos under the collective title *Eccentrism* in 1922 to inaugurate the Factory of the Eccentric Actor (FEKS). That year Eisenstein had a brief association in Petrograd with FEKS. The group would evolve from a theater workshop into a film acting group and then a film production unit. Collectively, the FEKS manifestos called for theater to break out of automatized language, gestures, and decor onstage and of the consequently automatized perceptions and reactions in the audience. The process entails deformation and decontextualization at every level of the theater—from the classical repertoire to incidental stage properties—and adoption of an alternative tradition of popular entertainments, including the circus, the variety show, and the screen comedy. The actor is presented to audiences more as a performer than a character, with an emphasis on physical action and improvisatory skill rather than psychology or inner motivation.

The Constructivist movement emerged in Russia at the time of World War I and rapidly became international in scope. It had widespread appeal among young Soviet artists and brought together into working relationships painters, architects, designers, printmakers, craftspeople, stage directors, and filmmakers. Its fundamental goal was to modernize traditional arts through the methods of industry and thus to make cultural experience a process of continuously active perception rather than one of static reflection. Through such innovations, the Constructivists argued, technics would replace style and functionality would replace beauty. In the West at the time, a Machine Age mentality also began to influence many aspects of culture, from painting to product design.

The language of Constructivist manifestos discards aesthetic terms in favor of those from engineering and industry. The work's calculated function and its selected materials determine form. In the visual and dramatic arts, where Constructivist innovations had the most enduring consequences, emphasis falls upon geometric shapes and functional, efficient interrelationships among the components of composition and ensemble. Elements of materialist thought and proletarian politics are evident in a number of Constructivist programs, such as Alexei Gan's *Constructivism* (1922): "We should not reflect, depict, and interpret reality but should build practically and express the planned objectives of the new actively working class. . . . Intellectual-material production is confronted with this problem: by what means, *how* to create and educate a group of workers in the sphere of artistic labor."[6] In rejecting art as a reflection or representation of reality, Gan substitutes an idea of art as a producer of reality with direct social utility.

By the time of *The Magnificent Cuckold* production, Meyerhold had organized the training of actors into a program of "biomechanics." Based loosely on studies in reflexology, behavior, and labor management, biomechanics purported to rationalize theatrical performance by means of scientific calculation. Physical instruction in biomechanics actually derived from techniques of the acrobatic circus and of the pantomime taken from commedia dell'arte. Meyerhold was adamantly opposed to the influence on actors of free expressivity through eurythmics, made popular by Isadora Duncan.

In a statement from 1922, Meyerhold applies the Constructivist rationale to acting:

Art should be based on scientific principles; the entire creative act should be a conscious process. The art of the actor consists in organizing his material; that is, in his capacity to utilize correctly his body's means of expression. . . . All psychological states are determined by specific physiological processes. By correctly resolving the nature of his state physically, the actor reaches the point where he experiences the *excitation* which communicates itself to the spectator. . . . From a sequence of physical positions and situations there arise "*points of excitation*" which are informed with some particular emotion.[7]

The objective psychology outlined here was given much currency at the time through the work of William James and the Russians Ivan Pavlov and Vladimir Bekhterev. Emotional states are considered to be immediate and reactive; they are the body's automatic responses to stimuli. The mental perception of emotion follows bodily reaction.

Through biomechanics the actor transmits to the audience the stimulation or excitation that will lead, secondarily, to the perception of emotion. The objective of Meyerhold's training method is to school the performer in the primary bodily forms in which emotion is always first experienced. This system is clearly opposed to the methods of acting advanced by Constantin Stanislavsky, Meyerhold's mentor at the Moscow Art Theater in the years 1898–1902. Stanislavsky's techniques entail the actor's emotion memory, inner motive forces, and sense impressions. They further require assimilation of imagined and remembered experience to convey a character's emotion and thus work on the audience's passions. These primary acts of mentation in the communication of emotion are clearly alien to biomechanical principles. In place of emotional identification of actor to character, Meyerhold treats the actor as an instrument to induce audience reaction directly, outside any concerns to render a character's inner psychology in cognitive form. Both schools of acting remained prominent in the first years of Soviet culture.

Anatoli Lunacharsky, the first Soviet Commissar for Enlightenment, formulated the relationship between artistic content and Bolshevik context in 1920 as follows: "if revolution can give art its soul, then art can give revolution its mouthpiece." The Commissariat of Enlightenment was the state agency of art, culture, and education and it remained under Lunacharsky's leadership from 1917 to 1929. Lunacharsky maintained a degree of independence from the Party's positions on culture in his direction of the Commissariat. In comparison with the tsarist censorship that preceded him and the Party dictates that eventually led to his resignation, Lunacharsky's policies were radical in their liberality. Modernist eclecticism and experimentation coexisted with established bourgeois tradition and militant proletarianism.

In Russian revolutionary thought, from Georgi Plekhanov in the 1890s to Lenin, propaganda is distinguished from agitation as the presentation of many ideas to a few people in the case of propaganda and the presentation of a few ideas to a mass of people in that of agitation. With the 1917 Revolution and the acquisition of the mass means of communication, the distinguishing feature of audience size became less relevant. In Lunacharsky's own definitions, propaganda is the elucidation of facts and logic according to the Bolshevik worldview and agitation is the excitation of "the feelings of the audience and readers and has a direct influence on their will."[8] Principles drawn from Eccentrism, Constructivism, and other avant-garde movements readily lent themselves to the purposes of agitation in the first decade of revolutionary culture.

Proletkult

Eisenstein worked with a number of stage companies but his longest association was with the Proletkult Workers Theater, one branch of the proletarian culture movement whose stated aim was to overthrow bourgeois traditions and establish a class-conscious, scientific, and collective art. In the early 1920s Proletkult welcomed the artistic license possible through avant-garde movements like Futurism and Eccentrism as effective devices in radicalizing the style and content of drama. In principle, Lenin opposed the rejection of inherited culture and branded it an act of "infantile leftism." In 1920 the Central Committee had rejected Proletkult and the Communist-Futurists in each movement's bid for Party recognition as the mandated style of new Soviet culture. A Party line on form and content for proletarian art did not gain dominance until the period of cultural revolution, 1928–32.

Eisenstein's first staged production with Proletkult, an adaptation of the Jack London story "The Mexican," opened for public performance in May 1921. As its designer, he sought to bring into the theater the vitality of popular spectator events. Reactionary characters were caricatured in exaggerated, clownish forms. The play's rival boxing promoters were presented through a contrast in primary shapes: round ones in decor, costumes, and makeup for the first promoter, square ones for the other. The only character to appear in naturally human form was the young Mexican boxer. This graphically contrastive approach to social typing remained Eisenstein's method in film design and direction.

The narrative momentum of *The Mexican*—whose original story is set in 1911, the year of revolt against Diaz—is toward the climactic spectacle of the staged prizefight, whose outcome determines whether or not the Mexican youth can further the cause of revolution through the purchase of rifles with his winnings. The original play script dramatized the prizefight only in terms of crowd reaction, with the event supposedly taking place backstage. Eisenstein's design placed a boxing ring in the auditorium center, surrounded by theater spectators. Fire regulations prevented fully carrying out this idea, so the ring was placed on an apron thrust into the auditorium, with the audience around three sides and extras closing the ring at the back. The integration of dramatic text and sporting event was designed to bring spontaneity and actuality into the theater. Rather than digest for the audience a reaction to an unreal, offstage event through characters, the boxing match becomes an immediate dramatic action. The actor is no longer an intermediary between event and audience but is a participant in an event presented directly, undigested to the audience. In the script, the boxing match was reflected across the boundary between stage and auditorium; in the production, the event is designed to stimulate a reflex in the audience.

By 1923 the Moscow Proletkult Central Theater was located in the former Morozov mansion. In April Eisenstein's production of the Alexander Ostrovsky play *Enough Simplicity in Every Wise Man* opened there.[9] A comedy from the nineteenth-century repertory in Russian realist theater, the Ostrovsky text was freely adapted by Eisenstein and his collaborator Sergei Tretyakov, who abbreviated its title to *The Wise Man*. They renovated the Russian classic into a nonstop burlesque on recent events, with characters transformed into figures relevant to Bolshevik politics. The main character Glumov, to take just one example, is the consummate opportunist in a parody of the unrevolutionary profiteers who were revived when the New Economic Policy was inaugurated in 1921. NEP brought restoration of the prerevolutionary money economy and of market business relations.

The Morozov mansion's salon served as the auditorium and spectators watched from steep banks of seats in front of a small circus ring. The juxtaposition of carnival atmosphere against aristocratic surroundings served to restate the production's parodic intentions. The performance offered clown costumes, acrobatics, slapstick, juggling, a tightrope act, current popular songs, and a brief film. Its knockabout acting style amounted to a satire on the conventions of nineteenth-century theater, in whose lineage Proletkult placed Stanislavsky's Moscow Art Theater.

During the same years of Eisenstein's Eccentrist productions, Brecht collaborated with the Munich folk comedian, cabaret performer, and clown Karl Valentin. In 1922 the two men prepared a midnight show called *The Red Raisin* to follow performances of Brecht's more serious comedy *Drums in the Night*. The Brecht-Valentin improvisation contained music hall routines and sketches. In the cases of both Eisenstein and Brecht, the development away from naturalism and psychological drama and toward gestural and presentational theater follows from an incorporation of popular entertainment forms. Both devised reflexive forms in order to underscore the dynamics of performance and frankly "sell" the audience the actor's gestures and movements. At that point in cultural history, the hegemony of academic theater is broken with a purposeful corruption of conventional acting styles and of the traditional repertory. In another interesting parallel, Brecht also incorporates a boxing arena in the theater auditorium in his 1927 music drama *The Rise and Fall of the City of Mahagonny*.

Eisenstein's production design for *The Wise Man* is similar to the on-stage Constructivist "machines for acting" erected in the theaters of Meyerhold and other directors. It is also representative of the Proletkult momentum away from proscenium staging and toward theater of the fairground and the street. With its large-lettered political banners and posters, *The Wise Man* mimics the street demonstration and integrates into the drama the word as a dynamic, material element. The play's dialogue was often subordinated to scenic elements of movement, gesture, and ensemble. In staging the dialogue, Eisenstein devised physical equivalents to convey idiomatic expressions. One character describes her predicament as "being up a tree"; a pole is immediately brought onstage and she climbs to its top. Another character is so furious that he is ready "to fling himself" at a painting; in an instant he runs across stage and dives through the picture. To literalize figurative expressions in these ways is to refamiliarize an audience with the material origins of metaphor. Similar verbal-visual materialization is later employed in Eisenstein's cinema to "lay bare" thematic devices, to use terminology from Formalism that will be discussed in the following chapter.

The Wise Man approached a terminus to theatrical traditions of language. When dialogue became unintelligible during performance because of noisy stage business, intensity in the actor's intonation and delivery were supposed to convey the semantic meaning. With a dominant purpose of provocation, words became salvos at the audience to break its passivity and stagnation. That such extreme stylization was at the expense of basic comprehension became quickly evident to Eisenstein, and performances of *The Wise Man* were soon accompanied by an explication and plot synopsis read at the outset. Nonetheless, the production remained popular with audiences and continued in the Proletkult repertory for nearly a year.

Eisenstein's theater work up to this point contained strong correlations with Meyerhold's methods. For both theater directors, dramaturgy is oriented principally to the performer and the spectator and only secondarily to the character contained in the play text. Direct impact on the spectator is their primary aim. While Stanislavsky maintained artistic goals of achieving authentic experience and real life within a confined, intimate stage world, their goal was to create a spectacle within the theater auditorium by linking stage to audience through direct presentation of the performance work. Meyerhold and Eisenstein in this period structured the spectacle around its emotionally active components, its points of incitement toward the audience. The circus seemed to them the purest form of emotional stimulation, one not in the service of ideas or refined beauty. There the body is vastly more important than either the voice or dialogue. The trick and eccentric act provide no foundation for an illusion of reality or for stability and objectivity in the naturalistic stage property.

In his memoirs, Yutkevitch recalls telling Eisenstein in 1922 of a favorite fairground attraction; the director quickly interrupted their conversation and explained that Eccentrist performances should be called "scenic attractions." Eisenstein reasoned that in Eccentrist theater, as at the fairground, the aim is to shock the spectator with a physical effect. In "Montage of Attractions," published in May 1923 in conjunction with *The Wise Man* production, he elaborates this line of thought:

An attraction (in our diagnosis of theater) is any aggressive moment in theater, i.e. any element of it that subjects the audience to emotional or psychological influence, verified by experience and mathematically calculated to produce specific emotional shocks in the spectator in their proper order within the whole. These shocks provide the only opportunity of perceiving the ideological aspect of what is being shown, the final ideological conclusion. (The path to knowledge encapsulated in the phrase, "through the living play of the passions," is specific to theater.) (W 34)

Eisenstein further insists that the devices of attraction are not limited to those of the Eccentrist trick, which is a stunt "complete in itself," apart from the spectator. Yet, Eccentrism remains central to the statement (which announces his work in "agit-attraction" theater as part of the "dynamic and eccentric" left wing in culture) and to *The Wise Man* production, according to an appended list of twenty-five attractions. Of that number, fourteen fully involve circus acts, from crude clowning to a climactic inclined-wire routine.

Another category of attraction is the image repertory of popular culture, acknowledged in the statement's references to Georg Grosz's storehouse of images and Alexander Rodchenko's compilation of photographic illustrations. Expressive movement is also one of the performance's attractions, but Eisenstein focuses less on the actor—and a transformation of emotion into excitation—than on audience reaction. His new dramaturgy holds that "the spectator himself constitutes the basic material of the theater." The design of a performance is to be governed ultimately not by an affective goal, but an ideological one: "to guide the spectator in the desired direction (frame of mind)." In the statement's vocabulary, ideology is the structure to immediate reality, which is lived sensually and psychologically. Unlike the emotional excitation and perception of affect that results from biomechanics, through attractions the aggressive stimulation of a spectator's affective system will lead, in the aggregate, to cognitive understanding. Ideology is the final, coordinating mental reflex to a succession of affective stimuli.

The other word in the phrase "montage of attractions" has direct associations with Constructivism. Photomontage had been a popular form since the turn of the century; Eisenstein recalled being fascinated as a child by French photomontage albums in the family library. (The first Russian director to apply the term to filmmaking was apparently Lev Kuleshov in 1917.) In the 1923 statement, *montage* directly carries the meanings of the French root: "assemblage," "fitting together," and more generally "construction," all terms that Eisenstein uses interchangeably at this point in his theory. The materials fitted together, according to "Montage of Attractions," are individual performance attractions, the corresponding audience response, and the aggregate interrelation between these first two factors. In his exposition of Constructivist principles, Alexei Gan makes a similar assertion: "The construction discovers the actual process of putting together. Thus we have the third discipline, the discipline of the formation of conception through the use of worked material."[10] Disclosure of the processes of composition, the third Constructivist discipline (the other two are tectonics and texture), correlates with the Formalist principle of baring the device and with reflexive principles of modernism generally.

For the 1923–24 Proletkult season Eisenstein collaborated on two new productions with Sergei Tretyakov.[11] In the magazine *LEF* (an abbreviation standing for Left Front of the Arts), Tretyakov proclaimed that "factographic" literature embodied a cultural mandate for the Soviet age as Tolstoy's epic realism had for nineteenth-century Russia. His new play *Do You Hear, Moscow?* was inspired by recent Communist revolts in Germany and Hungary, but its imagery and manner were that of Eccentrism and Grand Guignol. Some years later, Eisentein recalled that the production's *mise en scène* was intended to focus audience attention on discrete, concrete aspects of setting, gesture, and facial expression: "The composition singled out groups, shifted the spectator's attention from one point to another, presented close-ups, a hand holding a letter, the play of eyebrows, a glance."[12] The melodramatic plot presents antagonism elsewhere in Europe between the ruling class and activists who lead the workers in revolt at the play's close, during which a monumental poster of Lenin is displayed. To lend a greater sense of actuality to the scenes of revolt, Eisenstein scheduled the play's premiere to fall on the anniversary of the October Revolution, the same occasion on which its final scene is set.

Eisenstein's last production for Proletkult, the one that marks his departure from theater, was Tretyakov's *Gas Masks*, which was based on newspaper accounts of Soviet workers' efforts to seal a dangerous gas leak. Tretyakov composed the play for performance in an auditorium but Eisenstein, pursuing goals undertaken with his first Proletkult production of *The Mexican*, decided to stage it in the Moscow Gasworks. In keeping with the choice of a real locale and the actuality of characters, Eccentrist stylization in costuming, makeup, and behavior was discarded. The performance area included huge tanks and a network of conduits, ladders, catwalks, and scaffolds and was viewed from workbenches located on the plant floor. Theater was now brought to a real, functioning Constructivist environment, an actual factory for performance. With the audience surrounded by the noise and acrid odors of the gasworks, a spectator's experience of actual place was finally achieved. In another stroke of factographic dramaturgy, Eisenstein timed the last scene to coincide with arrival of the night-shift, when real workers replaced actors and ignited the gas jets. He subsequently commented, however, that the real factory environment negated the play's stage effects, dialogue, and action. *Gas Masks* closed after only four performances in March and April of 1924.

In its treatment of contemporary subjects, Eisenstein's theater work emphasizes qualities of actuality and immediacy over any properties of historicity. The Tretyakov text to *Gas Masks* contains a schematic conflict between the factory manager, a member of the NEP middle class who dissipates plant safety funds in drink, and his sickly son, who has joined the Komsomol (Communist League of Youth). The production does not seem to have treated this plotline critically, as a sentimental and bourgeois story form. The treatment of story form in Eisenstein's films will provide precisely such a critique. The *Gas Masks* production privileged an experiential impression of the tasks and dangers of modern production over any ideological inquiry into the forms of relations or means in the production process.

In the process of their Proletkult work together in 1923, Tretyakov and Eisenstein prepared a program for actors they termed "Expressive Movement."[13] Adapting the gymnastics training devised by the German Rudolf Bode, William James's schema of affective behavior, and Kleist's ideas on the marionette theater, their program approaches movement as the organization of "material forms in a spatial network and of organic processes in a temporal network" to achieve an "affective design." Expressive movement is a dialectical synthesis that arises from conflict between a body's conscious, utilitarian aims and its unconscious, instinctive reflexes. Eisenstein disassociated expressive movement from Meyerhold's biomechanics in stressing the disjunctive and contradictory aspects of bodily reflexes and motions. The trained actor is equivalent to the circus performer or athlete able to achieve efficiently concrete tasks, tasks that will induce in spectators psychological states through their motor responses. The actor is not expected to experience affectively an image, character, situation, or feeling. Rather, through motor skills, the actor transfers emotional experiencing, without its conversion onstage into sentiment, to "where it belongs, specifically to the auditorium." There, the spectator "reflexively repeats in weakened form the entire system of the actor's movements."

The affective paradigm of expressive attractions is preserved in Eisenstein's early theory on cinema. Other elements in "Expressive Movement" anticipate his first experiments in film form. Emphasis on "the approach to a movement" as a means of underscoring a gesture or an event develops into overlapped depiction of movement such as the *Potemkin* sailor's smashing of a dinner plate. Construction of the "collision of two motor movements" in acting anticipates the montage passage within the Odessa steps sequence when celebration turns to horror, a reversal marked by the recoiling movements of the dark-haired woman, depicted in extreme close-up. The expressive technique of "restraint" anticipates the delay and retardation of action through film montage, as in the bridge-raising sequence of *October*.

Film Construction

In general, the design concepts for Meyerhold and Proletkult productions of the classic repertory sought to urbanize and actualize the older plays. Even in the case of contemporary material, the dramatic text often became a secondary element amidst the modernized forms of its presentation. With other stage directors of the day, Eisenstein shared three essential goals: to make stage space dynamic, to isolate and enlarge actual details of the ensemble, and to incorporate material reality into the theater environment. To achieve the first objective, Eisenstein designed stage blocking to include chase tempos, quick changes in the action, scene intersections, and the concurrent performance of scenes. Kinetic stage machinery was used to represent the dynamics of the city and the interrelationship between modern man and urban environment. To achieve the second objective, his designs of the lighting, costuming, and blocking arranged to shift audience attention to details other than those emphasized through dialogue. The third objective was pursued by bringing into theater a degree of the topicality and factuality manifest in the newspaper, radio, and the photographic media.

Considerable efforts were made in this period toward "cinefication" of the theater, in Meyerhold's usage, to achieve the levels of actuality and materiality possible in film. (Government directives to bring cinema to the countryside, a source for the term *cinefication*, grew in earnest in 1922.) The Meyerhold production of *Earth in Turmoil* in March 1923, for example, involved an unprecedented number of large, real objects as stage properties. In substituting facts for fabrications in this drama of the Soviet civil war, Meyerhold brought onstage motor vehicles, field telephones, machine guns, a harvester, and a complete military kitchen. The Red Army costumes were actual uniforms, the actors wore no makeup, and the lighting was furnished by huge searchlights at the front of the auditorium. The production was subsequently performed outdoors, once with the participation of troops and cavalry. In the same year, 1923, a proletarian and futurist troupe named Theater of the Blue Blouse began performances of a simulated "cinema review," an evolution from the "living newspaper" and other presentational modes of theater developed for largely illiterate audiences. Known also as "living film" and "electrified theater," the program was performed under lights equipped with rotating filters that created the flickering effect of early cinema.

The *Do You Hear, Moscow?* and *Gas Masks* productions gave precedence to materiality of setting on the premise that modern popular and industrial forms offer the foremost means by which to represent the social and cultural raw materials available to Bolshevik artists. The means of representation were intended to accord with the axes of contemporary, material reality: the outward forms of rapid, heavy industrialization and an urban, proletarian worldview. The requirements of dramatic perform-ance, however, did not enable Eisenstein to construct a comprehensible materialist perspective. A new medium of representation seemed neces-sary.

One attraction in *The Wise Man* staging was film exhibition. Early in the play's action, theft of the character Glumov's diary is presented through a film clip that parodies American and French detective serials, then very popular among Soviet audiences. Later, the thief is shown on film arriving by car outside the Proletkult Theater, at which point the movie screen is darkened and the live actor portraying the character bursts into the auditorium. The thief carries Glumov's diary, which itself is a film attraction running a few minutes. The diary portrays Glumov's offstage activities and records the transformations of a clown into a swas-tika, a patient donkey, and a helpless infant.

While Eisenstein considered this film segment to have nothing to do with montage in cinema, it contains a variety of shot compositions. Shot transitions were managed through the same in-camera techniques of fad-ing and stop action used by the "trick film" pioneer Georges Méliès. A concluding film clip during the stage performance parodied the tradi-tional curtain call: Eisenstein appears onscreen against the playbill, filmed as background. He smiles and turns from side to side in the man-ner of Pathé's trademark rooster. For stage director Eisenstein, the film attraction offered another opportunity to contemporize theater through an incorporation of the mass media.

The diary and other material amounted to 140 meters of film, all shot within one day in March 1923. The leftist documentarian filmmaker Dziga Vertov had been assigned to instruct Eisenstein and his troupe, but he left the amateurs to their own devices after only a few shots were taken. The cameraman who completed the shooting was Boris Frantzisson, best known later for his work on the documentary *Turksib* (1929). Ironically, Eisenstein's fictional film actuality was reabsorbed into documentary proper when Vertov included portions of it in an anthology of *Kinopravda* material in May 1923. For the remainder of the decade Eisenstein was to argue against Vertov's methods, but in another ironic turn Eduard Tisse, cameraman and invaluable collaborator on all of Eisenstein's released fea-tures, had developed his skills over the previous seven years working in documentary film, including Vertov's unit. The collaboration with Tisse would begin in July 1924.

In its drama the film diary in *The Wise Man* imitates trick film and adventure genre series like that of *Fantômas*, directed by Louis Feuillade. As a film "document" of Glumov's activities, it parodies Pathé news digests and Soviet agitational newsreels, most pointedly the *Kinonedelya* (*Cinema Weekly*, 1918–19) and *Kinopravda* (*Cinema Truth*, 1923–25) series prepared by Dziga Vertov. The circumstances of Eisenstein's entry into cinema thus fully involve the two tendencies fiction and documentary, which historians and critics traditionally have used to divide and define the fields of cinematic representation. Dichotomies such as artifice/reality, montage/film shot, manipulation/disclosure, and formative/realist, which serve theorists like Siegfried Kracauer, Béla Balázs, and André Bazin, do not ultimately determine cinematic form for Eisenstein, as a later summary of his debate against Vertov will demonstrate.

The film archivist and documentary editor Esther Shub introduced Eisenstein to the principles of editing construction in cinema. Shub, the wife of Alexei Gan, held a position in the state cinema bureau that required her to remove or restructure offending material from imported films before their Soviet distribution. Of the feature films shown on Soviet screens in 1924, over 90 percent were produced in foreign countries. The re-editing of foreign films was thus a prominent element of the cultural scene; regular columns were devoted to the subject in the Soviet film press. With Eisenstein observing each step, Shub re-edited the two parts of Fritz Lang's *Dr. Mabuse der Spieler* (1922) into a single feature, an anticapitalist story released in March 1924 under the title *Gilded Rot*. The immense ideological potential of editing was confirmed to Eisenstein by similar revisions of the German film *Danton* (1921). With two simple cuts Soviet film editor Benjamin Boitler reversed the original meaning of a key scene and changed its political message to a sympathetic portrait of Robespierre. Such political translations of foreign films for Soviet audiences disclosed the medium's power to manipulate ideological codes.

In the years of Eisenstein's work for Proletkult, Lev Kuleshov was conducting a filmmaking workshop. By 1917 Kuleshov had defined montage as the result of the film artist's efforts to "compose separate filmed fragments, disordered and disjointed, into a single whole and juxtapose these separate moments into a more advantageous, integral and rhythmical sequence."[14] His workshop for film actors, design, direction, and montage originated in 1920 at the State Film Institute (known by its initials VGIK) located in Moscow. In 1922 he removed the workshop from the institute's facilities while his students remained registered there in order to qualify for diplomas.[15] The Kuleshov group was housed temporarily in Meyerhold's Zom Theater in Moscow in the early 1920s. The regular membership included individuals who were to become prominent in Soviet cinema, among them the directors Vsevolod Pudovkin and Boris Barnet.

Eisenstein and Grigori Alexandrov studied at the workshop for three months in the winter of 1922–23. In the training of actors, the Kuleshov workshop favored a system for the stage devised by François Delsarte and widely adapted in Russia at the time as an alternative to Stanislavsky's method. The Delsarte system involves a precise lexicon of gestures and poses that presume to replicate each of the emotional or psychological states possible within a dramatic character. Dance and rhythmic gymnastics were the rudiments for the actor in affixing each psychological moment in a character's development. By the end of 1923, with his own program on "Expressive Movement" developed as an alternative, Eisenstein opposed the metrical system of gesticulation for its segregation and displacement of the body's members from a unified center. It is important to note that at this threshold into filmmaking, Eisenstein argues for unity of body expression and image in the actor's performance, while soon he will experiment radically with fragmentation and isolation in its representation.

Kuleshov later recollected that while with the workshop Eisenstein and Alexandrov did extensive exercises on crowd scenes, which they prepared in the form of shooting scripts and shot lists. The workshop was also active in constructing "films without film," stage productions designed to simulate the nonstop action and rapid scene transitions of American film. These productions are another example of cinefication in Soviet theater and they embodied the plastic qualities Kuleshov extolled as "Americanism." In 1922 Kuleshov urged Soviet filmmakers to emulate the intense pace of editing in American cinema, the very quality that within five years will define Soviet cinema for world film audiences.

As the result of mounting documentary footage during the civil war period and of re-editing imported films for Soviet exhibition, Kuleshov was adept at montage. Through the workshop exercises he investigated further the degree to which film construction can create an impression of reality unique to the medium—reflective of, yet finally independent from, the material world. By composing along consistent orientation lines the movement of actors within shots taken in various locales, and intercutting shots of distant Moscow landmarks and shots of the White House taken from an American travelogue, Kuleshov demonstrated film's power to create its own "artificial landscape" or "creative geography." In simply matching the spatial cues of an actor's movements, the movements within the film frame suggest that disparate locales constitute a contiguous space for the duration of the editing sequence's linear continuity in its dramatic action.

The most famous of Kuleshov's montage demonstrations is now known as the Kuleshov effect. Working with a close-up of the Russian actor Mozzhukhin filmed in a comparatively expressionless pose (a shot acquired from re-edited material), Kuleshov intercut the close-up with different kinds of material to form three distinct sequences. As Pudovkin describes them, the close-up in one sequence is linked with a bowl of steaming soup, in a second with a woman's body laid out in a coffin, and in the third with a child at play.[16] Kuleshov and Pudovkin report that audiences interpreted the close-up strictly according to context, seeing in the actor's face hunger in the first sequence, grief in the second, and joy in the third. Many viewers additionally expressed astonishment over Mozzhukhin's dramatic range. The reported spectator response indicates that the two shots joined in each sequence are comprehended as one unit of meaning. Furthermore, a juxtaposition of two disparate shot contents is taken to resemble a causal relationship between the shots.

The Kuleshov effect marks an alternative to D. W. Griffith's methods, whose relational editing typically interpolates in close-up a detail in the setting (a significant object) or in the acting (a theatrical gesture) to heighten the emotion of a scene after the dramatic tableau is established. Kuleshov shows that the emotion and action can derive completely from the interrelationship of a facial close-up to other shots, without establishing in any other way the presence of the actor on the scene. Thus his technique demonstrated a greater freedom in dramaturgy and associational signification than was yet realized in the American story film.

For Kuleshov and his students it followed that montage constitutes the fundamental technique of cinema. In his words, which reflect Constructivist principles in the other arts, "with montage it becomes possible both to break down and to reconstruct, and ultimately to remake the material." These methods are to be strictly distinguished from those of the trick film, since montage achieves its effects "by organization of the material, rather than by a technical gimmick."[17] The fanciful tales and acts of magic in the films of Méliès, for instance, are achieved by means of special effects staged in his studio, arranged in the camera, and applied during processing. The new effect produced through montage in Kuleshov's workshop, on the other hand, results from the linking of relatively commonplace material. Montage endows the filmed material with greater autonomy from the profilmic events it records.

As Noel Burch has explained, the experiments in montage by Kuleshov and the first generation of Soviet directors took place at a time when the system of representation in Western narrative cinema was being consolidated.[18] That consolidation would mean a linear organization within the classical film narrative of spatial, temporal, acting, and editing codes. While the expressivity of film language was significantly enlarged by the Soviet masters of the silent period, Burch argues that each Soviet director—with the sole exception of Vertov—remained ultimately within the institutional mode of representation adopted from American and Western

European cinema. In counterargument to Burch's thesis, the present study will examine the nonlinear historiography that the montage of Eisenstein's silent cinema creates and its disruptions to narrative sequence through the intervention of discourse.

In Eisenstein's experiments at Proletkult with cinefication of the stage, as much as he tried to incorporate actual objects and real environment into the action, the theater's intractable spatial and plastic limitations did not permit any extensively new exploration into the interaction between character and milieu. Kinetic devices in stage construction and actors' movements enabled him to suggest the dynamics of this interaction superficially, but they failed to convey a materialist or dialectical concept of human action. Eisenstein's opportunity to work fully in cinema came in April 1924, when Goskino (the State Cinema production unit) accepted his proposal for a cycle of films on Russian political events leading to 1917.

In his first years as a filmmaker, Eisenstein considered the move from theater to cinema as the second formative break in his development, the first having been the change in career from engineer to artist as the result of the Revolution. Writing with radical fervor in 1926, he ridicules the idea of any mutual growth of theater and cinema. His essay describes their relationship as an antagonistic process of sublation until a point where theater reached the limits of its possibilities and, dialectically, cinema with its new forms of representation took over the process. Commenting about the cultural debates that preoccupied Meyerhold's company and Proletkult, he states categorically, "Theater as an independent unit in revolutionary construction, revolutionary theater as a problem, has virtually ceased to exist" (W 82). In this separatist attitude toward the theater, Eisenstein was in the company of filmmakers like Abram Room and Vertov.

The sum of these differences between theater and cinema in Eisenstein's development does not amount to an epistemological break in his artistic practices and thought, though in the rhetoric of that period he would sometimes claim so. There are strong continuities in matters such as typage, attractions, and a reflex model of audience response. The move into cinema does mark for Eisenstein a point at which his study of materialism and dialectical thought, begun in 1922, more fully provides a content for his work and an epistemology for understanding the processes involved in its creation and reception. Through the 1920s, that content is a history of class struggle.

CHAPTER TWO

Strike:
The Beginnings of Revolution

Eisenstein's first feature is the only completed film of seven for a proposed series titled *Towards the Dictatorship*. As originally conceived by writers in the Proletkult collective, the series was to be a historical survey of events leading to the October Revolution and Lenin's declaration of the dictatorship of the proletariat. The series outline, which was to include a film on 1905 and one on 1917, contains the rudiments for Eisenstein's second and third features as well. *Strike* entails, however, a more generic view of history than either *Battleship Potemkin* or *October*. The first film portrays not a single, documented sequence of events but a typical pattern of political agitation during the two decades before 1917, agitation that fostered a revolutionary outbreak in 1905. Lecturing in exile on the eve of the February Revolution of 1917, Lenin pointed to the 1905 uprising as "the *first*, though certainly not the last, great revolution in history in which the mass political strike played an extraordinarily important part."[1]

The proposal for the *Dictatorship* cycle indicated that the seven episodes "are impersonal throughout, only two have a mass character," *Strike* being one of these.[2] In its historical origins, the industrial strike is an illegal act and is thus equally an action against state authority. During the 1840s, Marx and Engels considered the strike a revolutionary means through which the proletariat developed political identity and consciousness as a class for itself. It was equally this new, illegal class's training ground for the inevitable social war. In Engels's words, strikes are "the military school of the working men in which they prepare themselves for the great struggle . . . ; as schools of war, the unions are unexcelled."[3]

Though trade unionism gradually gained legitimacy elsewhere in Europe over the course of the nineteenth century, under the tsars Russia's organized workers had no legal status. In her account of Russian history, the Marxist radical Rosa Luxemburg writes that the wave of industrial and general strikes culminates after a decade in the insurrectionary "moment" of January 1905, which "for the first time awoke class feeling and class consciousness in millions upon millions as if by electric shock."[4] From this perspective, the industrial strike is a historic event whose protagonist is the aggregate character of the working masses. The historian Sheila Fitz-patrick reports that the workers' movement centered in St. Petersburg, which rose to a general strike in the summer of 1914, provoked observers at the time to doubt the political prudence of Russia's mass mobilization for war beyond the empire's borders.[5]

In the Marxist critique of capitalist production, workers employed in the primary industries represent the most advanced political force within society. Moreover, mechanized production and the industrial organization of labor establish a proof for Marx and Lenin that the liberation of common humanity from lives of toil is a historical inevitability and not mere utopian fantasy. With such ideas in mind, Marx attended the great industrial exhibitions held in London during the 1850s and 1860s. With evident fascination in the new machinery, he gathered technical information and production statistics. Large-scale industrial reproduction of the instruments of production was for Marx the definitive historical feature of the modern age. The terms used in *Capital* to describe heavy industrialization are often mythic; it has a "cyclopean scale" and the power of Thor. Through the industrial revolution, humankind produces forces that rival nature's: "In Modern Industry man succeeded for the first time in making the product of his past labor work on a large scale gratuitously, like the forces of Nature."

From Marx's perspective on modern production we better understand the thematics of heavy industry in *Strike*, the battleship in *Potemkin*, modern armaments and machinery in *October*, and the tractor in *Old and New*. Their presence is material testimony to technological modernity and to a communist future predicated upon the industrial revolution. In Marx's estimation, the most persuasive testimony is the manufacture of locomotives and ships: "the construction of railways and ocean steamers on a stupendous scale called into existence the cyclopean machines now employed in the construction of prime movers."[6] Unlike the prime or unmoved mover of theology and philosophy, these prime movers are the modern, man-made impetus driving history forward. Thus, the locomotive and the battleship become apt metaphors for proletarian revolution. One of *Strike*'s scenes, for example, is set in an industrial yard heaped with the axle and wheel assemblies for railway carriages. Here, a revolutionary cell holds meetings for striking workers.

Production and Class Conflict

Released to the general public in April 1925, *Strike* has a narrative action divided into six segments whose separations are marked through a fade to another setting in combination with a dialogue or expository title insert.

With persistent shortages in usable equipment, Soviet movie houses and worker club theaters often had only one projector available. Thus the narrative segmentation in *Strike* probably corresponds to the reel divisions within release prints. Analyzed on the basis of content, these segments can be summarized as: the general situation among industrial workers; immediate cause of the strike; shutdown of the factory; repercussions among workers and their families of a prolonged strike; provocation by hired agents; repression of the working class.

After a shot of factory smokestacks that pour out black smoke, *Strike*'s first human image is of a fat, chortling stereotypical bourgeois, contextualized as yet only by the film feature's general title. A subsequent title card, "The Managing Director," identifies him generically. His milieu is established by an image of the steady traffic of clerks streaming back and forth through the swinging doors of an office. The film establishes a broader physical and social setting with an overhead tracking shot that runs the length of a factory floor. Subsequent shots specify the location as a locomotive works.

Heavy industry was of course a favorite subject for Futurist, Constructivist, and Proletkult visual artists, but its thematic possibilities appealed to Eisenstein as much as its graphic ones. The narrative throughout *Strike* stresses class aspects of the relations in production. In depicting the general situation among factory workers, its first section focuses not on working conditions or wage slavery but on management's surveillance and harassment of labor organizers. The first signs of fraternization among workers arouse the suspicions of a foreman and a company inspector, who report to their immediate superiors in the plant director's office. The chain of command is an intricate bureaucracy, leading up from the plant to the managing director, outward to the police and militia, and further up to the owners. The structure is a network of delegated authority and power, implemented through a series of messages and telephone contacts. A rapid montage of these brief telephone exchanges conveys the powerful control and implementation of information within the bureaucracy. The owners operate exclusively through this chain of intermediaries; at no time is there direct contact between them and workers. The workers have access only to the lowest ranks of secretaries and shop managers, who are officious and petty. The methods of organization among workers are later contrasted with this bureaucracy in order to convey the nature of class conflict.

The chain of capitalist command also extends down within the working ranks, where company agents and police spies operate. In order to infiltrate the workers district, undercover agents assume roles of an ice cream vendor, a blind beggar, and the exhibitor of a dancing bear. Optical devices are used to denote cinematographically their acts of spying. A gradual lap dissolve reveals a smirking villain beneath the guise of a pitiful beggar. The Lang film that Eisenstein observed being re-edited is full of such trick devices, as when a slow lap dissolve reveals the master criminal Mabuse in the disguise of a respectable old man.

In its characterization of counterrevolutionary agents, *Strike* presents them as animal figures in a bestiary of human treachery. Eisenstein freely develops the resources within the moving photographic image for the construction of caricature. His drawing activity was the initial phase of this exploration into the axes of substitution and comparison in the visual language of caricature. As a realistic and metonymic context for this set of visual metaphors, *Strike* provides the setting of a pet shop. One spy is equated to a monkey by a series of lap dissolves between the two in close-up as the primate sucks from a feeder and the man drinks from a bottle, both making facial tics as they do so. Agents Owl, Fox, and Bulldog are caricatured through similar uses of gradual dissolves and wipes. Formally, the contrivance of these optical tricks is made apparent through the montage's disclosure of the process. Thematically, the artifices of trick film defamiliarize the agents so that they are recognized to have no intrinsic, fully human identity.

To emphasize further their deception and inhumanness, *Strike* places the spies at a substantial distance from the immediacy of the strike action. Their presence is shown reflected in mirrors and shop windows, inverted in a daylight image reflected in the glass ball of a streetlamp, enshadowed in silhouette shots of them snooping and conspiring, and masked by the screen frame or matte inserts. In the pursuit of strike leaders, the spies' shadows come into view first. The theme of surveillance is reiterated by use of iris effects for transitions to new locales in the chase, and by close-ups of agent Owl's single open eye, which nervously watches his prey. Such compositions belong to the specular motifs that are to be found throughout Eisenstein's cinema. The word *specular* is used in this study in reference to the look, regard, or scrutiny directed by the camera or a character outward, a sense that admittedly departs from its primary dictionary definitions.

The physical contrast between police agents and the masses is total. An example from the first section is the swimming scene, designed as much for discursive presentation of the workers' physical beauty as for narrative purposes, as can also be said of the hammock scene in *Potemkin* and many sequences in *Que Viva Mexico!* Naked except for shorts, the workers are stalwart and self-possessed. Owl—a skinny, spectacled figure wearing an oversized hat—foolishly hopes to pass unnoticed as he spies on the workers. The bathers soon corner the spy, dunk him, then chase him off. Shown as essentially good-natured and unsuspecting, the workers react to espionage as a minor annoyance until the last two narrative segments, when they experience its brutal consequences. Narrative momentum thus far is sustained by the proletariat in physical, productive, and militant roles. Their antagonists are either on the periphery (in the case of police spies) or behind the scenes (in the case of the bourgeoisie) of worker activity and activism.

Owners and high executives simply do not work. Onscreen they either idly smoke cigars and chat or greedily consume liquor and delicacies while seated in overstuffed armchairs. What business they are shown to conduct is a momentary interruption of their leisure. Worker demands are handed to the owners on a silver tray by a butler, who himself displays distaste for even this remote contact with strikers. Capitalists are men of either plump or lean features and, regardless of physique, they remain immobile; only gratification of the senses or annoyance over labor disturbances animate them. Company underlings are generally thin and nervous in manner. Police agents, hired from the lumpenproletariat, are grotesque and hyperactive.

As Roberta Reeder has documented, these properties of caricature had great currency in Russian agitational and propaganda art in the first decades of this century.[7] The traditions of visual satire date back two centuries earlier in the case of the *lubok*, the popular Russian broadsheet print. Such forms were an integral part of revolutionary expression from 1905 onward. They served in the creation of antiwar statements in images by Mayakovsky and Kazimir Malevich. Political posters of the civil war period (1918–21) widely adopted lubok styles. The clown styles of Eccentrist theater utilized the stock types familiar also in agit-prop puppet shows. The New Economic Policy of the 1920s provoked a resurgence in the visual lexicon of the anticapitalist imagery utilized in *Strike*.

In contrast to the upper-class types, workers are athletic and fluid in their movements. The contrast is a difference in acting styles. The natural, easy behavior of workers is distinct from the capitalists' virtual paralysis and from their managers' and agents' oddity. Eisenstein has thus adapted the Eccentrist mode to visualize themes of class difference, making the same contrast between naked authenticity in the working class and elaborate cunning in the dominant class made in *The Mexican*.

Under heavy surveillance, workers at first conduct their radical activities in secret. But their organizing methods never resemble the clandestine maneuvers of the state. The call for workers to unite initially circulates in a handwritten note and soon after in printed form (a shot is inserted showing a press duplicating the message). Marking the close of the first section, the huge overhead crane moves forward scattering labor leaflets along the shop floor. Narratively, the first section establishes the organization and readiness for mass action in the working class. Labor meetings are later held outdoors to large gatherings; spies have no difficulty in locating them. With repression, the protest will take openly to the factory grounds and to the streets.

The film's second section presents the immediate circumstance that sparks an outbreak, the suicide of a worker named Jacob Strongine. The section opens with a repetition of the establishing shot of the workplace, a high overhead track of the factory floor. Prominent in the shot is a vast network of belts that transmit power to the presses and lathes below. At this distance, workers are indistinguishable from the machines they operate. A lower overhead track follows, and the belts now rise beyond the frame border to the transmission axle above, out of view. Now the machinists can be observed at their work stations. A collage shot follows the title, "A micrometer is stolen." Shown in the inset is a close-up of the workbench from which the instrument is taken. Enclosing this inset is a long shot of an aisle between rows of machines and down which the thief flees. This visual conjunction achieves the formal correlation of detail and milieu Eisenstein had sought with less success in the theater. Through a narrative ellipsis, identity of the thief is never established onscreen. The political discourse that organizes narrative events, however, identifies the thief as an *agent provocateur* in the employ of management and the police.

Jacob Strongine, the only character named individually in the entire film, rushes frantically to the shop managers after discovering that the expensive instrument is gone. The managers respond with accusations that he is a thief. Downcast, Jacob returns to his work area. The following shots are then mounted in accelerated succession: medium shot of the overhead network of belts; close-up of a noose made with a trousers belt; close-up of this belt snapped taut; medium shot of Jacob's dangling legs. Fellow workers untie the dead man and find a suicide note expressing the shame of being branded a thief. The visual analogy between Jacob's belt noose and the powerline belts succinctly conveys the alienated relationship of worker to workplace under conditions that deprive his class of control over the instruments and relations of production. At this narrative pivot, where an incidental theft and an individual's death set in motion extensive and massive consequences, the plot reveals work relations in the factory to be essentially property relations. This alienated condition is perhaps the most familiar and persuasive term in the subjective code of Marxism.

In the walkout that ensues, workers shut down the factory's power supply; the stilled transmission lines are shown in close-up. The sequence closes with an overhead tracking shot that reverses the camera movement of the establishing shot, as workers throw down their tools, leave their benches, and join the human tide swarming over machinery and rushing out of the building, directly toward the camera. The revolutionary outbreak is arranged often to project frontally from the screen at the viewer, in a form of direct address. Thereby, the narrative event becomes equally a rhetorical mode. By the conclusion of the second part, the factory locale is transformed pictorially from a mechanical and impersonal environment, a place of surveillance and treachery, to one humanized by the workers' activism. The concluding shot superimposes the image of three workers, defiantly crossing their arms, against that of a huge, turning dynamo coming to a halt. In scale, the workers are larger than the machine. The superimposition restructures the relationship between man and machine that previously prevailed. Narratively, it functions as an end-stop; rhetorically, it delivers an exhortation.

The two codes of Marxism operate concurrently in the presentation of Jacob Strongine's death. Shot composition and a Constructivist montage convey through objective correlations the relations of worker to machines and property within capitalist production. The narrative and rhetorical levels convey the subjective condition of alienated work under capitalism, as in the correlation of belt noose to powerline. By the conclusion of section two, an alternative relationship among workers, independent of the production process, has developed. The transition from moving to stilled transmission lines, marked by the close-up of Strongine's belt noose, signifies the cessation of routine work and the onset of revolutionary action. Accompanying this transition is a reorientation in dramatic focus, away from individual fate and toward the amassing of workers into a collective body.

With the factory shut down, workers enjoy an unexpected holiday. Part three shows them for the first time in a domestic setting. The workers district has a celebratory air, fathers are able to relax with their families, everybody joins in outings and music. The sunlit brightness of the scenes, the pictures of leisure they contain, and the relaxed rhythm in editing superinscribe one another in depicting the holiday atmosphere. Roland Barthes terms such practices of overstatement the "third meaning" in Eisenstein. Barthes finds in *Potemkin* and *Ivan the Terrible* that there exists beyond the informational and symbolic levels an excess of meaning, "a luxury, an expenditure without exchange; this luxury does not *yet* belong to today's politics, although it is *already* part of tomorrow's."[8] Barthes has located one of the utopian dimensions within Eisenstein's cinema.

The effect of such visual luxury is to create an *aura*, a term used here apart from the meaning of *uniqueness* Walter Benjamin associates with artworks prior to the age of mechanical reproduction. In *Strike* an aura is found, for example, in the luminous quality to the scene of a young worker and his wife bathing their child outdoors. Aura effects abound in the swimming scene, with its play of sunlight and motion, and in shots of workers agilely descending the axle and wheel assemblies to attend a meeting. In crowd scenes an aura is particularly strong because the rushing figures leave blurred, bright traces on the screen. The crowd shots bring to mind Cubo-Futurist studies in motion and light radiation by painters like Mikhail Larionov (who developed an aesthetic of Rayonism), Malevich, Natalia Goncharova, and, in Western Europe, Filippo Marinetti and Marcel Duchamp.

For Russian modernist painters, the traditional icon was a direct source for visionary imagery and the unique lighting effects of the aureole.[9] In cinema, an aura effect can be achieved through overlapped action, which Eisenstein explores in *Strike* but does not develop fully until *Potemkin* and *October*. The aura in *Strike*'s action shots enhances the workers' athleticism and dynamism. In static shots it monumentalizes and idealizes their stature. But this utopian surplus does not embrace the entire action and visuals of *Strike* as it does in *Old and New*.

In section three the workers' holiday comes to an abrupt end with arrival of the militia, which cordons off the district. Domestic bliss quickly sours as families go hungry and their few personal possessions must be pawned in exchange for food. The strike becomes a protracted struggle against starvation as well as against the ruling class. By the close of section three, bloody suppression of the workers' revolt has begun. Owners are shown sharing after-dinner cigars and liqueurs in a mansion. The surroundings with their Greek columns, grand stairways, and enormous open spaces can be described as Olympian. And like gods, the owners in cursory and negligent ways cause the deaths of men, women, and children.

Shots of owners at their leisure are next crosscut with shots of cavalrymen entering the workers district. After tossing aside the workers' proclamation, an owner proceeds to the more important matter of demonstrating the operation of a lemon squeezer. The accompanying title reads "Crush down hard . . . and then the juice," and is followed by a shot of workers being herded by cavalry officers. In self-defense the workers sit down, whereupon soldiers steer their horses into the seated group, brutally trampling some of them. The montage association between the two socially remote locales is the basis of a metaphor indicating that capitalists crush the workers. Within the locale of the workers district, shots of horses trampling workers is a metonymy for their being crushed.

The principal consistency in this montage sequence is a causal relationship rather than a temporal one. The two events are concurrent in a generic sense more than in a particularized dramatic context, since the sequence lacks the time cues that would unify them as discrete events in the narrative. A rhetorical figure of generalized causation in class conflict, into which the montage translates characters and events, advances the action. The literalization in this montage entails a chain of verbal-visual connotations. The ease with which the lemon squeezer crushes, of interest and amusement to the owners and of insignificance in comparison to brutal repression, is a literalized link between the lofty, casual world of capital and the violent, empathic world of work.

A further association arises from narrative ellipsis in the sequence. The owners do not explicitly order the state to mount a police action at this point. Just as owners need not dirty their hands to crush a lemon, they need not instruct the state as to the ruling class's best interests: the police and military are an instrument of convenience for the ruling class. At the close of the sequence, a panoramic view of workers fallen and slain is presented. This is followed by a close shot of the pulped lemon, which has fallen on an owner's shoe. A servant, using the list of worker demands, cleans up the mess.

In the fourth section, police arrest one of the leaders and offer him leniency in exchange for information. Eisenstein arranges the scene of this worker's capitulation around a moment of grotesque revelation. It opens with an attractive couple attired in evening wear shown, in full shot, dancing. A subsequent shot shows the worker and a police officer seated before a banquet table. They fill the foreground, but movement is perceptible in the background, amidst the entrées laid out on the table. The camera is set farther back in the next shots and, as the striker's defection to the police progresses, the rhythmic movement of a couple's legs is visible. Viewers gradually associate this movement to the first dancers and then realize that they are dwarfs. Once the defection is complete and the worker is led away, the dancers stoop down and gorge themselves on delicacies. The sequence's montage structure has involved viewers unexpectedly in a process of concealment and disclosure. Elsewhere in *Strike* this process is given graphic equivalents within the frame of a single shot through mattes and irises, which mask and then reveal. In these ways, thematic materials are literalized through the forms of graphic devices and montage associations, which in turn lay bear the themes.

In section five, scenes of grotesque humor are juxtaposed with scenes of horror. In an effort to incite a confrontation between workers and the militia, authorities hire provocateurs from the city's lumpenproletariat. *The Communist Manifesto* defines the lumpenproletariat as the " 'dangerous class,' the social scum, that passively rotting mass thrown off by the lowest layers of old society," which in revolutionary situations can be expected to play "the part of a bribed tool of reactionary intrigue."[10] From this sublayer of humanity the police recruit a criminal known as the King. Eisenstein makes him a mock god of the underworld who presides over a realm of sunken liquor casks, which house his entourage of whores and petty thieves. As the film's only royal figure, the underworld king is also an inverted image of the tsar. This characterization is an early instance in Eisenstein's cinema of the carnivalesque. The cultural modes of carnival, defined for modern criticism by his Soviet contemporary Mikhail Bakhtin, are employed here satirically while in *Ivan the Terrible* they convey implications of social tragedy. The carnivalesque is given full attention in the chapter on Eisenstein's last film.

The king and a band of hooligans set fire to a state liquor depot near an intersection where workers pass on their way back from a demonstration. This act of arson fails to incite looting or to break up the workers' march. Drunk on vodka, the provocateurs immolate themselves. Strike leaders sound an alarm, but the police order firemen to direct their hoses at demonstrators. Workers first react to the drenching as sport, but as the water pressure increases and the firemen draw closer, fun suddenly turns to terror. This narrative segment thus ends with a peripeteia, the device of sudden reversal in circumstances and emotional key that Eisenstein perfects in *Potemkin*.

In section six, authorities no longer seek a pretext for repression after the failure of attempts at provocation. Troops are ordered to overrun the workers district and a massacre of innocents ensues, with a soldier hurling an infant from the upper story of a tenement building. The climactic sequence in *Strike* is an associative crosscutting that links bloody repression with the slaughter of livestock in an abattoir. Like the earlier trope for repression, which hinges on the word *crush*, the climax is based on a literal construct. Introducing the sequence is the title "Brutalized." Eisenstein later described the filmic imagery as "a generalized 'plastic turn of speech,' approaching a verbal image of a 'bloody slaughter-house' . . . , 'a human slaughter-house' " (*FF* 252–53). This paraphrase of content and effect, however, does not adequately convey the sequence's subtle power and meaning.

The bloody climax is linked compositionally to the previous scene, set in a police station. In that setting, the striker who had earlier defected refuses to cooperate further with police. A captain, gloating that the strike has no chance of success, takes the striker over to a map of the city, spread out on a table. With a pen, the captain circles the workers district, indicating that it is surrounded by troops. He roars with laughter at the thought; the striker leaps forward and knocks the captain off balance. Once the prisoner is subdued, the captain slams his fist on the table in outrage, overturning a bottle of ink.

At this dramatic juncture, the montage makes a leap from the police station to events of slaughter. To make clear the montage associations, the description below lists in sequence the shot correlations; cuts are indicated by the paragraphing:

In close-up, the liquid spreads over the map, obliterating the circled workers district.

As the worker is removed, the angry captain (in medium shot) shakes his fists up and down, beyond the bottom of the frame.

Close-up of a hand clutching a knife, thrusting up and down at something below the screen frame.

In long shot, a mass of panicked workers charges down a ravine; their pursuers are not in view.

Previous close-up of knife thrusts.

Close shot of knife plunging into the throat of a bull.

Medium shot of the bull collapsing to the ground.

Medium shot of dozens of hands held up in a pleading gesture.

Medium shot of bull in convulsions, his legs jerking.

The transition is not simply from one story segment to the next, but is really a leap from a narrative event to a rhetorical figure, and through that figure to a consequent narrative event. The montage also marks a shift in form, from a conventionally theatrical mode (a scene staged and played out for the camera) to a dynamic pictorial association (prior to any "stage setting" for the event) conceivable only in the forms cinema allows.

Homogeneity of gesture is one basis for the sequence's compositional associations. Subsequent close-ups show blood gushing from the bull's slit throat and splashing into a pan with a movement like the spilling of ink over the map. The shock cut from the angry police captain to the stabbing knife, and the textural similarity between the ink and the blood, intensify the film's rhetoric of violence as they disjoin the narrative. The instantaneous switch in setting from police station to abattoir, so sudden as to cause an affective response before the new setting is cognitively identified, transforms the dramatized emotion of anger into a rhetorical figure for bloody repression.

The sequence's juxtapositions and reversals are equally expressive. The unexpected cut from a close-up of the stabbing motion, restricted obliquely within the frame, to a long shot of crowds of fleeing workers, streaming past the frame, is a form of enjambment of the rhetorical figure over into another narrative event. It also conveys a sense of the state's indiscriminate violence in suppressing such outbreaks. The police captain's moment of irritation is transformed into massive slaughter. In another of the film's peripeteia, the owners' indifference and the police agents' subhumanity—sources of satire up to this point—are revealed to have terrifying consequences.

Montage of Film Attractions

As originally scripted, the last image in *Strike* was to be an extreme close-up of the open eye of a dead bull. In an article written at the time he was working on its montage, Eisenstein said that this "film attraction" would avoid the artificiality of a staged death scene, with the liability of overacting by hundreds of untrained screen extras, and present instead an impression of actual death. The montage list specifies that the workers' panicked flight be shown in long and medium shots exclusively, while activity in the slaughterhouse is predominantly in close shots. If used, however, the planned image of the butchered animal's eye might have created confusing associations with the specular motifs and animal comparisons that are linked with themes of counterrevolution.

As mounted in the released film, the concluding images establish quite different associations. In long shot, a panorama of the massacred populace is seen; dead bodies fill the entire screen space. The camera begins to pan slowly, revealing the further extent of carnage. The title "REMEMBER" is followed by an extreme close-up that shows a man's staring eyes as they focus and respond to an event positioned in the place of the film viewer. The eyes look from a face recognizably belonging to the type of working-class features shown in the film story, but it is not the face of a recognizable character. The play of emotions in the look is suspended by the next title, "PROLETARIANS!," and then develops into wide-eyed horror, a reaction interrupted by a last title, "THE END."

The stare is fully frontal, functioning as both a reaction shot and a direct address to the audience. The image in a sense literalizes the plot device of recognition. Such literalization takes place not within the narrative but in a discursive summary, as does the association of slaughterhouse to massacre. The conclusive film attraction in *Strike* is a tendentious image, not dependent upon fictional continuity. In this sense, the devices of peripeteia and recognition here function first on a discursive level and second on a plot level.

In "Montage of Film Attractions" (1924) Eisenstein indicates that his first feature film is linked to his theater work "by a common (identical) *basic* material—the *audience*—and by a common purpose—*influencing the audience in the desired direction* through a series of calculated pressures on its psyche" (W 39). In theater he experimented with various principles of expressive movement to master that purpose through the actor, but in cinema he identifies the formative principle related to acting as the movement in *perception* of the filmed material. Cinema is the "art of comparisons." It is not characters, objects, or events that the cinema of attractions compares, but rather the chain of associations connected to particular characters, objects, and events.

Film attractions exercise "a definite effect on the attention and emotions of the audience" and thus concentrate audience emotion in the direction intended by the filmmaker (W 40). To achieve its purpose, montage construction "must be a tendentious selection of, and comparison between, events, free from narrowly plot-related plans" (*W* 41). Narrative is thus governed by discourse instead of plot, and its momentum is provided by the structure of attractions. This construction also entails "constant movement of the angle of vision in relation to the material," without adherence to any requirements of plot justification (*W* 46–47). A minor theme in the essay is Eisenstein's resistance to the plotline of an "ironclad scenario," in the language of a policy beginning to emerge from Soviet film management.

In the article "The Method of Making Workers' Films," published in August 1925, Eisenstein defined the purpose of *Strike* as "an accumulation of reflexes without intervals (satisfaction), that is, a focusing of reflexes on struggle (and a lifting of potential class tone)."[11] Irrespective of this model of ideological reflexology, transposed from his theater work, the film's narrative segmenting and development stands somewhat in contradiction to its historical contexts and political discourse.

Writing in 1906 on revolutionary violence, the Marxist and syndicalist Georges Sorel explains the mythos of the mass proletarian strike as the initiative for a victorious and "great *Napoleonic battle*" through which the state is overwhelmed in a catastrophic defeat to workers.[12] In contrast, *Strike*'s final directive, "REMEMBER . . . PROLETARIANS!," concerns a debacle in revolutionary history. While the importance to class unity of collective pathos is undeniable, the audience is not exhorted simply to remember the horror and pity of defeat rendered in the narrative. The discourse presents a cautionary lesson of history. Since 1921, concessions to capitalism under the New Economic Policy and direct suppression of the workers' opposition by the Party (as in the case of the Kronstadt revolt in March 1921) were factors that deferred the proletarian promise of 1905 and 1917. One political implication of the film's exhortation for Soviet audiences in 1925 seems clear: only through organized, monitored action can the proletarian revolution now be advanced.

Organization and vigilance were of paramount concern under Lenin, who proclaimed in 1918 the new nation's immediate task to be "prolonged and persistent struggle waged by stern, proletarian discipline against the menacing element of petit-bourgeois laxity and anarchy."[13] *Strike* consistently contrasts images of mass organization with images of anarchy. Though sparked by a spontaneous outburst, the factory shutdown is primed by the agitational propaganda of political organizers. Continuation of the strike requires planning and solidarity.[14] Workers generally maintain unity within their ranks in resistance to spying and provocation, but they fail to do so in the face of armed repression. By trying to escape from the military rather than preparing to defend themselves against it, the strikers are as suicidally anarchic as the provocateurs who kill themselves in the fire intended to discredit workers. In its panicked flight from soldiers, the corps of strikers disintegrates into a chaotic mob. One of its members is crushed to death in a doorway as a mass surges at that exit. In the closing sequence, especially in those shots where their pursuers are offscreen, numbers of people are trampled by their terrorized comrades.

The force in *Strike* that is strictly organized and disciplined is the tsarist military, depicted in insistently negative associations. To the extent that such associations succeed with viewers, the film's attractions confound the intended ideological reflex. A consistent understanding of its cautionary discourse seems possible only if the spectator is dispassionately critical of the depiction of stampeding workers. The model of ideological insight following, as a reflex, from a succession of attraction-stimuli does not adequately account for the montage structure from the police station scene through the conclusion. Rather, it is formal correspondences—such as the homogeneity of gesture in hand motions of the captain and the butcher and of texture in the ink and blood—that establish a coherent ideological discourse in the film's last section. Eisenstein's further experimentation with such correspondences will lead to the development of intellectual cinema.

A Materialist Approach to Form

Another theoretical statement accompanied the release of *Strike*: "The Problem of the Materialist Approach to Form," in which the principal concerns are historiography and aesthetics. Here Eisenstein reasons that the photographic media, as inventions of the industrial revolution, have a unique opportunity as art forms to render this revolutionary advance in man's productive relationship with the material world. He goes on to claim that the "revolutionary quality of *Strike* was exemplified by the fact that it took its renewing principle . . . from those that are *directly utilitarian*: specifically, the principle of the construction of the exposition of manufacturing processes in the film. . . . What was in *material* terms correctly ascertained was precisely that *sphere* whose principles might alone *define the ideology of the forms of revolutionary art just as they have defined revolutionary ideology in general: heavy industry*, factory production and the forms of the manufacturing process" (*W* 60). Machine Age aesthetics had already been established in the West, through artists like the photographer Paul Strand and the painter Fernand Léger, but Eisenstein argues for a materialist historical sensibility to accompany the new forms. With the example of artists like Eisenstein, Walter Benjamin developed his critique on "The Work of Art in the Age of Mechanical Reproduction."

The prominence Eisenstein gives industrial technology and productive practices contributes to a Marxist historiography in his cinema. Marx, by emphasizing technical inventions and new relations of production, construes history as a dynamic, materially determined process in which radical transformation is to be expected. In comparison to Marx, conventional history greatly delimits or censors the importance of actual, productive labor and consequently is silent on the creation of material life in a given era. The aspects of production activity and revolutionary action in his films are referents to material and class forces that create social value and produce history. Montage is the means for Eisenstein to pull filmmaking away from fixed forms of scenario and story genre and toward the project of treating historical revolutionary material.

The four silent films bear testimony to Eisenstein's fascination with and artistic utilization of industrial technology. When feasible, mechanical apparatuses discovered on location were used to facilitate shooting or were incorporated into scenes. The tracking shot of the factory interior in *Strike* is taken from the plant's overhead conveyor. Outside, in an industrial yard, footage is taken from a huge crane as it swings laterally. In *Potemkin* the ship's guns and engines play a prominent dramatic role. In *Old and New* the camera is attached to carts, tractors, and threshing tools. To familiarize audiences with the operations of a rifle and an internal combustion engine, Eisenstein exhibits cutaway views of their mechanisms in *October* and *Old and New*, respectively. To publicize industrialization in the agrarian sector, *Old and New* includes a sequence detailing the mass husbandry, marketing, and slaughter of pigs.

By a "materialist approach to form," Eisenstein also refers to the filmmaker's work on cinematographic materials. Explorations during the editing phase confirmed his belief that montage possesses an immense capacity for the production of meaning: in "the actual technique of exposition of *Strike* and the other parts of *Towards the Dictatorship*, there was, properly speaking, no script but there was a jump—subject: cue sheet—which was quite logical in terms of the montage essence" (W 59). The unexpected meanings that result from film location conditions and from the activity of mounting filmed material develop greatly the discursive dimension to his silent films. From such Soviet views on art as a productive process Walter Benjamin developed his ideas on the author as producer. Similar views also characterize Brecht's theater and theory. The "productive attitude" of epic theater as a premise "regards nothing as existing except in so far as it changes" and has as techniques "alienating the familiar" and a critical approach.[15] In conversation with Benjamin, Brecht praised the production aesthetic for its aleatory properties: "It can't be trusted. It is the unpredictable. You never know where it will end."[16] Jean-Luc Godard has expressed a comparable appreciation: "When montage effects surpass those of *mise en scène* in efficacy, the beauty of the latter is doubled, the unforeseen unveiling secrets by its charm in an operation analogous to using unknown quantities in mathematics."[17]

Eisenstein remarks at the outset of "The Problem of the Materialist Approach to Form" that "people are ready to trample with such fanaticism on any work in the field of form, branding it as 'Formalism' " (W 59). In addition to a generalized sense, the reference here is to the Russian school of linguistics and critical thought known as Formalism that predates the Revolution. Formalism had considerable influence on Soviet art and aesthetic theory during the early 1920s but was officially suppressed at the start of the 1930s. As the remark above indicates, by 1925 the movement was already under serious suspicion. Partly under the influence of Formalism, Constructivism and the Proletkult group viewed art principally as a matter of the work's materials, devices, and function, not one of inspiration, beauty, or the artist's biography.

The Formalist approach to "art as device," in Viktor Shklovsky's phrase, has a counterpart in the idea of art as production. Yuri Tynyanov, a founder of the Formalist movement and later Eisenstein's friend, writes in a 1923 essay entitled "The Idea of Construction" that in a literary text the "heterogeneous, polysemic character of material . . . depends upon the function and destination of this material" for its organization. The text's "constructive factor" and "dynamic form" determine the interrelationship of style and substance: "It can thus be said that one always perceives form in the course of an evolution in the rapport between the ordering and constructive factor and the subordinated factors."[18] Explorations of this rapport take graphic form in Constructivist posters and stage sets and in the work of Futurist poets like Mayakovsky and designers like El Lissitzky, who were closely associated with figures in the Formalist movement and who experimented with the dynamism of language and prosody on the printed page.

Reflexive texts like Sterne's *Tristram Shandy* and parodic ones like Gogol's *Dead Souls* held privileged status in Formalist literary criticism for laying bare their own devices of composition. Both kinds of literature "bare the device," whether through an account of their own making or by taking measure of other literary and verbal styles. Modernism, in its heterogeneity of materials and self-consciousness about style and substance, marked for Formalists a radical disjuncture from traditions of classicism and realism, with their conventions of "concealing" literary devices. Their emphasis upon properties of literariness leads to the conclusion that a text's subject matter is finally its own techniques, a conclusion that also holds true for Constructivist works in the other arts of the period. The raw material of cinema, Shklovsky stated, "is not the filmed object but a certain method of filming it."[19]

Like Eccentrism, Formalism considers the audience for an art work to be normally dominated by habit and automatized responses. Literature penetrates habituation through defamiliarization: it revives sensation by making strange the objects, environment, behavior, and language that surround a reader in everyday life. Thus, art's power of communication is always a power to revive perception. In Shklovsky's formulation, the purpose of art is to impart an experience of the object as if seen for the first time, not just as an object recognized. Plot, point-of-view, syntax, prosody, descriptive language, rhetorical device—in sum, all the materials of literary narrative or verse can cut a relexive path to the reader's understanding. The deformation and disarray of conventional elements in Eccentrist and Constructivist spectacles is likewise intended to renew audience perception.

Formalist analysis is often taken to be nonhistorical and exclusively synchronic. Later in the 1920s Formalist critics like Roman Jakobson defended its methods for their implicit acknowledgment of the effects of sociology and history on the evolution of literary forms. As practiced by artists of the period, Formalist explorations were unquestionably a conscious effort to disjoin and dislocate historical continuity. These acts of negation expose culture to be a formation subject to history and the same redirections as society, not a timeless, hieratic legacy. In laying bare the structure of conventions and devices, the Formalist artist openly offers the art work as a construct, as a product of the historical moment. Following a similar rationale, in their very preoccupation with contemporaneity Soviet avant-garde artists treat form as a provocation to new perception and as a materialization of the historical differential between present and past. Later in the century, art historians like Benjamin and Erwin Panofsky identify the technological form of the photographic media, and its implications for society, as an embodiment of a new materialist comprehension of reality.

The impetus to dynamize and defamiliarize in *Strike* extends from the individual shot to the narrative structure. Even the film's expository titles are subject to alterations in the manner of Futurist and Constructivist graphic innovations, with changes in type scale and the spinning design of one title intended to suggest the action of factory dynamos. In one sequence, photographs become comically animate. A police inspector looks at a file on informers and a still shot of four identification photographs, seemingly mounted on an album page, is shown full-screen. Suddenly the photographed agents come alive, looking right and left as they jut their heads outside the plane of the page. One of them jauntily hangs his hat on the front of the matte that frames his image.

Dziga Vertov was equally determined to revolutionize film form, but he and Eisenstein debated the inherent domain of cinema throughout the

1920s. His manifestos call for the "purification" of cinema from all past associations with literature and theater, which are now to be viewed as defunct legacies. In the place of fictional subjects and dramatic devices he offers film records of real objects, actual events, and ordinary people. The Vertov group, known as Kinoks ("cinema-eye men"), formed an experimental studio they termed a "factory of facts." In parallel with Tretyakov's factographic program, the Kinoks thought their new factualism promised an end to art and its confusion of representational codes: "We will explode Art's Tower of Babel." The leading principle of factography in film is the *kino-glaz* (cinema-eye), a precursor of some *cinéma verité* ideas. In a 1924 statement, Vertov asserts that the *kino-glaz*

> observes and records life *as it is*, and only then draws conclusions from these observations. . . . Hence the serious approach to news-reel—to that factory of film footage in which life, passing through the camera lens, does not vanish forever, leaving no trace, but does, on the contrary, leave a trace, precise and inimitable.
> The moment and the manner in which we admit life into the lens and the way in which we fix the trace that remains determine the technical quality; they also determine the social and historical value of the footage and subsequently the quality of the whole object.[20]

The Kinok program proposes no less than a new perceptual apparatus and a universal language of materiality.

Vertov wrote of the movie camera that it is a "mechanical eye" whose powers technology can perfect, while the human eye will always possess natural limitations. The camera's full potential is now necessary to any understanding of the industrial nations' rapid, diverse physical and social processes. Cinema-eye provides reality with pellucid properties, freed from the obscurely random motions of unframed life. A single film shot is an "object" that has privileged status above other objects in reality. Projected, the shot is able to reveal the material world in ways an unaided human eye cannot. Properly speaking, this cinema belongs to the category *actuality*, not documentary.

While Eisenstein was no less opposed to the confines of the story-film, he did not adopt the extreme position that fiction—or art generally—should be abandoned in favor of actuality. In comparison to a materialist approach to form, he considers factographic methods the *reductio ad absurdum* of filmmaking and labels Vertov's *Kinoglaz* (1925) the "formless" result of "primitive Impressionism," "pointillist painting," and "impassive consistency" (W 62–63). Brecht draws a similar conclusion in commenting on the style of direct photography of the 1920s: "less than at any time does a simple *reproduction of reality* tell us anything about reality. A photograph of the Krupp works or GEC yields almost nothing about these institutions. Reality proper has slipped into the functional. The reification of human relationships, the factory, let's say, no longer reveals these relationships. Therefore something has actually to be *constructed*, something artificial, something set up."[21] To the static, "manifest pantheism" Eisenstein finds in *Kinoglaz* he contrasts *Strike*'s dynamic construction and its ideological organization of filmed material (*W* 63). His contrast is additionally between a painterly, lyrical structure whose primary referent is the Vertov's own sensibility (an opinion Béla Balázs later will share) and *Strike*'s rhetorical, discursive structure oriented primarily toward audience response.

The basis for "attraction" in cinema for Eisenstein is the shot's photogenic properties, which give it ideographic meaning: "An idea expressed in its completeness is photogenic; that is, an object is photogenic when it corresponds most closely to the idea that it embodies" (*W* 56). Two examples of photogenic movement he specifies are that of an animal in nature and of a worker in the production line. To convey the idea of such movements requires "organization of the surface" of the screen (and thus within the shot) and orientation and juxtaposition of each surface with the following one in a montage succession. In mounting the shots, Eisenstein finds the Kuleshov "axial system" of organization limited in conceptual meaning through its principal concern with maintaining consistent spatial cues (*W* 57). What film attractions propose to convey is "the energetic purpose of material work" (*W* 58). (This proposition is analogous to Aristotle's *energeia*, activity motivated by thought.) In the practice of montage, then, presentation of an action is not to be dependent on the logic of behavior or superficial appearance, but follows the intended affect or idea of the sequence. As he develops montage in the silent period, Eisenstein disregards the emerging rules of matched orientation and action in constructing sequences of intensified affect or intellectual motivation.

In his polemical insistence Eisenstein overdraws the contrast, but comparison of *Kinoglaz* and *Strike* does substantiate a difference between the priorities Vertov gives to the filmed material for its own pictorial values and those Eisenstein gives to it for its reflexive potential. In opposition to the factographic principle, Eisenstein practices interpretation by means of selection and the transformation of reality and actual phenomena through montage. His cinema is a presentational medium, not a directly representational one, and it shares with other arts the means to form its materials narratively and discursively, and not simply to register them. For Eisenstein the film shot is a photo-reflection that remains to be constructed into coherent meaning. Actuality is the raw material for a filmic image. For the sake of a materialist conception, it often becomes necessary to defy the surface reality of the photographic materials through montage.

Vertov and Eisenstein are both materialists and both—particularly in this period of their careers—are dedicated socialists. When compared, their work offers two very different answers to the question of what role cinema should take in socialist society. In the case of both directors, the films themselves are far more complex and eloquent than the claims made for them in manifestos. In printed statements, Vertov proposes to depose aesthetics through the sheer actuality of Soviet modernization and cultural diversity. Eisenstein's declarations are aimed instead toward the development of a modern materialist aesthetic.

CHAPTER THREE

Battleship Potemkin:
Pathos and Politics

As originally scripted, depiction of the historic mutiny aboard the *Prince Potemkin of Taurida* entailed only forty-four montage segments from a total of over eight hundred in the scenario *The Year 1905* prepared by Nina Agadzhanova-Shutko in consultation with Eisenstein.[1] The *1905* scenario chronicles the year's major revolutionary activities in six parts: Russia's defeats to Japan in the winter months; Bloody Sunday (January 22), when the tsar's troops shot down hundreds of peaceful demonstrators in St. Petersburg; the popular uprisings in cities and countryside that followed; the general strikes of October and their suppression; a wave of counterrevolutionary terror and pogroms; and the worker insurrection of December in Moscow. The mutiny in June was to link parts three and four, with a cut from wind-tossed fields of grain to a stormy sea marking the transition. This montage association is a figure for the wave of revolution rolling across Russia. Calculating its importance in 1920, Lenin concluded: "Without the 'dress rehearsal' of 1905, the victory of the October Revolution in 1917 would have been impossible."[2]

The historical record shows that since the start of the Russo-Japanese War there had been insurrectionary activity among sailors in the Black Sea fleet, as when enlisted men destroyed officers' residential quarters onshore in November 1904. After the *Potemkin* mutiny in June 1905, sailors directed the ship toward Odessa, where a general strike was already in progress.[3] Strikers joined sailors ashore in a funeral procession honoring the slain seaman Vakulinchuk. In the course of the month, tsarist troops periodically attacked demonstrating workers and students, causing hundreds of casualties. At one point, the *Potemkin* fired several shells at the city, inflicting some damage to public buildings, but posing no military threat to the government since the *Potemkin*'s gunners refused to engage in combat.

The *Potemkin* steamed out to sea, challenged by a squadron dispatched from Sevastopol to break the mutiny. Seamen aboard the other ships refused to fire on the rebel vessel, which was briefly joined by another ship, the *St. George*. Within a few days the *Potemkin* left Odessa to seek amnesty in a neutral port. With its departure, the strike in the city weakened and tsarist troops regained control after waging a final attack. The *St. George* surrendered and the *Potemkin* went on to the Rumanian port of Constanza, where sailors left ship at the end of June. When one of the leaders, seaman Matyushenko, attempted to re-enter Russia two years later, he was arrested and hanged. The tsar's navy tried to efface this revolutionary episode by renaming the battleship.

Eisenstein confused the historical record by claiming to invent incidents and episodes for his film that subsequently were taken for fact.[4] One such claim involves the white tarpaulin thrown over mutineers in the order for their execution, a detail that in fact is included in eyewitness accounts of events shipboard. The massacre on the Odessa steps was often attributed by critics to Eisenstein's creation and he did little to correct this impression. In fact, on the night of June 28 during extensive rioting and looting by elements of the populace, cossacks and soldiers killed a large number of people in various locales of the city. These locales included the Richelieu Steps leading from the city center down to the harbor. A delegation of *Potemkin* sailors reported seeing many bodies in the port and on the steps when they came ashore at Odessa the next day. Eisenstein created a powerful transformation of the event in dissociating it from civil disorder, staging it in daytime and populating the scene with innocent civilians from the middle and working classes alike.

Lecturing before the 1917 revolutions about events like the *Potemkin* mutiny, which he mentioned specifically, Lenin emphasized their limitations in radicalizing history: "They flared up rather quickly; any instance of injustice, excessively harsh treatment by the officers, bad food, etc., could lead to revolt. But what they lacked was persistence, a clear perception of aim, a clear understanding that only the most vigorous continuation of the armed struggle, only a victory over all the military and civil authorities, only the overthrow of the government and the seizure of power throughout the country could guarantee the success of the revolution."[5] The mutiny Eisenstein represents in *Battleship Potemkin* ends not in the outbreak's dissipation or defeat but in revolutionary victory, with the vessel successfully challenging the squadron.

To charges that his film story is incomplete and thus historically inaccurate, Eisenstein responded in "Constanza (Whither 'The Battleship Potemkin')," an essay written in 1926 but unpublished until 1968. He writes there that his film narrative concludes at the event's political apex, which represents the maximum of revolutionary consciousness conceivable in the circumstances. Furthermore, the story closes "at this point where it had become an 'asset' of the Revolution. But the agony goes on" (*W* 67). Many of the film's most famous moments are reversals that convey agony, but its final sequence commemorates the mutiny as a prologue or exordium to 1917. Progressive radicalization of the Russian masses and an effective challenge to tsarist absolutism are fully apparent within the events of 1905. A standard Western text on Russian history states that the general strike that year may well be "the greatest, most thoroughly carried out, and most successful strike in history."[6]

For Eisenstein the recorded historical event is not isolated or conclusive. The original script's chronicle of a year's major revolutionary incidents is epitomized into the *Potemkin* episode, whose dramatized duration is only a matter of days. The film's entire compositional process—from revision of the scenario and development of a dramatic structure through location shooting and montage—is governed by the rhetorical figure of synecdoche or *pars pro toto*. The Odessa steps massacre stands for the whole of tsarist atrocities in 1905, starting with Bloody Sunday in St. Petersburg and on to the shooting of strikers in the Baku oil fields in August and the pogroms later. Rhetoric, organic form, and pathos in *Potemkin* would become set themes in Eisenstein's theoretical writing of the 1930s and 1940s. They are already evident in his commentary at the time, as in a claim that the film provides a " 'genetic' (constructive) amalgamation of the shots" (*W* 79).

Released in January 1926, *Battleship Potemkin* condenses the unfulfilled revolutionary movement of 1905 into a bloody but momentarily victorious episode and infuses the past with a sense of historic promise. Eisenstein stated years later that the mutiny is represented as "the character and spirit of the time [in] an attempt to grasp its dynamics, rhythm."[7] In this manner, the historiography the film constructs is progressive and utopian. As is often true in revolutionary history, a political or military setback can still strengthen class militancy. In immediate context, the mutiny is a spontaneous upsurge to protest bad food and harsh treatment. Lenin held that "the 'spontaneous element,' in essence, represents nothing more nor less than consciousness in an *embryonic form*."[8] The workers' revolt in *Strike* remains at a level of spontaneity and is finally abortive. In *Potemkin*, massacre is followed by advancement of the revolutionary cause.

Recalling the making of *Potemkin* twenty years after, Eisenstein attested that "the fortuitous became an integral component part of the film" (*N* 27). The roles circumstance played in determining artistic decisions during its production are now famous. Commissioned as an anniversary film, schedule constraints forced abridgement of *The Year 1905* chronicle finally to a single event. Weather conditions contributed to this abridgement when persistent cloudiness in Leningrad, the first planned location, compelled the crew to move south to Odessa to begin with later scenes. Stimulated by the dramatic and visual potential of the city's active port, broad streets, and the monumental flight of steps overlooking the harbor,

Eisenstein developed the originally transitional incidents set there into a representation of 1905 as a whole.

After a visit with Eduard Tisse to the major German film studios in March 1926, Eisenstein commented on the limitations of production methods evident in features like *The Last Laugh* (1924) and two films they saw during shooting on elaborate studio sets, *Faust* (1926) and *Metropolis* (1926): "The sets are devised in the mind 'once and for all' within predetermined limits and these sets cannot produce an independent charge from the material to add to the director's intentions. . . . This kind of limited number of simply pre-determined points of view removes the opportunity for new discoveries on the spot and does of course mean that directorial invention is impoverished" (*W* 86). Eisenstein opposed to this aesthetic (with which he would experiment in *Ivan the Terrible*) the aleatory situations and improvisations in form through which *Potemkin* was created.

Potemkin's visual character is often the result of material circumstances and directorial solution. One instance is the substitution for an actor with a day worker on the location crew, noticed by Eisenstein as the suitable physical type for the ship's doctor only minutes before shooting on these scenes began. Another is the experimental footage Tisse took in the harbor when the day's scheduled scenes were canceled because of coastal fogs. From this footage Eisenstein mounted the memorable visual requiem in honor of the slain seaman Vakulinchuk. In early shipboard scenes, the impressions of class domination and coercion result partly from constraints on location. The original *Potemkin* had been dismantled for scrap iron, but scouts found a sister ship named *The Twelve Apostles* moored along offshore rocks and now used to store munitions. After engineers turned the prow to face open water, for long and medium shots the camera had to be aimed from amidships directly forward, where the field of view was unobstructed by rocks, to sustain the illusion that the ship is at sea. Thus the dramatic tension and themes of oppression in the quarter-deck scenes—where the action unfolds within rigidly framed compositions—can be attributed to a combination of circumstance and design.

Pathos and Social Conflict

At the time of the foreign premiere of *Battleship Potemkin* in 1926 Eisenstein prepared a personal statement for the German press that reads, in part: "Tendentiousness in itself seems to me to provide a great artistic opportunity: it has by no means always to be as political, as consciously political as in *Potemkin*. . . . I have been criticized because *Potemkin* (and the German version has toned down the political purpose considerably) is too full of pathos. . . . Is not this pathos justified? People must learn to hold their heads high and feel their humanity, they must be human, become human: the intention of this film is no more and no less" (*W* 75). This expression of humanism corresponds with Marx's definition of communism as the acquisition finally "of real human life as man's possession and thus the advent of practical humanism."[9] It is not simply after but through the struggle of classes that the mass of men and women become authentically humanized. The subjective impetus of Marxism is to make history itself mankind's fully conscious practice, with the goal of a dis-alienated society. History and conscious life-activity will then be synchronous.

While early script drafts indicate division of the plot into four sections, during montage Eisenstein structured *Potemkin* into five parts indicated by number and title inserts, which correspond with the release print's five reels. Each title summarizes either a setting or an incident: "I. Men and Maggots," "II. Drama on the Quarterdeck," "III. An Appeal from the Dead," "IV. The Odessa Steps," and "V. Meeting the Squadron." The parts mark significant intervals in the dramatic action and thus function as acts.

The division into formal acts and the emphasis on pathos point to a model of traditional stage tragedy. The form was chosen, Eisenstein claimed fourteen years later, because culturally it has proven the most affective: "a pathetic structure is one that compels us, echoing its movement, *to re-live the moments of culmination and substantiation*" (*FF* 173). This claim for the film's traditional form partially reflects Soviet cultural policies of the 1930s. In 1926 Eisenstein writes of pathos in *Potemkin* as a negation of the methods that had become traditional in the dramatic construction of Western theater and film: "the positive effect (the pathos)—the stern appeal to activity—are achieved by three 'negative' methods, all of them the methods of passive art: doubt, tears, sentiment, lyricism, psychologism, maternal feelings, etc. These elements are removed from the harmony of their traditional composition with the resultant 'withdrawal symptoms,' with a suspension of reality and other pacifying effects. . . . These elements of 'right' art are dismembered and reassembled" (*W* 68). Agitational and ideological purposes, he goes on to argue, replace the conventional reduction of pathos to functions of audience appeasement and conciliation.

These formulations depart significantly from the classical description of tragedy. In Aristotle's *Poetics*, pathos refers generally to the realm of emotions and reactions undefined by logical thought. As a dramatic component, pathos is reported through the verse of the chorus or represented in a scene of suffering. Within the plot, pathos can be a provocation for the play's entire action. The affect of tragedy on an audience is specifically fear and pity. Its effect is to release and appease this affect through catharsis, thus reconciling the audience to the universal human fate imitated. The formal difference between the play's pathos and the audience's pity and terror, mediated through catharsis, is not present in Eisenstein's paradigm, which proposes an empathetic reflex in the viewer to each scene of suffering.

In the film, at least four formal factors contribute to its pathos and tendentiousness. First, the locus of action is carefully limited, particularly in comparison to the diversity of settings in *Strike*. There are three primary locales: aboard ship, mainly on deck during the first four parts; the quay where mourners gather; and the Odessa steps. In an early script draft the effect of this circumscription is diminished where a shot is indicated of a political meeting onshore in the opening sequence, which is otherwise set at sea. Crosscutting between these locales in the finished film is reserved for heightened dramatic moments, as when the citizens amassed on the Odessa steps signal their approval to the victorious sailors on ship.

Second, historical events of mid-1905 are condensed into a dramatic action whose duration is three days, marked by scenes set at dawn toward the opening of parts I, III, and V. In part I sailors awaken in their hammocks when seaman Vakulinchuk reads aloud from a revolutionary pamphlet: "Comrades, the time has come to act. What are we waiting for? All Russia is rising. Are we to be last?" Part III opens with a night scene and follows with shots of the harbor as dawn breaks. The body of Vakulinchuk lies in public on a quay. His martyrdom raises an appeal for support of the mutiny, which Odessa's citizens answer as the day advances; an accompanying title reads, "Along with the sun, rose the whole city!" In part V the mutineers hold a tense vigil in anticipation of the squadron's arrival. With morning, the crew readies the ship for action and soon achieves victory. The narrative structure thus develops a figure for a rising revolutionary consciousness and action.

Third, there is a marked circumscription of camera movement. In contrast to the relatively restless visuals of *Strike*, the camera in *Potemkin* is often stoically fixed. For example, a long overhead shot taken from amidships sets the scene for "Drama on the Quarterdeck." The sharply symmetrical contour of the deck space—divided by the jutting barrels of the main turret and tightly bordered by the shot frame—functions as a fixed referent as the sailors' revolt unfolds. The montage returns to this perspective regularly as the sailors break rank, the marines march on deck, the trapped mates are covered with a tarpaulin, and the rebellion intensifies. From this vantage point, the power struggle is territorial, with the commander trying to control the situation from the capstan, the main body of sailors taking their position at the turret, and the last group of rebels stranded on deck.

Fourth, to develop a stylistic of conflict and tension, Eisenstein abandoned the mixture of process shots and editing devices used in *Strike,* whose visual rhythm is often erratic and whose plot advances episodically. For the most part, the abrupt cut replaces the various wipes, masks, dissolves, and superimpositions applied so freely in the first feature. The abrupt cut preserves the clarity of the shot's organized surface. In each shot, the compositional message can be modified by purposeful movement of either the camera or the subject, as when the empty quarterdeck suddenly fills with victorious sailors. Consistent use of the cut in the montage of sequences and within each of the five parts emphasizes the properties of orientation and juxtaposition between individual shots. Fades are reserved to mark the conclusion of each part and transition to the next.

In respect to dramatic suspense, some aspects of *Potemkin's* montage are comparable to the accelerated parallel editing of a Griffith last-minute rescue. The delay in part II between orders to the firing squad and intervention by Vakulinchuk is prolonged by intercut shots of a life preserver, an imperial crest, and the ship's bugle. Eisenstein frankly admits that this sequence is melodramatically paced: "The action is slowed down and the tension is 'screwed' tighter" (W 118). In another respect, however, these inserts suspend the narrative momentum with objects that are insignia in a discursive order of meaning. While montage of such insertions will lead, with *October,* in the direction of intellectual cinema, its intention here remains at the level of film attractions, which Eisenstein now defines as "the new psychologism, the apogee of the psycho-effect elicited from the *object*" (W 68).

Through homogeneity of texture and of movement within the frame, there is linkage across the entire narrative of objective qualities within shots that correlate the thematics of social struggle. As a result, the meaning of class identification stimulated through pathos broadens in the course of the narrative. The opening shots of powerful waves crashing against a breakwater, sending up walls of spray, initiate a visually synonymic chain that is indicative of this broadening identification. Most immediately, the opening shots are linked in "Men and Maggots" to the boiling vat of inedible soup (seen from above) that provokes sailors to resistance. Subsequent compositions in the chain include the press of seamen in white on the quarterdeck during the uprising, seen often from a high angle, and streams of mourners flowing from the city's streets, bridges, and stairways to the vigil on the quay.

Once gathered at the vigil, the sea of humanity is quiet, as shown in a nearly overhead view. Steadily aroused by political speeches, the crowd is finally made turbulent by the anti-Semitic remark of a well-dressed man, who is quickly engulfed by provoked mourners (in another high-angle perspective). On the steps, tier upon tier of civilians hail the battleship; they become a panicked torrent when the militia attacks. In part V there is a tense stillness to the sea as the crew anticipates the squadron's approach. With the decision to challenge the naval cordon, the battleship breaks the sea into heavy whitecaps as it steams full speed ahead. With success of the challenge, the crew members flood the forward deck, waving their white caps joyously. In many of these last shots, the water's agitated surface and the crowded deck are seen from nearly overhead. The perspective and the objective qualities in composition are a thematic culmination to the views of boiling soup presented in part I.

This synonymic chain broadens identification from an incident of class conflict to a movement of social struggle. The class tendency of the conflict is denoted at several levels of the drama and imagery in parts I and II. With the scene of mourning, the Odessa populace (presented for now largely in terms of working and common types) extends sympathy beyond the martyred Vakulinchuk to an entire ethnic group in its reaction against the anti-Semitic heckler. (The intention in the original scenario to portray the pogroms of 1905 perhaps accounts for inclusion of this character in *Potemkin.*) The citizenry gathered on the steps in part IV distinctly traverses all class and other discriminatory lines, as the montage presents a diverse ensemble of individuals who all share the same fate. An elderly, refined woman wearing a pince-nez is accompanied by an adolescent girl. A plainly dressed mother urges her little boy to wave at the ship. A student with glasses and a white sweater cheers the boats. An elegantly featured woman in dark, fashionable jacket and feathered hat raises her veil and smiles; a handsome woman in white twirls the fancy parasol propped on her shoulder and waves. Between them appears a legless young man who moves about on his hands; he stops and waves his cap. The massacre that ensues is an act of war by the tsarist regime against Russian society.

A metonymic chain that extends across the narrative correlates the victorious rebels on the battleship at the conclusion with the ultimate triumph of the Russian people. Only two sailors are presented by name— Vakulinchuk and Matyushenko, historical figures in the mutiny. In the film their identities merge with the nameless common seamen. Aboard ship, Vakulinchuk's death becomes representative of oppression under the officer class. On the quay, it becomes representative of oppression of Russian society under tsarism. The metonymy that conveys this second correlation is a succession of titles and images connecting a close-up of Vakulinchuk on his simple bier with overhead shots of amassed mourners: "All for one / one / for all." The metonymy also introduces a tragic irony, since the individual's death will be followed by massacre.

Matyushenko, after being identified in an opening title as an activist, does not reemerge narratively until part V, where he acts as commander of the rebel ship. No title insert identifies him in this role, and his leadership is generically rather than individually heroic. (The historical record indicates that a surviving officer, Lieutenant Alexeyev, was placed by mutineers in the position of commander.) The fraternization between Odessa's citizens and the battleship's crew in parts III and IV has given a redemptive function to the closing action. *Potemkin*'s heroic unification of individual and the social body in opposition to state authority contrasts with *Strike*, where the corps of workers deteriorates into a self-destructive mob after one of the strike leaders is detained by police.

Differences in social class are presented as differences in physical type. The officers' slender, elegant features are an antithesis to the sailors' burly and common masculinity. In the first scene below deck, seamen sleep barechested in hammocks that crisscross their quarters. Muscular, almost sculptural, curves are framed by the geometrical patterns of hammocks and support ropes. In contrast to the sailors' easy, unselfconscious behavior, officers display a pride of class by assuming stern postures and hostile facial expressions. The ship's doctor, Smirnov, responding to protests that the ration of meat is spoiled, officiously removes his pince-nez to perform inspection. Curtly dismissing the claim, Smirnov turns on his heel. He pauses in a nearby passageway with the deck officer, and the two glare contemptuously at the sailors. As sailors approach, the deck officer gives them a condemning glance with one eye as he slowly turns his back.

Potemkin contains so many instances of officers squinting and glaring that a specular motif of the evil eye emerges. (Its fullest exposition comes later, in *Ivan the Terrible*.) In a series of close compositions, senior officer Gilyarovsky raises a rifle toward Vakulinchuk and takes aim with one eye open. At the moment he shoots, his face is shown in extreme close-up as the eye widens fiercely. A comic instance occurs after mutineers have toppled the ship's priest down a gangway. He feigns death, then briefly opens one eye to see if he can make an escape. The church's political role was suggested in an earlier montage that associates his handheld cross with an officer's regimental dagger. When the priest is first knocked down, the cross's lateral arm sticks in the deck like a knife blade.

In Smirnov's inspection of the meat, the pince-nez is folded together to make a magnifying lens. An accompanying close-up of the lens held next to the meat shows a swarm of maggots. Denying the now obvious truth of the sailor's claim, Smirnov makes the instrument serve the class purpose of distortion and injustice. The famous synecdoche trope of the pince-nez dangling from a thick hawser, after Smirnov has been tossed to sea, is equally a montage literalization of the overthrow of ruling-class perspective. A related literalization occurs at the vigil when the heckler is swarmed and drowned out by angered mourners.

While officers' glances are often one-eyed and sinister, the regard of sailors is invariably full, direct, and candid. After the crew has refused to answer mess call, three sailors are shown washing the officers' dishware. The youngest one slowly rotates a plate to read the inscription on its rim: "Give Us This Day Our Daily Bread." As the class irony of its words dawns on him, his face is shown in extreme close-up. Staring frontally, in a composition that is equally a narrative and a discursive image of recognition, the face registers anger and the eyes refocus in piercing rage. He smashes the plate, an action dilated and intensified through montage. In a sequence of eight shots taken from slightly different points of view, the sailor lifts the plate over his left shoulder and hurls it down, but before it breaks he is shown lifting and hurling it from his right shoulder as well. This is the first of several violations in the film of the strict axial system of edited action. The sequence, in marking the close of part I, is also a figure for the plot's swing of events into dramatic reversals; the figure is inaugurated earlier through swaying hammocks and the swaying, empty mess tables in the seamen's quarters.

With a narrative causality similar to that at the end of *Strike*, the incident of sailors' resistance in part I is met in part II, "The Drama on the Quarterdeck," with the state's readiness to wage massive counterviolence. The white tarpaulin brought to cover the mutineers before execution is first shown bundled up as officers haul it across the deck. In its first appearance, the tarpaulin is suggestive of the traditional shipboard shroud for a burial at sea. Part II's reversal comes when Vakulinchuk shouts to the firing squad, "Brothers! . . . Do you realize who you are shooting?" A young guardsman, seen in close-up, hesitates. The expression in his eyes indicates a new awareness of the situation; within moments, the guards lower their rifles. The squad's refusal to execute the condemned sailors is reiterated in part V when the squadron refuses to fire on the rebel battleship. In the narrative, progressive enlargement of the same type of event is used to represent growing confrontation and radicalization within Russia.

The crew's rebellion on the quarterdeck seems to be achieved when the title "Brothers! We've won!" appears. But elation is shattered the next moment as officer Gilyarovsky pursues and finally kills Vakulinchuk. Overlapped action dilates the event; successive shots, each taken from a different camera position or with a different lens, depict the movement of his falling from a moment prior to conclusion of the previous shot. Vakulinchuk falls over the side, landing on a large block and tackle suspended by heavy ropes. His death agony is portrayed in a series of baroque perspectives of his suspended posture. The extended, mannered embodiment of this event contrasts with the shorthand summary of Smirnov's death moments before through juxtaposition of his pince-nez and a hawser.

With Vakulinchuk's death the emotional tenor reverses from celebration to mourning. Peripeteia is equally a plot device and a rhetorical figure at this point in the film. It is given spatial equivalents through violations of the axial system of screen directionality. The launch that bears Vakulinchuk's body ashore is first seen moving in the direction of the frame diagonal, from right to left. This axis of movement is maintained in three of the sequence's other four shots as the launch moves the length of the frame in them. The sequence's second shot, however, depicts the launch moving gradually across the frame from left to right, a reversal of direction accented by the camera's slow travel with the action. Spatial reversal is used as well in the static compositions showing Vakulinchuk's body on display in a tent on the quay. A medium shot presents the body from waist up, arranged along the frame diagonal with the head toward the upper right corner. A close-up of the shoulders and head maintains this placement. The next close-up, however, positions the feet, pointing out of the frame, in the same corner. In these instances, spatiality is an objective property in the film attraction of reversal.

Manipulation of spatial relations in *Potemkin* also serves to heighten pathos. A commonly cited example is the scene of fraternization in part IV, when crafts under sail leave harbor with provisions for the battleship. Directionality is established as a movement from screen left (harbor) to right (battleship). The boats' gliding motions and their white sails set a celebratory atmosphere. Their seaward movement is the focus of attention by citizens on the steps. A few shots later in the sequence, however, show boats in the open sea moving in the other direction, seemingly toward shore. This break in the conventions of the axial system lends to the event's affect of spiritedness and independence.

Stanley Kauffmann has remarked that it is *Potemkin*'s distinction to present a conventional subject like oppression under tyranny from an artistically radical viewpoint. Of Eisenstein's purpose, Kauffman writes: "Clearly he felt that a new society meant a new kind of *vision*; that the way people saw things must be altered."[10] Such radicalization in viewpoint is most evident in the Odessa steps massacre with its spectatorial motifs and violations of axial space. The montage associations are motivated nearly as often by discursive functions as by narrative ones.

Except for four close-ups toward the end of part IV, troops are presented as a faceless menace. In graphic and spatial terms, the troops exert a relentless force pushing the populace downward, literally suppressing them. The compositional effect is at times underscored through a downward thrust of the camera as it follows the terrified flight of citizens. The mother and little boy from previous shots are tracked down the stairway. He is wounded and falls but the mother continues downward, with the camera preceding her. Suddenly aware the boy is missing, she turns to see panicked civilians trampling him. To portray the mother's reaction,

Eisenstein arranges a sequence of fourteen shots—six of the trampled boy (one of which reverses the direction in which the body is sprawled), five of the mother, and three of other civilians. The five reaction shots, three in extreme close-up, show the mother's eyes bulging in horror-stricken frenzy. Distributed evenly in the sequence, these shots prolong the duration of her agonized perception well beyond the conventions of screen time.

After reaching her son, the mother lifts his body and starts up the stairway to confront the soldiers. The tracking camera precedes her gradual upward progress, creating a graphic counterstress to earlier camera movement. She stops on a flight just below the front rank, its shadows engulfing her. With the officer's signal, troops fire on mother and child and march over the two dead bodies. This manner of isolating through montage the slaughter of individuals among the masses makes *Potemkin's* brutality far more affective than that in the tenement scene at the close of *Strike*.

Small, discrete groups seek protection behind the stairway's stone parapet. The elderly woman with a pince-nez rallies a contingent of four or five people to plead with the troops, in an action that unfolds as a violent inversion of part III's "Appeal from the Dead." Crosscut with tracking shots of their frightened movement are the sequence of the mother and little boy and one of a woman in lace shawl anxiously guiding a white baby carriage. In overlapped action, this woman is wounded and falls back against the carriage, whose spoked wheels cast a fragile shadow on the stairs, in contrast to the massive, uniform rank of soldiers' shadows. After several tense and uncertain moments in which the woman's body continues its fall, the carriage is propelled forward, out of control.

Interspersed in the sequence of the runaway carriage are two extremely brief, tight close-ups of the woman with a pince-nez, who now recoils in horror at something offscreen. Contextually, the viewer first assumes she is reacting to the escaped carriage, but this assumption proves false when, in an unforgettable montage illusion of action, an officer slashes her across the face with his sabre. The assailant and his victim are not shown on camera together: in four close shots his snarling face presses forward as he swings the weapon savagely, in a motion redoubled through montage; in a fifth, longer close-up the woman gasps in terror, the pince-nez shattered and her right eye streaming blood. Her reactions thus prove independent from the other two atrocities in the same montage association. Their relationship is contiguous in terms of pathos rather than dramatic space.

The brutality against the woman in pince-nez is a figure for an assault on perception. The mobility and mid-distance of the camera when she leads others in an appeal are indicative of her hopeful rationality. The stationary, tight shots of the attacker, who grimaces with an expression of absolute fury, on the other hand, show the woman to be a victim of an inexorable, soulless power. The shock image of her slashed face, with blood pouring from the eye socket, is in a sense an outcome of the recognition of brutality. Mounted in this sequence are four close-ups of the student with glasses and white sweater seen previously. In each brief shot his face is reflected in a mirror as he turns his head in horror at what he sees offscreen. While a script draft makes note of a mirror shattering above a stout man, the film does not establish the mirror as part of the setting. In fact, it may well have been used on location as a reflector for lighting shot compositions. Images of the student's mirrored look thus function outside the narrative, as a compounded response of pity and fear.

The massacre is avenged at the end of part IV when the rebel battleship turns its guns on military headquarters, an action that begins immediately after the image of the slashed woman. The dramatic impact suggests that the shelling was a more revolutionary act than the historical record would indicate. In any case, the footage shows toppling sculptural decorations, crumbling walls, and billows of smoke and dust clouding the wreckage from view. To avoid any misidentification in viewer sympathies, revolutionary counterviolence is treated through such displacements (the destruction of property rather than life), generalized compositions (the crowd surrounding the heckler), or euphemisms like the close-up of Smirnov's pince-nez entangled in a hawser.

Part V develops the theme of armed class struggle. The advancing, readied battleship, whose driving engines function as a visual refrain, is an image of the revolution's vanguard. In the confrontation with the squadron, two titles are separated by four compositions of the ship's heavy guns: "All for one / One for all." A reiteration of the phrase correlating Vakulinchuk with the mourners, the titles are followed by shots of crewmen embracing in anticipation. At this moment, the phrase applies to solidarity within the crew. With the ship's safe passage seconds later, it refers equally to fraternization among all sailors in the fleet. Disobeying orders, the squadron's crews have left their battle stations and now line the deck rails, waving their caps excitedly. The unification theme develops to its full extent. In close-up, the intent faces of three *Potemkin* crewmen look directly forward. The tense expression of one sailor eases and changes into a grin; the title "Brothers!" follows. The frontal regard here is similar to that at the close of *Strike* in functioning as a form of direct address to encourage an ideological reflex. In this case, it is an affect of relief and triumph, dramatized further in a rapid montage of ecstatic sailors.

As an anniversary film, *Potemkin* celebrates mass, revolutionary militancy. Though victory over reactionaries in the civil war was virtually complete by 1921, the Bolshevik government faced continuing economic and social divisiveness. Opposition on the left—from anarchists, Mensheviks, and Socialist Revolutionaries—made its greatest challenge to state authority with the uprising at Kronstadt, the island naval garrison near Petrograd that in 1917 had joined the revolutionary vanguard.[11] Preceded by factory strikes in Petrograd, the Kronstadt sailors and workers joined in a mass meeting on March 1, 1921, that resulted in demands for democratization of the Soviets, limited restoration of property rights, equalization in the rationing programs, and freedoms of speech, association, and labor organization. The Soviet government brutally suppressed the uprising in an assault that ended on March 18.

In research for the original *1905* scenario Eisenstein found that the *Potemkin* rebellion was a relatively forgotten episode in comparison to the mutinies in Sevastopol and Kronstadt that year. For Soviet audiences of 1926, the Kronstadt insurrections of 1917 and 1921 would be perhaps foremost in memory as correlates to the film's generic action. This potential historical association would redirect the ideological reflex, making the film less of an official work and more of a tendentious representation of class militancy. At the time of *Potemkin*'s release, Eisenstein wrote: "We must direct all our resources towards ensuring that art always exacerbates a current conflict rather than distracting audiences from it. The bourgeoisie is a great expert in smoothing over the critical questions of the present day" (*W* 69). The film's pathos is directed toward renewal in the spirit of class struggle. Pathos is thus a form of active, class-motivated recognition rather than simply an emotional experience. The essence of his cinema, he further asserts, is not to be found in an individual's emotions any more than it is to be in an individual shot. Rather, it is found "in the relationships between the shots just as in history we look not at individuals but at the relationships between individuals [and] classes" (*W* 79).

Typage

Eisenstein traces his approach to the selection and direction of the film performer back to the synthesis attempted in his theater work of "two separate lines of 'real doing' and 'pictorial imagination' " (*FF* 8). The first line can entail the casting of nonactors in roles that correspond to their actual occupations and the absence of makeup or special costuming, as in the *Gas Masks* production. The second line involves devices like the visual literalization of figures of speech used in *The Wise Man*. To Eisenstein's mind, their synthesis was finally unachieved in his theater work. The stage works that took the most materialist approach to form—*Do You Hear, Moscow?* and *Gas Masks*—revealed a "conflict between material-practical and fictitious-descriptive principles" that did not find resolution

(*FF* 8). Film through the means of typage and montage, however, can bring impressions of actuality into a necessary relationship with narrative and discursive constructs to explore the sub-scription of reality by ideography.

Typecasting is not synonymous with typage, though the practice may be one component of typage. Pudovkin, whose dramaturgy involves far more character development than Eisenstein's, explains the priority of type-casting as a function of the medium: "The conditionality of the film is not a property conditionality: it changes not matter, but only time and space. For this reason one cannot build up a required type artificially for the screen. . . . One cannot 'play a part' on the film; one must possess a sum of real qualities, externally, clearly expressed, in order to attain a given effect on the spectator."[12] The underlying principle here favors the least interference with or manipulation of reality.

In Eisenstein's work, the influences on film characterization came as well from his earlier interests in caricature, masked drama, and commedia dell'arte. The stereotypes and stock characters in these forms are culturally encoded and represent conventions and traditions through which reality has already been interpreted. Eisenstein explicates the figure of the Captain in commedia dell'arte, for example, as a type that derives from the history of Italy's struggle for independence from Spanish domination and thus as the result of a people's collective cultural production over a historical era.

Eisenstein's concept of typage is dialectical in its combination of the actuality in type-casting with the conventionality in stereotyping. An example on the practical level is the selection of a nonactor for the character Dr. Smirnov and then the use on him of artificial whiskers. Typage resolves the two sides of debate between acted film and nonacted film, an issue that Vertov vigorously pursued in the period. Typage does so by orienting the issue away from the matter of actuality as it is captured onscreen and toward a cultural basis in reality for understanding what the screen represents.

The purpose of typage is to present a perspective on character, not an individualized psychology of character: "it is important to us to create first and foremost an impression . . . of an observer, not the objective coordination of sign and essence actually composing character" (*FF* 127). According to a study of visual thought by Rudolf Arnheim, "type is the structural essence" that underlies the "abstractions characteristic of productive thinking" in art.[13] This view is largely shared by the art historian E. H. Gombrich, who proposes that all art is conceptual in that it originates in the human mind rather than in the visible world itself. In considering the unusually late development of caricature in the history of representational art, Gombrich concludes: "The invention of portrait caricature presupposes the theoretical discovery of the difference between likeness and equivalence. . . . All artistic discoveries are discoveries not of likenesses but of equivalences which enable us to see reality in terms of an image and an image in terms of reality."[14]

Where a factographist like Vertov hoped to remove any disparity in representational art between image and reality, Eisenstein insisted on the differential between photographic likeness and representational equivalence as a basis of meaning in cinema. Materialist construction of form, he explains, is conducted "not just through the *material* organization of the effective phenomena that are filmed but *optically*, through the actual shooting" (W 63). Reviewing the development of Soviet silent cinema some twenty years later, Eisenstein evaluates the difference between Vertov's principles and his own as a leap from "the *cinematographic eye* to the *image of an embodied viewpoint on phenomena*" (FF 233). Within his first two films, such embodiment is obvious in the spectatorial motifs, with the regard of revolutionaries direct and clear-focused, while that of reactionaries is sinister and myopic.

The film theorist Béla Balázs comments that in the juxtaposition of facial close-ups in Eisenstein's silent cinema "face faces face, and two different conceptions of the world clash in two different, unmistakable physiognomies." By presenting a viewpoint on characters, the director is "showing their class and showing it immanently. . . ; showing not man in his social class, but social class in men."[15] In part II of *Potemkin*, the close-up of a marine officer who smiles sadistically and fingers the curled end of his moustache seems to be, when isolated from the montage, a regrettable instance of clichéd villainy. But the image, which lasts no more than two seconds, is juxtaposed with other close shots in the sequence, notably three of a young guardsman who turns his head as the tarpaulin is brought on deck. The officer's withering, fanatical glare is set in opposition to the guardsman's averted glance, which reveals both intimidation and an unwillingness to obey.

The brief caricature of the marine officer functions as an abridgement in the thematics of social conflict. In 1921 Grosz published a collection of drawings entitled *The Face of the Ruling Class*. With their shiny top hats and fat cigars, his capitalists are identical to those in *Strike*. Typification of the conflict between officers and seamen in *Potemkin* through the conjunction of "Men and Maggots" is also strongly akin to Grosz's sensibility. In these cases, the social image is reduced to an equivalent drawn from the subjective code of class struggle.

In Eisenstein's imagery, class difference is a difference between visualization through stereotype of the bourgeoisie and through typicality of the proletariat. His treatment makes the ruling class into individualized caricatures, while by comparison the working class, seen in the hundreds in each film, seems an actual anonymous mass. In compositional terms, this is a difference between static, oblique designs and dynamic, normative ones. In regard to both physiognomy and camera point of view, the working class is an ideal type, distinctive for its physical power, artlessness, and collective identity. From this ideal all other social groups— owners, managers, military, priests, the lumpenproletariat—deviate. The antecedent in Marx for such typology is his Hegelian formulation that the proletariat realizes the Idea within history.

Concerning both character and story, typage has some affinities with the thought of Georg Lukács, where the typical relates specifically to the historical work of art. For Lukács the destiny of a typical character is not narrowly an individual fate but the dynamics of the historical situation which the work represents. Character thus does not simply become a static symbol of class; it is an expression of the process of social development through class conflict. Typical events, ordered into a plot, represent movement at a particular moment in history. (These specific properties of typicality have greater relevance to Eisenstein's later interests in epic character and individual heroism.)

Lukács considers typicality to be fully achieved in the realist fiction of Balzac and Tolstoy but does not regard it to be a property of avant-garde art of this century. The typical character is not an essential, universal, eternal, or final type, nor is it an ordinary, average, naturalistic specimen of humanity. The topical characters of tendentious literature are not to be mistaken for typical ones: "The typical hero reacts with his entire personality to the life of his age. . . . There is present this organic unity of profound individuality and profound typicality. The characters produced by schematists, on the other hand, are both above and beneath the level of typicality."[16] By this criterion typicality does not seem consistent with typage, which encompasses eccentricity at one level and collective rather than individualized identity at another. Furthermore Lukács disparaged advancement of a proletarian culture and replacement of the individual hero with the masses as protagonist.

Lukács is also well known for his condemnation of formalism for its aberrations from representational norms and of modernism for its interests in pathology, but the standard of historical typicality can admit to a degree these same properties. He justifies the stereotyped abnormalities depicted in caricature with an explanation that "artists like Goya or Daumier depicted the deformation of man under class society." In the period of capitalism's global expansion, novelists like Balzac had to reject concepts of beauty in life or of the integrated personality: "To be faithful realists they could only depict disharmonious, shattered lives, . . . lives inwardly warped, corrupted and brutalized."[17] According to Lukács's general definition, in a type "all the humanly and socially essential determinants are present on their highest level of development, in the ultimate unfolding of the possibilities latent in them, in extreme presentation of their extremes, rendering concrete the peaks and limits of men and their epochs."[18] Eisenstein applies a similar principle in rendering radical social transformation as a contrast between the idealized historical potential of the working class and stereotypes that make the ruling class seem anachronistic.

When Lukács locates typicality outside the standards of the nineteenth-century novel there is a conceptual latitude that permits further comparison with typage. He considers the portrayal of workers in Gerhart Hauptmann's play *The Weavers*, for instance, exemplary for taking about a dozen representative types and placing them in situations and interrelationships that form an artistic impression of the masses. From this dramatic technique, Lukács draws the structural principle: "The entire content of the art-work must turn into form if its true content is to bring about an aesthetic effect."[19] Considering the ordinary and topical nature of the characters in Hauptmann, this statement from the 1950s shows a tolerance for formalism and the mass hero not evident in Lukács criticism on epic realism in the 1930s and 1940s. At any rate, the sublation of content into form is the very basis of Eisenstein's montage, which in *Potemkin* creates the *idea* of the revolutionary masses as one of its effects.

Shock Effect

Primary to the pathos of *Potemkin* are its represented explosions of feeling. An instance is the rising emotion among mourners as they respond to the speeches of agitators. The scene registers a higher emotional key when first a peasant woman rips off her shawl and flails with it, then a young man wildly tears open his shirt. In a later analysis, Eisenstein describes this transition as one in which "the theme of mourning leaps into the theme of fury" (*FF* 164). When the film's peripeteia are considered— particularly the reversals from celebration to murder in part II and from fraternization to massacre in part IV—it is evident that shock effect is as important to the whole narrative structure as it is to the montage unit.

In some instances, images of graphic brutality mark an unexpected shift in emotion, as in *Strike*'s interpolation of actual butchery. The almost literalized assault on perception in *Potemkin*'s montage of the sabred woman in pince-nez has a counterpart two years later in Salvador Dali and Luis Buñuel's surrealistic violation of perception in *Un chien andalou* (1928). But that film's image of a razor slitting open an eyeball has qualities of actuality, gratuitousness, and symbolism (in its association with the image of sharp clouds passing the moon) largely absent from the image in *Potemkin*, which uses ellipsis and belongs to an immediate context of events. The shock effect of the Odessa steps sequence derives generally from its graphic and dramatic tensions rather than from its few violent images.

Instrumental in *Potemkin*'s creation of shock reflexes is the close-up, which is as important as montage to Eisenstein's practices of film construction. Properly speaking, for him this composition is not so much a close-up as it is a large-scale shot. Nor are its purposes primarily the selection or citation of detail for exposition. The unique properties of the large-scale shot for Eisenstein are made evident in *Potemkin*'s imagery of the rotten meat that is the immediate spark for mutiny. It is here, in disputing the sailors' claim that the carcass of beef is swarming with maggots, that the ship's doctor, Smirnov, removes his pince-nez to fold its lenses together and form a magnifying glass. Before the meat is shown again, the sequence mounts a tight shot that fragments the doctor's face, the folded pince-nez drawn to his one visible eye, which is grotesquely distorted. In the subsequent tight shot of infested meat, the folded pince-nez is brought next to the wiggling maggots. The composition's conjunction of lens and rotten meat is a trope that magnifies the conditions that oppress sailors.

The composition is also a reflexive statement on the practices of the large-scale shot in *Potemkin* as opposed to the traditions of close-up in the story film. Rather than an excision of detail for a closer perspective, this composition is a subversive intensification. A large-scale shot of putrefying meat is not an attraction one will find in the commercial cinema of the period. Another extreme, magnified shot of the carcass swarming with maggots is included in the sequence within which Dr. Smirnov is thrown overboard. It immediately follows the shot where the doctor hits the water's surface and leaves a wake. There is a graphic correlation of the foaming surface to the swarm of grubs on the meat.

With this specific shock attraction in mind, Eisenstein boasted that *Potemkin*'s effects are "linked together by a 'plot carcass' " (W 75). His film intended to do violence to the conventions of story film maintained not only by the features imported from European and American cinema, but in most Soviet releases as well. In 1925, movie theaters managed under NEP policies in the Soviet Union booked six imported films for every Soviet one. Sovkino, the new state cinema enterprise, developed policies that were frankly aimed toward commercial and entertainment objectives in competing for Soviet audiences. Lunacharsky officially supported these objectives: "There is one area in which we must imitate the bourgeoisie: we must wherever possible avoid tendentious films. . . . Our films must be just as attractive and just as entertaining as bourgeois films. The melodramatic form is the best form for cinema."[20] The Formalists

Shklovsky and Tynyanov warned that the predominance of such plot norms retarded the development of artistic devices specific to cinema.

In his admiration for *Potemkin*, Pudovkin stated that with this film "Eisenstein invented the cinema epithet."[21] While in Pudovkin's own films the close-up is governed more by dramatic continuity, for Eisenstein it allowed great flexibility in metaphoric and metonymic substitution. In its degree of freedom from scenic logic, the close-up can mark the modes of enunciation and discourse in a film text, as in the mirrored reflection of the student's reaction to events on the Odessa steps.

In "A Dialectic Approach to Film Form" (1929), Eisenstein relates shock effect to "dynamization of the inertia of perception—a dynamization of the 'traditional view' into a new one" (*FF* 47). As a precedent for this understanding, he quotes from the journal of Charles Baudelaire: "That which is not slightly distorted lacks sensible appeal; from which it follows that irregularity—that is to say, the unexpected, surprise and astonishment, are an essential part and characteristic of beauty" (*FF* 51). Walter Benjamin, in commenting on the importance of irregularity and the unexpected to Baudelaire's poetry, identifies these qualities substantively with modern urban life in general and formally with the methods of film in particular: "Technology has subjected the human sensorium to a complex kind of training. There came a day when a new and urgent need for stimuli was met by the film. In . . . film, perception in the form of shocks was established as a formal principle."[22] A similar premise underlies the reflexological model of the film attraction.

Benjamin had visited Moscow for two months in the winter of 1926–27 but did not meet with Eisenstein, who for part of that period was on location filming material for *The General Line*. During his visit Benjamin began to draft an article on *Potemkin* as a work of politically partisan art. In his commentary on the Eisenstein film Benjamin outlines ideas he will develop fully in "The Work of Art in the Age of Mechanical Reproduction." With the case of cinema generally, technical innovation has revealed the tendentious potential of all cultural forms: "Among the fracture points of artistic formations, one of the most powerful is film. Truly, with film a new *region of consciousness* comes into being." As distinct from the costume spectacles, contemporary adventures, and expressionist dramas produced at the German UFA studio, *Potemkin* specifically marks for Benjamin a new fracture point and epoch: "Here for the first time the movement of the masses has the outright architectonic and yet not at all monumental (i.e. UFA) character that establishes its viability for cinema. No other medium could render this turbulent collectivity, moreover none other could communicate either such beauty or the movement of such terror, such panic."[23] Benjamin concludes his article with a tribute to the tendentious insights of the film's typage in its innovative characterization of ship's officers through a collective mode distinct from the mode used to represent the masses. He recognizes Dr. Smirnov, for instance, as representative of a pattern of reactionary confederation between medical authority and state power familiar in German society during World War I.

In evaluating the potential of montage in radio and film on a later occasion, Benjamin designates its capacity to interrupt narrative as a potent structural principle for revolutionary art: "Interruption here has not the character of a stimulant, but an organizing function. It arrests the action in its course, and thereby compels the [audience] to adopt an attitude vis-à-vis the process. In the midst of the action, it brings it to a stop, and thus obliges the spectator to take a position."[24] An example of such interruption is *Strike*'s slaughterhouse imagery, which breaks linear development to the story's climax. It has the purpose, as an attraction, of stimulating an affect of horror. Additionally, that affect becomes a unit in the montage association with the close-up reaction shots which, in not belonging to the unity of story elements, establish a discursive position in regard to events.

Eisenstein, in his own subsequent analysis of *Potemkin*, terms each point at which the action undergoes an emphatic shift a "caesura" (*FF* 164). The caesura in part IV is marked by the title "Suddenly" and four brief large shots of a woman tossing her head so violently that her dark hair obscures her features. The film's whole narrative structure is divided near midpoint by a caesura. After the rising line of action that culminates with the success of mutiny and the unexpected death of Vakulinchuk, a dramatic pause is provided in the sequence of the harbor seen through morning fog. The rising action resumes when the crowd is stirred by the speeches of activists. In terms of the entire film, this caesura at the start of part III marks the transition from momentary, individual defeat to historic, collective victory.

The pathetic dimension is intensified through doubled actions like the sailor smashing a plate, the wounded young mother falling against the baby carriage, and the officer swinging his sabre. A similar effect is constructed into the entire Odessa steps sequence. Distant shots interspersed in the sequence reveal the soldiers' descent to be an overlapped action, with the front line stepping down from a position higher than that in immediately previous shots. The scene's space and time exceed the boundaries of everyday space and time. In carrying her murdered boy up the steps, the mother follows a path bordered by fallen bodies but cleared by a vertical panel of bright light leading to the troops. The lighting, which casts her shadow up the stairway, contradicts the continuity of shots depicting troops, whose shadows are always cast downward.

The film viewer is not disoriented by these nonnaturalistic compositions, however, for the montage establishes a context independent of the norms of spatial logic and, by thematic extension, beyond the norms of humanity. The sociologist and film critic Edgar Morin comments of Eisenstein's silent cinema generally: "Ideology is not plastered onto the film. It is not exterior to the film nor are the images simply pretexts. It seems to be born and reborn without end. . . . Cinema becomes instructive through its language of images and images only. . . . There is a coherent system in which the intensification and utilization of the images' affective power attains a logos."[25] With his next two films, Eisenstein explores the processes of ideological signification by means other than that of pathos.

CHAPTER FOUR

October:
History and Genesis

In Marx's historiography, proletarian revolution inaugurates mankind's genuine history. The progression of epochs in the economic formation of society—Asiatic, ancient, feudal, and finally modern bourgeois modes of production—arises from antagonisms between material conditions and social relations. With the material and technological revolution achieved in modern production, Marx sees an era beyond social conflict: "The productive forces developing in the womb of bourgeois society create the material conditions for the solution of that antagonism. This social formation brings, therefore, the prehistory of human society to a close."[1] The birth of society into a new order after epochs of human existence is a tenet of apocalyptic belief, as in the advent of the Messiah and the descent of the New Jerusalem. The signal marking complete regeneration is traced by Ernst Bloch from the thunderstorm and rainbow in astral myth and the King of Kings mounted on a white horse in Revelation to the popular assault on the Bastille.[2] The storming of the Winter Palace in Petrograd, both within Bolshevik culture and as rendered in *October*, is such a signal event announcing genesis.

From Marx's own perspective, development up to his era belongs in a sense to the unconscious, natural history of humankind. The materialist conception of history and the labor theory of value are the objective, scientific means of exposing legitimization of social antagonism according to God, king, or nation-state as false consciousness. From the critique of past and present, materialist history advances to make class struggle finally a conscious, universal purpose. This transformation promises to end the primarily commodity, impersonal dynamics of social relations. To adopt categories from the *1844 Manuscripts* and *The Communist Manifesto*, hitherto human productive activity largely instituted men and women's alienation from the products of their labor, from the productive process itself, from fellow humans—in sum, from their species being. With revolution against this cumulative past of alienation embodied in the private property system, the human era of free, conscious productive life activity and of history, properly speaking, begins.

The mythos to Marx's historiography is that genesis takes place in the future, not the past, of mankind. All recorded events are preparatory to that time when humans grasp themselves at the root, as the root, of existence. In notations made in 1844, Marx outlines this trajectory:

> *Communism* as the *positive* transcendence of *private property*, . . . as the real *appropriation of the human* essence by and for man; communism therefore as the complete return of man to himself as a *social* (i.e., human) being—a return become conscious, and accomplished within the entire wealth of previous development. . . . Communism is the riddle of history solved, and it knows itself to be this solution.
> The entire movement of history is, therefore, both its *actual* act of genesis (the birth act of its empirical existence) and also for its thinking consciousness the *comprehended* and *known* process of its *becoming*.[3]

Several ambitious art projects at the outset of the Bolshevik era attempted to convey this spirit of world-historical inception. Vladimir Tatlin's design for a monument to the Third International, first exhibited as a model in 1920, was projected to stand at twice the height of the Empire State Building and to house three functional units in different shapes and rotating at different speeds. Mayakovsky's verse drama *Mystery-Bouffe*, first staged in 1918, presents the antagonism between proletariat and bourgeoise as an apocalyptic contest for the future that spans heaven, earth, and hell. On May Day 1920 in Petrograd a mass drama titled *The Mystery of Freed Labor*, which chronicles a progression from ancient slave rebellions to the October Revolution, was staged in front of the former stock exchange to an estimated audience of thirty-five thousand. Another massive outdoor production, *In Favor of a World Commune*, followed in July 1920.[4]

Both the thematics and the montage methods of *October* and *Old and New* treat Marxist revolution as a spectacle of historical genesis and utopian potential. With a political irony not lost on Eisenstein, however, his years of work on these two films exposed the decline of revolutionary promise in the Soviet Union. The visionary and Futurist modes he employs in these two films had begun to fall silent by 1926, as indeed had many Soviet avant-garde movements. The 1927 Party conferences on literature and theater supported the legacy of classic works against the innovations of the avant-garde. Eisenstein knowingly adopted styles and intentions that met with increasing official disfavor.

In spring 1926 Eisenstein and the studio Sovkino reached agreement on a film about the movement for modernization and collectivization in the countryside to be titled *The General Line* as an indication of its promotion of Party policy on agriculture. The Eisenstein-Alexandrov scenario was approved in July and location work progressed through the end of the year in a variety of regions. Its production was suspended when Sovkino formalized a new contract with the Eisenstein unit to prepare an anniversary film for the October Revolution celebrations less than a year away. When ceremonies were held in Moscow in 1927, however, only selections from *October* were shown. The film was not put into release until March 1928. Its postponement was due in part to the difficulties of editing the extensive material filmed. Eisenstein explained in a statement to the press at the end of 1927 that he was working with material that would make two features with a combined length of 13,000 feet. The print of *October* released three months later measures 9,186 feet. Thus, over one-fourth of the material Eisenstein had planned to use was left out of the single finished film, which had considerably reduced the scope of his original intentions.

Party censorship also accounted for the film's delays and deletions. Alexandrov maintains that Stalin personally examined the work print and ordered the removal of scenes totaling nearly 3,000 feet. If this is indeed the case, it is an early example of Stalin taking personal control over public versions of Soviet history. One source in Eisenstein's research on the period was John Reed's eyewitness account *Ten Days That Shook the World*, the title under which *October* is frequently distributed in the West. Reed focuses on Lenin, Trotsky, and Anatoli Lunacharsky as the leaders of the Bolshevik Revolution but mentions Stalin only in passing since he played no central role. Once in power, Stalin banned the Reed book. All signs of the historic significance of Trotsky—whose alliance with Lenin brought the overthrow of Alexander Kerensky's Provisional Government and whose military skill preserved the revolutionary state through years of civil war—are absent from *October*. There is also evidence in relation to *Potemkin* that an epigraph by Trotsky, taken from his account of the 1905 revolution, had appeared in release prints and was later replaced with a citation from Lenin.[5]

In a letter to the French film critic and historian Léon Moussinac dated November 22, 1928, by which time production on *The General Line* had resumed, Eisenstein expresses alarm over vicissitudes in the cultural and political climate: "I'm afraid, very much afraid. And . . . the facts justify my fear. We aren't rebels any more. We're becoming lazy priests. I have the impression that the enormous breath of 1917 which gave birth to our cinema is blowing itself out. . . . People are beginning to notice heartbreaking symptoms of prerevolutionary times even among our avant-garde. . . . And what is worse, this is the tendency of the people for whom we are working!"[6] After submitting *The General Line* for studio clearance,

Eisenstein and Alexandrov were advised by Stalin personally that the film did not correspond with the reformulated Party line on collectivization. After addition of a revised conclusion, the film was released in October 1929 as *Old and New* since it was considered unrepresentative of the Party's new general policy on the countryside.

October and *Old and New* had become caught up in events that transformed Soviet history: defeat of the left opposition once led by Trotsky within the Party, an emerging policy of forced collectivization, the consolidation of state power by Stalin, the cultural revolution (1928–32), and the repudiation of NEP with the First Five-Year Plan (adopted in 1929 and declared fulfilled after four years). The cultural revolution, which receives full attention in Chapter 7, marks the end to an era of singularly diverse and experimental art that remains compelling and significant. By the time ten years later that Eisenstein's next film was completed, Soviet culture had fundamentally reversed both the climate for experimentation and the mood of revolutionary optimism experienced during its first decade.

The Historic Moment

As had become customary, Eisenstein's original scenario for *October* was epic in scope, extending from the February Revolution, events of October in Petrograd and Moscow, and the execution of Nicholas II to the assembly of counterrevolutionary forces, formation of the Red Army, and episodes of civil war concluding with the decisive victory at Perekop. The spirit of history *October* embodies is conveyed by the summary of Perekop's significance in an early script draft: "It was the Synthesis. It was the Gamut. It was the Kaleidoscope of all the heroic victories of the Red Army. It was the condensation of the agonising exertion of a whole nation such as history had never seen. . . ."[7] While *Strike* and *Potemkin* concern the pathos of social oppression and the necessity for organized action, *October* celebrates the inauguration of revolution. The intention to stimulate class identification through a visceral reflex is replaced by an effort to mediate through images and montage the process of history's transformation.

In his 1928 essay "Our *October*," Eisenstein refers to a historical break—an October—within his own film work. Indicating that development of revolutionary cinema will not continue in the direction of replacing character and intimate emotion by mass action and materiality set by his first two films, he explains: "the next stage will replace the presentation of a phenomenon (material, object) by a *conclusion* based on the phenomenon and a *judgement* on the material, given concrete form in finished concepts. Cinema is ready to begin operating through the abstract word that leads to a concrete *concept*" (*W* 104). In a letter to Moussinac later that year, he amplifies this explanation: "I think I'm ready to overturn my entire system. Thematically as well as formally. . . . This cinematography will be genetically ideological, for its substance will be the screening of . . . *begriff* [concept]. But there is no absolute *begriff*. They are always 'classical' (from the word 'class' and not 'classicism'). . . . *October* is the dialectical denial of *Potemkin!*"[8] The shift from affective to intellectual purposes corresponds with a reorientation from reflexology to ideography as the foundation of montage.

The events of 1917 in Russia mark historical changes that have in turn transformed our perspectives on the course of history. The events thus have a reflexive dimension for historiography. They reveal, according to Lenin, that history has a capacity far greater than even an advanced consciousness could comprehend:

> History as a whole, and the history of revolutions in particular, is always richer in content, more varied, more multiform, more lively and ingenious than is imagined by even the best parties, the most class-conscious vanguards of the most advanced classes. This can readily be understood, because even the finest of vanguards express the class-consciousness, will, passion and imagination of tens of thousands, whereas at moments of great upsurge and the exertion of all human capacities, revolutions are made by the class-consciousness, will, passion and imagination of tens of millions, spurred on by a most acute struggle of classes.[9]

An example of the excesses of historical content over the capacity to understand, the October Revolution as subject matter required from Eisenstein a method beyond the reaches of pathos and montage of attractions. Intellectual montage provides forms of association appropriate to the transformative, reflexive dimensions of revolutionary history.

In synthesizing and condensing events from February through October 1917, Eisenstein departs from the historical record in three major respects. Film titles indicate that the October 10 call for a general uprising set the date for October 25 (all dates correspond to the New Style calendar adopted subsequent to these events). Alexander Rabinowitch, in his historical reconstruction of events in Petrograd, points out that contrary to legend Lenin's resolution left the decision over the time and nature of the insurrection to the city's Bolshevik organizations.[10] In the film, as midnight approaches on the day of October 25, titles exclaim that time is running out. The concern for time—which is not the element of suspense it is during the mutineers' vigil in part V of *Potemkin*—here emphasizes the political delays that prevent the Revolution (traditionally dated October 25) from being announced until the early morning of October 26. The

Menshevik and Socialist Revolutionary parties are presented as temporizing factions whose uncertainty and unresponsiveness delay the course of history.

The film's second major departure from history involves the appearance of Lenin at its conclusion. The montage becomes kaleidoscopic after ministers in the Winter Palace are shown resigning to the Military Revolutionary Committee. A close-up presents a clock that reads 2:07 (in the morning of October 26). In rapid succession, images of the Winter Palace alternate with ones of clockfaces. Views of a young lad asleep on the imperial throne and of clocks arrayed and in motion across the screen are followed by close-ups of an audience applauding. Subsequent shots identify the new setting as the Smolny Institute. Lenin steps to the rostrum to announce "The Workers' and Peasants' Revolution is accomplished." In fact, Lenin made such a statement at Smolny on the afternoon of October 25 with Trotsky by his side. The declaration of victory made at Smolny in the early morning of October 26, though drafted by Lenin, was spoken by Lunacharsky. Lenin waited until the night of October 26 to appear and address the Congress. *October*'s conclusion thus condenses in a matter of seconds the proceedings of two days at the Smolny Congress.

A third departure from historical fact is made in the opening sequence. The first photographic image is the monumental statue of Tsar Alexander III, father of the tsar deposed during the February Revolution, Nicholas II. Seen from low angles and close distance to accent its grandiose appearance, the statue presents the crowned tsar seated in a throne, holding a royal scepter in the right hand and an imperial orb in the left. The regal trappings are subsequently isolated in close-up. Within moments, the common people swarm over the monument and fasten heavy ropes to its head and limbs. Following the title "February," the statue is dismantled. Though an effective metonymic figure for the fall of tsarism, razing the Alexander III monument was not a spontaneous event of 1917. In a 1918 poem, "It's Too Early to Rejoice," Mayakovsky impatiently demanded that the statue be destroyed: "And does Tsar Alexander still stand on Uprising Square? Dynamite it!" The Soviet government did not organize its removal until 1921.

The opening action also disregards geographical unity. The monument was located in Moscow while the historical events depicted occurred in Petrograd, but the film uses no establishing shot to set the action. It maintains continuity of events not through chronology or geography, but through compositional association. The second sequence presents in isolated details a Russian Orthodox ceremony that appears to give blessing to the new Provisional Government. The church metropolitan's vestments resemble Alexander's royal attire; shown in close-up, the cross in his right hand and the censer in his left are like the scepter and orb.

Where *Strike* and *Potemkin* establish a definable setting at their outset, *October* establishes a method of association in linking monuments and insignia to political activities.

An aspect of *October*'s "dialectical denial" of *Potemkin* is its uses of parody and comic structure in place of the previous film's pathos and tragic model. From a Marxist perspective, the generic plot structure underlying history is that of comedy—the climax of revolution will bring the end of state society, with its exploitative and alienated relationships, and the beginning of community. The very forces that make prehistory tragic, in the dissociation between potential being and material existence, ultimately bring resolution and unity. It is from such a perspective of history's comic outcome that Eisenstein renders events of 1917.

Strike and *Potemkin* portray tsarist troops for an affect of horror, but the forces of counterrevolution in *October* are handled farcically. One instance of farce is the unit of soldiers identified by a film title as the Women's Battalion of Death, which appears to be an intentional conflation of two actual units: the Moscow Women's Battalion of Death and the First Petrograd Women's Shock Battalion, which defended the palace in the last days of the Provisional Government. The pretension of violence in the brigade's name is satirized when these troops are shown preening and gossiping around Nicholas II's billiard table. Relevant to this comic tone is the consensus among historians that the Bolshevik rise to power in Petrograd was practically bloodless.

From *October*'s vantage point on tsarism and the Provisional Government as deposed institutions, they appear as comically inept and defunct forms of control. Kerensky's choice to house his government in the vast, baroque splendor of the Winter Palace, seat of the Romanov dynasty, is treated in the film as an anachronistic restoration of autocracy. With Kerensky's decision to continue the war declared by the tsar, the film's opening action is played in reverse, so that the Alexander III statue reassembles itself. Continuation of imperial policies is portrayed through montage contrasts of the palace's luxury with scenes of bombardment on the battlefront and of ration lines in the city.

In one of many comparisons of objects to individuals, a montage sequence combines shots of Kerensky with close-ups of a crafted gold peacock, one of the precious objets d'art that filled the Winter Palace. At one level, the comparison functions as a literalization of simile ("proud as a peacock") common to montage of attractions. At another, there are compositional correlations, stemming from visual equivalents and optical organization of the shots, that extend the comparison and its implications. Kerensky, standing pompously erect before portals to the tsar's bedchambers, is set through montage into mechanical motions imitative of the clockwork miniature's. The bright polish of his boots and gloves duplicates the sheen of the figurine's gold leaf. Acute camera angles contribute to this portrayal of Kerensky as a contraption and an artefact.

The Winter Palace and its treasures are represented as equivalents for the atavistic nature of Kerensky's leadership. Ornamental details like the crown with which he stoppers a flask, or the huge ivory tusks that frame him as he sits, seemingly enthroned, characterize the head of the Provisional Government as a ruler in the imperial and even tribal modes. These details, intercut with shots of the palace's ranked crystal, dishware, and porcelain miniatures, suggest that Kerensky plays at being tsar. The royal flask further implies that he is drunk with power.

In the film's most familiar parody of vainglory, Kerensky ascends the palace's main stairway to the accompaniment of the titles: "Supreme Chief / Minister of War and the Navy / Prime Minister / Etc., etc., etc. . . . Hope of the Country and of the Revolution: A. F. Kerensky." The sequence may literalize a verbal pun in Russian on "climb the stairs"; since *lestnice* means both stairs and ladder, it may refer to climbing a "ladder of success."[11] By overlapping shots, the montage retards Kerensky's progress so that he does not reach the next flight of stairs. Though futile, the stair-climbing sequence is one of Kerensky's rare active moments. Much of the time he is seen idly toying with priceless but useless objets. The inconclusiveness of Kerensky's efforts in the Winter Palace and, on a historical scale, of his response to the offensive launched by the reactionary General Kornilov stands in contrast to the decisiveness of the Bolsheviks' activism. The Formalist device of delay, intended to renew perception of the familiar, is adopted here and in the bridge-raising episode to render in the film material the phenomenon of retardation. Counterrevolutionary elements function as forces of delay in the momentum of *October's* events.

The ideographic organization of material presents the factions of conservatism and reaction through literalization, objectivization, and inanimacy. The Provisional Government's ministers appear first in petrified postures indicative of their powerlessness. Later, as the hour of resignation approaches, shots of their evening suits neatly laid out on chairs around a conference table show them to be already divested of power. In a montage association, Kerensky is equated with a plaster icon of Napoleon Bonaparte (who crowned himself Holy Emperor) and these two are equated with Kornilov, whose rallying cry is the tsarist motto "For God and Country." The comparisons have a basis in historical materials. Lenin issued a polemic in July 1917 against the "Bonapartist Kerensky" and his Provisional Government, and contemporary sources portray General Kornilov as having a fixation on Napoleon. Kerensky's failure to mobilize the defense of Petrograd against Kornilov's advance is mounted by *October* as a confrontation between two miniature Napoleons and, alternately, between two crude, featureless wood figures. This satiric demystification of their political ambitions concludes with a literalized act of iconoclasm: plaster Napoleons are smashed.

Equally relevant to *October*'s iconography and montage is the specific sense of Bonapartism within Marx's critique of state power under capitalism. In Marx's analysis of France's Second Republic and Second Empire, the career of Louis Bonaparte—first as elected president then as Emperor Napoleon III—exemplifies the potential for a chief executive to gain dictatorial power within an ostensibly parliamentary government. While not independent of capitalist class interests, the Bonapartist state develops a vast bureaucratic and military apparatus that becomes its own rationale for power; in this regard, it is often looked upon as a precursor of the twentieth-century totalitarian state. Capitalist development was unprecedented under the Second Empire: "industry and commerce expanded to colossal dimensions; financial swindling celebrated cosmopolitan orgies; the misery of the masses was set off by a shameless display of gorgeous, meretricious and debased luxury. The State power, apparently soaring high above society, was at the same time itself the greatest scandal of that society and the very hotbed of all its corruptions."[12] The centralized state power with a dictatorial leader at the head, its standing army and an entrenched bureaucracy are legacies from absolute monarchy whose historiography Eisenstein investigates in *Ivan the Terrible*.

In further demystifying the slogan "For God and Country," *October* inserts a series of religious idols into a montage of Kerensky, a church exterior, royal medals and brocade, the Alexander III monument, Kornilov, and Napoleon statuettes. The gods sequence is the film's clearest example of Eisenstein's new effort to develop through montage "direct materialization of a slogan" (W 105). The sequence opens with a baroque image of Christ enthroned against a rayonnant background, followed by an elaborate Eastern god with multiple arms radiating from its back. Eisenstein later identified the second image as the Hindu god Shiva; it is also in some respects reminiscent of Western images of the devil. The subsequent gods span Japanese, African, and Eskimo deities and finally rudimentary wooden figures. After the initial image, the gods are all non-Christian and there is a regression to more primitive forms until the montage again alternates Christ, Shiva, and the lacquered mask of a smiling face. Each image is uncontextualized, static and, by being brought into association with the strange gods of other cultures, despiritualized.

The momentum of the sequence is a critique of the signifier *God*, whose claims to universality and eternity, at least in Western religion, are contradicted. On a historical level, God is presented as a culturally defined, materially embodied construct. On a linguistic level, to use a term from the work of Roman Jakobson, God is presented as a shifter, an other-

wise empty sign dependent upon speaker and cultural context for its
meaning. The conjunction "God and Country" indeed has been evident
from the opening sequence, where the visual treatment of the Alexander
III monument accents perspectives that suggest religious traditions in
Byzantine art. This visual treatment presents Alexander III as a massive
icon, as a holy figure in autocratic terms. The Napoleonic imagery suggests a deity of the bourgeois era, revered in the form of statuettes. Thus
Eisenstein's montage correlates gods and rulers into an intertextual
system.

The film's mass scenes are infused with a sense of dynamism and purpose, contrasting with the inertness and dispiritedness of the leaders of
the Provisional Government and the counterrevolution, and of their slogans and deities. The masses in *October* are compositionally treated for
an effect of energeia not pathos and, in comparison to the first two films,
are presented through dramatic distance and abstraction. The July massacre in central Petrograd is filmed in stationary, extreme long shot. No
shocking, bloody details of the brutality are shown in the events on Nevsky Prospect. Only one close-up of a victim is shown, in the vignette of
irate bourgeois attacking a lone Bolshevik.

In reaction to the July demonstrations the Provisional Government had
major drawbridges raised in order to isolate worker districts from the city
center. The episode's developing tension is impersonal and almost purely
geometric. Fleeing demonstrators are shot down as they attempt to cross
a bridge; also killed is a white horse, which remains harnessed to an
empty carriage. Lying across the center juncture as the bridge begins to
open are several bodies, including those of a horse and of a young woman
whose long blond hair is lifted by the rising platform. Alternating general,
distant views of the bridge with close-ups of its understructure and of the
horse, the montage links this event with the ransacking of the *Pravda*
offices and the dumping of its issues into the river.

The title *Pravda* (Truth) is prominent in compositions of this last incident, and the "truth" set afloat is a summary image of the sequence's
representation of the July Days as the historical pivot between February
and October, between preservation and revolution. Only as the bridge
platform approaches vertical is the tension broken and the sequence concluded, as the white horse snaps loose and plummets into the water. With
the following sequences of the imprisoned soldiers who had rallied to
workers and the destroyed Bolshevik Party offices, the forces preserving
state power seem to have prevailed. Only with the mobilization of the
city's populace against the threat of Kornilov's troops is the momentum
toward revolution reestablished.

The sequence on fraternization between Bolsheviks and Russian troops
moves progressively from realism to abstraction. In a dramatic night

scene, organizers agitate within the Savage Division, a contingent of Caucasus soldiers that at first supports Kornilov. Group scenes alternate with one shots that single out the dissimilarities between urban Party workers and rural troops. To seal a coalition, Bolsheviks join them in the *lezginka*, the traditional dance of the Caucasus. The montage accelerates as the dancers compete in kicks and leaps performed in rain puddles; a shortening of shot length intensifies the pace. The action reaches a crescendo of whirling splashes, light and shadow. Interspersed with this climax to the dance are images of Kerensky, who is prostrate on the tsarina's bed with his head buried beneath a jumble of pillows. Jutting into the foreground are Kerensky's immaculate and motionless riding boots.

Perhaps the film's most abstract sequence is introduced among the events of October with the titles "The cyclists / are for the Soviets." This armed corps had primary responsibility for security around the Winter Palace. No dramatization of soldiers joining with Bolsheviks is presented. Rather, shots are mounted of bicycle pedals and wheels turning rapidly. Accelerated montage seems to quicken their motion further until the sequence cuts to the hands of Soviet delegates, who are applauding this news enthusiastically, and to scenes of mobilization toward the Winter Palace. The event of the cyclists' collaboration occurs in the last phase of revolutionary culmination. History, the montage suggests, reaches a moment of pure dynamism.

The perspective on the historical momentum of the masses resumes with the storming of the Winter Palace. On a discursive level, this final episode concludes the conflict between the slogan of preservation and reaction "For God and Country" and the slogan of revolution "For Peace. For Bread. For Land." On a semantic level, the conflict is between a theocratic exhortation and a social directive. Across the intertitles, these two slogans—more than indications of chronology or identification of persons and factions—are linguistic referents in the organization of visual imagery. Revolutionary objectives are first introduced in negated form by Lenin upon his return to Russia, in the Finland Station speech: "Down with the Provisional Government! / All power to the Soviets! / Long live the Socialist Revolution! / Socialist not bourgeois. . . . / of the capitalist ministers / Neither peace / Nor bread / Nor land." The locution "Down with" is reiterated on banners and titles in the July Days sequence. Revolutionary objectives are restated in positive form with the success of fraternization between Bolsheviks and troops, the major incident between the July Days and the events of October. The storming of the Palace is initiated as the titles "The time for words is past! / For Peace! / For Bread! / For Land!" are intercut with close-ups of artillery pieces being loaded.

With kaleidoscopic speed the montage shows revolutionary soldiers cross the square and enter the palace. When they reach the private quarters upstairs, soldiers are dumbstruck by an opulence alien to them. One lifts the seat of a plush chair to reveal a chamber pot. A tableau of Christ blessing Nicholas and Alexandra gives an absurd insight into the presumptions of power. Soldiers vandalize the tsarina's boudoir, scattering showers of feathers from her bedding, while in the palace cellars Red sailors smash racks of bottles, flooding the floor with wine. As in *Potemkin*'s action of the sailor smashing an officer's plate, but here on an epic scale, montage dilates these events to make visual luxury from the destruction. The ecstatic waste of the Winter Palace luxuries is expressive of liberation from the old order of signification.

In the midst of these incidents, an act of recognition is marked for the audience when caseloads of newly minted military decorations are found. As they are overturned and streams of the valueless medals pour out, the title "It was for this that they fought?!" is inserted. No speaker is identified in the visual context, which shows only a hand extending into the cases. The extent of reification contained in the imperial motto "For God and Country" is demonstrated in these enactments of overthrowing the palace.

October presents the Bolshevik Revolution as essentially a mass movement. Such a historical generalization is the center of debate in the West, but Rabinowitch's nonpartisan account reaches the following conclusion:

> In 1917 Lenin's prerevolutionary conception of a small, professional, conspiratorial party was discarded and the doors opened wide to tens of thousands of new members who were by no means without influence, so that to a significant degree the party was now both responsive and open to the masses. . . . The relative flexibility of the party, as well as its responsiveness to the prevailing mass mood, had at least as much to do with the ultimate Bolshevik victory as did revolutionary discipline, organizational unity, or obedience to Lenin.[13]

The film presents Lenin as a manifestation of the masses' energy and direction. Lenin does not control events but rather he appears at the pivotal moments when movement toward revolution is intensified. All three of Lenin's appearances in public are sudden and crucial. (His only other appearance is in the famous disguise he wore in order to get back from Finland to the Smolny Institute.)

The period between the February Revolution and Lenin's return to Russia in the spring is summarized in images of resumed warfare, the manufacture of armaments, and breadlines. Five titles, uninterrupted by visuals, mark the next stage of events: "Everything is as before. / Famine and war. / But— / At the Finland Station. / April 3." Shot compositions of a nighttime crowd—divided into images of a large mass, of small groups, and of an individual singled out—precede the next two titles: "—Him. / Ulyanov." The Cyrillic letters in the successive titles "HO—. . .—OH." ("But—. . . —Him.") are a graphic equivalent for the reversal marked by Lenin's return. The Lenin character does not appear until after a few further compositions of the crowd and political banners. After the speech, Lenin again becomes marginal to the thrust of events until October, when he returns from hiding. By the time of the Bolshevik call for a general insurrection, the Petrograd workers and militia have seized a large measure of power through their mobilization against Kornilov. By the time Lenin takes the rostrum at the Congress of Soviets to announce revolutionary victory, the event has already been enacted onscreen and announced to Congress delegates. While their applause is in progress, Lenin rises to formalize a *fait accompli*.

Clockfaces—singly in extreme close-up, a cluster of three, and a large number arrayed in two concentric circles around the cluster—are shown in rapid succession with announcement of victory. The times registered on them are not the same, nor are they consistent with regular time zones. Eisenstein later explained that his purpose in this imagery was to convey "a moment of victory . . . unique in history and in the destiny of peoples."[14] Here, as in earlier scenes of fraternization between Russian and German troops, *October* stresses the Revolution's original promise of universalism, a principle central to Lenin's Marxism and to Trotsky's tenets of permanent revolution. The sequence of clockfaces and delegates' applause includes glimpses of a lad fallen asleep on the imperial throne; he seems representative of a generation born of revolution. As Marie-Claire Ropars-Wuilleumier observes, *October* generates "the idea of revolution itself: not of October 1917, but of a world in revolution, where everything changes and is exchanged, even the image of revolution."[15]

October thus concludes with a utopian moment commemorating revolutionary history. This moment establishes a critical distance from the present, a distance Eisenstein also asserts in his 1928 letter to Léon Moussinac. The difference in meaning between revolution at its genesis and in its institutionalization over the intervening decade was great. Stalin introduced the theory of "socialism in one country" in 1925 and began to implement it as policy over the next years. *October*'s revolutionary universalism does not conform to the Stalin line. In an article accompanying the film's release, titled "The Battle for *October*" in reference to struggles over its completion, Eisenstein makes insistent charges against "*the fiercest enemy of all Soviet film: disorganization, administrative slowdowns and bureaucracy.*" The more candid phrasing about "lazy priests" in the Moussinac letter discloses his perception of an advancing counterrevolution within the state bureaucracy. In closing "The Battle for

October," Eisenstein expresses appreciation to Nikolai Podvoisky (a Bolshevik who in 1917 held to Lenin's radical line while Stalin wavered) and
"above all to the Petrograd proletariat (to whom we dedicate our film)."[16]
Eisenstein's critical distance from the direction being taken by the Soviet
state is more evident in *Old and New*, a work structured largely in the
utopian mode.

Cinema Speech

With the production and editing of *October* and *Old and New*, Eisenstein
started to elaborate ideas on film language. These ideas mark a shift away
from earlier inquiries, which mainly pursued affective and formal analogies to reflexology and pathos. In terms of structuralist linguistic theory,
what Eisenstein refers to as film language is closer in meaning to *langage*
(linguistic potential) and *parole* (a speech act) than to *langue* (a specific
language system). The basis for comparing film and the methodology of
language is its capacity to organize images into an intellectually, and not
just emotionally, tendentious form. He distinguishes a new approach from
the earlier literalization of metaphor: "Our understanding of cinema is
now entering its 'second literary period.' The phase of approximation to
the symbolism of *language*. Speech. Speech that conveys a symbolic sense
(i.e. not literal), a 'figurative quality,' to a completely concrete material
meaning through something that is uncharacteristic of the literal, through
contextual confrontation, i.e. also through *montage*" (*W* 80). The Formalist critic Boris Eikhenbaum, writing on film stylistics in 1927, reaches a
similar conclusion in defining the spectator's experience of montage: "For
a study of the rules of cinema (and montage above all) it is most important
to recognize that perception and comprehension of a film are inseparably
linked with the formation of an internal speech which links the separate
shots together."[17]

The gods sequence employs this principle of film speech. Jean Mitry
faults the gods sequence for its violations of the unity of space and time,
arguing that montage "is valid only insofar as it utilizes animate elements
(in the dramatic sense of the term), from which it derives its emotional
force and, at the same time, its concretely symbolic significance. Montage
loses its validity when it employs symbols which are chosen arbitrarily
and are imposed on reality instead of being implied by it."[18] The realist
preoccupations here, as in André Bazin, disregard contextual factors that
motivate and organize the images. The sequence is introduced by the
titles "In the name / OF GOD," which are indicative of social practices of
nomination. Juxtaposition of idols of deities from the world's religions advances a demonstration that the phrase's *designatum* or referent is plural
and thus, by the tenets of monotheism, nonexistent. In the context of the

successive images, the phrase is revealed to refer to a null class. It is an antithesis of the film's training sequence on firearms, announced by the title "Proletarian, learn to handle a rifle." This phrase has a *denotatum*, an existing referent, in the images of ammunition, firing mechanism, and rifle stock that follow and the process of loading and assembly that is demonstrated.

Bazin's realist objections to Eisenstein's montage in the silent period are that it "did not give us the event; it alluded to it" and that "the final significance of the film was found to reside in the ordering . . . of elements much more than in their objective content."[19] From the time of his polemic with Vertov, Eisenstein argued against objectivist and realist programs: "The representations of an object in the actual (absolute) proportions proper to it is, of course, merely a tribute to orthodox formal logic, a subordination to the inviolable order of things. . . . Positivist realism is by no means the correct form of perception" (W 142). The insistent recontextualization of images, the conceptual aspects of the montage associations, and the sheer rapidity of editing in *October* prevent any realist illusion while preserving an impression of materiality within the individual shot.

One recurrent feature of *October*'s nonliteral, intellectual montage can be described in terms of classical rhetoric: the overlapped or reprised actions that are used more frequently than in *Potemkin* and to an effect other than pathos. Among such actions are the dismantling of the Alexander III monument, the lowering of a cannon onto the factory floor, the bridge raising, the horse's plunge into the Neva, and, in parallel action, the opening of a gilded peacock's wings with the opening of ornamental doors for Kerensky. In these instances the visual structure is comparable to anaphora, the figure of speech in which the same word or group of words is repeated at the beginning of successive clauses. Unlike the repetition of sound, which can occur unintentionally, anaphora patently reflects the deliberation given to structure. In foregrounding its form of expression, anaphora is a reflexive device. Julia Kristeva defines the role of anaphora in signification as "the gest that *marks*, that establishes *relations* and eliminates entities."[20] Content in these sequences from *October* is never allowed to become inert or objective; instead, it is in constant development for its dynamic and relational significance.

Overlapped action lays bare the device of montage association and advances Eisenstein's purpose of "the emancipation of closed action from its conditioning by time and space" (W 177). The close-up enables further detachment of objects, human features, and architectural detail from their contexts and environments. Thus isolated and magnified, visual materials are freely associated without consideration of the dramatic unities. These formal features also contribute to an effect of defamiliarization, whose counterpart in Futurist art is *vosstaniye veschey*, "the rebellion of objects" against conventional denotation and contextualization. In contesting regularized meaning, Futurist objects function as a second-order language in which they are no longer signifieds but are signifiers.

Similar principles are fundamental to the alienation-effect (A-effect) or distantiation in Brecht's theater. His explanation of method reflects an adaptation of Formalism, Futurism, and film montage:

> The A-effect consists in turning the object of which one is to be made aware, to which one's attention is to be drawn, from something ordinary, familiar, immediately accessible, into something peculiar, striking and unexpected. What is obvious is in a certain sense made incomprehensible, but this is only in order that it may then be made all the easier to comprehend. Before familiarity can turn into awareness the familiar must be stripped of its inconspicuousness; we must give up assuming that the object in question needs no explanation.[21]

In assessing his development through the montage process on *October*, Eisenstein considers that now "methodology of the work has taken precedence over the construction of the work" (W 101). Construction is the principle of *Potemkin*, while this innovation in methodology he likens to *zaum*, the transrational or metalogical idiom developed by Futurist poets like Alexei Kruchenykh and Velimir Khlebnikov. A potential universal language "of pure concepts clearly expressed by speech sounds" was the poetic rationale for Khlebnikov's experiments in *zaum*.[22] Rather than a construction of affective meaning, *October*'s intellectual montage is a methodology of defamiliarization and reassociation intended to demonstrate a logic above the seeming transparency of reified social forms.

The general release of *October* came at the time of the Party Conference on Cinema (March 15–21, 1928). A principal resolution to issue from the conference was the stipulation that films be made in forms "intelligible to the millions." This slogan became a keynote in the cultural revolution that was beginning to unfold. *October* provoked much debate in the cultural journals over its intelligibility and historical facticity. In a forum conducted by *Novyi Lef*, Viktor Pertsov concluded: "*October* as a whole is a physiologically intolerable object. The ceaseless movement of the crowds, the masses, gives rise to a counterrevolutionary dream of the tranquility of interior shots, the sweet bliss of love scenes, the cosiness of individual experiences." Osip Brik, an editor of the journal, criticized the film for distortions that produce "the most commonplace historical lie."[23] In other publications, Esther Shub charged that the film's very staging of historical fact distorts history, and Adrian Piotrovsky faulted it for crucial historical omissions such as an account of World War I.

Mayakovsky joined Brik, Shub, and Piotrovsky in condemning the impersonation of Lenin in *October* by a worker named Vasili Nikandrov, whom Eisenstein typecast for the role. Mayakovsky considered the impersonation "not like Lenin but like all the statues of him," and Piotrovsky judged it to be a "*lubok*-style disguise."[24] Such critiques ignore the reflexive structure of *October*, which has no intention to actualize the person of Lenin in its representation of events. A mass spectacle, the film renders history as the outcome of forces beyond personality. The film presents Lenin as an image born of the revolutionary tide that destroys the icons of previous power. This iconoclasm reaches floodtide with the human mass that seizes the Winter Palace and disperses the properties of tsardom. In his miscomprehension of *October*'s iconoclasm, Brik faulted its construction of metaphors for not establishing their metonymic extension in the Winter Palace setting.

October had its defenders as well, most notably Anatoli Lunacharsky and Viktor Shklovsky. An originator of the Formalist concept of the delay device, Shklovsky praised the film for its "historiographical" inventiveness, "free treatment of objects" and a structure wherein "time is cinematically replaced."[25] The criticism of *October* by Pertsov, Brik, Shub, and Piotrovsky comes from the cultural left and acknowledges the value of avant-garde experimentation. The rightist position of "cultural revolution" is stated in a *Sovietskii ekran* editorial published at the end of 1928: "This Formalist madness, the play on the 'film shot' and its combination, are almost the besetting sin of our cinema, or rather not of our Soviet cinema but a sin passed on to us from the hostile bourgeois camp."[26]

Along with the Formalists, Eisenstein accorded content a functional and formative role in the art work. Writing in 1929, he states:

"Content" [*soderzhanie*]—the act of containing [*sderzhivanie*]—is an *organizational* principle.

The principle of the organization of thinking is in actual fact the "content" of a work.

A principle that materializes in the sum total of socio-physiological stimulants and for which form serves as a means of *disclosure*. . . .

Herein lies the production-based inseparability of the sum total of content and form from *ideology*. (*W* 154) [The translator's inclusion of original terms has been retained.]

The linguist Louis Hjelmslev reaches a similar conclusion in determining that ideology expressed in language pertains extensively to the "form of content."[27]

In accounting for the ideological aspects of art, Eisenstein determined
that classical aesthetic categories would have to be redefined in accordance with materialist epistemology. He found that the Russian term for
aesthetic form, *obraz* (which means "image" as well), is "itself a cross
between the concepts of 'cut' [*obrez*] and 'disclosure' [*obnaruzhenie*]" (*W*
154). These etymological roots, Eisenstein reasons, summarize respectively the classical and Marxist concepts of form: "These two terms bril-
liantly characterize form from both its aspects: from the *individually static*
(*an und fur sich*) standpoint as 'cut,' the isolation of a particular phenomenon from its surroundings. . . . 'Disclosure' characterizes image from a
different, socially active standpoint: it 'discloses,' i.e. establishes the social link between a particular phenomenon and its surroundings" (*W* 154).
Eisenstein's politically activist definition additionally relates the social
form of content in art, its ideology, to "the act of 'cognition' as an act with
immediate effects" in the political sphere (*W* 155). In their 1928 work *The
Formal Method in Literary Scholarship*, Pavel Medvedev and Mikhail
Bakhtin propose a criticism that aligns formal and sociological approaches
with the ultimate aim of developing a Marxist science of ideologies. Their
interests are directed equally toward types of ideological material and
environment and forms of social communication.[28]

Similar concerns motivate the study *Marxism and the Philosophy of
Language*, published in 1929 and attributed to V. N. Volosinov (a member
of the Bakhtin circle). The critique of ideology remains undeveloped in
Marxism, this book asserts, because too often it has been confined to issues of consciousness alone or to explanation through a mechanistic, undialectical determinism. An ideological phenomenon is not only part of
material and social reality, it at the same time reflects and refracts reality
outside itself. By definition, then, *"Everything ideological possesses semiotic value"* and the critique of ideology necessarily involves problems
in the philosophy of language. Consciousness arises by virtue of the signs
it contains and exists through the exchange of signs in social interaction,
through a "chain of ideological creativity and understanding."[29]

Ideology is not limited in sense to false consciousness or dominant ideology. *Marxism and the Philosophy of Language* proposes another category—behavioral ideology—to account for ideology at an experiential
level. This realm embraces the inner and outer speech that provides
every instance of behavior and conscious signification with meaning. Ideology occurs at the level of *parole*, with the understanding that the whole
social milieu (and not narrowly the *langue*) organizes an individual's utterance. Activities within the sphere of behavioral ideology have great
power in periods of historical transformation: "Compared to an established ideology, they are a great deal more mobile and sensitive: they
convey changes in the socioeconomic basis more quickly and more viv-

idly. Here, precisely, is where those creative energies build up through whose agency partial or radical restructuring of ideological systems comes about."[30]

These works of criticism, like *October*, are part of a Soviet intellectual movement in the 1920s to compensate for the neglect by Marx, acknowledged by Engels, of the formal and formative factors of historical materialism—the development of institutions, ideology, and culture in the superstructure—in favor of objective factors in the economic base. Such lines of inquiry would not survive the cultural revolution that had just begun.

CHAPTER FIVE

Old and New:
History and Utopia

While based in historical subject matter, the narratives in Eisenstein's first three films are oriented toward the future event of the October Revolution, in part as a consequence of their purpose as commemorative works. With *Old and New* the trajectory toward a culmination of revolution originates after October, in the immediate present. Eisenstein explained the utopian spirit he meant to convey through this film in conversation with Jean Mitry in 1929:

What I want to do now is to exalt the pathos of everyday existence, of ordinary things, and to find within [the] ordinary the sense of collective enthusiasm. I want to polarize in one fact, be it an unexciting fact, all the passions, all the hopes in man's reach, all the things which give him reason to live. I want—I should like—to create images which radiate deep meaning, meaning beyond what they show on their face, but still grounded in the visible, as if the object or fact presented on the screen were the "sign" of a psychic movement, of an impulse, of an inspiration, the sign by which man recognizes himself in that which he has assigned to himself as a purpose.

Thus the image, which becomes a way to incarnate and fix an ideal or a paroxysm, can engender ecstasy as being the sublimation of that ideal.[1]

The montage structure in *Old and New* does indeed present an energeia of the everyday and a projected intentionality from within the man-made world.

At times Lenin wrote passionately on the revolutionary principle of hope and of a need to dream. In *What Is to Be Done?*, his major work prior to the 1905 Revolution, he urges "We should dream!" and quotes approvingly the nineteenth-century literary critic D. I. Pisarev, who believes the "rift between dreams and reality causes no harm if only the person dreaming believes seriously in his dream." Lenin adds: "Of this kind of dreaming there is unfortunately too little in our movement."[2] Bol-shevik utopianism gained wide currency during the 1920s through *The ABC of Communism*, which was prepared in 1919 by Nikolai Bukharin and Evgeni Preobrazhensky as "an elementary textbook of communist knowledge."

Mirroring the ambitious program adopted at the Eighth Party Con-gress held in March 1919, *The ABC of Communism* projects a new social and historical dimension: "Human culture will climb to heights never at-tained before. It will no longer be a mass culture, but will become a genuinely human culture. Concurrently with the disappearance of man's tyranny over man, the tyranny of nature over man will likewise vanish. Men and women will for the first time be able to lead a life worthy of thinking beings instead of a life worthy of beasts."[3] Manifest in this vision of the future is a restatement, in the subjective code, of Marxism's pur-pose of ending alienation in bringing human prehistory to a close. The first years of Soviet society, as historian Richard Stites has documented, animated many revolutionary dreams.[4]

Soviet Policies on the Countryside, 1923–30

At the time Eisenstein and Alexandrov wrote their original literary sce-nario *The General Line* in May and June of 1926, the Party maintained a gradualist approach to transforming the peasantry into a collective soci-ety, following the position Lenin had adopted. In a 1923 article "On Co-operation," Lenin advised: "It will take a whole historical epoch to get the entire population into the work of the co-operatives." He perceived a general reorientation in the Bolshevik movement: "We have to admit that there has been a radical modification in our whole outlook on socialism. The radical modification is this; formerly we placed, and had to place, the main emphasis on the political struggle, on revolution, on winning polit-ical power, etc. Now the emphasis is changing and shifting to peaceful, organizational, 'cultural' work."[5] With regard to Soviet peasants this ed-ucational, almost evolutionary, approach represents Lenin's effort at rec-onciliation after the devastating hardships experienced from 1918 to 1921 with the economic policies of War Communism, which included forced seizures of grain stocks, and the famine of 1921–22, when an estimated five million died.

The peasant commune in Russia originated within the feudal system of landholding, not as a voluntary form of mutual assistance. To facilitate exploitation of the serfs, the commune had become a compulsory institu-tion by the middle of the eighteenth century. The emancipation in 1861 recognized the *obshchina* or *mir*, the village commune and council, as the primary political institution of rural life, but peasants remained in

debt to estate owners and the government for land that often amounted
to less than what they had cultivated for their own needs as serfs. The
first phase of the Bolshevik Revolution in the countryside entailed the
seizure of lands from the gentry and their redistribution among peasants.
Redistribution left both the *mir* and the smallholding, family cultivation
system intact. The family land parcels were not consolidated but dispersed, often into strips scattered miles apart from one another.

In 1926, over 90 percent of the peasantry still lived and worked in a
mir. The alternatives sponsored by the Soviet government took two
forms: the *kolkhoz*, a collectively owned and operated farm making deliv-
eries to the state at fixed prices; and the *sovkhoz*, a state-operated agricultural enterprise paying wages to peasant workers. These new modes
had not significantly altered food production. In 1927, collective and state
farms produced only 4 percent of the total agricultural output. For a rural
population of over 120 million there were only 18,500 trained agronomists
in the Soviet Union.[6]

The Fourteenth Party Congress of December 1925 continued to accept
the institutions of small landholding and the rural market system as elements of the New Economic Policy. Collectivization was part of the Party
program, but as a distant goal. The Fifteenth Party Congress of December 1927 passed a hastily drafted platform on agrarian matters predicting
that backward customs would be modernized over the years through the
example of collective, mechanized methods. At this point, official policy
left change entirely to the choice of the individual peasant.

To secure grain for the cities, Stalin imposed emergency measures for
the first six months of 1928 and sent troops into the countryside to intimidate peasants and make confiscations. Opposition members within the
Party, led by Nikolai Bukharin, challenged the policy's legality and denounced it as a campaign of state terror. In the face of resistance from
peasants and lowered planting and harvesting, the government retreated
from these measures by July and restored market management of the
rural economy. In reaction to the instability in the state's policies, food
production declined in the period 1928–29.

In November 1929 Stalin announced a "Great Turn" in Party policy
concerning the agrarian question: a turn toward rapid, forced collectivization and against the kulaks. Party rules divided the peasantry into three
groups: poor households, which normally did not even own a work horse;
middle households, which owned one or two horses and means of production whose total value was less than 1,600 rubles; and *kulak* (literally,
"fist") households, owning means of production in excess of 1,600 rubles.
(For comparison, an industrial worker's annual income averaged between
600 and 700 rubles; the average price for a work horse was 140 to 150
rubles.) Kulaks were defined in Party terms as "rural capitalists." They

profited from their own fields and from leasing out implements and horses. In terms of the local market economy, kulaks often functioned as merchants and moneylenders. In 1927 the Party estimate on the number of kulaks in proportion to the total peasant population was 2 percent. By the time two years later that the Party targeted kulaks, the estimate had risen to 5 percent. Middle peasants comprised over 70 percent of the rural population.

Western historians agree that Stalin's collectivization program was impulsive and haphazard in conception and without precedent in Party theory. The Party apparatus was largely unprepared for this massive redirection in policy. Enforcement was nonetheless swift and unsparing. In the first two months of 1930, according to government reports, nearly eleven million households (a figure equivalent to half the rural population) were collectivized into the kolkhozes. The government's determination to eradicate suddenly the established infrastructure of food production in its own country represents a unique situation in world history. The state relented in its pace of transformation in March and millions of households left the kolkhozes later in 1930. The "Great Turn" policy remained intact, however, and the campaign was reintensified over the next four years. In the period 1932–33 as a result of the collectivization campaign there was a famine whose devastation exceeded that of the famine ten years earlier.

Where Lenin foresaw the emergence of socialist society in the countryside through force of the example of collective work, Stalin found in the countryside a last battlefront in the class war to win socialism in one country. Imposed collectivization and rapid industrialization were the primary objectives of the revolution from above that Stalin had undertaken. By the time of Stalin's fiftieth birthday in December 1929, the revision of Bolshevik history to promote a personality cult was also underway. The history of Marxist revolution was soon to be rapidly and radically rewritten. The utopian Bolshevik manifesto *The ABC of Communism* had been reprinted and translated many times in the decade, but with the Party's censure of Bukharin and Preobrazhensky in 1929 the book became unavailable in the Soviet Union. By that time the two Bolsheviks had split over the issues of Party leadership, economic control, and policy toward the countryside. Stalin exploited these divisive issues to conquer these two and other rivals within the Party.

Eisenstein's work on *The General Line*, originally undertaken in 1926, resumed in June 1928.[7] The script version for *The General Line* upon which production was based in 1926 and the one upon which it resumed in 1928 bear the same inscription, a quotation from Lenin: "There are conditions when the exemplary organization of rural labor, even at the very smallest scale, has a more important meaning to the State than the work of many branches in the central government." In February 1929 the completed feature received approval from the Sovkino administration. But Eisenstein and Alexandrov were obliged to make revisions after official criticism of the film, again initiated by Stalin, for inadequate representation of Soviet modernization in agriculture. The production crew went on location in April and May to the northern Caucasus and the sovkhoz named "Giant" near Rostov, on the Don River. Montage was completed by the time Eisenstein left for Western Europe and the United States in August. Though he took a print with him abroad, the film was not released in the Soviet Union until October 1929.

The film's lengthy production schedule falls within the period when the Party was involved in an ambiguous process of decision making, "constantly changing their directives because they had no definite system of objectives," in historian Moshe Lewin's words.[8] Eisenstein's film had been retitled *Old and New* when released so as not to be taken as representative of the Party's rural policy, which remained indecisive until its historic redirection by Stalin in November. In December 1929 Stalin went further and established "liquidation of the kulaks as a class" as state policy. The dynamics of revolution imagined in *Old and New*, in contrast, come not from a powerful state leader but from within peasant society, in an idealization of Lenin's evolutionary outlook. In his thinking about film form at the time of montage on *Old and New* Eisenstein was influenced by the erotic symbolism in Emile Zola's naturalist fiction, the experiments in language and genre in James Joyce's *Ulysses*, which he first read in early 1928, and his own ideas for a screen treatment of Marx's *Capital*. None of these influences would accord with new cultural policies.

The Utopian Projection

In the course of their revisions to *The General Line* scenario, Eisenstein and Alexandrov shifted dramatic focus exclusively to the present and future.[9] The original 1926 literary script opens with scenes of class warfare in the countryside years before the Bolshevik Revolution. As Steven Hill and Vance Kepley have pointed out, at this stage the scenario had strong links to *The Year 1905* project and to *Potemkin*. In the scenario's first part, the wave of revolution in 1905–6 reaches the peasantry across the Russian empire. This event is dramatized around Evdokiya Ukraintseva, who loses her husband in the strife. Named emblematically to represent the vital Ukraine region, this character is a "soldierette" waging the struggle for transformation of rural existence. Early scenes that summarize conditions in the countryside disclose the backward customs that lead to absurd property divisions, class divisions between poor peasant and kulak, and the migration of peasants to the city in search of work. The 1928 scenario opens with a more generic, less historically specific scene of peasant back-

wardness. The central character is now given the actual name—Marfa
Lapkina—of the poor, illiterate peasant from Konstantinovka Eisenstein
had cast in the role. Marfa returned to her home province during delays
in the film's production and continued to live there after its completion.

From the point where the peasant woman joins the village cooperative,
most of the major events drafted in the 1926 and 1928 scenarios remain
in the film. But the tone of revolutionary optimism is more thorough in
the released film than in the earlier scenarios. In the scenario drafts the
misery of peasant life is embodied in the constant presence of flies that
swarm around animal and human alike. The contemporary rural scene is
set amidst mud and dampness in this manner in the 1926 draft: "Flies
intimidate everyone. Flies land on exposed portions of flesh. And both
people and beasts have to toss and turn, shake their heads and wave their
hands." In both drafts the peasant woman's ultimately erotic and utopian
dream begins as a nightmare in which her last cow appears before her,
dying. In the language of the 1928 scenario, Marfa first dreams: "The cow
showed its ribs, showed its skinny legs, its dry udder, the bones on its
croup, its sad eyes, tear-ridden, pasted up with shitty flies." Such suffering weighs like a nightmare of the peasant past on her. The Russian terms
mukh (fly) and *mukh'* (suffering) function as verbal-visual homonyms in
the scenario's imagery, which the film's visuals do not render in this specific fashion.

The peasant nightmare of decay and starvation is the pivot to a dream
vision of vitality and abundance that follows, much as the putrid meat is
the immediate spark for mutiny in *Potemkin*. Interestingly, the peasant
woman's vision is devised in the early scripts as a temptation scene: "In
the sky, in a pair of clouds, in the radiance of the sun's rays, like Mephi-
stopheles, a pedigree bull appeared." In sequences subsequent to the
dream, the 1926 and 1928 drafts detail laboratory experiments conducted
at a state agricultural station, which are left more generalized in the released feature. The first experiments scripted involve flies and controlled
hybridization, causing selective mutation. On this model, the improve-
ment of livestock and grain is projected to prodigious degrees: sheep with
additional milk glands to nurse their multiplied offspring, wheat fields as
tall and dense as forests. This transcendent advance is figuratively a negation (breeding experimentation that begins in the laboratory with flies)
of the negation (suffering). The initial nightmare dimension to the dream
is absent from *Old and New*, as is the explanatory and metaphoric sequence of fly breeding. Instead of the accent on the pathos of suffering in
The General Line drafts, the *Old and New* release develops a pathos of
ecstasy.

One member of the production crew on *Old and New* was Andrei Burov, a Constructivist designer hired to build models of the film's dairy

cooperative. The modern agricultural laboratory whose exterior is seen in the film is in fact a full-scale prototype prepared by Burov. This projection through models of an architecture of the future corresponds with Constructivist practices in the first years of Soviet society when, given the material and financial limitations, there was virtually no opportunity to realize new designs on a large scale. Artists like Vladimir Tatlin and architects like the Vesnin brothers freely explored modernist styles of form and function in their plans for public structures.

Writing in 1923 about such explorations, Boris Arvatov praised their vision of the future, even if now unrealized: "Taking root in the bosom of the historical process such a utopia becomes a material force, which organizes mankind. . . . If a 'materialized' utopia is at present only alliteratively similar to a 'realized' utopia, then one conclusion must follow: *help to realize the path indicated.* Or, finally: develop, continue further, reform, but do not turn aside. May this individual attempt, this romantic leap across the abyss turn into a collective, deliberate collaboration."[10] Eisenstein persists in Futurist, visionary romanticism in the late 1920s while architects like the Vesnins had returned to more conventional styles.

More recently, Herbert Marcuse and Ernst Bloch have argued that the utopian principle is fundamental to the historical materialism of Marxism. For Bloch utopianism and the principle of hope are a cultural impulse able to transform history: "a 'cultural surplus' is clearly effective: something that moves above and beyond the ideology of a particular age. Only this 'plus' persists through the ages, once the social basis and ideology of an epoch have decayed; and remains as the substrate that will bear fruit and be a heritage for other times. This substrate is essentially utopian, and the only notion that accords with it is the utopian-concrete concept."[11] In *Old and New* visual luxury and an excess in signification produce a similar cultural surplus.

As a narrative, *Old and New* tells a simple, exemplary story. Though divided into six episodes in the final shooting script, the film action in release print is not separated into formal or titled acts. The first episode, set in spring, introduces peasant life and the film's nonactor heroine, who is identified in titles by her actual name, Marfa Lapkina. The second episode introduces a state agricultural officer, who addresses a village meeting to encourage peasants to form a collective. Marfa is the first to answer his appeal and she is joined by a few others, while the majority remains wary. During a drought, local priests and villagers join in a religious procession through the parched fields. Their prayers fail to bring rain. In the meeting room of the new kolkhoz a cream separator is tested before an audience of peasants.

In episode three Marfa finds a group from the collective dividing the

common funds among themselves and she tries to stop them. The agronomist intervenes and persuades them to return the funds, which are being saved for the purchase of a bull. That night Marfa falls asleep over the
cashbox and dreams of nature's vast fertility. Later she travels to the district's sovkhoz to buy the bull. Upon her return, a wedding ceremony is
conducted for the bull Fomka and his mate. Episode four depicts the grain
harvest. Peasants with scythes compete among themselves but stop in
amazement when a mowing machine is set to work. Marfa travels to a
tractor factory in an effort to expedite an order for machinery. In episode
five, peasants poison the bull during her absence. Marfa returns to report
that the tractor will be delivered and she learns of Fomka's death. The
tractor makes an entrance in episode six and after a minor breakdown it
begins to cultivate the land. The finale introduces a transformed Marfa,
who now drives a tractor for the collective.

Eisenstein enumerated a full spectrum of topics relevant to the subject
matter of his film: "komsomols in the countryside, cultural enlightenment, movement of rural correspondents, cooperation, the new family,
atheism, the women's movement, differentiation of the peasantry, deku-
lakization."[12] His treatment of themes is predominantly binary, through
oppositions such as old/new, male/female, animal/human, human/ma-
chine, individual/peasant society, kulak/poor peasant, bureaucrat/worker,
static/dynamic, and religious faith/communist belief. Marfa Lapkina, like
the lad asleep on the imperial throne in *October,* represents the first
generation of liberated Russians. As protagonist and epicenter of the thematic oppositions, her destiny is to participate in transforming the old
social order. At the conclusion she stands on the threshold of a heroic new
world, but the heroism of her action, like that of Vakulinchuk, is essentially collective.

Marfa is introduced into the plot by a series of progressively closer
shots and then, after a tight close-up, by progressively longer ones and
the title "One among Millions." When her cow collapses in exhaustion
after futilely trying to draw a plow, she is shown in medium shot shaking
her fists in frustration. This portrait is match cut with a medium shot of
Marfa making a similar gesture but in a different locale. The new setting
is revealed to be a village meeting, at which she speaks in favor of the
proposal for a peasant cooperative. The surprise montage transition marks
a conversion of personal dissatisfaction into agitation for social aims. Marfa
is exemplary in her potential for a new personality, which is latent in the
masses as a whole.

To depict the economic situation developed over centuries by Russian
property customs, Eisenstein makes thematic use of wipe cuts. Titles
state "When brothers separate / They divide the farm / In half" after the
opening dramatic action shows a peasant family, crammed into a low,

smoke-filled hut, rising stiffly and reluctantly from their sleep. The meaning of the statement is rendered in long and then successively closer shots
as two brothers are shown sawing a rural dwelling in half until finally the
montage isolates in close-up the blade cutting through timbers. At this
distance, camera point-of-view is reversed several times as a figure for
divisiveness and disruption. Following the horizontal motion of the
blade—thus establishing a causal relationship between the two montage
units—wipe cuts reveal first open fields and then, as the house is dismantled, the gradual partitioning of the land by fences in a succession of cuts.
Trick film devices are used reflexively here to render property division as
an "unnatural" process. There is a closing vista of patchwork small plots
across the countryside.

Possessing only a cow, Marfa visits a kulak to ask the rental of a horse
for her spring plowing. Differentiation between kulak and poor peasant is
presented through caricature and compositional contrast. As she arrives
at the kulak's property, the camera emphasizes a sturdy, well-stocked
barn. In several shots the foreground is dominated by livestock as Marfa
is seen in diminutive scale in the background. Both the barn and the
house are decorated with intricate, whitewashed fretwork around their
eaves and windows. The kulak's wife wears an elaborate haircomb that
appears to repeat this ornamental pattern. The kulak couple are well fed
to a point of obesity, with their plump faces rounding into double chins.
At the moment Marfa requests a loan, the kulak's oversized head, with its
delicate curlicue of an ear, looms in the foreground and obliterates her
from view. The gigantism and disproportion here are obvious expressions
of differences in social scale. The uses made of depth of field are entirely
separate from the dramatic continuity between foreground and background a realist like Bazin favors. Instead, the shot's photographic depth
in *Old and New* establishes planar and iconic conflicts for an effect of
montage within the shot.

To visualize the mechanization of agriculture, Eisenstein released the
camera from its customarily stationary position in his filmmaking. Early
in the film the camera sluggishly reverse tracks, in a high-angle setup,
before a weak cow Marfa has yoked for the plowing. This sequence is
crosscut with another reverse tracking shot, taken from the same angle,
of two harnessed peasants dragging their own plow. The overview provided by the high-angle perspective and the montage association convey
the beastly, ineffective drudgery of unmechanized labor. Late in the
story, the camera rides on a wide, tractor-drawn tiller. At ground level, it
films the machine's effortless cultivation of the earth.

Resistance to mechanization and collectivization derived in part from
the inertia of age-old habits, superstitions, and beliefs. The episode of the
religious procession during a drought is arranged as a critique of peasant

ideology. Its montage is organized through a key camera movement, a vertical panning action connecting views of the sky with images of the earth. In the opening shot, the camera tilts down from a bell tower cross silhouetted against a cloudless sky to the tower base, where billows of dust are raised by the procession leaving the church. The vertical camera tilt is resumed in following the actions of faithful peasants, who throw up their arms to heaven and then hurl themselves to the arid earth in prayer. The camera then moves horizontally along with the procession until it stops in anticipation as the sky darkens. A series of close-up portraits is mounted, isolating peasants as they press their faces to the ground in hope and humility, and the montage tempo quickens as gusts of wind blow across the parched soil. To suggest the desperation and futility of their efforts, Eisenstein inserts associations in close-up that link the wax dripping from a priest's candles, starving sheep who foam at the mouth, and peasants who sweat profusely in their fervor.

The duration of shots increases, slowing the tempo, as it becomes evident that prayer has failed. A priest looks quizzically at an ornate barometer, which is indistinguishable from the procession's church treasures. When the sky brightens, the camera—now objectively stationary—is positioned at a greater distance from the procession. In a calculated allusion to the opening low-angle view of the bell tower, a priest is shown holding his cross up to heaven in a final plea. Other priests sheepishly raise their eyes heavenward. The peasants slowly rise from the ground and dust themselves off. The sequence concludes with close-ups of their faces registering failure and disillusionment.

These close-ups are used to make a subtle transition from the religious procession to the cream separator demonstration. The individual portraits of peasants continue, but a dark background indicates that the scene has shifted from an outdoor setting to an indoor one. The peasants' facial expressions modulate from disbelief to curiosity. Eisenstein has commented that the two sequences interrelate as variations on a theme of "doubt and ecstasy" (*FF* 77). The tonal reversal from exterior to interior lighting is paralleled by a contrast between the harsh glare reflected by gold icons and the rich luster of the utilitarian separator. The separator is first presented out of focus to accent its luster and to lend it an aura. The icons and the machine both become tests of peasant convictions. In writing about the sequence Eisenstein poses the machine as an antithesis to the icon that retains an equivalent affect: "It is not the Holy Grail that inspires both doubt and ecstasy—but a cream-separator" (*FF* 77).

The separator demonstration ultimately confirms belief in the power of mechanization. At its culmination, peasant faces are illuminated by the cream that has splattered them. The spirit of the moment reverses the termination of the procession, when their faces are darkened by shadows

and their expressions are drawn in doubt and frustration. The phallic imagery of cream jetting from the machine's spouts counterpoints previous
imagery of dust rising from the sterile earth. The process of demystification Eisenstein has used here is distinct from *October*'s gods sequence,
where there is a purely discursive manipulation of objects as empty signifiers. The procession and demonstration maintain an identical, immediate narrative context in order to dramatize a reflex in peasant consciousness to objects within the film's social sphere. Furthermore, utility is
demonstrated as a basis for new belief.

Eisenstein explained this reflex to Mitry in the following terms: "Imag-
ine what a piece of bread can mean to a hungry man. All his wishes, all
his needs, all his hopes become concrete around this one material thing.
That's what the cream separator meant for Russian peasants just after the
Revolution. It is not its existence as an object which is important, it is
what it represents, what it means, what it implies: a moment in peasant
consciousness, the total overthrow of the conditions of existence, the
transformation of the ancestral way of life."[13] This idea of the social form
of value is fundamental to principles Marx formulates at the outset of
Capital: "It is value . . . that converts every product into a social hiero-
glyphic," and the attachment of value to an object "is just as much a social
product as language."[14] In the procession and demonstration sequences
the association between objects and faces in reaction shot dramatizes a
popular determination of value.

A functional difference between exchange value and use value is elaborated in the next sequence. After recovering the savings peasants had
begun to divide among themselves, Marfa counts out the money and returns it to the cashbox. With a smile of great satisfaction, she puts her
arm across the box's top and rests her head there. She sleeps to dream of
a majestic bull the kolkhoz will purchase.[15] The shift in mode of representation conveys a transformation from quantity (a monetary sum) to quality
(a mythically virile bull). The shift is also consistent with the finding in
Capital that the exchange value of an object has no systematic, quantitative ratio to its use value. Value is not a technical relation but a social
relation.

With the separator's successful operation, the peasants' collective joy
is registered in montage that combines milk and water imagery. This imagery is expanded during Marfa's dream of the bull, a vision that reaches
orgasmic intensity. In it, abstract compositions of swirling, flowing milk
and water are followed by naturalistic scenes of livestock nursing their
offspring and glimpses of a mechanized milking operation. Presumably
Marfa's dream coincides with a change in circumstances since the predicament of drought ceases to be a narrative conflict at this point. Instead,

the story leaps forward to Marfa's visit to the district sovkhoz for the purchase of a young bull.

The transition to this new locale occurs within the imagery that illustrates Marfa's dream. The film's discrepancies and ellipses in the unities of space, time, and narrative action are not motivated by discursive purposes as in *October*, but by a projective momentum toward resolution of antagonisms within peasant society and between the human and the natural. Marfa's tour of the sovkhoz's modern facilities causes her to exclaim, "Is it—can it be—a dream?" This is conventionally the first question of a visitor to any utopia. Both she and the film spectator see a "good place" that is as yet "nowhere," since the model collective is in reality a mock-up constructed for *Old and New*.

Ernst Bloch, the philosopher most concerned to develop utopian components in Marxist thought, defines humanity as being true to its essence through active hope, which gives present behavior future purpose. Bloch's definition reasserts the premises on species being in the *1844 Manuscripts*. Human existence is a trajectory and its one constant is change. As they pursue free, conscious life activity, humans project a future and strive to attain it. In the context of social alienation and exploitation, the potential life activity is a disruptive force. Hope is an "anticipatory illumination" that acts like an explosive upon social and ideological orthodoxy. Hope materializes in history as force: "There is nothing soft about the conscious, known hope; rather, it has a strong will: this is the way it should be; this is the way it has to be. The inclination to wish and to want burst forth with zest, the intensity of excess, of surpassing."[16]

Mundane events like the breeding of cows are rendered in *Old and New* with a similar surplus of meaning. The sequence opens with a procession of the village girls holding garlands, as though a peasant marriage is being held. The bull and a cow are ceremonially introduced and the montage tempo quickens to suggest the bull's sexual arousal. After the bull rushes forward—in a movement accelerated by the editing—images of explosions are presented. For the premiere, Eisenstein inserted brief clips containing only splashes and strokes of color on film stock.

The mechanization introduced by the collective is also treated with an eroticized surplus of imagery. In contrast to opening scenes where old, handheld plows shallowly scratch the land's surface, later images overflow with thick swathes of soil turned by the cultivator upon which a camera is anchored. At the close, a squad of tractors till the land in a concentric design evocative of previous compositions of swirling milk and water. The film's non-narrative imagery of liquids and soil is worked into abstract or geometric patterns and offered as modernized agrarian symbols of fertility.

The procreative power of the machine is comically indicated in the scene where the tractor driver, attempting to repair a stalled motor, positions himself on the vehicle in a variety of suggestive positions. Marfa, embarrassed and amused, offers her petticoat for oil rags. Marfa's posture—toes turned in, her skirt lifted slightly and face turned to the side—makes the scene appear like a moment of adolescent sexual exploration.

The Soviet director in whose films erotic imagery and folk motifs are most prominent is Alexander Dovzhenko, whose origins and imagination are tied to the Ukrainian land. In *Earth* (1930), his film on collectivization and kulak resistance, machines are not naturalized or given utopian meaning as in *Old and New*. When the collective's new tractor breaks down in *Earth*, peasants refill the radiator with urine. In its attention to natural cycles, life cycles, and to relationships of family and class, *Earth*'s imagery connects three principal events: a grandfather's death, his grandson's murder, and the birth of a child to that young man's mother. The father, who had once opposed any change in village life, refuses a church service for his son and requests a funeral conducted by the local Soviet youth brigade. Dovzhenko intercuts with the burial procession scenes of the mother in labor and of the young man's fiancée tearing at her own clothes in grief. In the closing shots to *Earth*, rain washes fields and orchards and their heavy fruit falls to earth. Dovzhenko's affirmation of life is based in scenes of pristine nature, irrespective of the machine or the collective. Renewal remains at a level of archaic archetype, with the promise of transcendence brought by spring.[17]

Eisenstein, on the other hand, employs agrarian archetypes in order to realign nature with a new, mechanized culture. In one correlation, the sound and movements of the grasshopper are multiplied in the noise and mechanisms of a wheat harvester. In other cases the film uses such correlations for montage contrasts in a critique of the reification of social issues into natural conditions. One example is the montage unit introduced with the title "Peasant Spring" and containing variations on three shots: 1) rain clouds moving overhead; 2) an immensely pregnant woman shown in profile against a barren tree; and 3) a starving cow in close-up. This montage unit is also a deliberate experiment through cinema in the laconism of the haiku form.

Old and New concludes on a village road, where a tractor has stopped beside a haycart in which a young couple relaxes. The tractor driver is dressed in a leather outfit with goggles and is at first unrecognizable. A smile then identifies the driver as Marfa, whose story is reprised through a series of close-ups taken from earlier scenes. The close-ups mark the stages of her transformation from the typical peasant victimized by natural and social conditions. Now she is a liberated social being, master over nature, free from determinism by gender. A romantic element is introduced when the young man leaves his girlfriend, who wears peasant dress, to embrace Marfa.

The reprise conventionally functions in the Hollywood story film to validate the actor's or actress's image as a screen star. In *Old and New* it is a device for epitomizing social processes in terms of individual character. Though she is the heroine, Marfa is treated through narrative and visuals as an equivalent for her class and is always placed in typical rather than individualized circumstances. Marfa's story does not develop along the lines of psychological conflict or romantic complication. Eisenstein substitutes consciousness for psychology and an eroticized environment for emotional intrigue. In farcical transpositions from the attractions of romantic and heroic cinema, Marfa's first beaux are the phallic cream separator and the gigantic bull of her dreams.

Intellectual Cinema

With its method of characterization in mind, Eisenstein wrote of *Old and New*: "The construction of this film as a whole . . . adheres to a basic constructive process. Namely: a conflict between *story* and its *traditional form*" (FF 77). Through ideographic story-telling Marfa is treated as a configuration for the interaction of social forces. As a consequence of his interests in *Capital* as a screen project in this period, Eisenstein is most explicitly Marxist in explaining his form of filmmaking: "the collision of two factors gives rise to an idea. . . . So, montage is conflict. Conflict lies at the basis of every art. (A unique 'figurative' transformation of the dialectic.) The shot is then a montage cell. Consequently we must also examine it from the point of view of *conflict*. Conflict within the shot is: potential montage" (W 144–45). A dialectical dynamic organizes the film material from a cellular level of foreground/background oppositions, for example, within the shot. At a larger structural level, the same dynamic organizes thematic oppositions within story materials and the opposition of this specific story form to conventions of the sentimental drama about women's problems.

Marfa's initial conflict is with the peasant conservatism she has inherited. She triumphs over backward, individualist consciousness when she first volunteers for the collective. Her concluding advent as a tractor driver telescopes a process that in previous stages of social development had taken epochs: a transformation of consciousness through material change in the means of production. An almost abstract dynamism is reached in the film's combination of images of machines and industrial processes with images of the four primary natural elements, some of which show earth and liquid transfigured by these processes. This dynamism reiterates the themes of revolutionary transformation.

Another story convention *Old and New* contradicts is socialist realism, which was emerging in the late 1920s as a dominant narrative mode and would be mandated within a few years as the official Soviet style. The cultural campaign for art that presents a prototype socialist "living man" at its center originated in the RAPP organization (Russian Association of Proletarian Writers) in 1927. At a conference held in September 1929, a RAPP resolution condemned the "tendency to regard content purely as raw material for formal experiments" as "hostile to Soviet cinema."[18] In "Perspectives," an essay published in March 1929, Eisenstein rejected the trend toward the RAPP model as a deviation of culture backward, to outmoded traditions: "Filling the screen with 'living man' would mean precisely . . . 'unsuitable progress' " (W 159). He saw in the "living man" prescription a priority for content that is adverse to his own reflexive uses of form: "the dynamic, active and effective *act* of 'content' as 'containing within oneself' has been replaced by an amorphous, static and passive understanding of content as *contents*" (W 153).

From the cultural program of socialist realism followed reductive and prescriptive political wish fulfillment in Soviet art for the next three decades. Unconditional idealization of a "new Soviet man" evaded any contestation of the status quo, which is a necessary function for the authentic utopian principle, even within revolutionary culture. In 1929 Eisenstein took an adamant stand against this advancing cultural line: "Cinema can— and consequently must—convey on the screen in tangible sensual form the pure, dialectical essence of our ideological debates. Without recourse to intermediaries like plot, story or living man" (W 159). Eisenstein also rejects interior characterization and psychologism in favor of a social, ideographic treatment of the protagonist. *Old and New*'s visual structure is formally, not psychologically, centered on Marfa and its dynamics are contrastive, transformative, and projective.

Eisenstein remained outspoken in his objections to the consolidation of realism in Soviet culture during 1929. He disparaged the "regular 'ranking table' of officially designated harmony" that "returns periodically and unfailingly in periods when absolutism is in the ascendancy." He further asserted, to continue a quotation cited earlier: "Positivist realism is by no means the correct form of perception. It is simply a function of a particular form of social structure, following on from an autocratic state that has propagated a state uniformity of thought" (W 142). With Stalin's growing acquisition of personal power, the implications of this last statement are radical and far reaching, but they are not put fully into imaginative form until *Ivan the Terrible*.

In *Old and New*, political satire and visual dynamism establish a critical distance from the ideology of the contemporary Soviet state. Through caricature, the iconography of Lenin, and persistent emphasis on revolution from below rather than from above, the film sets the spirit of the Bolshevik Revolution against political circumstances that prevail a decade later. Like priests and kulaks, bureaucrats are made into grotesques through the severe closeness and angularity of the camera setups. The tractor requisition sequence opens with an acute low-angle shot of an office interior. A manager dictates to a secretary as a typewriter cylinder juts across the frame into the foreground. In this perspective, the office machine is monstrously enlarged and appears aggressive. The deformation is a critical commentary on bureaucrats' delusions of grandeur and their petty interference in matters. An administrator officiously appends documents with stamps, seals, and his own baroque signature, which is as intricate as the fretwork that decorates the kulak's house.

Statuettes of Lenin are displayed on office desks in the tractor factory. By the late 1920s portraits, statues, and busts of Lenin were displayed throughout the Soviet Union. A foreign visitor reports that even in peasant huts he commonly found an inexpensive print of Lenin's picture, often placed next to a religious icon. While Lenin strongly resisted public adulation in his last years, with his death a cult rose around him. Stalin was instrumental in initiating the Lenin cult and had positioned himself by 1929 as the "best Leninist" among Bolsheviks.[19] Concerned only to turn out more paperwork and red tape, clerks and managers in *Old and New* wipe their fountain pens on the Lenin statuettes. In this environment, Lenin has become a worthless souvenir of a revolution now reified and lost in state bureaucracy. The ironic spirit of this scene is similar to the 1922 Mayakovsky poem "Lost in Conference," one of the few new Soviet literary works to gain official praise from Lenin. The poem satirizes bureaucracy for its insistence on routine to the exclusion of human concerns, its ritualized procedures and jargon, and its unproductive methods. In praising Mayakovsky for the piece, Lenin said, "I do not know whether it is good poetry, but I promise you he is absolutely right from a political point of view."[20]

The presence in *Old and New* of two characters who bear a remote resemblance to Lenin—the state agronomist and a factory manager—is an answer to the criticism of *October* over the impersonation of Lenin by Nikandrov. With these two characters the resemblance is put to divergent uses. The agronomist's features suggest a Lenin in his thirties or forties, that is, in the period of revolutionary ascent. The factory manager, when he is first glimpsed, suggests a caricature of Lenin in old age, had he lived on. With the collective's requisition order for a tractor stalled in the labyrinthine bureaucracy, Marfa and a political worker storm the offices of the factory manager. Seen initially with head bent down, as he idles over a newspaper, the manager bears a likeness to Lenin that causes Marfa and the worker to gape. When the manager finally looks up, the illusion is broken. With a monumental bust of Lenin prominent in the background, the worker invokes the example of "The Leader" and demands the requisition be expedited. The manager is thus commanded to follow the revolutionary spirit that has lent Lenin to canonization in the first place. Otherwise, Lenin remains a mere appearance, a plaster icon, in Soviet society. As an alternative to these trends of effacement and petrifaction of the revolutionary heritage, Eisenstein projects in *Old and New* a permanent revolution, a continuously dynamic impetus in nature, consciousness, and society and in their productive interaction.

Eisenstein wrote at this time about development of a new montage principle based on the "visual overtone." Prior to *October*, his montage had relied primarily on *"dominants,* i.e. the combination of shots according to their predominant (principal) sign. Montage by tempo. Montage by the principal direction within the frame. Montage by length (duration) of sequences, etc. Montage by foreground" (*W* 181). The earlier principle accords fully with a Formalist premise advanced by Yuri Tynyanov, who asserts that literary structure "involves the foregrounding of a group of elements—the *dominant"* and that "a work enters into literature and takes on its own literary function through this *dominant."*[21] Montage of attractions and the structure of pathos share this Formalist attribute in being oriented toward producing a dominant affect, which is often done through the image's sensationalism and a basic montage tempo.

Overtonal montage is based in the organization of compositional variations within the shot: "In combination with a calculation of the secondary resonances of the actual filmed material this produces, by analogy with music, the visual *overtonal* complex of the shot" (*W* 183). Having issued with Pudovkin and Alexandrov in August 1928 a statement on the potential of contrapuntal sound in cinema, Eisenstein now makes explicit reference to the overtonal technique in modern composers like Debussy and Scriabin in selecting a term to designate his new method.

Eisenstein considered *Old and New* his first film to exploit fully visual overtones. Vladimir Nilsen, assistant cameraman on *October* and this film, indicates that Eisenstein and Tisse began to experiment freely with artificial lighting only after they had mastered the geometry of shot composition, which is primarily a matter of line and dimension.[22] Fortuitous elements in lighting and in the panchromatic range of black and white cinematography had provided visual overtone to *Potemkin's* images of a mist-shrouded harbor, but now more extensive control over light value and tonal density was gained. The result is greater potential for montage within the shot. Instead of allowing the foreground to dominate shot composition, Eisenstein increasingly juxtaposed it with other compositional elements.

Overtonal association among shots, as in the gods sequence, entails a "conflict-juxtaposition of accompanying intellectual affects" that can produce an "intellectual overtone" (*FF* 82). One additional resource explored in *Old and New* is the variation in meaning of the same camera perspective in different social contexts. Low-angle composition is used in the procession sequence for images of priests imploring God and in the outdoor meeting for images of the agronomist introducing the idea of collectivization. Both perspectives represent the peasants' point of view, but the priest is seen from a kneeling position while the agronomist is seen from a standing one. When peasants are seen in reverse shot, the camera is placed in an unnaturalistically high and removed position in the first case and in an eye-level position from the speakers' platform in the second. The implications of this variation are clear: the procession is an otherworldly appeal that belittles peasants while the meeting is a communication among equals. The slightly elevated angle of the platform is indicative of political guidance and advancement. Marfa steps from the peasant masses up to the platform to take a vanguard position.

Through visual overtones, intellectual cinema extends the correlation of shots to attain counterpoint between entire sequences, as already examined in the relation of the religious procession to the cream separator demonstration. At the start of the subsequent dream sequence, as Marfa falls asleep over the cashbox, the cream separator is prominently featured in the background. Its presence links Marfa's dream with the demonstration and evokes associations of productivity and social ecstasy. Marfa dreams *in* its context and her dream thoughts are rendered not as private or repressed but as collective and liberating. The montage ellipsis from the dream into Marfa's visit to the model collective implies that utopian drives are both personal and social and that they are a force in transforming reality.

Through earlier study of the Japanese language and his recent research on the subject, Eisenstein identified the oriental ideogram as a linguistic counterpart to intellectual cinema. In the 1929 essay "Beyond the Shot" he postulates that hieroglyphs—the rudiments of the ideogram—like shots, the units of montage—are a means of constructing concepts. The combination of two simple hieroglyphs, he writes,

> is regarded not as their sum total but as their product, i.e. as a value of another dimension, another degree: each taken separately corresponds to an object but their combination corresponds to a *concept*. The combination of two "representable" objects achieves the representation of something that cannot be graphically represented. . . .
> Yes. It is precisely what we do in cinema, juxtaposing representational shots that have, as far as possible, the same meaning, that

are neutral in terms of their meaning, in meaningful contexts and series. (W 139)

The ideographic method of montage—discovered with the police station/ slaughterhouse correlations in *Strike* and developed in *October* and *Old and New* to include conceptual contexts within the shot—thus finds confirmation in a *langage*.

While scholars have challenged the reliability of Eisenstein's account of written Japanese and Chinese, it should be recalled that he confines his examples to ancient hieroglyphs and their simplest surviving forms. In these, he finds a direct correspondence between representation and signification that is not readily apparent in later, complex forms. This analysis accords with Western studies on oriental language available at the time. To the list of scholars cited in his essay—Jean-Pierre Abel Rémusat, Frederick Victor Dickins, and Yone Noguchi—can be added Ernest Fenollosa, the American orientalist, poet, and curator of Japanese art. In "The Chinese Written Character as a Medium for Poetry," edited by Ezra Pound and first published in 1920, Fenollosa considers the character to reflect metaphor, which he defines as "the use of material images to suggest immaterial relations." He stresses that "relations are more real and more important than the things which they relate." The structure of metaphor visible in some Chinese characters is a "bridge whereby to cross from the minor truth of the seen to the major truth of the unseen."[23]

Like Fenollosa, Eisenstein attributes to ideographic languages a process of intellection based in visual perception. For his Soviet contemporaries Pudovkin and El Lissitzky, the graphic artist and designer, the hieroglyph seemed an ideal model for a purely visual and potentially international language. From the literalization of metaphor in montage of attractions, Eisenstein advanced to a purpose wherein "thinking in images is displaced at a certain stage and replaced by conceptual thought" (W 140).

The eighteenth-century printmaker Sharaku and Kabuki theater are for Eisenstein two persuasive cases of ideational art. Sharaku, whom he considers "the Japanese Daumier," created a woodcut series of costumed actors' portraits, which entail substitutions of equivalents for likenesses. Eisenstein quotes art critic Julius Kurth to the effect that "general compositional juxtaposition is subjugated to a purely semantic purpose" in these character portraits (W 141, 142). In August 1928 a Tokyo troupe of Kabuki actors performed in Moscow, where Eisenstein attended performances. Soon after, he wrote enthusiastically on the unexpected juncture between Kabuki and intellectual montage. Kabuki's conventionalism in stage environment, costume, speech, gesture, sound effects, and music induce in the spectator the "direct *perception*" of ideas. Furthermore, its "*perfect* equivalent of visual and sound" images offers a guide to the future of sound film (*W* 116, 119).

Eisenstein also notes analogies between acting practices in Kabuki and the presentation of actors through montage. Japanese performers denoted alterations in a character's emotional state by means of changes in costume and makeup onstage under concealment of the *kurogo*, the black-clothed stage assistants. He finds this to be a "decomposed" method of acting, without transitions, and considers it related to the laconism of imagist forms in Japanese poetry—the tanka and haiku (*W* 149). It completely violates the continuous, individually psychological method of naturalist traditions in Europe.

Eisenstein favors the nonnaturalistic approach because it replaces "a single changing face by a whole gamut of faces of varying dispositions" (*W* 148). Accordingly, in *Old and New* he eliminated any gradation between the polar contrasts in a single character's facial expression. As an example, he cites the cream separator demonstration: "Here the psychological process of the play of motives—faith and doubt—resolves into the two extreme states of joy (certainty) and gloom (disillusionment). In addition, this is heavily underlined by light (which by no means conforms to real life)" (*W* 148–49). The effect of such montage abridgements is to turn the face shown in close-up into a kind of mask whose expression is an objective depiction, a denotation, of an emotional state. The reprise, in close-up portraits, of Marfa's experience of modernization accents this quality.

The nature of this stylization in screen performance is similar to what Brecht identified as distantiation or the "alienation-effect" in Chinese stage acting. But what Brecht describes as a function of the actor is in Eisenstein's cinema primarily a result of direction and montage. Camera setups and compositional tone impart objectification and conceptual perspective to acting performances that may well entail naturalism in their execution on the movie set. This presentational and ideational approach has affinities with the linguist Volosinov's category of behavioral ideology, in which the structure of an individual utterance is determined by the immediate interpersonal situation and the broader social milieu. Marfa is not only a representative of her class; the emotions she displays are class determined. In opening scenes Marfa's exhaustion and submission are expressive of the poor peasant's conditions, which in turn impoverish consciousness. With success of the cream separator, the ecstasy she experiences is social behavior conveying a change in class perspective. Her impatience and anger in the factory offices reflect a consolidation in class consciousness and militancy.

Eisenstein summarizes in 1929 his discoveries in montage made over five years of filmmaking practice. As a rationale within his own current artistic purposes, he cites Lenin's synopsis of dialectics: "an endless process of deepening human perception of things, appearances, processes, and so on, from appearance to essence . . . , from co-existence to causality and from one form of connection and interdependence to another, deeper, more general" (*FF* 81). Eisenstein offers intellectual cinema as an instrument of perception designed to develop a dynamic comprehension of reality whether it be practical or abstract, immediate or historical. He specifies the dialectical function of montage in "the conflict between normal conceptions and particular representations as a dynamic—a dynamization of the inertia of perception" (*W* 162). A full range of compositional conflicts is organized to produce ideographic perception. Within the shot these include conflicts in axial direction, scale, volume, mass, light intensity, and depth of field. Within the sequence they include conflicts in camera angle, camera distance, directionality, tonality of lighting, dramatic content, and the conflict "between an event and its temporal nature," as in overlapped action (*W* 145).

Within the film as a whole, Eisenstein now favored "a polygamy of approaches, styles and genres" (*W* 102). The result is less a structured form than a dynamic, intertextual process. One aspect of such heterogeneity in *Old and New* is the juxtaposition of a machine environment with an atmosphere of eroticism. Eisenstein acknowledged the Zola novel *La Bête Humaine* as the source for such a juxtaposition. A second approach is the composition of an abstract conclusion through the accumulation of physiological detail, much as in the fictive processes of James Joyce. Another heterogeneous approach is the treatment of documentary sources and social science reports as literary material for the scenario, as in the case of *The General Line* drafts. With *Old and New* Eisenstein had begun to explore the direct treatment of polemical issues and the "de-anecdotalization" of events in the course of a film that also makes use of narrative material and dramatized conflicts (*W* 96).

Eisenstein developed intellectual cinema in the course of exploring the ideological relationships between reality and film image. Intellectual cinema attempts to rectify the disjunction between historical reality (*October*) or a projected reality (*Old and New*) and the human processes of perceiving it. That disjunction is identified by Marx as the deficiency of materialist thought until his elaboration of a new, activist materialism: "The chief defect of all hitherto existing materialism—that of Feuerbach included—is that the thing, reality, sensuousness, is conceived only in the form of the object or of *contemplation*, but not as *human sensuous activity, practice*, not subjectively. . . . The question whether objective truth can be attributed to human thinking is not a question of theory but is a *practical* question. Man must prove the truth, that is, the reality and power, the this-sidedness of his thinking in practice."[24]

In clarifying the aims of intellectual cinema, Eisenstein seems to reiterate Marx's statement deliberately: "It must restore to science its sensuality. To the intellectual process its fire and passion. It must plunge the abstract process of thought into the cauldron of practical activity. Restore the splendor and wealth of gut-felt *forms* to the emasculated speculative *formula*" (W 158). The last two silent films, and the *Capital* project undertaken in the same period, endeavor to provide through montage structure visual and dynamic equivalents for the individual activity of intellectual perception and the collective, historical process of revolutionizing consciousness.

CHAPTER SIX

Dislocation:
Projects, 1929–32

Eisenstein and his two closest collaborators, Grigori Alexandrov and Eduard Tisse, left Moscow for Berlin in August 1929 en route to
the United States, where they intended to make their first sound feature.
During his European tour Eisenstein had no reason to believe that his
productivity as a filmmaker was to be interrupted, having released four
films in as many years. While in Paris in April 1930, he signed a contract
with Paramount Studios that provided for motion pictures to be made in
both Hollywood and Moscow. But American financiers and Soviet officials
were to prevent the completion of Eisenstein's film projects for the next
eight years.

In 1929 Eisenstein anticipated that an adaptation of Marx's *Capital*
would be the culmination of intellectual cinema and a dialectical approach
to film form. But in the period 1929–37 many events contributed to a
dislocation and disjunction in Eisenstein's career and to a reorientation in
the treatment of history in his cinema. Principal among these events are
his extensive travel in the capitalist West, his prolonged contact with the
historical and cultural diversity of Mexico, the emergence of sound technology, interference with his filmmaking activities through the dictates of
commerce in Hollywood and of ideology in Moscow, and the broad control over Soviet art under the policy of socialist realism.

With a sense of revolutionary immediacy and optimism, in *The Communist Manifesto* and *Capital* Marx brings history fully up to the present
and the modern forms of capital production and finance in order to establish the preconditions for social transformation. On the other hand, it is
with an ironic sense of the fate of modern revolutions to date and a sense
of society's potential for reversion that Marx approaches history in *Class
Struggles in France* (1850) and *The 18th Brumaire of Louis Bonaparte*
(1852). These two works analyze patterns of paradox that transect epochs
of history. *Class Struggles in France*, for example, measures "revolutionary advance" by "its immediate tragicomic achievements" and by its defeat at the hands of "a powerful, united counter-revolution."[1] In making
Ivan the Terrible, the only film he was to complete whose scope ap-

proaches that of the *Capital* project, Eisenstein turns to a comparable
tragicomic historiographic mode.

Capital

In Eisenstein's estimation, intellectual cinema made possible the direct
treatment of dialectical thought. With the advances in form reached
through work on *October* and *Old and New*, and with characteristic play-
fulness, he announced in a notebook entry for 1927: "CAPITAL, a new
work on a libretto by Karl Marx. A film treatise."[2] At the same time, the
project would serve a serious social function since education campaigns
had not reached tens of millions of adult illiterates. In the main, the Soviet masses could not read Marx for themselves. In an audacious response
to the Soviet campaign for a cinema "intelligible to the millions," Eisenstein contemplated experiments in cinema to make *Capital* intelligible to
the unlettered and the politically unschooled.

As subjects to include for a cinematic critique of political economy,
Eisenstein considered contemporary portraits of the industrialist Krupp
and the potentate Aga Khan. About the latter figure he notes: "cynicism
of shamanism carried to the extreme. God—a graduate of Oxford University. Playing rugby and ping-pong and accepting the prayers of the faithful." Another subject, suggested by Daumier's caricatures of the French
parliament under Louis-Philippe, was a film satire of "capitalism and its
puppets." Though he found "endlessly possible themes for filming in
CAPITAL ('price,' 'income,' 'rent')," the formative goal of the project remained Marx's method. Accordingly, a "complete departure from the factual and anecdotal," achieved in sequences of *October*, was to structure
the *Capital* film as a whole.

The content was not to be a story or themes contained by cinematic
form but was to be itself a method, the *forms* of dialectical thinking: "In
the new cinema, the established place of eternal themes (academic
themes of LOVE AND DUTY, FATHERS AND SONS, TRIUMPH OF
VIRTUES, etc.) will be taken by a series of pictures on the subjects of
'basic methods.' The content of CAPITAL (its aim) is now formulated: *to
teach the worker to think dialectically*. To show the method of dialectics.
This would mean (roughly) five nonfigurative chapters. (Or six, seven,
etc.) Dialectical analysis of historical events. Dialectics in scientific problems. Dialectics of class struggle (the last chapter)." The ordering principle of the imagery would evince the logic of dialectical method.

Intellectual cinema was not to be dependent on sound technology for
the exposition of ideas. Eisenstein calculated that no more than 10 percent of the soundtrack for *Capital* would entail spoken dialogue. The 1928
statement stresses that nonsynchronized juxtapositions of visual and aural

images "provide an even greater opportunity than before of speeding the idea contained in a film throughout the whole globe, preserving its world-wide viability" (W 114). The theatrical and naturalistic uses of sound in the first generation of American talkies impressed Eisenstein as antithetical in form to a genuinely international cinema.

In order to give *Capital* "the form of a discursive film," Eisenstein contemplated a "de-anecdotalization principle" that would diminish storyline to a level of *historiettes*, of petty events. Seeking "an adequate triviality for the 'spinal' theme," he identifies an example within literary modernism: "In Joyce's ULYSSES there is a remarkable chapter of this kind, written in the manner of scholastic catechism. Questions are asked and answers given. The subject of the question is how to light a Bunsen burner. The answers, however, are metaphysical." The chapter in question is the seventeenth, identified by Joyce critics as the "Ithaca" section. As in *Ulysses*, in the *Capital* project the methods of representation—rather than the persons or events represented—are foregrounded, textual dominants.

The project also utilizes shot composition to disclose ideology. Referring to a subject conceived in 1926 while in Berlin, Eisenstein notes: "Absolutely special will be the problem of the image and frame composition for CAPITAL. The ideology of the unequivocal frame must be thoroughly reconsidered. How, I can't yet tell. Experimental work is needed. For that, it's 'madly' necessary first to make THE GLASS HOUSE, in which the (usual) idea of the *frame* is what happens to the *structure of things* in the fragments of OCTOBER and in CAPITAL's entire structure." With the extensive use of glass in Bauhaus architecture and design in mind, Eisenstein imagined for *The Glass House* a completely transparent apartment building in an American city as his setting. Only doors would remain solid, as a token of conventional privacy. Morality and order are preserved as long as old social habits of nearsightedness and narrow focus are maintained. When this conditioning weakens, criminality and catastrophe ensue. Neighbors become rapt spectators to a suicide by hanging and a murder by arson. The extent of this indifferent, cruel voyeurism is expressed in images where "walls, floor, and ceiling seem made of faces."[3]

The "transparent" meaning of bourgeois life—the direct, uncensored perception of material and social reality it seems to offer—proves illusory in *The Glass House*. Spatial and social relations among objects and persons become problematic with the perspectives in depth, overlapped images and unprecedented points-of-view afforded by the glass walls and floors. Effects of juxtaposition and conflict, until *Old and New* gained mainly through the montage of shots, are now to be achieved frequently within the single frame. The "unequivocal" nature of the compositional frame—its univocal signification—is thereby voided. At the level of method, these innovations would compel audiences to revise their normative processes of perception and interpretation.

The affect that best characterizes intellectual cinema, according to the notebook entries, is "*Lachsalven!*" Eisenstein anticipated that a salvo of laughs would accompany the spectator's sudden, unexpected insight. The economy of expression and comprehension in intellectual cinema is analogous to the psychical economy of wit Freud describes in his 1905 study *Jokes and Their Relation to the Unconscious*. Freud's metapsychology accounts for verbal humor as a temporary regression to primary process responses (the realm of the unconscious and instinct) by means of material structured through operations of the secondary process (the domain of reason and language). Eisenstein, at this point in his theoretical investigations, poses questions of form mainly in terms of logic, method, and social language. Within a few years, however, his interests will turn increasingly toward primary process thinking.

Humor in the *Capital* film was to serve conceptual aims: "The elements of the *historiette* itself are thus chiefly those which, in the form of puns, provide the impulse towards abstraction and generalization (mechanical spring-boards for patterns of dialectical attitudes towards events)." With the exception of authentic pathos in a final section on class struggle, the film's banal story skeleton would amplify sentiments to levels of the grotesque and farce. Eisenstein cites as the guideline for construction of a historiette a critic's comment on "the advantage of irony over pathos." The notebook also quotes approvingly a passage from Georg Grosz's autobiography where the artist comments on the mass hysteria of wartime Germany: "It was a delightful time, when everything was saturated in the symbolism of war, when every jar of artificial honey was decorated with an 'iron cross, second class.' "

As additional subjects within the film, Eisenstein considered a day in the life of an average man, events linked in a progression from a bowl of soup to the sinking of a British ship, and an "analysis of a centimeter of silk stocking." Even a topic as ordinary as the last one embraces fundamental social matters from commerce, competition, and morality ("the silk manufacturer's fight for the short skirt") to exploitation ("Indian women forced to incubate the silk cocoon by carrying them in their armpits!"). The project here treats a matter central to "A Critique of Capitalist Production," as Marx's *Capital* is subtitled.

Marx fully demonstrates the dialectical method in the early chapter "The Fetishism of Commodities and the Secret Thereof," which demythologizes the bourgeois form of value. Confusion and mystification arise because capitalist political economy dissociates commodities from the productive process, making a concrete social relation between individuals assume "the fantastic form of a relation between things." The bourgeois order of things is thus ironic in the duality between the imagined independent status of commodities and their social, productive origin. Their imagined status is the same as a primitive religious illusion. For Marx, the extreme of bourgeois fetishism is found in the designation of gold as the universal standard of value: "When the producers of coats and boots compare those articles with . . . gold or silver, as the universal equivalent, they express the relation between their own private labor and the collective labor of society in the same absurd form."[4] Bourgeois economy is ironic in that it both conceals and reveals a fundamental truth. The truth it reveals, in absurd form, lies in the universalized standard of value. Positing gold, a socially useless commodity, as that standard conceals the genuine universal, which Marx identifies as labor. Much as his dialectic stands the Hegelian method on its feet, the labor theory of value rectifies the "fantastic form" capitalist production takes. His critique of value retranslates commodities from fetish objects back into productive processes and social relations.

Eisenstein's notebooks propose a visual fantasia on relations within Western commodity culture. One set of associations would link the dinner table to international conflict: "Pepper. Cayenne. Devil's Island. Dreyfus. French chauvinism. *Figaro* in Krupp's hands. War." Anticipating by over twenty years the exposés by Evelyn Waugh and Jessica Mitford on modern American funeral customs, Eisenstein sketched the following episode: "In America even cemeteries are private. 100% Competition. Bribing of doctors, *etc.* The dying receive prospectuses: 'Only with us will you find eternal peace in the shade of trees and the murmur of streams.' " Another episode would concern a mailbox for foundlings. Having read a newspaper account of such a deposit box outside an Athens orphanage, Eisenstein comments: "Absolutely brilliant material, 'compressible' to the point of 'bloody irony.' Bourgeois culture and philanthropy." Visual puns, juxtapositions, and patent absurdity are the satiric devices intended to reveal alienated conditions within commodity culture.

Walter Benjamin has closely identified Marxism with the satiric mode: "Marx, who was the first to undertake to bring back the relations between people from their debasement and obfuscation in capitalist economics into the light of criticism, became in so doing a teacher of satire who was not far from being a master of it."[5] A similar spirit of Marxist irony is to be found in a German work contemporary to Eisenstein's *Capital* project, the Kurt Weill–Bertolt Brecht *Mahagonny* collaboration. First performed in July 1927 as a cycle of songs and orchestral music, the full opera *The Rise and Fall of the City of Mahagonny* premiered in 1930. Brecht's libretto presents a consumer culture in which the only capital crime is a person's lack of money. The inhabitants of Mahagonny have no spiritual beliefs, only materialistic drives. When the city is destroyed by bankruptcy, its citizens take to the streets in violent, absurd protest under the slogan "For the Continuance of the Age of Gold."

Through visual satire the *Capital* film proposed to invert and expose the social processes of symbolization in bourgeois culture. In turn, a rupture in the normative process of perception would be effected: "A normal perception occurs, and then there's a break in the perception of something outside the logic of the ordinary. This moment is held, and then, at a given moment, a restructuring of ordinary perception takes place." The project's method shares with Marx's critique an analytic approach that starts from society's banal realities. This approach accords with the commentary Lenin made on dialectical method: "In his *Capital*, Marx first analyzes the simplest, most ordinary and fundamental, most common and everyday *relation* of bourgeois (commodity) society, a relation encountered billions of times, viz. the exchange of commodities. In this very simple phenomenon (in this 'cell' of bourgeois society) analysis reveals *all* the contradictions (or the germs of *all* the contradictions) of modern society."[6] Even while the content of the social object analyzed is scant, the form of dialectical analysis is complete.

Increasing centralized control over Soviet culture made the *Capital* project infeasible, especially by a non-Party artist like Eisenstein. Even the comparatively open-minded administration of Sovkino, the studio that produced *October* and *Old and New*, thought its most successful director was being presumptuous: "We have no ideological supervision, nor can we say that ideological supervision is in the hands of Comrade Eisenstein, who hopes to find the correct ideology hidden in Marx's *Capital*."[7] This official rejection is itself profoundly uninformed, for with *The German Ideology* and *Capital* Marx differentiates historical materialism and dialectical analysis from ideology. The Sovkino statement is representative of the dogmatism and obscurantism that grew from the cultural revolution. As subsequent events confirm, the strict administration over Soviet culture opposed any adequate popularization of Marx, perhaps from fear that the regime would be recognized as un-Marxist.

In the mid–1930s Eisenstein incorporated dialectical method in the program of film direction at the VGIK (All-Union State Cinema Institute). Dialectical structure, however, did not remain the basis for film form in his later theory and filmmaking. To some extent, the limitation put on Soviet thought in the Stalin era accounts for the change. Unlike Marx and Lenin, Stalin had no training or serious interest in philosophy. In an assessment of Marxist thinkers, Richard T. De George observes of Stalin that in "dialectical materialism he remained always a neophyte," yet "his scant writings on the subject dominated Soviet thought."[8] Stalin's writings de-emphasize dialectics as a theory of knowledge and make dialectical method subservient to Party policy. As a consequence, Soviet philosophers published no original work on dialectics in the 1930s or 1940s.

Eisenstein's announcement in 1932 of a film project on the twilight of capitalism is an early indication of his move away from a cinema of manifestly dialectical form. Before returning to Moscow, he stated to German reporters: "I would like to create one day, on film, a kind of modern *Götterdämmerung*, a visual history of the deaths of the Titans, of Basil Zaharoff, Löwenstein, Krüger, Deterding—a kind of Pergamon frieze, possibly with Richard Wagner's music post-synchronized."[9] The persons named are all heads of industry whose financial and political interests were international in scope. This project contrasts with ideas for the *Capital* adaptation where a banal event, a historiette, was to unfold dialectically to disclose global contradictions and interrelationships. The scale for Eisenstein's *Götterdämmerung* is world-historical from the outset. In conception, its form and style are mythic and operatic rather than dialectical.

American Tragedies

Once in Hollywood with Alexandrov and Tisse, Eisenstein proposed *The Glass House* as his first feature for Paramount, but he was unable to compress the various scenes he had sketched into a single plot to satisfy the conventions of American story film. The next project, an adaptation of Blaise Cendrars's novel *L'Or*, resulted in the scenario *Sutter's Gold*, which draws on ideas and formal devices dating back to the *Capital* project and the 1928 statement on sound. Its narrative focus is John Sutter, the Swiss immigrant who became a successful California farmer only to see his fields ruined with the discovery of gold in 1848.

From an ironic perspective on gold as a standard of value, Eisenstein's scenario describes the destruction of agricultural land by mining operations: "Sutter is maddened by . . . sounds. And now to them is added the renewed sound of the picks, and of stones piled high out of the river, stones encroaching and burying under them the fertile fields. Stones rapidly being built into mountains that crush under them all trace of the fertility that went before this terrible symphony of sounds."[10] At the height of his real wealth, Sutter is depicted as an agricultural industrialist, having introduced mechanization and the organization of field workers. Mankind's productivity is celebrated in an early scripted sequence through a catalogue of occupations, which Eisenstein composed in the epic styles of Whitman and Sandburg. With the gold discovery, men are seen to abandon their various tasks to pursue the sole endeavor of prospecting; this sequence visually dismantles the rich diversity of human productiveness.

The notation for a "terrible symphony of sounds" is indicative of Eisenstein's design for audiovisual montage. Only a few features at this time—among them Alfred Hitchcock's *Murder!* (1930) and Vertov's *Enthusiasm* (1931)—achieve similar innovations. To convey Sutter's emotional distress, the sound level was to reach a "Colossal" pitch. There was to be a Sutter march melody based on concrete music: "The sounds of the blacksmith's instruments, the girl's giggles, the neighing of the horse, the screams of the man losing his teeth, the flute, the choppings are all arranged in this rhythm although they retain their natural and recognizable sound." The symphonic presentation of character would be resolved with a "death chord running tremblingly to its crescendo." To accompany the scene of Sutter's death, the following material is outlined:

> His diabolic laughter joins the other sounds.
> The shriek of his son dying in the fire.
> The song of the elements around Sutter.
> The rolling of the wagon wheels pronouncing his name.
> The roaring of the mob.

The scenario's most powerful visual metaphor is the desert, which is the landscape of American tragedy in the film. As an immigrant wandering across the continent, Sutter crosses great stretches of desert until he finally settles in California's Central Valley. With the gold rush, his cultivated acreage is turned to wasteland. In the period of his retirement, the Sutter estate burns down to "a black desert." Sutter is in his last years a morose, fearful man who spends days absorbed in the reading of *Apocalypse*. This bleak scenario was rejected by Paramount on the grounds of cost, but the decision also reflects the studio's ideology.

The last project Eisenstein attempted in Hollywood was an adaptation of the Theodore Dreiser novel *An American Tragedy*. Paramount had owned screen rights to it since publication in 1925 but all the contracted treatments—including ones by D. W. Griffith and Ernst Lubitsch—had been refused. Eisenstein valued the novel's store of material detail and acute observation of American speech and customs, but its impartial, unassimilated actuality presented problems: "This epic of cosmic truth and objectivity had to be 'screwed together' into a tragedy, which was unthinkable without the direction and the emphasis provided by a particular world-view" (W 228). The novel's characterizations convey Dreiser's concept of human "chemism"—that is, human action as a reactive compound of ideals, emotions, biology, heredity, and circumstance. Discarding the novel's chemic theory of human behavior, Eisenstein identifies the fate of young Clyde Griffiths as neither individual nor cosmic but as necessarily

social. The death of the factory girl Clyde has made pregnant frees him
to court a society girl and pursue the moneyed life.

Eisenstein considered the murder scene the interpretative crux but
thought that the extended courtroom drama in the novel's third part left
thematic development of this crucial event "logically not to the plot but
to the processes of law." To provide a determining tragic context, he
found it imperative "to sharpen the *actual* and *formal* innocence of Clyde
within the specific act of committing the crime." The tragedy is attributed
to the class structure of "a society whose very mechanism drives a rather
characterless lad to such a predicament and then, invoking morality and
justice, puts him in the electric chair" (*W* 230).

In the scenario, contrasts between owner and laborer in work, income,
and life-style are absolute. When Clyde first sees the house of the manufacturer Samuel Griffiths, his uncle, the youth "yields himself to the luxury of reflecting on his connection, however humble, with this gorgeous
family." A montage transition is indicated: "The mansion slowly fades in
the darkness. . . . And in the darkness the factory looms roar, and the
steam machinery hisses, and out of the clouds of steam appears working
a perspiring, wet, miserable-looking Clyde." Wealth gained through exploitation has precedence over blood ties at this point in the narrative.

Eisenstein continues an analysis of the form of value in capitalist society with this project. When Clyde takes a job as a hotel bellboy, the
exchange of his first tip is dramatized as an awe-inspiring moment. As
detailed in the vignettes of hotel life that follow, Clyde's holy lucre is
increased by trading on man's appetitive instincts and corruption. On the
soundtrack, "Fifty cents" is the refrain to a celebration of the mystique of
money: "An unknown voice is heard screaming it and a smile almost of
exaltation brightens the whole face of Clyde. 'Fifty cents.' Still louder
screams the strange voice, and together with the cry the orchestra is
heard playing a wild, happy march. As though at High Mass the music
peals forth, and the hotel resembles a mighty cathedral." When Clyde
dares to steal his first kiss from the factory girl Roberta, he is described
as smiling "as he smiled that day when he earned his first money, and
heard that grand music." Later, in the company of the society girl and
her friends, Clyde discovers that wealth acts upon him as an intoxicant
and aphrodisiac. His sexual impulses, however, are fulfilled only with the
ill-fortuned Roberta. The same grand music accompanies their consummation, suggesting that sex substitutes for cash at this moment.

As in the case of Sutter, characterization of Clyde was to entail extensive audiovisual montage. A "symphony of music, laughter and the natural sounds" would convey his elation during a weekend with the rich set.
The scenario's dominant audio mode, however, is dissonance. When
Clyde considers killing Roberta, ambient sounds become grotesque and

shrill: "A whisper becomes the whistle of a storm, and the storm cries out 'Kill,' or the whistle of the storm becomes the movement of the street, the wheels of a streetcar, the cries of a crowd, the horns of motorcars, and all beat out the word: 'Kill! Kill!' " The murderous roar subsides into a whisper again, at which point a low, unemotional voice reads a newspaper account of a boat accident resulting in death. The script also has Clyde act in disharmony with his surroundings in a number of instances: dashing frantically in a tranquil setting, falling down without any apparent cause, and standing motionless in the midst of a busy crowd. Joined, the audio and visual tracks would thus raise the effect of dissonance to a third level.

Studio executive David O. Selznick professed admiration for the script as serious art but thought the finished film "cannot possibly offer anything but a most miserable two hours to millions of happy-minded young Americans."[11] Paramount refused to put it into production and terminated the studio's contract with Eisenstein. The adaptation was assigned to Josef von Sternberg who, working from an entirely different script, made Clyde's fate an individual matter, independent of social factors. Dreiser vigorously opposed the Sternberg production, which was released in 1931 despite the novelist's efforts to bring a court injunction against Paramount. Upon his return to Moscow in 1932, Eisenstein attacked the American movie industry's Production Code and the Hays Office for promoting reactionary racial and social views and for preventing any serious political dissent from reaching the screen.

Que Viva Mexico!: Living History

Determined to complete a film in the West, Eisenstein contracted next with Upton Sinclair and the novelist's wife, Mary, for a motion picture on Mexico. Eisenstein's interest in Mexican culture had been raised some years back by the John Reed account *Insurgent Mexico* (1914) and by the painter Diego Rivera's visit to Moscow. Rivera had shown his mural paintings in Mexico to the touring poet Mayakovsky, who described them in a travel account Eisenstein read in 1928: "On dozens of walls, the past, present, and future history of Mexico is represented. . . . Modern art in that country had its origins in the ancient, colorful, unsophisticated folk art of the Indians, not in the decadent eclectic forms imported from Europe, and . . . the idea of art is part—perhaps not yet quite consciously so—of the idea of the struggle and liberation of colonial slaves."[12] Eisenstein was fascinated with the dynamic correlation of past to present, and stated upon departure for Mexico in December 1930 that "the struggle of progress is still very real" there.[13]

The Sinclairs conceived of the Mexico project as a commercial and artistic enterprise and stipulated in the contract that "the picture will be non-political."[14] Eisenstein, accustomed to ideological supervision, placated his American financiers and Mexican censors by submitting an inoffensive story outline while filming freely on location. In a letter from Mexico, he virtually warns Upton Sinclair of this evasion: "It is true that you are in the same position as was Sovkino when we were shooting *Potemkin*—we had such a lot to do, that nobody in Moscow knew what we were doing!" At the stage of Eisenstein's arrangements to return to the Soviet Union, Sinclair promised that all the Mexican footage, which had been processed and stored in Hollywood, would be forwarded upon the director's arrival there. Events in the interim, including the discovery by American customs officers of sexually graphic drawings by Eisenstein on Christian subjects, irreversibly estranged Sinclair from the Soviet director and he severed all agreements.

The film stock exposed in Mexico and shipped to the States totalled more than 200,000 feet. This figure represents a running time of some forty hours, but it includes numerous duplicate takes made as a precaution since daily rushes were not available on location. A number of film releases have been made from the exposed footage, but it scarcely needs to be said that none of them represents an Eisenstein film.[15] In spite of the unfinished form of *Que Viva Mexico!*, it remains possible to discuss his filmmaking practices in this period, particularly through evidence in the study film Jay Leyda has prepared.

Having completed over a year of principal photography, Eisenstein stated: "*Viva Mexico* in the theoretical research field is before everything a 'shot' (camera angle) picture: I think I have solved (anyhow for myself) the montage problem (as a system of expression). This picture has to analyze the same laws on their other degree—the 'shot.' "[16] Now not simply a montage cell, the shot contains within itself a system of representation. Writing in 1946, Eisenstein explains the reorientation in these terms: "In my early films I was . . . attracted by the mathematically pure movement of montage concepts rather than the 'thick' strokes of the accentuated shot" (*IM* 44). In viewing the compiled Mexican footage, filmmaker and critic Jacques Rivette has noted the "absolute independence" and unique "interior" of each Eisenstein shot.[17]

During the first months in Mexico, Eisenstein completed the essay "The Dynamic Square," based on his address concerning innovations in screen dimensions to the Academy of Motion Picture Arts and Sciences in Hollywood. In notes for *The Glass House* in 1928 he had contemplated "a monster screen—four times the usual size."[18] While Eisenstein welcomed experimentation with screen size and proportions in "The Dynamic Square," he was concerned that any new format would continue to function as a proscenium space, thus "approximating the cinema to the stage" (*FE* 60). With the Hollywood sound film, set design and shot composition stage the action within inflexible, closed boundaries: "Incorrect handling of sound is at the point of ruining the *pictorial* achievements of the screen" (*FE* 48). For alternatives to static theatricalism, Eisenstein offers "as an example and an ideal, the framelessness of a Japanese impressionist drawing" (*FE* 56).

Que Viva Mexico! establishes an open, frameless pictorial style in its almost exclusive use of exterior location shots. Screen space is relative and contiguous rather than absolute. Shot composition creates an impression of spatial extension relative to the frame rather than an impression of enclosure, as in the constriction of action on-deck in *Potemkin*. In other words, the profilmic area captured by a shot clearly exceeds the frame boundaries. It is to this property of extension and excess that Eisenstein refers in noting the shots' "extravagance."[19] He also proposed that a "*dynamic* succession of *dimensions*" be created onscreen (*FE* 52). One means of doing so within the same shot is through a prolonged moving camera take. With fewer technical resources than were available for the silent films, Eisenstein still arranged on location in Mexico the most elaborate traveling shots in his cinema to date.

An initial script treatment comments that cultures and customs in Mexico are "violently contrasting." They coexist yet are at the same time "centuries away" from one another and as a consequence no single plot, no whole story, would unify the work. Instead, "the contrasting independent adjacence" of cultures is taken "as the motif for constructing [the] film: 6 episodes following each other—different in character, different in people" (*FS* 251). The script underwent revision and expansion in the fourteen months Eisenstein traveled and filmed in Mexico as he maintained a spontaneous approach to story material and to production on location. The scenario Eisenstein prepared for publication provides an idea of the film's narrative modes and structure. Some scenes, however, were intentionally omitted to avoid censorship and one entire episode ("Soldadera") was left unfilmed. The placement of episodes in positions three and four varies in some of the director's notes, but the published scenario reflects the order Eisenstein most frequently outlined for *Que Viva Mexico!* at the time he was filming.

The scenario identifies the six episodes as "four novels framed by prologue and epilogue."[20] While the initial treatment calls for "a rhythmic and musical construction" to bind together the episodes, the published scenario indicates that each episode is accompanied by a Mexican folk song and that the audiovisual structure will "create a vast and multicolored Film-Symphony about Mexico." The episodes are also distinct in geographical setting, narrative type, temporality and historical period, social milieu, and in the visual style that governs composition and acting.

Reflecting this stylistic diversity, each section was dedicated to a different painter.

The prologue or overture is set in the Yucatan and presents the burial of a young man according to Mayan ritual. It is dedicated to David Siqueiros (with specific reference to his fresco "The Worker's Burial") and specifies accompaniment by a Mayan drum rhythm and high-pitched chant. An aura of timelessness is indicated for the event. A pre-Columbian order of "Stones—Gods—Men" is evoked in portraying "realms of death, where the past still prevails over the present." Shot composition is predominantly static, sculptural, and architectonic. Like stone temples and carved gods, the Mayan Indians are shown in fixed postures and immobile positions. The anthropomorphic origins of their deities are disclosed through compositions that match human profiles with stone idols; Indians are posed with closed eyes to accent their resemblance to the ancient, blank-eyed figures. The petrification of landscape, ruins, and inhabitants alike conveys a sense of their existence as prehistoric.

Images of great vitality are reserved for the funeral procession, which is captured in complex, prolonged sequence shots. Bearing the open coffin on their shoulders, six Indians make measured progress through a cactus-covered terrain. Unlike the ironic distance of the camera in tracking the religious procession in *Old and New*, here the camera's closeness and deliberate movement convey dignity. The visual contrast to their otherwise stationary positions suggests the Indians' potential for change in burying the past. The potential is for historicized life, and the prologue's symbols of death will be transformed in the epilogue into images of life and a triumph over prehistory.

Each of the four novels dramatizes the passions of man and woman with an intimacy unprecedented in Eisenstein's cinema. "Sandunga" is a celebration of life in a tropical society free of political and religious conflict. It is dedicated to the Mexican painter and art historian Jean Charlot and was to be accompanied by a festive Oaxacan popular song—slow and sensual in tempo—of the same title. The lush fertility of setting makes a diametric contrast to the prologue's stony landscape. The place is again timeless, but it embodies vital forces rather than prehistoric and mortal ones. The story mode is romance and embodies a lyrical spirit. The indigenous culture is depicted as a maternal paradise; the heroine's name is Concepcion. One of Eisenstein's sources notes of this region, Tehuantepec, that "the women, famed throughout the land for their beauty, are distinctly superior to the male not merely in ability, but in prestige and status among their people."[21] Eisenstein represents marriage as the principle of serene, eternal life in the culture and, in this, the novel contrasts with the marital tragedy and marital farce in episodes that depict the Spanish colonial heritage.

"Sandunga" creates the image of a golden age in Mexico's heritage, of an original culture where social relations are simple, unmediated, and procreative. It opens with sunrise in the tropical forest and an "irresistible call to life." The sensuous, lyrical qualities in visual style are present in earlier films, but social tranquility remains unthreatened for the first time in Eisenstein's cinema. The first days free of work in *Strike* have a holiday air, but it is broken quickly by hardship. The restful beauty of the *Potemkin* sailors asleep in hammocks is shattered by an officer's brutality.

"Sandunga" portrays a monetary society, but the form of value remains in functionally human terms. There are no signs of poverty or class conflict. The capital Concepcion gains through trade is accumulated on a necklace of gold coins, which is a decoration enhancing her natural beauty, her allure. The necklace serves as her dowry; the study film contains lap dissolves from its large coin pendant to the future husband, who sits suspended in a hammock. The husband removes the necklace once they arrive in their new home. The next scene shows the couple with their first-born child. Monetary exchange and accumulation are thus seen to unite individuals and increase life immediately.

"Maguey" is set in the era of Porfirio Diaz's dictatorship, at the beginning of this century, and depicts conflict between a hacienda owner and the Indian peons who work his maguey fields in the cultivation of the plant for an intoxicant called *pulque*. In an unfinished essay of this period, Eisenstein associates the maguey with the visual style of José Orozco.[22] The novel also utilizes the geometry and simplicity of folk art designs. Its music was to be based on the peons' plaintive melodies sung at the start and close of each work day. The dramatic mood is dominated by "aggressiveness, virility, arrogance and austerity," and the courtship of a young peon and his fiancée ends in tragedy.

Massive walls and an army of guards protect the landowner in his hacienda, which is one of many "former monasteries of the Spanish conquerors." Only cactus and agave grow on the region's dry plateaus. The maguey is a towering agave with thorny leaves and is the source of the liquor that "drowns sorrows, inflames passions." No images depict peons in their own living quarters; the maguey groves define their social existence. At dawn peons gather at the outer hacienda wall. They are wrapped against the morning cold in serapes that give them the shape of rudimentary statues, a form reiterated by the shadows they cast on the wall. This imagery gives additional meaning to the prologue's theme of men and stones. Under the watch of guards, workers leave for the fields. In this stark, menacing environment the young Sebastian breaks from work to meet with Maria's family and arrange a marriage.

The *hacendado*, "a good-natured old man," has invited neighboring landowners for a feast that day. Greedily drinking pulque and slavering on their moustaches, they are presented in caricature as descendants of Spanish colonialists. Their guards are mestizo henchmen in bandoliers and jackboots. In the afternoon Sebastian, following colonial tradition, goes to present his fiancée for the hacendado's blessing. He is prevented from accompanying Maria inside and she is subsequently raped by a guest. Having waited for hours, Sebastian intrudes upon the party in search of Maria and struggles with her abductor. The peon is forced from the hacienda but he returns shortly with three comrades. After raiding the hacienda arsenal, they engage in a gun battle with guards, who pursue the rebels into the fields. Three are captured and the fourth is left for dead. The captives are buried up to their shoulders then trampled to death under galloping horses. Close-ups detail the interplay of the victims' innocent, suffering eyes. The fourth peon regains consciousness in time to witness their execution. His eyes, as in *Strike*'s final extreme close-up of a worker's face, register the event's horror. Maria is released from the hacienda and discovers her dead fiancé in the fields.

"Fiesta" is also set prior to the revolution of 1910, in the Diaz era, and concerns the Spanish colonial influences in Mexican institutions, social customs, religion, and culture. Dedicated to Francisco de Goya, its style is baroque. The narrative mode in "Fiesta" is ironic in the treatment of Indian peoples, satiric in that of Spanish descendants. The featured rituals of the church, the bullfight and courtship are accompanied by colonial music. The scenes of worship during the feast of the Virgin of Guadalupe, the patron saint of Mexico's Indians, stand in thematic and visual counterpoint to the rebels' execution in "Maguey." The contrasts delineate the historical and cultural ironies of the Spanish Conquest. Indian worshipers in the procession wear stylized masks and costumes to represent conquistadores. The braided, decorative chains one Indian wears to symbolize mortification of the flesh are, in truth, tokens of how Spanish ideology has imprisoned native consciousness.

In a grotesque display of devotion, many Indian penitents advance on their knees to the Virgin's shrine. Some bear stone crossbars on their shoulders in imitation of Christ. Close-ups of Indians with their heads partially covered by heavy black cloth capture the tone of exquisite suffering found in baroque paintings of martyrs. Within such iconography, the name of the peon rebel, Sebastian, reflects ironically on Catholic culture. Though martyred in a savage manner, the agony of the Christian Sebastian is often painted—notably by Mantegna and Perugino—as a sensual, almost elegant, sacrifice. The execution of the peon Sebastian and his two fellow rebels is, in contrast, vicious and unredeemed. Images of Maria with the dead body of her fiancé evoke scenes of the Virgin Mary attending Christ after the Crucifixion. One dramatic irony is that Maria has been sexually violated. The script's narrative rationale is that Mexico's only savior is revolution, which its people undertake in 1910. From Eisenstein's perspective in 1930, that revolution is yet to be incarnated.

The connections between church and state in modern Mexico are presented as a military alliance. Black-robed friars bear staffs and death's heads that make them appear like a clan with the human skull as its totem. (The visual correlation is reworked in *Alexander Nevsky* to render the Teutons' Christianity as a barbaric creed.) In a series of his Mexico drawings, Eisenstein interweaves images of the Crucifixion, the bullfight, and homosexuality to suggest an erotics of ritualized death. A crucified matador, his arms nailed to the bull's splayed hindquarters, puts the animal to death with a sword thrust guided by the man's penis. One sequence taken for "Fiesta" relates homosexual carnality to political domination. At the corrida a soft-bodied gentleman is seated next to a slender, raw Mexican lad. This bourgeois exhibits *aficion* for the bullfight and a lustful interest in his young companion, whom he alternately pokes and hugs.

"Fiesta" centers the matter of Spanish cultural influence in a story of adulterous love. A jealous husband discovers his wife in the arms of her lover, a picador, and draws an ornate Spanish pistol. As he is about to fire the weapon the lovers escape death by a "pure miracle," which is left unspecified in the published scenario. In the genre of popular religious legends, Eisenstein subsequently explained, the lover is transformed into an old patined crucifix such as those found in Mexico's baroque churches. With a satiric twist worthy of Luis Buñuel, the jealous husband then drops his pistol in order to kneel down and pray before the cross.

The unproduced "Soldadera" novel is epic in mode, presenting a "tumultuous canvas of uninterrupted movements of armies, battles and military trains which followed the revolution of 1910." The *soldadera*—the common-law wife of a guerrilla soldier—became a heroic figure in John Reed's account of the Mexican Revolution and in murals by Orozco and Rivera. The popular song "Adelita" provides a musical refrain to the action, and the concrete sounds of the march, camp, and battle were further accompaniment. An unbroken continuity of life is achieved through the *soldadera*'s strength and perseverance. She gains another man, and a father for her infant, promptly after burying her first husband. Prepared to follow the new husband back into battle, she receives word that the civil war is over.

Scripted for this episode, as well as for "Sandunga," is an extranarrative interrogation of characters that inserts an authorial presence manifestly into the fiction:

Suddenly the loud voice of the author calls to Pancha:
—Say, "Soldadera." . . .

Pancha stops, turns her head toward the camera, first she just
stares; then, pointing her finger to her breast, she inquires silently:
"Did he call her?" The Voice, again:
"Where art thou going, woman?"
She turns pensive, smiles enigmatically, shrugs her shoulders, as
if ignorant of what to answer, parts her hands in the broad gesture
women are apt to make when saying:
— "Who knows?" (*Quien sabe* . . . ?)

This innovation in audiovisual montage anticipates the degree of reflexive
intervention into the classical film narrative later found in the cinema of
Ingmar Bergman and Godard.

The epilogue is set on November 2, All Soul's Day on the church cal-
ender but celebrated in Mexico as the Day of the Dead. An expression of
Indian heritage, the day is popularly observed with banquets in grave-
yards, carnivals that mock death, and candies in the shape of skulls and
skeletons. The episode's visual style is inspired by José Guadalupe Posada, the illustrator and—with the 1910 Revolution—radical publisher
who through his *calaveras* caricatured politicians and social types. The
soundtrack was to combine the noises of contemporary urban and industrial Mexico with carnival voices and music.

To avoid censorship, the published script simply indicates that the festival celebrates a "victory of life over death, over the influence of the
past." Other production notes outline an impression of "Industrial Mexico
enslaved by the Police Force." Eisenstein later stated that the 1910 Revolution had become by the Calles era (1924–34) a shabby spectacle of
officers parading in front of the president in a formation spelling out
MEXICO. Using full-sized skeletons, the epilogue presents a gallery of
calaveras in the costumes of a bishop, a society lady, a capitalist, a Spanish dancer, and a toreador. In a critique of contemporary Mexico, an act
of unmasking represents the continuation of class struggle. The bourgeoisie removes masks only to reveal human skulls; workers and peasants remove mask skulls to reveal smiling faces. This contrast is a commentary
on the morbidity of colonial, Catholic culture.

The epilogue's sense of rebellion is better understood in light of the
Mexican poet Octavio Paz's reflections on the national spirit. Paz writes of
the annual Day of the Dead celebration as "a revolt, a sudden immersion
in the formless, in pure being. By means of the fiesta society frees itself
from the norms it has established. It ridicules its gods, its principles, and
its laws: it denies its own self. The fiesta is a revolution in the most literal
sense of the word. In the confusion that it generates, society is dissolved,
is drowned. . . . To express it in another way, the fiesta denies society as
an organic system of differentiated forms and principles, but affirms it as

a source of creative energy."[23] The epilogue to *Que Viva Mexico!* intimates Mexico's revolutionary potential through the vitalism of its popular, native cultural heritage. Eisenstein characterized that potential as "the life-giving social principle which is self-affirming."

Eisenstein had previously studied the myths and languages of other cultures in the work of anthropologists like Sir James Frazer and Lucien Lévy-Bruhl and philologists like Wilhelm von Humboldt. Now in an environment of non-European folk customs, ancient heritages, and "the fantastic structure of prelogical, sensuous thinking—. . . from daily communion with those descendants of the Aztecs and Toltecs," his theoretical interests moved toward forms of primitive and mythic consciousness (*IM* 211).

The rich visual cultures of Mexico renewed Eisenstein's habits of drawing. He later described their influence on his graphic style as one of refinement in the use of line to an exact but abstract manner. In drawings from this period, Eisenstein's concern is not with a finished or static represented form. Rather, he is preoccupied with the dynamics of the figurative process. Fundamental to his method is a clean line, without any modeling or shadowing to indicate the illusion of three dimensions. Eisenstein considers the graphic line to be principally a dynamic movement, a function, a route to ideas, rather than a means of fixing a likeness. In particular, the "graphic skeletons and lineal edges" found in both pre-Columbian artefacts and the contemporary popular arts were an inspiration (*IM* 46).

In his Mexican drawings, sharp contours identify the subject through means of extreme economy. Drawing serves essentially as a mode of delineation. The graphic instrument functions as a marking tool that segments the graphic plane. The desired effect is not to solidify or stabilize the subject matter, but rather to formulate concepts about the subject matter, much as in his earlier practices of caricature. Eisenstein now associates this purpose with an intellectual affinity for principles of movement and generation and for dialectical, sensual thought generally. Graphic space is made into a site of dynamic conflict, of contestation against conventional forms and against perspectives in the third dimension. Graphics are a medium of metamorphosis, visual metaphor, and ideational play.

The Mexico drawings encompass a broad critique of class society, the colonial heritage in culture, and the "perversions" of religious mystery. The graphic line itself serves an analytic, dissecting function. For Eisenstein, the line produces an incisive, rudimentary outline or shape for his subject. And as often as not, the line demarcates a site of conflict and contradiction, of antagonism and antithesis. This graphic practice is distinct from treatment with chiaroscuro, where contour is in transition between light and dark and form can remain ambiguous or indefinite. When warranted by his scenic concept, Eisenstein employed devices of chiaroscuro. In *Sutter's Gold* the migration of miners and profiteers was envisioned as a descent of locusts upon California, darkening then consuming a fertile land. From the late 1930s until his death, Eisenstein fully employs a graphic environment of shadows and darkness.

While Eisenstein was filming in Mexico, a condemning evaluation of his work was published in a 1931 issue of the Soviet journal *International Literature*. With the intention to challenge Eisenstein's stature in world cinema, the critic Ivan Anisimov faulted him for "technical fetishism" and other "petty-bourgeois limitations."[24] In a letter sent to Mexico in September of that year, Esther Shub attempted to be candid about a Soviet political climate now hostile to Eisenstein: "I fear delays. You need to return as soon as absolutely possible to the USSR. . . . I'd like to explain very concisely and totally why I am hurrying you and so insistently asking you to return. It's not possible to write truthfully about this."[25] Two months later a blunt threat from Stalin was relayed through Upton Sinclair. In a cable to Sinclair dated November 21, 1931, Stalin charges that Eisenstein "IS THOUGHT TO BE DESERTER WHO BROKE OFF WITH HIS OWN COUNTRY STOP AM AFRAID THE PEOPLE HERE WOULD HAVE NO INTEREST IN HIM SOON."[26]

A tableau from *The Wise Man* production at the Moscow Proletkult Central Theater. The classic play is transformed into a burlesque and circus act.

The capitulation of a worker to police in *Strike* is rendered as a scene of grotesque revelation.

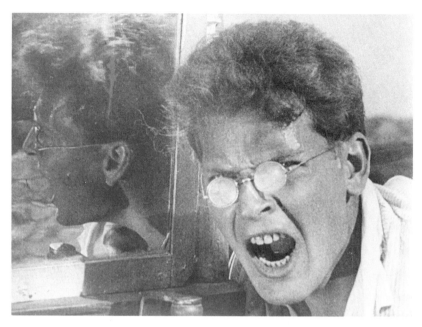

In *Battleship Potemkin* the student reacts in horror to atrocities committed on the Odessa Steps. The student's mirrored look functions outside the narrative as a compounded response of pity and fear.

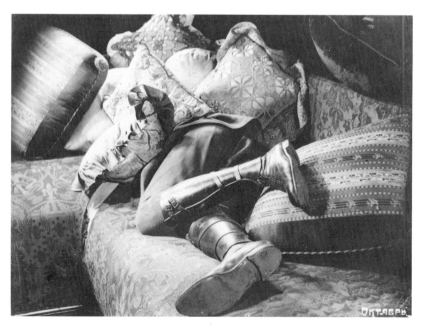

Kerensky seeks refuge in the lap of luxury at the Winter Palace in *October* as he fails to mobilize the defense of Petrograd against Kornilov's counterrevolution.

The modern agricultural laboratory in *Old and New*, a prototype prepared by Andrei Burov. Its Constructivist and Bauhaus style is a utopian projection for an architecture of the Soviet future.

An image from the Day of the Dead fiesta in *Que Viva Mexico!* that indicates the vitalism of a popular, native heritage.

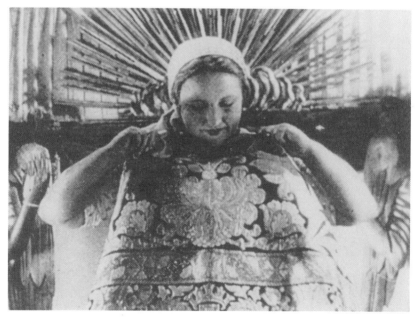

Peasants dismantle a local church in *Bezhin Meadow*, an event of ecstatic contact between two cultures. The visual alignment of religious images and vestments with the young collectivist expresses an animate and mass spirituality.

The historical leader depicted in *Alexander Nevsky* as a *bogatyr*, the mythical knight of superhuman prowess in medieval Russian epic. Such iconography supported the cult of leadership fostered in the Stalin period.

The tsar's coronation in *Ivan the Terrible*, part 1. Ivan's clairvoyant gaze is fixed in a direction above the specular drama of palace intrigue.

The absolutist in *Ivan the Terrible*, part 2, surrounded by the *oprichniki*, his secret entourage and army, dressed as monks. The tsar's sovereign power is exercised as a state religion.

CHAPTER SEVEN

Disjunction:
Projects, 1932–37

A month before Eisenstein, Alexandrov, and Tisse returned to the Soviet Union in May 1932, the Party Central Committee had announced that the numerous and often contentious literary groups were to be disbanded and a single body, the Union of Soviet Writers, would be established. The Party approved socialist realism as the accepted style of Soviet literature, thus bringing to conclusion the period of cultural revolution that had begun in 1928. During the years of Eisenstein's absence from the Soviet Union, the campaign of criticism against modernism and formalism had intensified. The termination of an era of artistic experimentation and stylistic pluralism was completed with the state's new control over cultural life and its extension of the socialist realism mandate to all the arts in the period 1932–35.

Direct accusations and denunciations of Eisenstein's artistic formalism became more frequent and increasingly vehement in the course of the 1930s. The dangers of deviation from the official line prompted Alexander Dovzhenko to warn his colleague publicly at the All-Union Conference on Soviet Cinema in January 1935: "I'm convinced that in more ways than one his erudition is killing him, no! excuse me, I did not mean that word; I wanted to say is disorganizing him."[1] Many artists involved with avant-garde movements early in the Bolshevik Revolution, and who had been able to pursue their artistic innovations during the 1920s, were convicted of formalist "crimes" during the 1930s. A campaign against Meyerhold, for example, began with the institutionalization of socialist realism. His theater company, which had influenced a generation of Soviet stage and film directors, was closed. Though he had been a Party member since 1917, Meyerhold was arrested in June 1939 and died in detention seven months later. A number of the Soviet artists murdered by the state in these years were unquestionably Marxists. They include two of Eisenstein's close collaborators, the writers Isaac Babel and Sergei Tretyakov. Brecht esteemed Tretyakov as his mentor in Marxism.

Eisenstein's preoccupation with the dangers of the political situation is disclosed in the essay "Word and Image," written in 1938 and published a year later. To demonstrate the inner process of representation, Eisenstein engages in free association in the essay: "By way of example I shall take the first couple of situations that come to me from the multiplicity of imagined pictures. Without weighing them carefully I shall try to record them here as they occur to me. 'I am a criminal in the eyes of my former friends and acquaintances. People avoid me. I am ostracized by them' " (*FS* 40). The imagined scenes of a public trial and condemnation Eisenstein goes on to detail in the essay are a thinly veiled commentary on the purge trials.

It is known now that not a single prominent film artist was exiled or executed in this period, but Eisenstein and his colleagues in cinema had no assurance that they would be spared. That they were appears to have been essentially a matter of Stalin's personal taste. While Stalin directly oversaw the political trials of old opponents among the Party leadership like Bukharin, the accused among writers, artists, and intellectuals were left mainly to the secret police and Party apparatus. Stalin greatly enjoyed movies and obliged others in the Kremlin to watch favorite films with him repeatedly. In 1937 Dovzhenko recounts the experience of viewing *Chapayev* (1934) with Stalin, who enthusiastically recited its dialogue from memory.[2] The Soviet historian Roy A. Medvedev has speculated that Stalin possessed a genuinely protective concern for film artists.[3] Although the secret police had prepared cases against some film directors, Stalin never permitted their arrest.

Cultural Revolution, 1928–32, and Socialist Realism

Though the cultural revolution coincides with the period of the First Five-Year Plan, its political processes differed from the plan's primary campaigns. Rapid industrialization and total collectivization were the two main thrusts of a revolution from above directed by Stalin in the period. The process of change in Soviet culture, in contrast, was in significant measure initiated from below rather than from the Party leadership.[4] The Party did promote an atmosphere of class war in cultural and intellectual matters starting in 1928, but there is evidence that Party leaders did not develop a well-defined mandate for the Soviet intelligentsia until as late as 1931. Political mobilization for proletarian hegemony in culture as the official Soviet policy originated largely among middle-level Party intellectuals and among activist arts organizations. The proletarian revolution in culture took place with a degree of spontaneity and broad-based initiative that would not be conceivable after 1932.

The course taken in Soviet literature established the pattern for cultural revolution in the other arts. The All-Russian Association of Proletarian Writers (VAPP), formed in 1920, had as its main force a group of young

Communist journalists who sought to become a Party representative in cultural matters, but the Central Committee did not sanction this role nor did VAPP benefit from the determined support of anyone in the Party leadership. Before 1928, the Party had no "hard line" in cultural matters, which meant that there was no concerted Party intervention on behalf of proletarian interests. In the course of 1928, the Soviet state's accommodation with diverse literary movements came to an end while the Party remained officially at a distance from cultural policy.

As a result of the First All-Union Congress of Proletarian Writers in April and May 1928, VAPP was absorbed into the Russian Association of Proletarian Writers, RAPP. Formed in 1925, RAPP stood against bourgeois canons, modernist subjectivity, and formal experimentation, and in favor of the recruitment of artists from the working class and the establishment of a distinctly proletarian culture. Though it was without direct Party authority, the proletarian cultural movement served the purpose of segregating among the intelligentsia opponents to the restructuring taking place in the Party leadership. RAPP positions gained dominance in the cultural front by 1931, but the organization never gained Party sponsorship. Once RAPP had served the purposes of class warfare over issues of culture it was summarily dissolved along with other proletarian groups by the Central Committee decree on the reorganization of culture in April 1932. With that reorganization the Party became directly active in overseeing the arts.

Stalin intervened personally in cultural matters only on occasion during the 1920s, making all the more consequential the concern he took with Eisenstein's *Old and New*. A "great turn" in Party cultural policy was marked by Stalin's open letter published in the October 1931 issue of *Proletarskaya revolyutsiya*, the leading Soviet journal on history of the revolutionary movement and the Party.[5] Though occasioned by his objections to an article by a young historian on pre–1917 Bolshevism, the Stalin letter was a broad indictment of the discipline of Soviet history for its lack of vigilance against alien and enemy ideas, such as those of Trotsky on Party history. The letter was a battle signal for cultural revolution in the history profession that brought the profession's normal activities to a halt for a period of several months. Purges in the profession immediately took place. Only one historian at the Soviet Academy of Sciences who held a post prior to 1929 remained on staff at the end of 1932.

Stalin's letter marks the first publicly official determination by a Soviet leader of a sanctioned interpretation on a purely intellectual matter. It had the effect of announcing a prohibition over work that the Party could deem ideologically incorrect. Truth in intellectual life would now be determined by Party authority. Historians began to anchor universal, eternal principles upon the account of Bolshevism the Party advanced under

Stalin. The past was to be thoroughly rewritten under the pressure of contemporary realpolitik. History as a discipline of objective critical analysis, even when based on Marx's principles of critique, became politically unsafe. The Society of Old Bolsheviks, an association whose membership consisted of Party members active in the Revolution and whose purpose was to preserve the heritage of 1917, was abolished in 1935 by Central Committee decree. Historical truth was now a matter of determining ideological correctness or deviation on the basis of Stalinist policies.

After the cultural revolution, Soviet intellectual life developed in the direction of a compulsory conformity and orthodoxy. Between 1932 and 1936 most of the cultural policies that emerged during the proletarian period the previous four years were reversed. The Union of Soviet Writers founded in 1932 included bourgeois and other non-Communist writers on equal terms with those from proletarian background or with Party membership. Many conservative intellectuals, identified during the proletarian episode as bourgeois fellow-travelers or class enemies, were allowed back into positions of cultural authority. Nonconformist intellectuals, avant-garde artists, and Old Bolsheviks, however, were targeted as enemies of the Soviet state.

With the Sixteenth Party Congress of 1930, Stalin gained unprecedented ideological hegemony. From this date Soviet history was officially regarded as having entered the period of socialism. In the cultural sphere, socialist realism was deemed the only artistic approach suitable to this new historical phase. The term was coined in 1932 in announcing formation of the Union of Soviet Writers. Guidance by the aims of socialist realism became one of the union's statutes. The meaning of socialist realism was debated in the period up to the First Writers' Congress in 1934. Maxim Gorky argued in favor of socialist realism in the understanding that it continued the critical realist traditions of nineteenth-century literature.

Debate over its meaning ended when Andrei Zhdanov, a secretary of the Party's Central Committee, and other Party representatives delivered addresses at the 1934 Congress to enforce socialist realism as the canon of Soviet literature. Zhdanov fashioned the definition that socialist realism is a combination of lowly, everyday reality with the heights of heroic promise. In practice, the Party increasingly favored literature that promoted myths of heroic individual leadership. The measure of literary truth became *partiinost* or "party-mindedness," guidance by the Party's social policies. Party authorities left the definition of socialist realism general so that it would accommodate future determinations in cultural doctrine and ideological mandate.

The content of socialist realism in Soviet literature is typically schematic and its form is purified of the stylistic devices of naturalism and subjective symbolism. Contemporary subject matter is treated as an affirmation of the "reality" of mankind's achievement of socialism in the Soviet context. With historical subject matter, Russian nationalism and the political foresight of the most powerful tsars, like Ivan IV and Peter I, are given priority. Katerina Clark has argued that socialist realism is a system of literature that is best understood as a modern ritual.[6]

After Eisenstein began to consider a screen adaptation of Marx, he jotted down a prospective inscription, dated April 8, 1928: "CAPITAL will be dedicated—officially—to the Second International! . . . The formal side is dedicated to Joyce."[7] Upon his return to the Soviet Union in 1932 Eisenstein vigorously defended modernist experimentation with form and cautioned that no new revolutionary realism could be created through administrative decree. Art made according to Party slogans he considered "accommodating trash of the present" (FF 95). His 1932 essay presenting the montage design for An American Tragedy specifies that Joyce's methods will be adopted to connect Clyde's "feverish race of thoughts intermittently with the outer actuality" (FF 103). In his plans for An American Tragedy, inner monologue displaces intellectual cinema as the rationale of film structure.

In 1933 Eisenstein argued that sound film's specific domain as a representational art is a "reflection of reality in the movement of the psychic process," while theater's is "a reconstruction of the actions and deeds of man as a social being" (W 248). This distinction between the psychological reality of cinema and the social materialism of theater is a diacritical element absent from his earlier film theory. Previously, Eisenstein distinguished cinema from theater on the basis of its formal properties (principally, the close-up and montage of shots) and on cinema's superior capacity for materialist and dialectical representation.

By 1934 Eisenstein's position on modernism had become politically dangerous, with official condemnation of Joyce at the First Congress of Soviet Writers. There, the Party functionary Karl Radek described Ulysses as "a dung heap, swarming with worms, photographed by a movie camera through a microscope."[8] To counter such degeneracy, Radek promotes the hygienics of socialist realism. While Georg Lukács also condemned Joyce's modernism as empty, "unhealthy" formalism, in this period Ernst Bloch found some social validity in the montage of images and subjective discourse. Brecht selectively valued methods of inner monologue, simultaneous registration, and shorthand abstraction, but Eisenstein was alone in his outspoken, unqualified praise of Joyce. A few months after Radek's speech denouncing Ulysses, Eisenstein lectured on Joyce, praising his "microscopic treatment of phenomena" as necessary for an understanding of modern culture and sensuous thought.[9]

At the All-Union Conference on Soviet Cinema in 1935, Eisenstein summarized his current investigations in culture and psychology and identified inner speech as the basis for a new theoretical synthesis. (In this period Meyerhold also considered experiments for achieving in theater the effect of internal monologue.) Eisenstein's conference address was published the same year, in English translation under the title "Film Form: New Problems." Embodied in primitive thought and the modernists' interior monologue alike, inner speech underlies as well *the whole variety of laws governing the construction of the form and composition of art works*" (*FF* 130). In stating this claim, Eisenstein characterizes aesthetic experience as a regression in thought processes. Eisenstein is aware that he has placed art on a continuum with mental states like "infantilism, schizophrenia, religious ecstasy [and] hypnosis" condemned by socialist realism as the preoccupations of a decadent modernism (*FF* 145). In justification, he explains that enduring works of art embody a dual process: a "progressive rise along the lines of the highest explicit steps of consciousness and a simultaneous penetration by means of the structure of form into the layers of profoundest sensual thinking" (*FF* 144).

Ideas on inner speech had been elaborated already in the work of Boris Eikhenbaum, Valentin Volosinov, and Lev Vygotsky. Volosinov's 1929 study approaches inner speech as dialogical communication "in close dependence on the historical conditions of the social situation and the whole pragmatic run of life."[10] Published in 1934 but suppressed in 1936, Vygotsky's *Thought and Language* differentiates inner speech from external speech as closer to thought in its structure and in its tendencies toward abbreviation, predication, primary words, and pure meanings.[11]

With a rationale similar to Freud's in *Totem and Taboo,* Eisenstein and Vygotsky approach inner speech as the residue in consciousness of earlier developmental stages, both culturally and ontologically. For Eisenstein, the properties of inner speech most immediately related to aesthetic experience are "non-differentiated thinking," "identification of image and object," and the participatory illusion (*FF* 132). For an example of these properties, he points approvingly to the identification between actor and role through Stanislavsky's subjective method, which he had rejected in the 1920s as an undialectical psychologism.

In Mexico Eisenstein had made the following self-evaluation: "My theoretical work has come a long way from its position prior to my departure. Fortunately, it's headed in the direction of ever-greater simplification, clarity, and scale."[12] That direction is indicated by subsequent references to the unity of opposites as the essential principle of dialectics. The 1935 conference address claims that a "most curious 'dual-unity' " constitutes the dialectic in works of art (*FF* 144). In contrast to previous theory, however, the dual-unity is not comparable to the principal objective and subjective codes original to Marxism. References in the address are not to Marx's dialectical critiques of history and capital production, but to Engels's investigations into anthropology and physical science in late works where Engels concluded that natural phenomena are proof of a universal and eternal dialectics.

Eisenstein cites Engels's general theorem that dialectical method provides an "exact representation of the universe, of its evolution, of the development of mankind, and of the reflection of this evolution in the minds of men . . . [with] constant regard to the innumerable actions and reactions of life and death, of progressive or retrogressive changes" (*FF* 144). Where *The German Ideology* proclaims that there is only one dialectical science, the science of history, Engels's scientism maintains that humanity and nature are subject to the same dialectical laws. His unfinished work in this area was edited and first published in 1925 in Moscow as *Dialectics of Nature*. Its self-sufficient, value-free, universal science of dialectical materialism—not subject to historical change or real Marxist critique—served the purposes of Stalin's revolution from above.

Applying Engels's theorem to aesthetics, Eisenstein represents the unity of form and content as a " 'dually united' interpenetration" (*FF* 145). His 1935 address concludes with a renunciation of intellectual cinema as a reductionist, tendentious attempt to make form and content identical in its representation of Marxist critique. The function of form is now to be expressive and affective rather than methodological and critical. Though ultimately unsuccessful in terms of his own career, Eisenstein's attempt at conciliation with socialist realism can be seen in the proposition that the dual process of art will unite elemental sensual thought in form with advanced political consciousness in content as Soviet cinema enters "its classical period" (*FF* 149). Contrary to Eisenstein's proposition, conformist political content legitimized an unimaginative, exhausted classicism in Soviet socialist realism.

Soviet Film Policy, 1928–38

Calls for proletarian revolution in Soviet cinema began to appear in film publications at the end of 1927. Within the proletarian campaigns, *Potemkin* was frequently acclaimed as a benchmark while *October* and *Old and New* were faulted for being formless in plot and excessively formal in visual treatment. Within the administration of the Soviet studios, the goal of profit from domestically produced entertainment films remained foremost. One Sovkino slogan of the mid–1920s was "10 per cent ideology and 90 per cent commerce."[13] The strongly plotted movie drama with a conventional hero was clearly the preference among paying audiences in the Soviet Union throughout the 1920s. The growth in domestic film production reached a height in 1928, with the release of 109 new Soviet features. This output was sustained in 1929 with 106 domestic releases.

The majority of these released features did not belong to the category of avant-garde art long prized in world film history. The Soviet cinema avant-garde struggled to survive over the next decade. The loss of artistic freedom among Soviet filmmakers was not the result of a sudden coup, but an outcome of intervention and censorship that increased from 1929 on. Party groups gained a formal presence in the film studios in 1929. At that point, Party terminology began to shape the discussion of cinema within the film industry and the film press. There was also at this time a purge of Soviet films that had remained in distribution over the years, among them Kuleshov's eccentric farce *The Extraordinary Adventures of Mr. West in the Land of the Bolsheviks* (1924). Administrative censorship became far more active. By an estimate made in a Soviet editorial published in *Na literaturnom postu* in February 1930, the proportion of films banned by Glavrepertkom (the State Repertoire Committee) rose from 3 percent in 1928 to 38 percent in the first quarter of 1929. Of the films produced at Sovkino in the latter period, 55 percent were banned.[14]

The distribution figures for new Soviet films drops to an average of only 42 releases per year for the period 1933–38. A major cause of the decline was the prolonged process of conversion to sound technology in Soviet production and exhibition. In 1934, the 45 films released are divided almost equally between silent (24) and sound (21) productions. The proportion shifts in favor of sound films only in 1935, when they total 64 percent of film production. The introduction of sound technology into the Soviet film industry marks a redirection from the utopian promise of an international language of cinema, at least among the avant-garde Soviet directors of the 1920s, to the immediate tasks of technical development and a bureaucratic mandate to increase the number of profitable sound films for the domestic market.

Overseeing this period of change in the Soviet film industry was Boris Shumyatsky, appointed in February 1930 as chairman of Soyuzkino, the newly centralized Soviet film organization. The central administrative office was redesignated twice under his tenure: in February 1933 to GUKF (State Directorate for the Cinema and Photographic Industry) and in January 1937 to GUK (State Directorate for the Cinema Industry). Shumyatsky's background was not in the film industry but rather in the Party apparatus and then with the Central Committee.

In a speech delivered in July 1932 Shumyatsky criticized montage as an overvalued device and held it responsible for the sacrifice of content to form in Soviet cinema. He also condemned the "plotless" film as powerless in regard to both ideology and entertainment. In a later address, Shumyatsky singled out the montage of attractions as a particularly odious stylistic practice. The standard of socialist realism was first invoked in the

film press in December 1932. Under its mandate the scriptwriter began
to assume a more accountable and determining role in the creation of the
finished film. Within the general Soviet industrial plan, cinema production was expected to be economically self-sufficient. Shumyatsky regarded a strong story-line to be the basis for a commercially successful
entertainment film.

   In administering the Soviet film industry Shumyatsky instituted a system wherein a producer was assigned to a film project to oversee its development at every stage. He based this system on the Hollywood production model, which he would observe firsthand in visiting film capitals
in Europe and the United States with a Soviet delegation during summer
1935. Shumyatsky organized central script departments and placed them
under the management of Party members. The producer and an ideological supervisor were empowered to require revision at every stage of production, from treatment and shooting script to final editing. The studio's
annual production schedule was guided by a thematic master plan.

   While Lunacharsky had pursued the development of an entertainment
cinema in the 1920s, the Commissar of Enlightenment also supported the
artistic ambitions of Soviet directors. Shumyatsky judged the continued
support of an avant-garde in Soviet cinema to be a luxury the industry
could ill afford in the 1930s. Shumyatsky also tried to foster the development of a new Soviet popular genre, socialist comedy. He lavished praise
on *The Happy Guys* (1934) and *The Circus* (1936), two musical comedies
directed by Grigori Alexandrov after he left the Eisenstein production
group. But the new genre gave no latitude for satire, especially where
Soviet society is concerned. In his book *A Cinema for the Millions* (1935),
Shumyatsky makes the unimaginable claim that were Gogol and Chekhov
alive their comic vision "would in the Soviet Union acquire joie-de-vivre,
optimism and cheerfulness."[15] In responding to such suggestions, Eisenstein asserted in a 1937 article that Soviet development of the genre
should "preserve the tradition of the bitter laughter" of Russia's nineteenth-century comic masters (*N* 111). It must be noted, however, that in
Alexander Nevsky corrosive humor is directed solely at German characters, while the comedy on Russian topics remains light and harmless.

   By 1935 only one cinema journal was published regularly, *Iskusstvo
kino* (Art of Cinema) in Moscow, and its pages were frequently occupied
by discussions of Party aims and the Second Five-Year Plan. The All-
Union Conference on Soviet Cinema in January 1935 formalized the centralization of the film industry in terms of both business and ideology, a
process that had been in progress since the 1928 Party Conference on
Cinema. The 1935 conference also affirmed Shumyatsky's priorities in
film production and the plan for economic self-sufficiency. Conference
discussion centered on the correct forms socialist realism would take in

cinema, the ideological goal of a medium intelligible to the millions, the past mistakes of artistic experimentation, and the reasons for decline in the completion of films. The conference's presiding official, Sergei Dinamov, a Party activist, declared the values of a new Soviet cinema to be optimism, heroism, and the dramatic story form. The director Leonid Trauberg, an outspoken participant in the discussions, judged *Potemkin* to be no longer serviceable as a standard for Soviet cinema. In the face of such repudiations of the international achievements within Soviet silent cinema, in an essay published a year earlier Eisenstein offered the montage structure in *Potemkin* as an example of "irreproachable purity and culture in our film language" (W 294).

The 1935 conference established *Chapayev*, directed by Georgi Vasiliev and Sergei Vasiliev, as the benchmark for Soviet cinema in the era of socialist realism. The year of its release, *Pravda* published an editorial in praise of *Chapayev*, the first time the central Party paper had given a film such attention. The film is a close adaptation of the novel *Chapayev* written by Dmitri Furmanov and published in 1923. Before turning to fiction, Furmanov had been extensively involved in administration and journalism as a Party advocate. The novel is based largely on actual events of the civil war, when Furmanov had worked as a head of political affairs with the Red Army regiment commanded by Chapayev, a legendary figure from the peasantry. In the 1930s the novel was officially cited as an exemplar of socialist realism, even though it preceded the term for this genre by nearly a decade.

In his book *A Cinema for the Millions* Shumyatsky praises the film *Chapayev* as the summit of Soviet cinema and a model for socialist realism in the medium. In his estimation, the film's directors "have depicted superbly the positive heroes and the positive features but they have not been afraid to show in their film a number of the negative aspects that existed in the Red Army at that time." Shumyatsky estimates that the negative aspects are treated "realistically and truthfully" to the degree that "the film depicts in every negative feature the traces of its demise."[16] Such an admission of the negative only to the extent that it is a priori self-defeated is entirely consistent with the "small inoculation of acknowledged evil" that functions within myth on the political right as described by Roland Barthes.[17] *Chapayev* offered an unproblematic redaction of the early Soviet period, while the complex living truth of that period preserved in such organizations as the Society of Old Bolsheviks was being eliminated.

A major cause for the reduction in the number of new Soviet films released in the 1930s was the new ideological strictures in culture. The official ban on Eisenstein's *Bezhin Meadow* in 1937 was by no means a unique turn of events. Production statistics for the years 1935–37 indicate that a number of projects were either abandoned or terminated. In 1935, of the 130 films planned, 45 were completed. In 1936 the number of films planned rises to 165, while that of films completed is only 46. In 1937, the GUK reduced the number of projects to 62, and the films completed declined to 24. Denounced in the Party press for sabotage of the Soviet film industry, Shumyatsky was arrested in January 1938 and executed in July that year. Semyon Dukelsky was appointed head of the film industry and served until the installation of Ivan Bolshakov over the newly formed State Committee for Cinema Affairs in June 1939. Bolshakov would become the first Minister of Cinema in 1946.

An Unfinished Cinema

Faced with mounting evidence that the *Que Viva Mexico!* material would not be sent to him in the Soviet Union as promised, Eisenstein turned to the development of other projects. In the course of 1932 he made proposals for the theater and some plans for stage productions, including one of Zola's *Thérèse Raquin*, the kind of naturalistic work that would be condemned under socialist realism. In August 1932 Eisenstein began work on the scenario *MMM*, a fantasy and satire for which he intended to cast actors from the eccentric genre of 1920s Soviet screen comedy. *MMM* was titled after its hero Maxim Maximovitch Maximov, a Soviet bureau chief for Intourist who has just assumed his post. The comic action was designed to range across the course of Russian history as Maxim summons people from all social castes to join the contemporary corps of shock-workers and Komsomols (members of the Communist Youth League). In one reflexive sequence scripted for the film, the intersection of different epochs becomes so labyrinthine that the camera retreats from the dramatic action.[18] In the process, the camera discloses that the characters are standing on a gigantic chess board. Also revealed are the film's scriptwriter and director, perched above the action and engaged in discussion over the best way to untangle the current confusion of story lines.

Such modernist relativism, which Eisenstein acknowledged as analogous to the methods in Pirandello's theater, found no support in the studio administration. *The Black Consul*, a script on the Haitian revolution against the French empire, is another project in this period that did not advance into production even though Paul Robeson made himself available for the lead role. Eisenstein also conceived the historical panorama *Moscow*, whose tapestry structure resembled that planned for *Que Viva Mexico!* The new film was intended to approach its subject through episodes drawn from contrasting and diverse epochs, from Russia under the boyars, the reign of Peter I, and up to the massive construction of the

Moscow subway system in progress during the early 1930s. In addition to its historical subject matter, *Moscow* was to feature a primal schema based on imagery of the natural elements water, earth, fire, and air. In 1934 the Moscow studio declined to sponsor this project.

In the course of the two years following his return, Eisenstein became fully involved in the instruction and training of Soviet film artists. During 1928 he had offered a seminar in direction at the State Cinema Polytechnic (GTK). This educational unit was elevated to the highest rank as the State Cinema Institute (GIK) in 1930, in no small measure as a result of Eisenstein's efforts.[19] In 1932 he assumed a regular position with the GIK in the directors faculty. Eisenstein developed a master plan for the institute's curriculum in film direction at the same time that he wrote a summation of his theoretical and practical work in the volume *Direction*. The curriculum Eisenstein devised, and which was in part instituted, was a four-year course of study that involved literature, philosophy, psychology, art history, and natural science in addition to theater arts and cinema.[20]

In March 1935 Eisenstein began to prepare a director's shooting script for *Bezhin Meadow* based on the literary scenario by Alexander Rzheshevsky, which the studio administration had already approved. Over the next two years of production Eisenstein was forced to make major revisions in both the story and the visuals. For his original script Alexander Rzheshevsky took the title from a Turgenev short story. In that story Turgenev's central character is a homely but courageous lad named Pavlusha who, though uneducated and raised on folk truths and tales of ghosts and demons, is a pragmatist free of superstition. In response to companions' fears about evil omens, he has an ordinary explanation for the natural cause of each unnerving sight or sound.[21] The script's main character, Stepok, is modeled on the contemporary Soviet hero Pavlik Morozov, a member of the Komsomol killed by relatives when he attempted to stop their act of sabotage. The nonactor Eisenstein cast in the role was not attractive in person, as Jay Leyda notes in his production diary, but his screen image projects the precocious strength of temperament Turgenev described.[22]

The Rzheshevsky scenario traces a cultural revolution in Soviet peasant society, where the Komsomols struggle against the old laws of patriarchy. The screen story opens with scenes of the countryside in spring and then reveals Stepok by the body of his mother, dead after a beating by Stepok's father. The father remains in his crude hut and, in a drunken rage over Stepok's association with the Communist Youth League, he delivers a curse: "If a son betrays his father, slaughter him like a dog."[23] Stepok and his younger sister leave home for the safety of the village collective. Peasant saboteurs invade the local church, where they are captured by collectivists. Taken under escort along the main road, the prisoners are threatened by field workers until Stepok defuses the crowd's anger with a quickwitted joke and a joyful dance. The collectivists dismantle the local church and convert it into a meeting house. Stepok's father and fellow counterrevolutionaries disarm their guards and flee into the woods. Around the grain fields, young pioneers form the nightly watch against incendiaries. The father fires a rifle and Stepok falls to the ground, mortally wounded. To the dying boy, the father repeats his curse on a son's betrayal: "When the Lord God made Heaven and Earth and people like you and me, my son, He said: 'Go forth and multiply. But when the son betrays the father, kill him like a dog.' " With his remaining strength, Stepok succeeds in alerting other guards to the saboteurs' attack. At dawn, Stepok dies with the *nachpolit* (local chief of political affairs) by his side.

Eisenstein completed principal photography for nearly two-thirds of this material. He did not rigidly follow the script, and widely improvised even on the sound stage. Partial visual analysis of the first version of *Bezhin Meadow* is possible on the basis of frame enlargements and the compilation film constructed by Naum Kleiman and Sergei Yutkevitch. This visual material displays a correlation between men and gods like that in the prologue to *Que Viva Mexico!* While *October* and *Old and New* exposed religion as mythology and ideology, the two later films valorize the mythic consciousness at the core of religion. At work on *Bezhin Meadow*, Eisenstein wrote: "If we turn to the immeasurable treasury of folklore, of outlived and still living norms and forms of behavior preserved by societies still at the dawn of their development, we find that what for them has been or still is a norm of behavior and custom-wisdom turns out to be at the same time precisely what we employ as 'artistic methods' and 'technique of embodiment' in our art-works" (*FF* 131). Rather than project the utopian potential of mechanization or collectivization, the film presents communal society as the humanization of religion.

The father, whose features suggest an Old Testament figure, personifies ancient and repressive Russian orthodoxy. The settings associated with him are dark and menacing. When Stepok visits home for the last time, the grandmother—who in profile looks like a predator—brandishes a heavy, ornate Bible at the boy. Exaggerated perspective, foreshortening, and expressionistic lighting contrast this setting with the bright outdoor life of Stepok and the collective. In leaving his father's home, Stepok escapes the forces of darkness and gains a benevolent family. The father's murder of Stepok, which occurs at nighttime, is a sacrifice exacted by the old, wrathful family order.

The church, a protector of this order, is first shown as a battleground between counterrevolutionaries and collectivists. Saboteurs barricade themselves behind an iconostasis, their rifles aimed through its scrollwork. Dismantling of the church symbolically ends the old familial and spiritual order. This action is not an orgy of destruction, as Party censors claimed. It is instead congenial, particularly in comparison to the bacchanalia Eisenstein had staged for the storming in *October* or that he had read in D. H. Lawrence's *The Plumed Serpent*, where Mexican Indians throw Catholic relics to the flames.

The dismantling is an event of ecstatic contact between two cultures. Peasants are intrigued with the church treasures but not in awe of them as religious symbols. Faces are illuminated by reflections from gilded icons. There is a resemblance between old bearded peasants and paintings of church fathers. Shot compositions align the facial and bodily features of young collectivists with religious images to express an animate and ordinary spirituality. As with *Que Viva Mexico!*'s assertions of human vitalism over religious morbidity, one lad holds up a church death's head at which he grimaces in mockery. In great amusement, peasants and their children costume themselves in clerical robes and regalia. A prelate's crown rests comically askew on a boy's head.

In the dismantling scene, one biblical figure is transposed to the Soviet era. A peasant giant stands between the altar's main pillars as Samson stood between pillars of the Philistine temple. But where Samson was brought captive for the Philistine's amusement and commits suicide in destroying the temple, the Soviet Samson makes sport of razing the Russian Orthodox altar. In doing so, he creates a public, open meeting place from the holy, partitioned sanctuary. *Bezhin Meadow*'s spiritualization of the new differs greatly from the Party piety and ritualism conventional in the Stalin period. In a Stalinist poem by O. Minikh, for example, an oil worker is fatally injured while fighting a fire and, using all his remaining strength, he writes in the sand: "What a pity. I am dying without becoming a member of the Party."[24]

Stepok's death is sensual and passionate. The night scene opens with meditative, somber compositions of mists over the landscape. Bathed by moonlight, lovers meet and embrace in the birch forest. After Stepok is shot, his death throes are enacted as a dance, with a dramatic irony that brings to mind the murder of Vasili as he dances in *Earth*. The religious context relates Stepok's murder specifically with the Passion. While the church's baroque crucifix represents Christ's martyrdom with grotesque religiosity, Stepok's death is an event of ecstatic transfiguration. The sun rises at the moment the boy dies. His body is borne through ripe grain fields by a procession of pioneers.

A corps of youths fills Stepok's place. This narrative closure accords with the "negation of the negation" Engels posits as a general law of dialectics. A key example he develops in *Anti-Dühring* is the growth-germination-death-proliferation cycle of cereal grasses like wheat. In Engels's dialectics, negation of the negation is a mythos of regeneration: from death arises new life in greater numbers. Noting that for the procession a wide-angle lens was selected for both close and long shots, Leyda paraphrases Eisenstein's explanation: "Less corrected lenses, such as the 28. and the 25., . . . give a wide and sharply rounded image, producing a positive sense of strain in the spectator. These shots, coming near the end of the film, should bring a calculated expansion of the heart, and here the greatest tension of both lens and of composition (far and near) may be advisable."[25] Optics are thus intended to facilitate audience identification with the closing moments of ecstasy.

Eisenstein's plans for audiovisual montage involved extensive non-naturalistic effects. When peasants encounter the captured saboteurs on the highway, they shout and whistle in anger. The soundtrack becomes less realistic as peasant hostility rises, until human voices become sirens in pitch and intensity. At this point, visual imagery embodies the acoustical effect: saboteurs are buffeted by the noise. After Stepok's joke discharges the peasants' anger, their laughter visibly sways the surrounding fields and trees.

The montage of speech and image was designed to intensify the drama of family conflict. In their confrontation, the father speaks in monologue while Stepok maintains an unyielding silence. The editing did not maintain the conventional two-shot and shot-reaction shot composition. In one montage, the back of Stepok's head fills the frame while offscreen the father reaches a new peak of rage, which is heard with this visual image of silence. In some two-shots the father's uncontrolled anger contrasts with the grandmother's steady, diabolical stare; two forms of malediction are cast at Stepok.

After censure of the original material during production, Isaac Babel joined Eisenstein in early 1936 to rewrite the script. The assignment was among the last of Babel's sanctioned professional activities. In the course of 1937, publication of his works ceased. Babel was placed under arrest in May 1938 and he died while in retention in March 1941. The filming of *Bezhin Meadow* resumed in the period August to October 1936 with the new script and some new casting in prominent roles. Eisenstein began work on the film's montage in November. On March 17, 1937, all post-production work on *Bezhin Meadow* ceased and the film was entirely banned upon orders of the GUK administration. At the end of March a three-day forum on the failures of *Bezhin Meadow* was conducted.

In the *Bezhin Meadow* script revised by Babel and Eisenstein the general conflict between saboteurs and collectivists remained unaltered. The conflict between father and son, however, was muted from a mythic struggle between old and new beliefs down to a personal and emotional drama. The father is a kulak motivated more by simple possessiveness than by biblical vengeance. In the death scene Stepok cries out in anguish to his father, who responds: "I am here. They wanted to take you away from me. But I would not give you up. My son is my blood."

The second scenario deletes the action of dismantling the church, with its sacramental overtones. To make the context more contemporary and secular, scenes at a tractor station are added and the role of a Party adviser is expanded. A moment of tribute to Stalin is also included. As the night watch forms, Stepok tells fellow pioneers the story of a revolutionary who, before 1917, staunchly endured a beating when caught with radical literature, which he continued to read. Stepok concludes, "Later, he won the revolution." The story is taken from legends about Stalin's militant youth. Eisenstein's few praises in print for Stalin are made in this period as well.

In making revisions, Eisenstein and Babel reduced the story's ecstatic temper and minimized the unconventional audiovisual montage. Despite these concessions and closer bureaucratic supervision, production on *Bezhin Meadow* was terminated. The official explanation by Shumyatsky, published in *Pravda* on March 19, 1937, condemned Eisenstein for developing story elements and imagery independent of the approved script. Shumyatsky censured the film for its "biblical and mythological types," a "pathos of destruction," and the "elemental character of revolutionary forces" it represents.[26] This ideological criticism is accurate in that *Bezhin Meadow* imagines the transformation of a primal, unmerciful patriarchy into a new fraternal order guided by an ideal patriarch. The unfinished film promised a vision of ecstasy much in the cultural spirit of *Que Viva Mexico!*

In April 1937 Eisenstein issued a statement of self-criticism in which he rehearses the faults officials had found in *Bezhin Meadow* and pledges to eliminate the "anarchistic traits of individualism" that remain in his cinema and theory. The self-criticism enumerates the film's formalist mistakes: "The hypertrophy of the settings: the den instead of a hut, the distorted foreshortening in the camera shots and deformed lighting effects. Decorations, scenic effects, lighting—the setting instead of the actor. The same applies to the characters: the image displaces the actor. It is no longer a living face but a mask, the extremes of a generalized 'typification' divorced from the living face, a static image which resembles a frozen gesture."[27] These formal qualities were all intentional. When Eisenstein undertook *Ivan the Terrible*, he knowingly repeated the same "mistakes."

As well as its continuation of typage practices, *Bezhin Meadow* applies in cinema conventions common to Asian theater. The renowned Chinese stage performer Mei Lan-fang and his company appeared in spring 1935 at a Moscow theater conference whose participants included Brecht, Eisenstein, Tretyakov, and Erwin Piscator. Eisenstein recorded on film a scene from the Chinese troupe's repertory to preserve a demonstration of its techniques. In his essay on the performances, Eisenstein values the properties of antirealism in Chinese theater that emphasize imagery at the expense of the concrete.[28] Within these conventions, a concrete stage property can lend itself to a number of recontextualized and ideational meanings.

Stimulated by the same theatrical example, Brecht advanced his ideas on stylization and the distancing effect to be achieved through schematic acting. According to Brecht, the distancing effect proposes to externalize expression and behavior in order to reveal "the gest relevant to society, the gest that allows conclusions to be drawn about social circumstances." In distancing imitation and empathy, the social gest gives spectators "the chance to criticize human behavior from a social point of view, and the scene is played as a piece of history."[29] In Brecht's epic theater no "pure" emotion is intended, nor is character independent of a social mask.

Eisenstein's public confession in 1937 is properly understood in light of his later reflections on the fate of his mentor Meyerhold. Weighing Meyerhold's refusal to retract his theories or compromise his art, Eisenstein drew the following lesson: "Philistinism ensures calm, stability, a deep-rootedness, and the pleasure of recognition . . . where the absence of it condemns a too-romantic nature to the eternal doubts, the searchings, the vicissitudes of fate, and often to the fate of Icarus, to the final way of the Flying Dutchman" (*IM* 161). With the success of his next film, *Alexander Nevsky*, Eisenstein inoculated his career with another dose of philistinism to avert a comparable destiny.

With the ban on *Bezhin Meadow* Eisenstein destroyed the hundreds of work drawings he had prepared during the two years of production, an act that was uncommon for him. The period after *Bezhin Meadow* through the work on *Ivan the Terrible* is increasingly dominated with studies in shadow and darkness under the influence of artists like Goya, Piranesi, and James Ensor. Piranesi's gloomy architecture in the *Prisons* series of engravings was an acknowledged source in sketches for the urban environment during earlier centuries in the proposed film history *Moscow*. Approaching black-and-white cinematography now as composition with "a spectrum of single-tone values," Eisenstein developed a number of projects on the thematics of life's colorfulness "devoured by black." A 1940 proposal for a film on the medieval plague was based in the graphic idea of society progressively engulfed in blackness. A film portrait of Lawrence of Arabia was to examine the shadowy psychological recesses of a "dreadful inner confession of nihilism, of spiritual bankruptcy, and Dostoevskian despair" (*IM* 249, 252). Throughout this period, Eisenstein explores the expressiveness of chiaroscuro, the obscure and troubled aspects of character, and the darkly menacing properties of setting. The full palette for coloration in black is realized in *Ivan the Terrible*.

CHAPTER EIGHT

Alexander Nevsky:
The Great Man in History

During production of *Alexander Nevsky* in the period January through October 1938, Eisenstein reassured studio bureaucrats and Party critics of the film's self-evident, unequivocal political content in developing "the main, the only, the unswerving patriotic theme" (*N* 39). At the film's premiere on November 23, 1938, Stalin is reported to have embraced the director and praised him as "a good Bolshevik." The political rehabilitation of Eisenstein in Soviet society resulted from a combination of factors, including changes within the Directorate for the Cinema Industry, early Party supervision of the *Nevsky* project, and the director's own careful political calculations.

In accounts by close associates, Eisenstein is shown to have been acutely aware that professional survival depended upon decisions made at this juncture in his career. Studio executives had offered Eisenstein a choice of two biographical subjects for his next film, the thirteenth-century leader Alexander Nevsky or Ivan Susanin, the seventeenth-century peasant who gave his life to save that of Michael Romanov, founder of the dynasty that ruled Russia from 1613 to 1917. Eisenstein chose Alexander Nevsky because the subject entailed an earlier, less documented and researched period of history. In conversation with fellow director Mikhail Romm, Eisenstein confided at the time: "Whatever I do the historians and the so-called 'consultants' won't be able to argue with me. They all know . . . that the evidence is slim. So I'm in the strongest possible position, for everything I do must be right."[1]

Eisenstein may have considered that the biographical subjects proposed to him represented a choice not only between two eras but between two movements in Soviet art as well. As a protagonist, Ivan Susanin belongs with the typical heroes of proletarian art like Marfa, who projects the masses' potential through exemplary action. In *Old and New* this heroism takes generative, open, and spontaneous forms that shape history in terms of a promised future. The emphasis in socialist realism, on the other hand, is on legendary heroism mandated by state authority. A process of restoration in the prestige of Russia's national heritage and powerful autocrats had been underway for several years in Soviet culture. In contributing to this restoration, *Alexander Nevsky* presents history as monumental and hieratic through a devotional treatment of the past.

The prototype for the common hero in the 1930s was established with Alexei Stakhanov, the young worker who set productivity records for the coal industry in the 1930s. Proclaimed by Stalin a national hero, Stakhanov became the model for great individual exploits, not only in industry but in science, technology, and exploration as well. The new hero was designated by a family name, *stakhanovite*, rather than by a group title (such as *udarniki*, "shock workers") or a common, generic first name (such as Marfa). An epithet frequently applied to the *stakhanovite* was *bogatyr*, the term for a mythical knight in medieval Russian epic that conveys the connotation of superhuman prowess. *Stakhanovite* art serves a culture of elitism and authoritarianism in place of the egalitarianism and collectivism of proletarian art.

Stalinist Historiography

During World War I, Lenin had denounced "Great Russia" ideology and at the Eighth Party Congress in 1919 he opposed Great Russian chauvinism in the matter of nationalities within the Soviet Republic. In the Bolshevik Revolution's first decade, when Soviet artists turned toward history it was commonly to the immediate past and with an eye toward contemporary revolutionary themes. A standard Soviet textbook—M. N. Pokrovsky's *Brief History of Russia*, published in nearly ten editions through the 1920s—is representative of this cultural attitude. A two-volume work, the *Brief History* covers the feudal and tsarist period from the fourth through the nineteenth centuries in one volume and the revolutionary decade 1896–1906 in the second. Its Marxist interpretation differentiates between periods on the basis of economic structure rather than on political institutions or the succession of rulers. There is little emphasis on personalities, reigns, palace intrigues, or wars. The text rejects any historical explanation of national events as the result of individual leadership. Over the previous century, great-man versions of history had been advanced by thinkers as different as Goethe, Hegel, Carlyle, Nietzsche, Emerson, William James, and Bergson. Pokrovsky treats such historiography as an idealist fallacy that serves the ruling powers of its era.

In the *Brief History* Russia's past becomes a matter of class struggle and of transformation from a feudal economy to a mercantile society and then a capitalist one. Alexander Nevsky receives no attention in the text and only brief mention in the chronological tables. Of feudalism, Pokrovsky makes the following summary statement: "Its essential feature is that all the land with all its inhabitants is the possession of a small number of warlords, who together with their armed retainers rule over the working masses."[2] In terms of this revolutionary historiography, Nevsky's era is an exploitative and socially undeveloped period.

Pokrovsky denied a role in history to exceptional individuals and thus he scorned the supposition that powerful tsars determined Russia's historical development.[3] He also rejected the historical premise that social reform in the course of history was the result of an autocrat's policies. From his perspective, "revolution from above" was inconceivable. The territorial expansion of Russia under the tsars is condemned in the *Brief History* as socially unjust. Subsequent to Stalin's 1931 open letter on history, the schematic and strict economic-materialist approach taken in historiography by Pokrovsky and his followers was officially discredited. Soon after Pokrovsky's death in April 1932 (by natural causes), the Party instituted policies that certified narrative as the correct form for Soviet history and encouraged glorification of the national tradition.

In a 1934 decree circulated among historians and again in a public repudiation issued in 1936, Pokrovsky's *Brief History* was officially denounced for errors in its methods and interpretations. In concert with socialism in one country, the Party advanced nationalism and a reclamation of the tsarist past. With a patriotism unknown in the Revolution's first decade, Soviet culture promoted pride in former territorial expansion and campaigns of national defense and in Russia's power as a nation-state in European and Near Eastern affairs. That Stalin sought counterparts among Russia's medieval heroes and tsars is evident in a Red Square speech of 1942, at the time of Nazi advance on Moscow. He appealed to soldiers and citizens to follow the inspiration of founders of the fatherland like Alexander Nevsky and Dmitri Donskoy, the ruler who defeated occupying Tartar forces in 1380. Stalin proclaimed Nevsky a national hero and created a military order in his name.

With this proclamation, Stalin completed a Soviet campaign that revived the tsarist tradition of revering Alexander Nevsky as a patriot and military leader. The thirteenth-century "Tale of the Life and Courage of the Pious and Great Prince Alexander" is narrated in the style of a saint's life. The first known *vita* of a secular figure in Russian church literature, it venerates Nevsky for defending his country and Eastern Orthodoxy. In 1380 his remains were revealed and the Vladimir churches began to observe the day of his death as that of a saint. In 1547, during the reign of Ivan IV, the Russian Orthodox church canonized Nevsky. In the early eighteenth century Peter I transferred the prince's remains to the site where St. Petersburg was soon to be built and, in 1725, the honorary royal Order of Alexander Nevsky was established.

The active rehabilitation of Russia's tsarist past is symptomatic of the counterrevolutionary direction the Soviet Union takes under Stalin. To cite another relevant indication, in 1933 Stalin reinstituted the internal passport system that was a longstanding policy under tsarism but had been abolished by Bolsheviks after 1917 as an illegal restriction of civil rights. As a hero for the Stalin era, Nevsky is an appropriate figure. His saintliness represented no obstacle for Soviet audiences since adoration toward Stalin was becoming common in the media. Weighing the epithet "Saint" in relation to Nevsky, Eisenstein considers it less a matter of ecclesiastical meaning than one of popular homage, expressive of "the *highest possible appreciation* of merits, such merits for which usual epithets like 'brave,' 'dashing' and 'wise' were insufficient." His authority was paternal. "Adoring crowds" did not distract Nevsky from the nation's cause, though he often had to restrain them with "stern words of warning" (*N* 40). Stalin cultivated a kinship of greatness to make himself the direct descendant of powerful father figures in Russia's past.

The *Alexander Nevsky* assignment developed from the literary scenario *Rus* written by Pyotr Pavlenko, a Soviet novelist who conformed to socialist realist orthodoxy. Pavlenko remained on the project to work closely with Eisenstein on the film's final script. In some accounts of the 1930s by survivors of Stalin's terror, Pavlenko is a sinister figure. Nadezhda Mandelstam, widow of the poet Osip Mandelstam (who died in exile in December 1938), reports that Pavlenko was given permission by the secret police in 1934 to eavesdrop on their nighttime interrogations, including that of her husband.[4] The assignment of a Party-approved artist to "consult" with a suspect artist became common in the Stalin years.

The Pavlenko-Eisenstein script contains a historical transubstantiation whereby the deceased Alexander Nevsky is made flesh in Dmitri Donskoy, his great-great grandson, who secured Russia's eastern border with victory over the Tartars. In an unproduced scene that originally concluded the narrative, a proposed matching shot seams together events separated by over one hundred years: Nevsky's funeral procession and Donskoy's campaign. This montage association is designed to redeem the unheroic actions of Nevsky in the matter of Russia's eastern and southern frontiers. Nevsky came under the sway of Tartar power and collaborated with the Golden Horde in maintaining Russian obedience to the Eastern khans. His alliance with the khans is customarily interpreted as a strategy of appeasement devised to allow Russia to secure her endangered western and northern borders and to protect the weaker principalities of Novgorod and Vladimir from Tartar invasion.

The fact remains, however, that Tartar garrisons were maintained in Russian regions and heavy foreign taxes were imposed on the populace. Novgorod rose in revolt against the Eastern presence, but Alexander Nevsky helped suppress the popular liberation effort. Early Soviet historians openly recount these events and offer them as counterevidence to the saint legend.[5] The Pavlenko-Eisenstein script, on the other hand, represents Nevsky as independent of the Eastern khans. For the facts of Russia's subjugation to the Golden Horde with the collaboration of Nevsky, the script substitutes scenes of Donskoy's later Eastern victory. The film script greatly advances the legend of Alexander Nevsky as it suppresses a significant portion of the historical record.

Glorification of the tsarist past was unknown during the silent period of Soviet cinema. As late as 1934, with the release of Alexander Feinzimmer's *Lieutenant Kije*, tsarist politics were unsparingly satirized. The film's script, written by Yuri Tynyanov, involves a military officer who exists only on paper. While Tsar Paul I is convinced of the man's existence, in order to put an end to the fiction his aides stage a funeral, at which Paul weeps. Paul was a tyrannical, unpredictable ruler with a preference for Prussian military customs and under him St. Petersburg became the scene of endless parades and ceremonies in the 1790s. The script gives Feinzimmer and Sergei Prokofiev, who composed the musical score, occasion for broad farcical and mock-heroic strokes. *Lieutenant Kije* employs eccentric acting techniques from the silent era and it borders on black comedy in the depiction of Paul's militarism and despotism. The grotesquerie on Russian subject matter in Prokofiev's score was the kind of music condemned in *Pravda* two years later in an editorial critical of Dmitri Shostakovich's latest opera.

By the late 1930s Soviet films no longer present Russia's tsarist past through satire or invective. Pudovkin's *Minin and Pozharsky* (1939), scripted by Viktor Shklovsky, is indicative of the new historical trend. This spectacle film dramatizes the alliance between the commoner Kuzma Minin and Prince Dmitri Pozharsky in the popular war they led against Polish domination in the early seventeenth century. Shklovsky and Pudovkin's reconstruction of the period emphasizes a progressive element within Russia's aristocracy and shows the prince to be a patriot acting on behalf of the masses. As well as being anti-Polish at a time when Germany and the Soviet Union negotiated the partition of Poland, the film takes a conciliatory attitude toward the role of the ruling classes in Russian history.

In his report to the Seventeenth Party Congress, held in 1934, Stalin distorts Marx's thinking on social equality under communism and brands the goal of egalitarianism "bourgeois" and "infantile."[6] As early as 1931 Stalin had expressed admiration for Peter I with an explanation that it was an error of vulgar Marxism to discount the role of great individuals in history. Autocracy was justified because Peter alone foresaw Russia's destiny and pursued it through Westernization and modernization. In 1721 Peter had himself acclaimed "Father of the Fatherland, Peter the Great, Emperor of All Russia." A similar glorification of Stalin as supreme father of the Soviet Union became central to his personality cult. In his radio speech declaring to the Soviet people war on Germany, he pronounced the official slogan for the national cause: "The Second War for the Fatherland" (the first was fought against Napoleon under Tsar Alexander I). A revival of tsarist nationalism, the slogan also points toward the paternal iconography fostered in Stalinist culture.

Tracing the dissemination of Stalinist ideology through prose and poetry, Katerina Clark finds that from the mid-1930s through the war years literary content advances a distinctly paternal model of society. The new man or woman proved Soviet superiority—whether it be in industry, technology, or culture—as a loyal son or daughter of the State with Stalin as helmsman and father.[7] The epithets automatically attached to Stalin's name sound a litany in praise of a supreme father. A sample of the leader cult rhetoric is contained in the lead article to a 1936 issue of the journal *October:* "All the thoughts and feelings of our great people are turned toward him, the father of the Soviet Union, the bright sun of humanity, the greatest genius of our age, toward our dear Stalin."[8] At times a neoprimitive note is struck in the formulas: "the leader of mankind, the chieftain of the people."[9] Customs of filial obedience were promoted within the Party and among the populace.

The Party purges of the 1930s left no influential eyewitnesses of the October days and the early Soviet years to challenge a new version of events. The revisions to Bolshevik history establish Stalin's rights of copaternity with Lenin for the 1917 revolution. A film on this period that gained Stalin's praise is Mikhail Romm's *Lenin in October* (1937), which premiered as part of the twentieth anniversary celebration. Alexei Kapler's script has Trotsky, Kamenev, and Zinoviev act in cowardly and traitorous ways, while Stalin is Lenin's indispensable collaborator in engineering the October Revolution. Not the massive, frenetic, seemingly spontaneous action Eisenstein depicts in *October,* the Revolution Romm presents is managed by great leaders with the assistance of businesslike Bolsheviks and orderly militiamen. With Lenin's proclamation of the Revolution's success at the Congress of Soviets, Romm's film has Stalin appear in the immediate background and the screen frame encloses a double portrait.[10]

Stalin delighted in seeing himself portrayed in drama and film and *Lenin in October* was shown frequently in the Kremlin. Romm received a commission to direct the sequel, *Lenin in 1918* (1939), in which the part of Stalin is taken by Mikhail Gelovani, who was to play the role in over twenty films through the remaining years of Stalin's life. Insight into Stalin's sensibilities as a film viewer is provided by Milovan Djilas, who observed the Soviet leader during the customary after-dinner screenings: "Throughout the showing Stalin made comments—reactions to what was going on, in the manner of uneducated men who mistake artistic reality for actuality."[11]

The autocratic nature of Stalin's involvement with Soviet culture is vividly conveyed in an incident recounted by Viktor Shklovsky concerning production on *Alexander Nevsky*.[12] During the final stages of editing, the studio was instructed late one night to rush the film to the Kremlin for a private screening. At the time Eisenstein was still at work on a reel containing an early scene of civil strife in Novgorod. In the haste to deliver the film, this reel was left behind. After Stalin viewed the rough cut and expressed his delight, no one dared inform him that the film he approved was incomplete. *Alexander Nevsky* was thus released in an incomplete version; the reel in question has not been recovered. Were it not for the fate of prominent artists like Meyerhold, Babel, Tretyakov, and Mandelstam in the 1930s, this incident might seem simply an example of grotesque political farce.

An Iconography of Leadership

Pavlenko and Eisenstein acknowledged indebtedness to the earliest accounts of Alexander Nevsky for their film script. Probably written, in the original version, by a member of Alexander's retinue, the "Tale" was rewritten around 1280 by an unidentified cleric and this more religious version was embellished by later church scribes. In a fifteenth-century text, Alexander's power is said to be that of Samson and his God-given wisdom that of Solomon, placing him above the already exalted plane of the bogatyr.[13] His military exploits are depicted as a holy campaign to preserve the Eastern church and are accompanied by accounts of visions and miracles. His victory in battle at Lake Chudskoe is proof that "god glorified Alexander." A miraculous event is described in connection with Alexander's burial and the "Tale" concludes with the coda "Glory be to God, who glorifies his saints, forever and ever."

As reflected in Eisenstein's three sound films, Soviet culture in the Stalin period advances a social division that makes for individuation only among a select leadership and for an anonymous collectivity at all other levels. The masses are entitled to a few leader figures from among their ranks, like Alexei Stakhanov, but these invariably serve the greater glory of the supreme leader. The Great Leader, through his fatherly concern and wisdom, guides the common people toward a historic future. *Alexander Nevsky* concentrates on heroic individuality as the visual dominant.

Panoramas of a land littered with weapons and skeletons of soldiers killed in battle stand as prelude to the drama. Prominent in the foreground of one shot are two skulls, one still topped by a helmet. (The composition evokes imagery from *Que Viva Mexico!* and is perhaps Eisenstein's valedictory tribute to this unfinished film.) The first foreign threat depicted is from the East. A Tartar convoy containing Russian prisoners stops near the banks of Lake Pleshcheyev and demands tribute money from the fishermen. A Russian adolescent, encountering these invaders for the first time, looks on dumbfounded as villagers drop to their knees at the command of a Mongol horseman. Both his astonishment and the truth of Russian servitude are accented by use of the screen frame. A shot in which only a man's legs are in view is followed by a shot of his lowered body, now fully in view. In composition, the montage makes tangible the man's act of lowering himself in obeisance to a foreign master. A blow from the horseman causes the adolescent to fall as well.

In a visually literalized sense, Prince Alexander Nevsky stands as the alternative to such subjugation. With Russian and Mongol voices raised in argument, Nevsky turns from the net he holds in the lake's shallow waters and, in a close shot that identifies him for the first time, complains: "What's the bellowing about—you'll frighten the fish!"[14] Leading the other fishermen, he strides to the roadside and, without any sign of deference, warns the Mongol soldiers to stop their harassment. At this, a warlord draws back the curtains of his palanquin and, learning of Alexander's identity, descends to meet the renowned prince. The Eastern tyrant advises Nevsky to join the Golden Horde as a military commander in a manner and voice that is ironic, flattering, conspiratorial. The demeanor of the Russian prince is direct, severe, independent. With a voice that "reverberates like a manifesto," as the script describes it, Nevsky refuses: "We have a saying—die on your native land, don't abandon it." The warlord returns to his cart, ascending over the back of a kneeling slave.

With the warlord's departure, Nevsky remembers the fishing nets he has left and rushes back to the lake. A light, comic effect is created in foreshortened shots of the prince running through ankle-deep water, making him appear like a prancing youth. In the plain broadcloth of fellow fishermen, he at first does not have the appearance of the great victor over the Swedes at the River Neva, the deed that gained him the epithet Nevsky and that—historically—had taken place two years prior to events in the opening action. The initial impression of princeliness is not based on artificial distinctions but on his fearless assertion of patriotism.

One-shot compositions encode his status as a natural leader, with background panoramas that connect him with water, the land, and the skies. The warlord, in contrast, is shown in severe low angles against bleak, featureless backgrounds. Nevsky is in his native element and stands as leader among his people. The iconography of the supreme patriot as a saint carries an intimation here that Nevsky, like Christ, is a fisher of men. The people, for their part, confide in him and trust his judgment. The relationship of leader to people possesses an apparent social asymmetry. By film's end, Nevsky seems monumental and infallible.

Eisenstein indicates that a major problem encountered in writing the script was in developing scenes to convey Alexander's genius, which he defines as "an ability to apply deductions drawn from minor chance instances to unexpected major phenomena" (*N* 44). In its dramatization of Nevsky as he is engaged in forming military strategy against Teuton invaders, the film gives functional roles to common sense and folk truths to signify his status as a popular leader. As Nevsky and a soldier are reconnoitering frozen Lake Chudskoe, the soldier's horse falls to the icy surface. The embarrassed rider complains to his mount, "What are you slipping for?," to which Alexander musingly responds, "Hooves slipping?" This moment's reflection is translated a breath later into an important decision: "This is the place to attack their cavalry, right here. . . ."

A second inspiration comes when the armorer Ignat recounts a folktale to soldiers gathered around a fire in camp. To the men, "The Hare and the Vixen" is merely an amusing, risqué story. To Nevsky it provides the kernel for victorious strategy. The tale tells of a hare who outfoxes a vixen. The hare maneuvers her between two birch trees and announces, "Better say bye-bye to your maidenhood." While the men laugh Nevsky muses, "Between two birch trees. . . . And pounced?" The tale's punchline prompts him to devise a pincer tactic to pin and devastate the Teuton battle wedge. The scene portrays Nevsky as a desexualized personality. He does not share in the soldiers' ribald pleasure; he is above carnality. In the film's subplot lesser characters have romantic interests, but Nevsky has none.

The legendary heroism in *Alexander Nevsky* differs from the typical heroism in the Vasilievs' *Chapayev*, where the famous Red Army commander of the civil war period is an earthy, passionate, and fallible character. In one memorable scene, Chapayev plans battle tactics on a cluttered dining table with the use of potatoes and an aide's pipe. Characteristically, in the battle that follows he does not use his own stated tactics. Though Furmanov, the region's Bolshevik commissar, has some success in instilling discipline and political consciousness in Chapayev, the leader loses none of his raw energy, humor, or spontaneity and remains a folk hero throughout the film.

After the first scene, Nevsky is put at an increasing distance from the populace. Before delegates from Novgorod are permitted into his humble quarters, Nevsky changes his plain tunic for a finer one, more suitable to his rank. The costume change prefigures personality changes that follow. In accepting the petition to protect Russia, Nevsky accepts the sacred mantle of his country's cause. His boldness and supreme leadership are signaled by a refusal to defend and a promise to attack. Nevsky no longer stands among the people but above and in front of them—positions the film visually reiterates, even in scenes where Nevsky is surrounded by soldiers and commoners. The burden of patriotic leadership falls on Nevsky alone and separates him increasingly from the common people.

The common folk heroes are Ignat and the two warriors Vasili Buslai and Gavrilo Oleksich. According to Eisenstein, in the original scenario the armorer was meant to embody the people's patriotic spirit, while each warrior was to reflect an attribute perfected in Nevsky's personality. Vasili was to represent boldness and Gavrilo wisdom, but these distinctions are lost in the film itself as the two compete over the maiden Olga. They display the masculine sexuality absent from the characterization of Nevsky. Their exaggerated manliness and battlefield prowess place them in the epic tradition of the bogatyr peasant knight, whose prodigious exploits earn him social rank. In figures like that of the *stakhanovite*, Stalinist culture promoted a similar meritocracy.

Use of the epic type should be distinguished from typage, which functions in Eisenstein's silent films to represent the divisions and dynamics of class conflict. Such conflict is broached and then deflected early in *Alexander Nevsky*. Novgorod's merchants voice strong opposition to the commoners' plea to summon Alexander. Their policy is appeasement on the grounds that trade can continue only if war is avoided. At a public assembly, they occupy prominent positions atop the tribune. Popular consensus prevails, however, and patriots gain elevated positions on the platform. What at first appears like class conflict quickly becomes a question of Russian patriotism. Having worn fisherman's sackcloth at the film's opening, Nevsky is subsequently absolved of class considerations. This is to say that the film's intentions are mythic rather than ideographic or historiographic. Similar transpositions operate in Stalin's reclamation of the tsarist past.

In making a patriotic leadership myth of Russia's feudal past, *Alexander Nevsky* makes the same myth for the Soviet present, as is suggested in Eisenstein's comment "I was making a film that was, first and foremost, a *contemporary* one" (N 37). In explanation of Nevsky's "saintliness," he states: "The gist of the matter lies in the true popular love and veneration which surround the name of Alexander Nevsky to this day. In this sense the epithet is highly revealing. It shows that that hero and man of genius saw far ahead of what he was doing: he saw Russia great and unified. And the people felt it in the commanding personality of Alexander Nevsky" (N 40). In logic and rhetoric, this statement echoes the cult of leadership under Stalin.

That a perspective other than historical materialism controls the narrative is nowhere clearer than in a speech by Domash Tverdislavich, who is initially called upon to defend Novgorod: "A great misfortune is approaching, it will require great men of us. I am not the one you need, but another—a man with a stronger hand and a clearer head, one whose renown is spread throughout the realm, and who is known to the enemy. . . . And that man, brothers, is Prince Alexander Yaroslavich!" In later scenes the film's visuals tend to treat Nevsky as a living monument. Shots of Nevsky are frequently static and ponderous, and compositions are weighted down with his heroic presence. Mounted and armed in battle he often seems like an overscale equestrian statue. The stasis and monumentality in visual treatment becomes especially noticeable in comparison to *Chapayev*, in which the hero frequently seems uncomfortably constrained by the screen's frame. Nevsky is always perfectly posed within the frame.

Toward the film's conclusion Nevsky praises and reproves the Russian people. Victory has been won and the populace has assembled in Pskov. Nevsky begins with a stern caution against betraying the national cause: "It's all shouting and more shouting, with not a thought for the battle, gentlemen of Pskov and Novgorod. But you may rest assured that I would make war on you too, whip you mercilessly, if you were to let the battle on the ice go for nought. . . . So remember it well, tell your children and your grandchildren. For if you forget, you will be a second Judas—Judas to the Russian land." With approval of the popular assembly, Nevsky sets the Teuton foot soldiers free and suggests exchanging the knights in barter for soap. The proposal arouses great mirth among the people, who are stopped short with a disapproving look and chastening words from Nevsky: "You're all ready to be entertained, all full of jokes." Similar warnings and threats against internal wreckers of society and enemies of the state are common to Stalinist literature.

The romantic-comic business of settling the contest between Vasili and Gavrilo for Olga's hand follows. Vasili's domineering mother presses Nevsky to decide in favor of her son, who timidly pronounces Gavrilo bravest of the two. To compensate his mother for having defied and shamed her, Vasili takes the hand of Vasilisa, a heroine of the battle. Alexander smiles approvingly at the two matches and announces that the revels may begin. His position in this comic sequence is, by figurative implication, that of a benevolent father standing to the other side of a domineering mother.

In the closing dramatic shots the patriotic hero Nevsky speaks as the nation's patriarch. Positioned directly in front of the camera and in close shot, he addresses viewers in a commanding manner: "Go and tell all in foreign parts that Rus lives. Let people come to us as guests without fear. But he who comes with a sword shall die by the sword. On this Rus stands and will forever stand!" Though *Alexander Nevsky* remains largely within the leadership cult and the official style, it does not reach the extremes of heroism and paternalism found in films on Stalin of the 1930s and 1940s.

Gelovani's impersonations of Stalin are worshipful and wooden. A pipe often provides character business and, accompanied by the actor's fixed stare and knitted brow, it serves as a token of Stalin's deep intellect. Typically there is a key dramatic scene in which Stalin deliberates the people's fate. Only a few moments alone in silence are needed for the nation's wise father to set a historic course. With *Ivan the Terrible,* Eisenstein was to challenge openly this leadership myth.

Alexander Nevsky's narrative and iconographic structure maintains the premise that the nation can defend against its enemies only through a strong leader. Not least among these enemies are disloyal Russian elements. Two prominent characters conspire with the Teutons: Pskov's mayor Tverdilo, the historical figure who betrayed his city, and Ananias, a fictive creation who appears to belong to a mendicant order. Tverdilo's betrayal of Russia is open while that of Ananias, named after the early Christian in the New Testament who is struck dead for lying, is covert. Both characters are the object of anticlerical satire. Tverdilo, unaccustomed to Latin liturgical rites, entangles his hands in trying to cross himself in the new manner. The two display servile obedience and are often seen in postures of slavish worship toward the Teuton knights and monks. Tverdilo's treachery is epitomized in the scene where he stabs the patriot Ignat in the back. Once captured, Tverdilo is paraded into liberated Pskov draped in an ass's harness and bells and then left to the people's judgment. Through an ellipsis similar to one in *Potemkin,* a crowd engulfs Tverdilo until he disappears from view. Satiric elements and visual euphemism isolate Tverdilo's fate from any associations to violence committed by Russians. Ananias has already been destroyed on the field of battle by Vasilisa.

By the time of production on *Alexander Nevsky,* a Soviet film genre on the theme of foreign threat had emerged. Over the two-year period 1938–39, six anti-Fascist films were released, but among them only Eisenstein's film depicted a defense taken on Russian soil against foreign aggression.[15] In *Alexander Nevsky* the foreign enemy is a faceless, mechanical, relentless force and its troop formations appear at first to be an invincible battery. The depiction suggests a comparison between German armored knights and Nazi panzer divisions, whose destructiveness was just becoming evident. The Teutons engage in a slaughter of innocents. Knights throw infants into the fires of the devastated city of Pskov as a monk intones, "Die in order that ye may be saved." But *Nevsky* does not rival *Strike* or *Potemkin* in visceral details of mutilation and slaughter. Bloody images scripted—such as that of a decapitated Russian volunteer—do not appear in the finished film. In another case, the script has Russian troops seize the bodies of fallen comrades and thrust them onto the spears of

advancing Germans as a defensive measure, a scene which has no counterpart in the released film.

Views of wartime horror in *Alexander Nevsky* are for the most part
confined to early film scenes depicting the German sack of Pskov and are
based on a conjunction of three images: soldiers' spears mingled with
Latin crosses, the hangman's crossbar and noose, and the smoke from
fires of pillage and execution. In the Roman church's name, Teuton strategy depends upon the decimation of civilian populations and a scorched
earth policy. The scenes additionally evoke impressions of barbaric practices in modern warfare, such as the Fascist devastation of Guernica in
1936.

To convey the terror such tactics create, Eisenstein includes segments
of extra-diegetic action comparable to one montage within the Odessa
steps sequence. After general views of the destruction in Pskov we see
women, many with infants in their arms, cower and recoil from some offscreen threat. This action is repeated two times in the scene, but at first
the composition is not a reaction shot in the conventional sense. Breaking
the editing sequence of shot-reaction shot, which establishes a cause-and-
effect relationship, Eisenstein shows the effect before disclosing its cause.
The first reaction, like the moment of panic when the dark-haired woman
on the Odessa steps turns her head wildly, discloses utter, uncontrollable
fear. The women recoil a second time in reaction to a Teuton order given
to execute the men of Pskov and a third time in reaction to the approach
of Teuton footsoldiers ordered to seize the children.

The corps of monks is perhaps more terrifying than the German
knights and troops. Almost as large in number as the army itself, the Latin
order is cloaked and cowled in white and each cleric bears a staff-length
cross. Ranked in unbroken lines with the soldiers, the order is a featureless, seemingly inexorable force. In a reversal of the conventions of color
symbolism similar to the reversal found in Melville's *Moby-Dick*, as Eisenstein later commented, the utter whiteness in the Teutons' apparel is
associated with cruelty, oppression, and nihilism. There is a single black
figure among the Teutons, the sinister monk who blesses Russian infants
thrown into the flames. His gnarled, predatory features lurk within a
black cowl. The spiritual leader of the Latin crusade is an old and frail
bishop whose sharp features are expressive of the church's fanaticism. The
crosses monks bear are more like implements of war than signs of holi-
ness. Later, when the German rear camp is overrun, the monks raise
their crosses as battle weapons.

Spiritual truth is fully on the side of Russian patriots and those who
die for the national cause are martyrs. Pskov's military leader Pavsha is
bound, beaten, and finally drawn by ropes up the side of a church tower.
Suspended above the carved relief figure of an angel, at the moment of

death he tells survivors to summon Alexander. The sanction of his dying plea indicates that only Alexander will gain the country's salvation. Later, on the eve of battle, the fallen Domash is carried back to the Russian camp. As Alexander looks down on the corpse, he vows that German soldiers shall not advance on the homeland. The scene has all the appearances of a sacred occasion.

Comic touches are set against images of terror in early scenes. Before we see any of their faces, Teuton knights are individuated by their headgear, while regular soldiers wear identical helmets whose eye and mouth slits form a cross. The knights' full-face helmets are adorned with personal insignia that caricature the invaders' reputation for invincibility. These range from spikes, vanes, animal horns, and replicas of regal birds to an oversized, open hand. Another comic effect is created by having the old bishop and the black monk act as leaders in the Teuton camp. Their small, stooped, scampering movements make a humorous contrast to the master knights' self-conscious grandeur. While the German vanguard is literally encased in steel, the mass of Russian peasant volunteers are minimally equipped and possess an appearance of human vulnerability and courage. Eisenstein's scenes of combat evoke both an original kenning for battle— "web of men"—and the early Renaissance battleground images painted by Paolo Uccello.

Before it is clear that the tide of battle will turn in favor of the Russians, there are several scenes of epic buffoonery. Ignat, exchanging blows with an enemy soldier, gives a professional opinion on the temper of Teuton steel. Nevsky and Vasili playfully criticize the quality of the armorer's own work, injuring his professional pride. Without a helmet through much of the battle, Vasili remains highly visible in the tangle of lances, men, and horses. He pauses to lift a keg of ale from a Russian supply cart, drinks it in one long gulp, wipes his mouth, rubs his hands together, and rejoins the battle that has continued unabated around him. For Vasili warfare is great sport and he wields a sword as though he were in a woodchopping competition. When the sword breaks he is tossed a pole, with which he batters an enemy knight, bashing his helmet down until it is locked shut. The imagery of superior Russian phallic prowess is unmistakable.

The humorous tone indicates that Russian victory is a foregone conclusion. Without the suspense, peripeteia, and pathos of *Potemkin*, the Battle on the Ice is a patriotic and often comic epic. When repulse of the Teutons turns to rout, the action is accelerated. Filmed in summer under cloudless skies, the battle scene required special lens filters and slow camera speeds to suggest the icy expanses and low skies of a Russian winter. Projected at normal speed, shots of Germans in retreat produce a hurried effect associated with slapstick chase scenes. Fleeing across the frozen lake, the heavily armored knights break through the ice near shore. Camera shots are held until their helmets' insignia and plumage have sunk out of view and bubbles rise to the water's surface. The Teutons' inhuman and mechanical appearance, which is at first terrifying, has become ridiculous by the time they are last glimpsed. Comic elements carry over into the victory celebration as the romantic ties between Vasili, Gavrilo, and Olga are further complicated, then resolved.

Opera in the National Defense

At the time of their collaboration on *Alexander Nevsky*, Prokofiev invited Eisenstein to direct his new opera, *Semyon Kotko*, a heroic piece set in the Revolutionary period. Prokofiev explained: "I somehow *a priori* believe in Eisenstein—as an opera *régisseur!*"[16] Eisenstein declined, however, and he was soon fully engaged in preproduction on *Ferghana Canal*, a historical film panorama set in central Asia whose contemporary episode would concern the massive Soviet construction of a canal in the region. When this film project was canceled Eisenstein did go on to stage an opera production—Wagner's *Die Walküre* at the Bolshoi Theater in November 1940, during the period of the Soviet-German Nonaggression Pact (August 1939–June 1941).

In the first scene of *Alexander Nevsky*, choral song completely precedes the dialogue. Fishermen peacefully at work and peasants on surrounding hills join voices to sing "It was on the River Neva," which recounts the Russian victory over Swedish invaders. Then a Tartar entourage arrives to interrupt the harmonious mood, and dramatic dialogue begins. The subsequent choral piece, "Arise people of Rus," incorporates elements of nineteenth-century Russian opera with folk music traditions. First sung following the summons of Alexander at Lake Pleshcheyev, the vigorous composition is a rallying cry to mobilize peasants. Volunteers emerge from fields and huts to march to Novgorod. Though in context a marching song, its presentation relies on conventions of the film soundtrack rather than those of opera; that is, the verse is not dramatically delivered onscreen. In heroic measure a male chorus intones, "No enemy foot shall tread Rus, / No armies shall enter her bounds." It is joined in the final stanza by a female chorus to sing the lines "Fame and glory to her living warriors, / Everlasting honor to the dead!" The next scene, set in Novgorod, is accompanied with an orchestral arrangement of the choral music. The song itself is taken up three times in the scene and at points dramatic dialogue overlaps the choral verses.

The most sustained passages of high opera in *Alexander Nevsky* are in the night scene following the Battle on the Ice, as Russian women search for loved ones among the wounded and dead on a frozen plain. The aftermath of combat makes an uncannily quiet sight. A faint, sparsely orchestrated theme rises gradually on the soundtrack. The chords darken and the theme is more forcefully articulated as women approach from a distance. When Olga comes forward a restrained, mournful theme is stated at a higher volume. After naturalistic groans of a fallen soldier are heard, Olga's mezzo-soprano aria begins. She remains in long shot and at times the aria is punctuated by the voice of a wounded patriot calling out a woman's name.

The scene's epic and pathetic seriousness is carried in Olga's verse:

> From their wounds warm, red blood like rain was shed
> On our native soil, on our Russian fields.
> He who fell for Russia in noble death
> Shall be blessed by my kiss on his dead eyes.

The theatrical appearance of this scene, produced entirely in a studio, is appropriate to the operatic style. The aria and accompanying music stop when Olga reaches Vasili, who despite his own wounds is aiding the more severely injured Gavrilo. In an effort to stir him back to life, Vasili swears that Gavrilo has acted braver in battle and thus wins Olga. The two men, drawing on their remaining strength, stagger across the battlefield with the support of Olga. The opening orchestral theme resumes by this point, but its pathos is lost with the unintentionally comic sight of two rivals in love on their last legs.

The most distinctive element in the soundtrack score is the comic. Prokofiev had returned to the Soviet Union in 1932, having left in 1918 for the United States and residing there and in Europe for a fourteen-year period. The first Soviet work he completed was a film score composed in 1933 for *Lieutenant Kije*, the farce on tsarist militarism. In keeping with that film's story line, the music is rich in irony and parody. Alert to the socialist realism mandate in Soviet art, Prokofiev published a statement in 1934 that distinguishes works in music of great artistic ambition from those which are simply popular in their intentions. Characterizing himself as a composer in both categories, Prokofiev announced his commitment to create "lightly serious" and "seriously light" music that would be accessible to all Soviet listeners.[17] The film music to *Alexander Nevsky* clearly follows this stated purpose.

Humor in Prokofiev's works can range from the lyrically capricious to the grotesquely satiric. His humor—like that of other Russian composers such as Modest Mussorgsky and Shostakovich—is a popular element that often derives from a descriptive use of musical effects, as in *Peter and the Wolf* (1936). In a serious vein, discordant counterpoint and graphic noise are employed in Prokofiev's *The Age of Steel* (1927) to portray the sounds of factory work and urban life. Collaboration with Eisenstein required

Prokofiev to create descriptive music of a peculiar sort. In celebration of Russian victory, medieval musicians play pipes and drums with great enthusiasm. The director's original plan was to film matching shots to the music Prokofiev composed for the occasion. When the composer failed, as Eisenstein tells it, to discover "what precise effect should be 'seen' in his music for this joyful moment," they tried an opposite approach. Production designers fashioned prop instruments and Eisenstein "shot these being played (without sound) visually" (FS 158). With the visual material at hand, Prokofiev composed musical equivalents to accompany the actor instrumentalists' pantomime.

In *Alexander Nevsky* there is also descriptive music of the conventional kind that imitates natural sounds and physical movements. In the Russians' rout of Teuton knights, the correspondence creates satiric effects. Using phrases and rhythms from vaudeville and film chase music, the score combines this clownish flavor with an uptempo Russian theme that conveys the exhilaration of victory. Recorded over this music are heavy, prolonged notes from war horns in a restatement of earlier music announcing the German attack. In its reiterated form, the German theme is deflated. No longer the battle cry of a noble and invincible army, it now suggests the last cries of a wounded, pursued animal. The chase comes to an abrupt end when ice breaks under the weight of German armor. Kettledrums, cymbals, and lighter drums provide a harsh, dissonant tone in accompaniment to the noise of breaking ice. The German horn theme is repeated a final time over shots of knights sinking from view. The enemy's martial music grinds to a comic halt as the last knight disappears: a horn glissando runs ridiculously down the scale as bubbles, their sound amplified, rise to the water's surface.

More original musical-visual satire is contained in scenes with the Teuton monks. They deliver a Latin chant whose text, apparently composed by Eisenstein and Prokofiev, reads: *Peregrinus expectavi / Pedes meos in cymbalis* (A foreigner, I expected / My feet to be shod with cymbals). Its verse bordering on nonsense, the chant is a musical antithesis to the stirring, patriotic Russian songs. Structured somewhat like a Gregorian chant and sung like a dirge, the Latin hymn characterizes the invaders' bloodthirsty religiosity. When first heard during the sack of Pskov, the hymn's melody is dark and forbidding. On the eve of battle, in a church service to bless the army, monks in white chant the hymn as the black monk accompanies them on a small pipe organ. The organ's rasping sound, in combination with close-ups of the monk's grotesque, cadaverous face, caricatures Teuton spirituality. When the soldiers assemble for combat, chanting stops but the black monk continues to play the organ. Without choral embellishment and played to the percussive tattoo of horses' hooves, the music's religious tone disappears and its essential military nature becomes fully evident. The organ theme is repeated later when the German monks attempt to use their crosses as battle axes against Russian soldiers.

A contrast in musical styles restates the conflict between Russians and Teutons. Russians are portrayed through clearly stated, warm harmonies with an emphasis on strings and woodwinds in orchestration, and through melodies based in folk idioms. The musical impression is of a people self-sacrificing, united, and heroic and of events that cause sorrow but that ultimately reforge the people's will. Program music, in wide disrepute in Europe during the century, was in strong Soviet favor. Its external, naturalistic, and pictorial qualities accorded with socialist realism, which denounced the tendencies of modernist music as subjective and pathological. Modernist traits in Prokofiev's most ambitious Soviet compositions ultimately led, in 1948, to criticism by the Central Committee of the composer for a grotesque and satiric temperament and a failure to express the greatness of Soviet reality.

Prokofiev's modernist experimentation in the *Alexander Nevsky* soundtrack is judiciously limited to Teuton themes in creating a sound portrait of barbarism. Most strongly stated in scenes of the Pskov sack and the knights' "swine" formation, these themes are complex and polytonal in construction, heavy and mechanical in their rhythms, and strident in instrumentation, with emphatic drums and shrill brass. Prokofiev used technical shortcomings in the sound-recording process to advantage in capturing the low, fearsome notes of German war horns, whose sound in the bottom registers is noticeably distorted. The ugliness and dissonance that result represent Russia's enemies as repulsive and inhuman. Restatement of the Teuton themes reduces them to ridicule in their final versions.

The anti-Fascist parody and farce in *Alexander Nevsky*, perhaps its most original element, brings to mind two superior films of the period, Chaplin's *The Great Dictator* (1940) and Ernst Lubitsch's *To Be or Not to Be* (1942), in which the mystique of German invincibility is exposed as a lunatic absurdity. With actual war being waged against Fascism, fiction film could fight only a mock battle and an effective artistic weapon was mockery itself. In an appreciation of *The Great Dictator*, Eisenstein suggests the film is Chaplin's comic vengeance against Hitler for having appropriated the Tramp's famous little moustache (*N* 199–202). Through satiric manipulation, the pomp and regalia of the Third Reich—its uniforms, salutes, symbols, monumental art and architecture, and mass rallies—are presented as the third-rate stuff of man's fantasies of conquest and power. Though the Eisenstein and Chaplin films contain scenes of military domination and religious persecution, they both comically assert a confidence that German vainglory will prove self-destructive.

Art comes into conflict with the Nazis in *To Be or Not to Be* and art—second-rate art at that—wins. The ham actor Joseph Tura (Jack Benny) is called upon by Polish patriots to impersonate two members of the Nazi occupation forces. The impersonations are successful because Tura's ham acting looks natural and is convincing in the new roles. Another minor actor parades around Warsaw disguised as Hitler; his success indicates that there is nothing intrinsically unique or superior about the Führer. In full-dress uniform the figure looks like a supernumerary from some absurd opera or costume spectacle. While political farce in *To Be or Not to Be* reaches the proportions of black comedy, it does not in *Alexander Nevsky*. The flavor of black comedy is present, however, in the grotesque style of *Ivan the Terrible*.

By comparison to Eisenstein's earlier theories and proposals on sound, *Alexander Nevsky* seems conventional. The 1928 statement on sound cinema specified that its artistic development depends on use of the soundtrack as "an independent variable combined with the visual image" (*W* 114). Audiovisual disjunction and nonsynchronization would preserve the montage principles of juxtaposition and collision. Ten years later the model for sound cinema is a "unity of fused musical and visual images, *composing the work with a united audio-visual image*" (*FF* 177–78). At least according to the original definitions, *Alexander Nevsky* is truly a sound film and not a talking picture. Ironically, Alexandrov—a cosigner to the 1928 statement—established himself as a director in the 1930s with conventional musical comedies.

Direct speech in *Alexander Nevsky* is subordinate to music and action. Due as much to technical limitations as to directorial choice, there is a minimum of recorded dialogue in the action sequences. In dramatic scenes, on-camera dialogue is delivered from stationary positions, which were held in order to maintain sound quality under marginal recording conditions. The resulting alternation of wordless action with scenes of dialogue, delivered in static tableaux, creates a structure like that of opera. The characters' words, particularly Alexander's, seem to be delivered in recitative.

Postsynchronization of material other than music was not used extensively. Where naturalistic sound effects are added, they usually serve immediate narrative purposes. In the early scene of Nevsky's reconnaissance on Lake Chudskoe, the clatter of horses' hooves on ice and the noise of Gavrilo's horse slipping down onto the frozen surface function in Nevsky's formulation of strategy. During a segment of the Battle on the Ice unaccompanied by music, the clash of metal and a dull roar of soldiers' groans and exclamations rise on the soundtrack. There is, however, no use of sound perspective or directionality. Volume remains at the same level as the action shifts from long-shot to close-up.

The sound of cracking ice at battle's end marks the success of Nevsky's strategy. Accompanied by music and itself amplified and percussive in tone, the sound of cracking ice is conveyed more as a musical element than as an actual noise. The same can be said of the closing effect of bubbles gurgling to the water's surface. The illustrative uses of sound, and the minimalization of naturalistic sound effects, lend further styliza- tion to *Alexander Nevsky* in the directions of opera and epic.

The 1928 statement rejects "every mere *addition* of sound to a montage fragments" and its uses for an automatic coloration of dramatic action. These practices would only increase the "inertia" of individual montage pieces and would severely lower the possibilities for juxtaposition (W 114). Yet it is precisely in terms of audiovisual homogeneity and illustra- tion that Eisenstein analyzes a sequence from *Alexander Nevsky* in the three "Vertical Montage" essays of 1940 and 1941 (translated as chapters 2–4 in *The Film Sense*), which have been considered essential in the his- tory and theory of sound cinema. Termed by Eisenstein the "dawn of anxious waiting," the sequence contains twelve shots and precedes the Battle on the Ice. The infinitesimal detail of his analysis, covering more than forty pages, inflates a sequence whose screen time is about two min- utes and whose simple purpose is to create a mood of tense expectancy on the eve of battle.

Composer Hans Eisler has found Eisenstein's analysis to be based on a fallacious analogy between visual properties and musical notation under the mistaken assumption that notation is directly equivalent to the music in performance.[18] The claims in "Vertical Montage" about the spectator's emotional modulations—said to be perceptible within individual mea- sures of the Prokofiev score and corresponding elements within individual shots—are not readily verified when the sequence is viewed in the con- text of the whole film. Nevertheless, the analysis remains important for an understanding of the direction Eisenstein's thinking takes in the pe- riod of socialist realism. The concept of vertical montage is drawn from the notation on an orchestral score, where vertical structure indicates the interrelationship of all the instrumental elements at a particular moment. Through the progression of the vertical line horizontally, harmonic com- position unfolds. In the case of audiovisual montage, Eisenstein treats visuals as another "staff" that corresponds with the line of musical com- position.

To demonstrate the methods of vertical montage, Eisenstein selected a sequence whose constituent shots are static in content. In matching the sequence's seventeen musical measures with its twelve shots, "Vertical Montage" reprints the staves above diagrams of the shot compositions. In terms that vary among light tonality, linear values, graphic structure, and dramatic content, each shot is found to have direct congruence with its accompanying music. In music, compositions primarily vertical in their texture are termed homophonic and are simultaneous, consonant, and harmonious.

In the 1928 statement, the goal of sound cinema was announced to be "a new *orchestral counterpoint* of visual and sound images" (W 114). A contrapuntal or polyphonic structure in music places emphasis on horizontal texture and successive effects. In analyzing the "dawn of anxious waiting" as a temporal and horizontal structure, however, Eisenstein emphasizes the consistency and continuity in audiovisual composition from frame to frame. The editing of shots is based on a principle of their serial unity. Though the visual material in each shot is static—as it is also among the shots edited together—the eye, according to Eisenstein, moves across the pictorial composition in a manner exactly analogous to the music's movement and reads each shot in a strict left-to-right direction in the same manner that a musician's eye reads the accompanying Prokofiev score.

Nonsynchronization is no longer Eisenstein's goal for sound cinema. "Vertical Montage" predicts a future cinema that synchronizes all human senses. His previous concepts of dialectical method and intellectual cinema are not in evidence in Eisenstein's theory and applied criticism of the early 1940s. Where once dialectical conflict served as the paradigm for film form, Eisenstein now pursues organic synthesis and unity. In "Vertical Montage" Wagner stands as an ideal of the creative artist and thinker in having left the legacies of synaesthesia and the *gesamtkunstwerk*. The possibilities for a supreme art form that opera represents for Wagner, sound cinema now represents for Eisenstein. Writing shortly after *Alexander Nevsky*'s release, Eisenstein claims that the goal has been attained: "here—in cinema—for the first time we have achieved a genuinely synthetic art—an art of organic synthesis in its very essence . . ." (*FF* 193–94). Eisenstein's affinities for Wagner at this time are reflected in his concentration on myth, organicism, sensuous thought, and primal emotion.

Another summary of Eisenstein's new approach to form is presented in the 1939 essay "The Structure of the Film," which devotes much attention to the artist's temperament. Personality and creative vision—not class and ideology, as in theory of the silent period—are the axes of analysis. Organic structure, unity, and ecstasy have supplanted conflict, discontinuity, and collective pathos in Eisenstein's critical vocabulary. The individual creator holds priority of place in great art, where "the theme and content and idea of the work of art become an organically continuous unity with the ideas, feelings, with the very breath of the author" (*FF* 174). Where form in intellectual cinema establishes ideological perspective and critical distance, in organic cinema form fuses author, content, and individual spectator.

An analysis of *Potemkin* in "The Structure of the Film" identifies each dramatic unit as a "cellular organism" that fuses with the other units (*FF* 163). The organic principle of construction creates a nonconflictual relationship between film and viewer: "Each spectator feels himself organically related, fused, united with a work of such a type, just as he senses himself united and fused with organic nature around him" (*FF* 161). Previously, in Eisenstein's actively dialectical and materialist approach to structure, each montage unit is a fragment of representation that collides with other fragments, continually recontextualizing the film event for the spectator. The ideological affect of shock at the cognitive level that Eisenstein once claimed for *Potemkin* is replaced by an affect of ecstasy, which occurs at a level of depth psychology.

Rather than foster a collective, class identity for audiences, the ecstatic affect enhances individuated, subjective experience: "The spectator not only sees the represented elements of the finished work, but also experiences the dynamic process of the emergence and assembly of the image just as it was experienced by the author. . . . The strength of the method resides also in the circumstance that the spectator is drawn into a creative act in which his individuality is not subordinated to the author's individuality, but is opened up throughout the process of fusion with the author's intention" (*FS* 32–33). Fundamental to Eisenstein's new theoretical synthesis, then, are principles of authorship, individual psychology, and a participatory mystique that stand in direct opposition to those principles of constructivism, mass politics, and dialectical critique that define his theory in the silent period.

Eisenstein's emphasis on personality and adherence in aesthetic experience reflects the consequences to Soviet society under Stalin of a cult of the leader's individual genius, rectitude, and power. In its first decade Soviet film culture had thrived on political theorizing and debate among artists. With the establishment of state unions for each art and the imposition of socialist realism, Soviet artists were barred from effective political life. The dissociation of art from activist politics is evident in Eisenstein's completed sound films, which represent societies that are statist and absolutist. Eisenstein's previous dedication to issues of modern history and revolutionary transformation is replaced by interests in society's earliest forms and primitive thought.

Compared to Eisenstein's silent films, *Alexander Nevsky* seems static and hieratic. While these qualities are present to a considerable extent in the two *Ivan* films as well, there they are aspects of a historical critique. *Alexander Nevsky*, on the other hand, is immobile and monumental in conformity with the Soviet leadership cult. For the duration of the Soviet-

German Nonaggression Pact *Alexander Nevsky* was withdrawn from distribution along with other Soviet films in the anti-Fascist genre. The film was re-released with great success domestically and in the West following Germany's attack on the Soviet Union in June 1941. *Alexander Nevsky* clearly had an influence on another famous patriotic film of the period, Laurence Olivier's *Henry V* (1944).

In a statement of intentions made during production, Eisenstein indicates that by design the film treats the figure Alexander Nevsky in the vein of folklore and nationalistic myth and not in the spirit of revolutionary history.[19] To Eisenstein's credit, he did not slavishly serve the cult of Stalin as did filmmakers like Mikhail Romm, the painter Sergei Gerasimov, and the sculptor Merkourov. But the iconography of *Alexander Nevsky*, it must be said, exhibits the self-important heroism ridiculed in Eisenstein's previous films. Eisenstein revives the spirit of iconoclasm when he creates his next film portrait of a national hero newly proclaimed by Stalinist culture.

CHAPTER NINE

Ivan the Terrible:
An Inversion of History

Two projects that followed the completion of *Alexander Nevsky* influence the historical perspective, themes, imagery, and visual style of *Ivan the Terrible*. Given the commission in December 1939 to stage Wagner, Eisenstein approached *Die Walküre* as a drama of "historical consciousness" at a primitive stage when "man envisaged nature as an independent being, now gracious, now austere, at times echoing his own feelings, at others opposing them" (*FE* 89). The stage design and sets provided an animistic environment, with mountain scenery moving in tempo to physical action. To capture man's socially undifferentiated being, Eisenstein devised pantomime choruses. Hunding is at times enfolded by a horde of kinsmen and servants that comprises a shaggy, hydra-headed shape representative of a hunting pack. *Ivan the Terrible* employs similar primitivist effects to portray atavistic tendencies in the political order.

Starting in March 1940, Eisenstein drafted ideas for a film biography on Alexander Pushkin to be titled *The Love of a Poet*, a subject he periodically returned to over the remaining eight years of his life. The political drama of Pushkin's career in autocratic Russia held compelling interest for the Soviet director during the 1940s. One of the first scenes developed in the script is taken from the Pushkin play *Boris Godunov* (1825), whose democratic tendencies led tsarist censors to ban its staging for forty-five years. The script scene contains Tsar Boris's monologue, "I have attained the highest power." In response to the people's discontent and his regime's unpopularity, the tsar says in scorn, "Such is the judgment of the mob: seek then its love!"[1] Not romantic love but individual supremacy and popular resistance are the first themes the director evolves for the Pushkin project.

Addressing a state conference on "Problems of Soviet Historical Films" in February 1940, Eisenstein cites *Boris Godunov* as instructive for the Soviet rehabilitation of Russia's tsarist past and he paraphrases Pushkin's definition of tragedy as follows: "What takes place in tragedy? What is its goal? Man and the people. Individual human fate and the fate of the people." To Boris's monologue, "I have attained the highest power," he contrasts the drama's last scene, "The people stand mute." For a comparison, Eisenstein explains that the difference between the tsar's psychology and the people's will is the same as that between Romm's *Lenin in October* and his own *October*, which has "no historical personages and no historical leader."[2] The implication is that the figure of Lenin in his *October* is not a historical character according to the canons of socialist realism or the cult of leadership. Lecturing to students in 1946, Eisenstein again evokes the political drama in *Godunov:* "The people in the course of the tragedy develop an awful power. They have grown, and by the last moment they adopt by their silence an active judgment on the events before them" (*FE* 160–61).

Pushkin's *Boris Godunov* had long been an interest of Meyerhold, who planned during 1936 for its production the next season at his theater. The state's interference and final closure of the Meyerhold Theater prevented its staging. At the time of Meyerhold's arrest and imprisonment in 1939, Eisenstein intervened to save and preserve the theater director's personal archives. A month after Meyerhold's death, Eisenstein cites *Godunov* at the state conference on historical film in making his comments on fate and political power. The film director transported the Meyerhold archive with him from Moscow to Alma-Ata during the period of work on *Ivan the Terrible*. Leonid Kozlov suggests that *Ivan* incorporates the traditions of Meyerhold in its theatricalization of history.[3] One of Meyerhold's famous stage performances as an actor was in the role of Ivan the Terrible.

In the Pushkin play, there is an imaginary connection between Boris Godunov and Ivan the Terrible through the Pretender who passes himself off as Ivan's fourth son, Dmitri, thought by some to have survived Boris's murder plot against him in 1591, seven years after Ivan IV's death. Prominent in the dramaturgy of Eisenstein's *Ivan* are the tsar's actions as a performer and an impersonator who has a theatrical sense of political intrigue and state affairs. Among the many character models Eisenstein utilized for Ivan are Saturn, who devoured his children, the rebel angel Lucifer grieving the separation from his Creator, and Rustum, the father in Persian legend who killed his son Sohrab in battle. Mythic conflict between father and son was relevant for Eisenstein to the artistic relationship to his "spiritual father" Meyerhold and to political relationships under Stalin's patriarchy.

In Eisenstein's staging of *Die Walküre*, the last act's "Magic Fire Music" was a crescendo of color and audiovisual sensations. A scarlet flame within a ring of blue fire was projected against a bronze background and led to an azure backdrop sky, with these tones varying in value. Eisenstein also elaborated an intricate scheme of color for *The Love of a Poet* to make Boris Godunov's monologue into a "color nightmare." The montage list depicts the scene as a phantasmagoria of gold, orange, violet, and red, with the colors whirling together to create an oily texture. Eisenstein was able to experiment with these ideas in part 2 of *Ivan the Terrible* after some Agfa color negative was acquired among other spoils of war.

Eisenstein's first notes for *Ivan the Terrible* date from January 1941 and he continued to shape the scenario as filming started in April 1943. Prokofiev joined the director at that time in the south of Kazakh Republic, to which Soviet filmmakers were evacuated during the worst months of war. The complete screenplay, written by the director without collaboration or immediate supervision, was published in December 1943.[4] On location and at the Alma-Ata studios, the production team shot footage for almost the entire first half of the script and for segments of the second part. Eduard Tisse directed the cinematography for exterior scenes, while interior scenes were assigned to Andrei Moskvin. Previous work with directors Kozintsev and Trauberg in the Eccentrist mode prepared Moskvin for the extreme stylization in Eisenstein's handling of actors.

Ivan the Terrible, part 1, was released in January 1945 and a year later Eisenstein was awarded the Stalin Prize for the film. At the time he was finishing montage on part 2. The published screenplay contained so much material as to require a proposed third feature. At a celebration in his honor in February 1946 Eisenstein suffered a heart attack. Political censors did not accept part 2 for general release, and condemnation by the Party Central Committee followed in September. After a personal interview with Stalin in the Kremlin in February 1947, Eisenstein was permitted to resume production on part 3, which was to incorporate approved material from the banned film, but his heart condition made further filmmaking impossible. The ban on part 2 remained in effect until 1958, ten years after Eisenstein's death and five years after Stalin's.

During the Kremlin interview, Stalin, accompanied by Vyacheslav Molotov and Andrei Zhdanov, instructed Eisenstein that the political errors of Ivan IV in the campaigns of terror were his hesitation and attacks of conscience: "Ivan the Terrible executed someone and then he felt sorry and prayed for a long time. God hindered him in this matter. Tsar Ivan should have been even more resolute."[5] Molotov and Zhdanov complained that the film depicted Ivan's policies as the result of neurotic conflicts rather than patriotic aims. Another motive behind official condemnation of part 2, unstated during the 1947 interview, was the leadership's increasing moderation of traditional nationalism once World War II had concluded and the resumption of Party supremacy in Soviet life.

The complete screenplay to *Ivan the Terrible* presents an even darker view of history than that in the two finished features. In some respects, *Ivan the Terrible* should be accounted an unfinished film. Part 2 and the planned part 3 nearly divide between them themes and kinds of historical action that in part 1 are joined. Part 2 gives prominence to psychological intrigue and interior scenes while part 3 emphasizes military exploits and location exteriors. In this regard, the Ivan of part 3 might seem a safer subject ideologically, one on the order of the patriotic hero Alexander Nevsky. But the last part stands also as a resolution to the drama of political terror that develops in the first two films. His writings in the years 1946–48 give no indication that Eisenstein considered conforming to Party prescriptions on the historical image of Ivan.

In the original screenplay, the plot is strictly chronological and with its linear narrative adheres to a 1934 Party decree on the correct representation of historical events. In citing this decree in his 1940 address on history and film, Eisenstein comments that "every class attempts to so interpret its past as to establish the rationality of its own existence."[6] The first dramatic scene in the screenplay presents the boy Ivan witnessing his mother's death by poison and is followed with him holding an official audience. In the third scripted scene nursemaids remove the boy's ceremonial robes and prepare him for bed as one old nurse sings the lullaby, "Ocean sea, Azure sea, . . . Glorious sea." At the screenplay's final moment the song is repeated when Tsar Ivan, after prolonged strife with Russian and foreign foes, finally reaches the Baltic Sea.

Commenting on the screenplay in 1944, Eisenstein remarks that its linear chronology establishes a causal connection between the impressions of Ivan's childhood and later policies of his regime: "the series of childhood traumas *coincides* along an emotional index with objectives the adult sets before him."[7] In the sequential chronology of the screenplay, Ivan's biography represents the struggle of a modern autocrat against a feudal aristocracy. The film *Ivan the Terrible,* as a contemporary version of history, represents that struggle as a complex of tragedy and the grotesque, of intimate psychology and social consciousness, and of progressive and regressive dynamics. The narrative code of psychological determinism is altered and politically recontextualized with the positioning of the childhood scenes in part 2 of the finished film at a decisive moment in Ivan's adult life. The film's biographical plot renders the Stalinist orthodoxy of Ivan's heroism as a historical paradox. Eisenstein made *Ivan the Terrible* with an awareness that the great-man version of official history constitutes an inversion of the preeminence mass movements and collective heroism have in his cinema of the 1920s.

Contemplating the 1848 revolution in France and Louis Bonaparte's coup d'état of 1851, and comparing this sequence of events to the first French Revolution and the crowning of Napoleon I, Marx brooded that the "tradition of all the dead generations weighs like a nightmare on the brain of the living." In this context, Marx makes his famous addendum to Hegel: "Hegel remarks somewhere that all great, world-historical facts and personages occur, as it were, twice. He has forgotten to add: the first time as tragedy, the second as farce." History's tragedy of the original French Revolution and the First Empire has its farcical, inverted image in the 1848 revolution and the Second Empire. The counterrevolution in France teaches the following history lesson: "The social revolution of the nineteenth century cannot draw its poetry from the past, but only from the future." With France's return to autocracy, in Marx's view, humanity is defeated and state power is consolidated through political regression: "Instead of *society* having conquered a new content for itself, the *state* only appears to have returned to its oldest form."[8]

Ivan *Grozny*

The promotion of Ivan as a Soviet national hero is unique to the Stalin years. In Pokrovsky's standard *Brief History* of the 1920s Ivan IV and tsarism are assessed as Bonapartist formations: "With the Muscovite Tsars begins the development of the 'State principle.' It found its embodiment in Ivan the Terrible, . . . who is represented from a variety of angles as the impersonation of a *State that stands above classes*."[9] At least one Soviet silent film contains a vivid portrait of Ivan IV and his era—Yuri Tarich's *Wings of a Serf* (1926), a story about a serf who invents a flying machine and, after demonstrating it for the tsar, is condemned to death as a sorcerer. Soviet reviews comment on "the sly and calculating spirit, the brutality, the gross sensuality, and the morbid isolation" in the characterization of Ivan and on "his unlimited despotism."[10]

Evaluating the representation of tsarism in Soviet silent cinema, Eisenstein wrote in 1928: "The 'great' and 'illustrious' personages of the past ruled the fate of millions according to their limited views. They were 'gods' invented out of whole cloth. It is time to reveal the truth about these paid romantic heroes. The concealed traps of official history must be exposed. We want to know the social basis of these fabulous figures. . . . Ivan the Terrible as a personality in the manner of Edgar Allan Poe will hardly interest the young Soviet worker" (*FE* 26). The interpretation of history here follows Marxism's subjective code, as indicated further by Eisenstein's amplification: "The story of Ivan the Terrible should go on to tell how he became absolute monarch, head of a dominant aristocratic class." With reference to *October*'s iconoclastic perspective on Russia's last tsar, Nicholas II, its director remarks: "In a motion picture lasting an hour and half, all the years of tinsel, falsehood and deception are dispersed" (*FE* 27).

Ivan IV's legendary political stature is conveyed in the epithet *grozny*, "the Terrible." Exemplifying practices that Machiavelli's *The Prince* advanced two decades earlier, Ivan IV cultivated an image of intimidating, unpredictable power. *Grozny* has affinities with traits connoted by the revolutionary pseudonym *Stalin* ("man of steel"). Claiming that only Ivan IV, Lenin, and he had instituted a state monopoly over foreign trade in Russia's history, Stalin identified the tsar as a statesman in the socialist mold and as his direct forerunner. Stalin credited Ivan IV with the unification of major provinces into Great Russia, the suppression of boyar power, and liberation from obligations to the Tartar Golden Horde. Historians, however, commonly date these developments fifty years earlier and associate them with Ivan IV's grandfather, Ivan III, who reigned in the period 1462–1505 and gained the epithet "the Great." Stalin's preference for Ivan the Terrible, and his misattribution of such formative events to this tsar's era, is indicative of the arrogance of Stalin's own absolute power. In the period of World War II, Stalin gloried in a historical analogy that is profoundly incriminating from most other perspectives.

During the purges Stalin explicitly linked the Party's action to Ivan's campaign of terror against internal enemies. Stalin considered the *oprichniki,* Ivan's secret entourage and army, a modern instrument of power. While editions of the *Soviet Encyclopedia* in the 1930s wrote of the oprichniki as a force oppressive to aristocrats and peasants equally, by 1946 the *Encyclopedia* disclaims its reactionary and ruthless attributes.[11] The rehabilitation of Russia's tsarist past under Stalin revived prerevolutionary social hierarchies, including old ranks, distinctions, decorations, and uniforms. Official condemnation of *Ivan the Terrible,* part 2, contains the charge that the film represents the progressive army of the oprichniki as a band of degenerates similar to the American Ku Klux Klan.

In the early 1940s a novel by Valentin Kostylyov and plays by Alexei Tolstoy and Vladimir Solovyov elevated Ivan IV as a modern national leader. While drafting the screenplay in 1942, Eisenstein explained his own historiographic method as comparative: "It is advisable to approach *different* historical stages each in *a different manner;* what is progressive in the epoch of the Russian Renaissance of the 16th century may be profoundly reactionary for the end of the 19th and the beginning of the 20th centuries!" In the Renaissance context, Ivan's centralization of power and unification of the state is "historically progressive and positive," as were the statist activities of "Louis XI, Charles VIII, Elizabeth of England, Catherine de Medici."[12]

In publishing the screenplay a year later, Eisenstein significantly revises the list of Ivan's political peers in a prologue commentary. Retaining only Catherine de Medici, the prologue names Charles V, Philip II, the Duke of Alba, Henry VIII, and Bloody Mary. The lesser-known Duke of Alba was a professional Spanish soldier serving Charles V and later Philip II who occupied the Netherlands in 1567 and established a tribunal popularly known as the Council of Blood that, according to his own claims, executed eighteen thousand people. Reference to two events in the century is added: "The Fires of the Inquisition and the Night of St. Bartholomew." The screenplay's historical context thus places considerable emphasis on terror as an institution in Renaissance politics.

Commenting on the topic of democracy in 1945, Eisenstein identifies its heroic historical prototype as Abraham Lincoln. Inspired by the John Ford film *Young Mr. Lincoln* (1939), Eisenstein esteems Lincoln as a truly popular leader, a great humanist, and "an embodiment of Karl Marx's favorite quotation from Terence: 'Nothing that is human is alien to me.' " As an index to Lincoln's humanism, Eisenstein cites many of the epithets by which he was commonly known, such as the Great Emancipator, the Great Heart, Honest Abe. Considering such epithets "an almost faultless criterion in establishing the historical relation of the people with their governments and leaders," Eisenstein cites the instance of Ivan Grozny as a reflection of the awe and dread this tsar induced among the common people (*FE* 143–44). Compared to the iconography developed in *Young Mr. Lincoln* or *Alexander Nevsky*, Eisenstein's Ivan cannot be accounted a popular, democratic leader.[13] Rather, he is a tormented individual greatly estranged from Russia's masses.

Tragedy, Eisenstein held, is inseparable from the legendary image of Ivan in the Russian mind, where the tsar remains a figure "fearsome and alluring, fascinating and terrible, in the full meaning of the word—tragic in his inner struggle with himself, a struggle which he inseparably tied to struggles against the enemies of his country." While at work on part 2, the director finds the popular image so "romantic, mysterious, at times sinister," as to make the tsar seem like a character "taken directly from melodrama." Characterization in the manner of Poe is now relevant to a Soviet understanding of Ivan IV. Ivan "effected a complete revolution in establishing absolutism" through the force of a personality that also exhibited tendencies toward isolation, self-dramatization, and merciless rage.[14]

Ivan the Terrible adopts Renaissance conventions of tragedy born of revenge and at the same time it is a modern tragedy about political power and individuation in the Renaissance. Party censors charged that part 2 portrays Ivan, "a man of strong will and character, as a man of no will and little character, something like Hamlet."[15] While filming part 1, Eisenstein confided in a letter to Tynyanov his anticipation of such official criticism: "Presently, on the *human* plane of *Ivan the Terrible*, I am endeavoring to convey the leitmotif of autocracy as the tragic fatality that results from an absolute ruler's solitude. *One*—unique—and *one*—solitary, abandoned by all. You well understand that this is exactly what I first, in the scenario as in the film, strive to *replace*."[16] This tragic leitmotif becomes strongly evident in part 1 when it is analyzed together with part 2, as it always should be.

Eisenstein conceived Ivan as an extreme character, but not as the pathological personality Party censors alleged. In commentary made within *Nonindifferent Nature* in the years 1945 to 1947, Eisenstein associates Ivan with tragic heroes in a tradition that extends from Shakespeare to Dostoevsky and wherein the complexity of character transcends issues of pathology. Eisenstein insisted that the historical Ivan was not insane and that his film's characterization avoids the psychological dualism of a split personality. Ivan's character is divided, but the divisive forces do not originate in personality alone. The film presents a pathology not of the individual per se but of the *polis*. In autocracy, politics and personality form a historical unity. The state *is* Ivan, particularly in consideration of his traditional status as Russia's first tsar.

Tragic crisis, according to Eisenstein, can be conveyed through character conventions of "inner tension . . . and the psychological outbursts of transport from adoration to denigration of the adored, from hate to love, from meekness to beastliness and that 'divine frenzy' in which all the depths of . . . pathos is revealed."[17] All these personality traits are present in the complete *Ivan the Terrible*, which becomes an increasingly interior tragedy in its representation of absolutist Russia. Eisenstein sought to achieve the unity of personality and history found in the work of Shakespeare and Dostoevsky. Though eccentric and alienated, Hamlet and Raskolnikov are characters who—through the authors' historical genius—profoundly represent the conflicts of their times.

In terms of politics, Ivan's tragic fatality is his estrangement from the Russian people. In terms of personality, it is his obsession with the Russian state. Statism is Ivan's mania. The psychology of character is based on an effect Eisenstein terms "the inhumanity of the system of images in *Ivan the Terrible*" (*IM* 29). His dramaturgy consciously draws upon Seneca, Marlowe, Jonson, Webster, and—as fellow director Kozintsev noted—"the mannered theater of horror."[18] *Ivan* shares with revenge tragedy emphasis on the hero's hesitation and aberrant behavior, the possibility of madness, and scenic displays of terror. The motive of vengeance in *Ivan*, however, is often displaced and depersonalized.

The Plot of Russian History

With proletarian revolution, according to *The Communist Manifesto*, history itself is overthrown: "In bourgeois society . . . the past dominates the present; in communist society, the present dominates the past."[19] In *Ivan the Terrible* the bearing of past on present is extensive, complex, and decisive. Within the film plot, Russian history takes a grotesque, dire turn. The sixteenth-century context of Catherine de Medici, Bloody Mary, and Ivan Grozny, of the St. Bartholomew's Day Massacre, the

Catholic Inquisition, and the executions of boyars, pertains deeply to the shift in twentieth-century Europe toward totalitarianism, political terror, and mass extermination.

As autocratic figures, Ivan IV and Alexander Nevsky differ greatly. In Eisenstein's historiography Nevsky's leadership is patriotic, Ivan's statist. Biographical material on the earlier figure is essentially confined to legend and hagiography. Ivan belongs to the first full era of Russia's documented history, but he is also the subject of vast legend. The historical record contains several tendentious portraits of Ivan's personality left by political adversaries, and Ivan cultivated the image of dread ascribed to him by political foes. The other primary documents are Ivan's own proclamations and correspondence, which comprise an enigmatic self-portrait. Ivan instituted a new right of autocracy in crowning himself at age sixteen with the title tsar in accordance, he proclaimed, with God's will. Though sometimes claimed as Ivan IV's innovation, this coinage of Greek-Roman origins (*Caesar*) had been a title first used in official documents by his grandfather, Ivan III.

The treatment of sixteenth-century history in *Ivan the Terrible* entails considerable compression, transposition, and excision of events. As conceived in the full screenplay, the narrative spans nearly forty years of Ivan's life. The earliest scene, the death by poison of Ivan's mother, dates to 1538. Ivan's withdrawal to the Alexandrov Palace and subsequent return to Moscow, events that conclude the filmed part 1, took place in the winter of 1564–65. The execution of Vladimir Staritsky, which concludes the filmed part 2, occurred in 1569. Events represented in part 3 of the script range in date from 1569 (execution of the Basmanovs) to 1573 (death of Malyuta) and 1577 (the year of Ivan's most successful campaign against Livonia).

The planned closing scene of Ivan beside the Baltic Sea amounts, historically, to a wish fulfillment, for the tsar never secured a major Baltic port. In scripted dialogue, one of Ivan's enemies reports that "the Estonians, the Latvians and the Lithuanians are fighting on his side." The three Baltic states were not in fact brought under Russian control until the 1720s, with the conclusion of Peter I's prolonged war of expansion in the north. Estonia, Latvia, and Lithuania gained independence after World War I, but with the Soviet-German Nonaggression Pact they again came under Russian control and, in 1940, were annexed by the Soviet Union.

Significant biographical elements are deleted.[20] Ivan married five times in these years but only his first marriage, to Anastasia, is depicted. The tsar's first-born son, Dmitri, died in infancy. The child appears in one scene to part 1, but the film makes no mention of the loss. Nor is there mention of Ivan's younger brother, Yuri, who was born with such severe physical and mental impairments that he was never considered for the succession and who died in 1563. Historical records present Vladimir Staritsky, Ivan's cousin, as a proven military commander and a worthy candidate for the throne. Contemporaries remarked the strong ties between Ivan and Vladimir, who was honored by the tsar as the bravest prince at Kazan. The film character Vladimir Staritsky is a simple-minded fop pushed toward the throne by his mother, Euphrosyne, the tsar's aunt. In some respects the character is a composite portrait of Yuri and the actual cousin of Ivan. The film strongly encodes the intimacy of the two figures by having Ivan's mock coronation of Vladimir parody the wedding celebration of Ivan and Anastasia.

The narrative techniques in *Ivan the Terrible* are related to the telescopic method of storytelling Eisenstein had planned for *Ferghana Canal* in 1939. Epic in breadth, the proposed film was to span centuries of history through sudden temporal leaps. Eisenstein considered the resulting narrative perspective a temporal depth of field, through which the history of three epochs, separated by centuries, appears continuous. Part 1 of *Ivan* telescopes events that covered a full year historically. Two early scenes represent four events from 1547: Ivan's coronation (January 16, Old Style); the wedding of Ivan and Anastasia (February 3); the fall of the Kremlin bells and the great fire and riot in Moscow (June); and the tsar's first campaign against Kazan (undertaken in December).

On film, the first two events are divided into separate scenes by a fade-out and a fade-in used conventionally to indicate a lapse in time. The filmic convention is reinforced by the first scene's closing dialogue, in which Euphrosyne bitterly reports, "The marriage is fixed for St. Simon's Day." The subsequent three events, however, are presented as one continuous scene, starting with the tsar's wedding and concluding with his raising the people against the Tartars. The extent of the scene's historical compression will not be apprehended by viewers unfamiliar with this set of events, but its dramatic and thematic telescoping is apparent. In sequence, the three events establish a continuum unifying Ivan's personal life (the wedding) with the goals of national unity (the tsar wins the trust of a rebellious populace) and patriotic defense (he refuses to pay tribute to emissaries from Kazan).

In including Malyuta Skuratov in the scene of rebellion that disrupts Ivan's wedding celebration, the film makes a significant historical transposition. The bearded Malyuta emerges from the mob to threaten the tsar with a heavy stanchion. Unarmed by Prince Kurbsky, Malyuta listens intently as Ivan dispels the mob's hysteria with his reasoned, plain eloquence, and the rioter is converted to Ivan's cause. In the siege of Kazan, Malyuta acts as a munitions expert, mining Tartar fortifications. The strategy was actually devised by the Danish engineer Rasmussen, who is represented in a few shots set at Kazan but is not identified by name. As it stands, the Kazan sequence depicts Malyuta as a Russian commoner whose native ingenuity provides the winning tactic. Historically a petty nobleman with estates near the Lithuanian frontier, Malyuta Skuratov entered the tsar's retinue in the 1560s, over ten years after the events depicted.

The dramatization of Anastasia's death as a murder by poisoning is Eisenstein's fabrication. No such interpretation is offered in current biographies of Ivan. Yet the scene transposes into drama the "poisonous hatred" of boyars toward Anastasia, in Ivan's words.[21] In the tsar's lengthy correspondence with Kurbsky, documents that Eisenstein drew upon freely, Ivan makes no accusation of murder in his wife's death, but he charges that the animosity of priests and counselors greatly weakened her health. Anastasia was buried in 1560. In 1564 Prince Kurbsky, fearing arrest and execution, fled Russia to live in exile.

The film telescopes these two events into one scene, set in the cathedral of Moscow. Anastasia's body lies in a heavy, open casket that is raised on a narrow platform. Ivan balances awkwardly on the platform in silent yet demonstrative mourning. Metropolitan Pimen recites from the Psalms of David while Malyuta reports to Ivan the defections of boyars. The tsar receives the simultaneous messages in silence. His first outcry is an anguished self-doubt: "Am I right in my heavy struggle?" In his preoccupation with the "great task" of leadership, Ivan experiences political grief. His deepest personal anguish is aroused by news of Kurbsky's flight, dialogue that is accompanied by a close-up of Anastasia.

Death and defection isolate Ivan, but when Pimen reads "I have sought consolation but without finding it," Ivan rises to proclaim: "The Tsar of Moscow has not yet been brought to heel!" The scene ends with Ivan's decisions to form a private army—the oprichniki—and to leave for the Alexandrov Palace, where he will await a summons from the Moscow populace. The scene's compression of biographical and historical events thus develops an inherently intimate situation (mourning) as Ivan's political drama (his self-doubts as tsar, the defection of Kurbsky), an individual drama that determines Russia's destiny (his decisions to strengthen autocracy). The *oprichnina* (the peculium or separate property) was the tsar's official territory and military corps. In political terms, the oprichnina was the state apparatus for autocracy.

Ivan the Terrible attributes no revolutionary grandeur to the masses. The people appear first as an ignorant mob driven to riot. Among them is a beggar simpleton, a film role played by Pudovkin. He shouts that the tsar is bewitched and further arouses the mob, but he is easily subdued by Ivan's wit and wisdom. The film's simpleton character resembles a *yurodivy*, or spiritually gifted fool. A yurodivy figures prominently in

Mussorgsky's adaptation of the Pushkin drama into his opera *Boris Godunov*, which concludes with the holy fool's lament over the darkness and "tears of blood" that have befallen Russia.

In *Ivan the Terrible* the tsar selects one man from the mob—Malyuta—to become his most trusted adviser. At times in affection, at times in rancor, Ivan calls Malyuta his "dog." The epithet contains a historical reference to the oprichnik insignia, a dog's head and broom, and dramatically it intimates Ivan's alienation from the common people. The characterization of Malyuta is the film's most extended representation of a commoner. When Ivan expresses his lofty purpose, it is most often as "the Great Cause" or "the Great Russian State," not "the people."

The siege of Kazan follows the mob scene at the royal wedding celebration. The conjunction of these two scenes suggests a causal relationship: in answering a foreign threat Russia's masses are transformed into a disciplined, loyal army. As the men march into battle, their ranks form long, narrow lines whose curved shape anticipates the line of pilgrims to Alexandrov at the film's close. In both the battle and pilgrimage scenes no topographical evidence explains the curved formation of people. It becomes apparent that the formation is abstract and decorative. Ivan guides the military action from a distant, elevated command post. Thus, in both the battle and pilgrimage sequences the masses are spatially—and dramatically—subordinate to the tsar. No mass scenes are scripted for part 3. The Russian people are referred to indirectly, in a scene of royal penance conducted after the tsar's massacres. With Ivan present, a monk accounts for his victims, who number in the thousands. The masses figure there only as absent victims of terror.

A feature prominent in the legends of Ivan IV is his tendency toward fits of remorse and religious devotion. At these times he would vow to leave the throne and retire to a monastery. Ivan actually placed a Tartar prince on the Russian throne for one year in the 1570s. In the drama of intrigue and disguise that concludes part 2, Ivan dresses and crowns the simpleton Vladimir as tsar. Informed of the plot against his life, Ivan makes his successor the murder victim through this symbolic abdication. The feast service involves a grotesque masquerade of power, and its inversions strongly accent the masculinity of Ivan and his oprichniki. Young Fyodor Basmanov appears in a woman's peasant costume and a mask with long braids of hair. He leads the soldiers in a frenzied dance, during which they grasp at his disguised body. To close the mock coronation, Ivan prostrates himself before the effeminate Vladimir, who now occupies the throne.

Before leaving the feast to enter the cathedral, Ivan and the oprichniki don plain black cassocks and cowls and Ivan becomes indistinguishable from his black-robed band. The community Ivan joins, however, is more like a masculine horde than a religious order. Vladimir remains in regalia and leads the procession. According to the oath they chant—"Renounce kith and kin, forget father and mother"—the oprichniki are a political and military brotherhood. The pledge taken in the film is adapted from the harshest version of the oprichnik oath, recorded in Kurbsky's history of Ivan IV. Ivan's brief abdication and loss of identity amount to a temporary, symbolic reversion to an earlier form of rule, the masculine clan.

With the subsequent murder of the pretender Vladimir, Ivan emerges from the oprichniki to reclaim his throne. In the political coda that follows, Ivan declares victory in the internal struggle for a unified state: "In Moscow, we have struck down the enemies of Russian unity." Speaking from the royal throne, he announces a campaign against foreign enemies. The coda does not appear in the original script. It would be inappropriate there, since internal terror continues in part 3. In the script's action, Ivan discovers that the elder Basmanov has broken the oprichnik oath. As a test of loyalty, Ivan orders Fyodor to execute his father. Though the son carries out the sentence, Ivan immediately suspects him of treason. The tsar orders his arrest, with the brutally ironic explanation: "You showed no pity to your father, Fyodor. Why should you pity or defend me?" Young Basmanov lunges toward Ivan, but he is felled by a fatal dagger thrust. Ivan's protector is the German mercenary Staden, a member of the oprichniki. With his dying breath, Fyodor denounces Staden as a spy. With these sudden twists, the tsar's protective brotherhood is exposed in part 3 as a murderously corrupt institution.

In parts 1 and 2, Ivan is a man of policy and conscience whose regime is maintained through systematic terror and murder. The historical focus falls upon the rationalization of state power through despotic means. The task of forming a nation-state is responsible, on a dramatic level, for Ivan's extreme behavior. In a scripted scene for part 3, the list of the state's victims, read in penance, drives Ivan into a fury of self-punishment: "Tsar Ivan bangs his forehead against the flagstones in a rapid sequence of genuflections. His eyes swim with blood. The blood blinds him. The blood enters his ears and deafens him. He sees nothing."

In shifting the film's childhood scenes to part 2, Eisenstein deflects the psychological determinism constructed in the original script, where the childhood scenes open the narrative. The scenes function in part 2 as a disclosure of the cruel circumstances under which Ivan inherited the throne. Ivan recounts the nightmare experiences to former intimate Fyodor Kolychev, now the prelate Philip, in a desperate effort to regain his allegiance. Ivan's fear of isolation borders on hysteria. The death of his mother is Ivan's earliest experience of isolation. It is also his first conscious experience with the boyars' murderous plots. Narrative telescoping links the death of his mother in Ivan's childhood depicted in part 2 to

Ivan's adult experiences in part 1 through her warning: "Watch out for poison! . . . Beware of the boyars!" Boyar violence is mainly reported in this childhood scene; the murder itself is not enacted onscreen. Both the warning and the violence have already been fulfilled in the film's plot, with the poisoning of Anastasia. Thus, by telescoping and transposing elements of the story, the plot puts personal experience and state action into an interdependent relationship rather than a linearly causal one.

The other childhood scene depicts Ivan's first act of execution, which is the narrative equivalent of his first act as Russia's autocrat. The act, in other words, is formative in both a psychological sense and a political one. The film's boyar and regent Shuisky is a composite of two historical figures, the cousins Ivan and Andrei Shuisky. In his letters, Ivan IV recounts a scene from his early years when Ivan Shuisky, in a show of disrespect, placed his feet on the bed of the tsar's father. Ivan Shuisky died of natural causes in 1542 and the regency passed on to his cousin Andrei. In 1543 Ivan ordered the arrest of Andrei Shuisky and placed him in the custody of the kennelmen, who beat the regent to death. The film scene in which Shuisky is sent to his death thus telescopes into one action events and persons separated in history by over a full year. The scene is equally an act of revenge and an assertion of autocratic power. After putting his feet on the mother's bed, and fearing no reprisal, Shuisky trades insults with the young prince. Though intimidated by Shuisky, who threatens the frail thirteen-year-old, Ivan impulsively cries out, "Seize him!" The prince is visibly shocked when his personal guard, the kennelmen, carry out the order.

With the seizure of Shuisky, a regal hauteur flashes in Ivan's eyes. This look reiterates the decorative motif of the Imperial double eagle, adopted as Russia's national emblem in the time of Ivan III. Ivan's royal look is seen often in part 1; the coronation, the siege at Kazan, and the decision to form the oprichniki are instances. The scene from Ivan's youth in part 2 dramatizes its origins. The exercise of power first brings the look into the adolescent Ivan's eyes and he makes a historic decision: "I shall reign alone! Without the boyars! I will be Tsar." These lines are delivered with the adolescent Ivan staring steadily into the distance, in a pose of historical farsightedness.

The earliest childhood scene in part 2 takes place when Ivan is eight years old. Throughout that scene, the regard in his eyes is one of nightmare terror. His features and eyes express isolation and insuperable fear. This look returns to the mature Ivan in scenes of emotional loss: the death of Anastasia, the flight of Kurbsky, Philip's condemnation of his actions. In such scenes, no line divides the dramas of personality and politics. Autocracy is a politics of personality.

In conclusion to the scene of Ivan's mourning over Anastasia in part 1,

Fyodor Basmanov becomes "wedded" to the tsar's historical purpose, which is formulated in these words: "By the people's summons I shall gain limitless power. It will be like a new coronation, enabling me relentlessly to consummate my great task!" Ivan can be construed as a popular leader only to the extent that the people act in conformity to the tsar's destiny. Ivan's new coronation and renewal of purpose is a consummation of power, a political ecstasy, presented mainly through montage with dialogue at a minimum and the "poisoning" theme on the music track. The montage places Ivan's attention equally on Anastasia and Fyodor Basmanov. With the sequence's exchanged and shared regards, Fyodor becomes Anastasia's successor.

The tsar's wedding immediately followed his coronation in the first two scenes. The mourning scene culminates with a new coronation declared and an exchange of political and emotional vows. Ivan promises to found an immortal empire: "Two Romes have fallen. Moscow is the third. She will stand firm, for there never will be a fourth!" With these words as the scene's closing dialogue, Ivan stands over Anastasia's coffin, her white robes gleaming in the cathedral's dimness. A medium shot of Ivan postured over the coffin is followed by a close-up of Fyodor, with his worshipful gaze directed at the tsar and the background illuminated by torches. For a time, Fyodor will be Anastasia's equal in devotion to the tsar. But, in part 3, Ivan will feel betrayed by this male helpmate.

Ivan's pledge to found a "third Rome" should be explained. The promise of a third Rome had been made in the reign of Ivan's father, Vasili III. From the perspective of Eastern Orthodoxy in the sixteenth century, a new center for the Christian church was needed. The title was given to Moscow by Russian Christians in the belief that the city was endowed with the sanctity that once belonged to Rome, center of the Catholic West, and to Constantinople, the "new Rome" of the Orthodox East. Schism between the Eastern and Western churches had existed for centuries. Since the mid-fifteenth century, Constantinople had been under Turkish rule and thus in Ivan's time a new Christian capital seemed necessary.

In degree and in explicitness, the film gives state violence greater impact than boyar violence. To be sure, much of the story details the boyars' strategies to oppose autocracy, to murder Anastasia and later Ivan. The film's plot, however, makes greater dramatic point of Ivan's sudden, extreme countermeasures. In terms of the story's causality, Ivan's actions against boyars appear as reactions against serious provocations. But the plot's logic reveals the initiative for terror to be largely Ivan's own.

Ivan's first mature decision to execute boyars is dramatized shortly after the adolescence scene in part 2. Ivan's account of personal oppression and terror fails to persuade Philip to join an alliance of the Orthodox church and the state on the tsar's terms. Instead, Philip gains the right to intercede on behalf of boyars condemned by the tsar. In the next scene, Malyuta warns Ivan against such dangerous compromises and offers to circumvent the formal agreement: "You've made him promises . . . You can't go back on your word . . . I understand . . . So we must see that the Tsar's word is respected and . . . wipe out the traitors too. . . . I'll give my soul for the Tsar. I'll go to hell if need be, but I'll keep the Tsar's word."

The tsar's pledge is outwardly honored while his darker purpose is clandestinely achieved. Malyuta is to serve, in effect, as Ivan's soulless, Machiavellian alter ego. The elder Basmanov, who first suggests the policy of forming the oprichniki, is another accursed, ruthless alter ego. The thickset, shaggy-haired appearance of Malyuta and Basmanov contrasts with Ivan's gaunt features, which are further accented by his long, stringy beard and hair. In a number of close-ups Malyuta and Basmanov are, individually, brought into intimate proximity with Ivan. Compositionally, the figures suggest two sides of a single personality. Ivan approves Malyuta's mission with the words: "You'd give your soul for the Tsar? . . . Eh, dog? . . . Be off with you! . . . Do what you have to do. By God's will, be judge and executioner." In point of fact, it is Ivan's will that commissions Malyuta, as the tsar discloses in a moment of doubt that follows. Once alone, Ivan questions: "By what right do you set yourself as judge, Tsar Ivan? . . . By what right do you wield the sword of justice?"

The next scene is set in Anastasia's bedchamber, where Ivan realizes for the first time that his wife has died of poisoning. Montage of the poisoning scene in part 1 has informed viewers of the exact circumstances of her death even though Ivan remains ignorant of them. In handing the poisoned drink to his wife, Ivan served unknowingly as an accomplice. In part 2, Fyodor Basmanov implants in Ivan the suspicion that Anastasia was murdered by Euphrosyne and the boyar families. Though the young oprichnik was not present at the death scene, Ivan is instantly convinced of the boyars' treachery. The recognition scene that takes place in Anastasia's bedchamber is thus based on circumstantial evidence and Ivan's intuition. The tsar hurries to the courtyard where Malyuta conducts executions. The henchman pronounces sentence on three boyars and raises a sword over their bowed heads. Ivan's arrival coincides with the sound of the sword's fall. His only spoken reaction is: "Too few!" In the original script there follows a sequence depicting mass anti-boyar terror. Oprichniki were to be shown "tearing forth to wreak harsh justice," like a storm sweeping Russia. Shots of pillage, confiscation of property, and summary executions are also scripted.

With the elimination of such exterior action, part 2's attention to palace intrigue and psychological terror is intensified. Euphrosyne's plot to place Vladimir on the throne and Ivan's counterplot occupy fully half of the narrative. The assassination attempt and Ivan's reversal of it develops in a single, continuous action that moves from a banquet hall, across a court-yard, and into the cathedral. The sequence is composed of over 230 shots. The action and imagery constitute another displaced coronation and wedding scene. Reversal and inversion form the basis for the whole film's configuration of Russian history and its specular drama. Moreover, these functions produce "the inhumanity" Eisenstein attributes to the system of representation in *Ivan the Terrible*.

A Historiography of Russian Terror

Stalin's personality cult reinstituted the ideology that individual political genius is necessary to the plot of history. *Ivan the Terrible* is a nightmare vision of autocracy as a historical necessity. The film presents the tsar as victorious in the struggle to establish for Russia the royal prerogative *L'état, c'est moi*. The film dramatizes consolidation of the state in terms of the tsar's increasing isolation. This historical tendency contradicts the Marxist premise that history is not determined by rulers but by classes.

Victory in the state revolution is achieved with the murder of Vladimir, represented as a farcical pretender to the throne. According to historical accounts, Vladimir Staritsky died at the hands of oprichniki. There is no factual evidence connecting the acolyte Peter Volynets with his death. The execution scheme Ivan devises in the film incorporates elements from one of the tsar's legendary acts of murder reported in the popular and colorful *History of the Russian State*, written in the early nineteenth century by Nikolai Karamzin. Eisenstein describes the portrayal of Ivan's reign in the Karamzin history as one of "insensate terror worthy of a Caligula."[22] In 1568 the tsar summoned to the Kremlin Ivan Chelyadin, a former governor of Moscow. He commanded that Chelyadin be dressed in royal attire and enthroned. Ivan kneeled before the mock tsar in homage, then rose and stabbed Chelyadin fatally. Subsequent histories have discarded this and many other stories of Ivan's horror as unreliable. By the time the tsar regains the throne at the close of *Ivan the Terrible*, part 2, however, film audiences come to recognize him as a ruler of sinister ingenuity.

Within the film, formation of the nation-state is based upon a chain of political betrayals and murders. Executioners in one period of Ivan's reign of terror may become its victims in a later period, as do the Basmanovs. In the case of Peter Volynets, an assassin recruited by boyars to murder Ivan becomes the tsar's ally. The vicissitudes in Peter's fortunes are indicative of the extreme political and psychological precariousness in the Russian state. An acolyte under Metropolitan Pimen, Peter is selected to assassinate the tsar as one "pure in heart." The assassination is conceived as a suicidal mission, so the church performs last rites over the youth before sending him forward. When Peter is apprehended and brought before Ivan in the cathedral, the youth cries out that he will not speak even if threatened with torture or execution. Ordering Peter released, Ivan bows before the youth in gratitude for "it was not only a fool he killed . . . but the Tsar's worst enemy!" The last glimpse of Peter Volynets in part 2 is accompanied by oprichnik vows, sung in chorus with the guard still in their clerical robes, to purge Russia of "her savage enemies" and "to shed with my own hands the blood of the guilty." Peter cowers in the cathedral shadows, face hidden in his hands. As the fingers of one hand clench, his right eye appears, staring in horror toward the tsar's men.

Peter's doubt and anguish over his political status intensifies in part 3. The assassin gains an audience with Ivan and falls to his knees, sobbing that he is impure and unworthy of service to the crown. Peter's self-abasement is absolute: he pleads to be executed. The script notes that Ivan has anticipated this act of humiliation; he draws close to Peter to soothe and reassure him with "fatherly" attention. In the confession that follows, Peter alleges a broad conspiracy against the tsar that involves the Russian principalities of Pskov, Novgorod, and Moscow itself. The circumstances of such a confession suggest Eisenstein's own era. From the 1930s until his death, Stalin fostered similar suspicions of pandemic conspiracies against his leadership.

Feeling betrayed on all sides, Ivan turns to the confessor Eustace for counsel. The monk fanatically calls for the destruction of Novgorod: "Shake the whole soil of Rus, as it sees how a great Sovereign goes to punish traitors!" Ivan chooses the course of massive terror even though he regards the monk with a cunning look of suspicion. Upon his return to Moscow, after the destruction of Novgorod, Ivan exposes the monk as a boyar conspirator.

In a subsequent military campaign, Peter becomes an inseparable companion to Malyuta. At moments, the younger man is characterized as a comic sidekick to the old warrior. After Malyuta's death, he is the tsar's closest surviving political associate. Figured in this affiliation with Peter Volynets is another legendary aspect of Ivan's personality: inverse behavior. Historical evidence of such behavior is to be found in Ivan IV's acts of abdication and debasement as well as in his fluctuation between displays of piety and outbursts of cruelty. The rituals of the banquet hall in part 2 entail many political inversions, including elevation of a royal subject—Vladimir—to the throne and symbolic demotion of the tsar.

Sexual inversions are also involved, notably Fyodor's dance in female costume and the intimacy of Ivan and Vladimir, which is visualized through extensive analogy to the scene of Ivan and Anastasia's wedding. The symmetry of shots depicting the royal couple locked in an embrace in part 1, with the court assembled for a feast, is a sign of political stability, however temporary. Food is served from platters ornamented with gilt swans. The movements of servants and banqueters form an ensemble in harmony with the scene's nuptial song. In part 2, Ivan and the retarded Vladimir head an oprichnik feast. The drunken, playful prince falls into the tsar's arms. Dishes are served from ornamental black swans, which are hurriedly brought in. The banquet's music is rapid and dissonant.

The transition from banquet hall to cathedral in part 2 traces an inversion in the tsar's conduct, marked by his exclamation: "The farce is over! Enough of this ungodly revelry!" Suddenly sober, Ivan orders the merrymakers to address themselves to God. They obey the command with a change in attire from brocaded silk to the black broadcloth of penance and mortification. Overtonal montage marks the transition with a shift from color in the banquet scene to the blue and white tonality of the procession scene. One of the last shots in color shows the female mask Fyodor had worn, now lying forgotten on the floor. The oprichnik chorus shifts from a profane ballad to a somber, devotional chant. The rituals of the cathedral, undertaken at Ivan's order to "remember the hour of death," serve as a subterfuge to preserve the tsar's life and put to death a usurper. By the close of the cathedral scene the chant, delivered now at full volume, is revealed to contain vows made to the state, not to God.

A climate of unpredictable repression results from Ivan's negative, antithetical conduct. One scene scripted for part 3, and set in the Tsar's Hall at Alexandrov, parodies religious devotion and celebrates political terror. The tsar and his oprichniki, clothed in monastic habits, conduct a ceremony for the dead boyars. Fyodor Basmanov, as mock priest, delivers the litany. The script continues: "He is amusing himself with Ivan's favorite jest: he holds a Psalter in front of himself upside down." In sharp falsetto, Fyodor leads a chorus in an impious hymn recounting the slaughter of Ivan's enemies. Oprichniki accompany the grisly lyrics with a ritual dance and the clang of drinking cups. At the center of the festivities sits Ivan, aloof and melancholy. Suddenly the tsar rises to interrupt the chorus and dance with a somber reminder: "The duty of a Tsar's Man—this duty is no jesting matter." In the next moments Ivan makes accusations that lead to liquidation of the Basmanovs.

There are significant historical analogies between actions of the oprichniki under Ivan and the Great Purges of the 1930s. The oprichniki carried ceremonial brooms symbolic of their purpose to sweep away enemies to the tsar. With the stabilization of Ivan's state rule the oprichnina was destroyed and its practices disavowed. The tsar conducted an execution of chief oprichniki in 1571. Within Communist Party terminology the *chistka*—literally, a sweeping or cleaning—referred to the periodical purge of undesirable and enemy members within Party ranks. Ivan's later destruction of his earlier apparatus of power has direct parallels with the fate of key Stalin agents from the major purges of the mid–1930s, men like the former head of secret police, Genrikh Yagoda (executed in 1938), and his replacement, Nikolai Yezhov, who prepared the treason case against Yagoda and then himself disappeared in 1939.

The film represents the process of Ivan's nomination "the Terrible" in part 2's church play sequence. After a scene in the Staritsky palace, where bodies of dead boyars have been gathered for burial rites, Ivan visits the cathedral in the company of oprichniki. They enter as a performance of "The Fiery Chaldean Furnace" is underway. It tells the story from the Book of Daniel of the captivity of Shadrach, Meshach, and Abednego by King Nebuchadnezzar and the Chaldeans. Choirboys sing of their bondage, "To a Tsar unrighteous / And the most evil on all the earth." As the play's action and choral song continue, Ivan confronts Philip, who orders the tsar to submit to the church's authority and to dissolve the oprichnina. The choir stops as the men continue to argue and Ivan silences Philip. In the stillness, as they glare at one another, a young boy points at Ivan and asks loudly, "Mother, is that the terrible and godless Tsar?" In a fury, Ivan turns in the direction of the child and an amused Vladimir. Ivan's expression withers the smile on the idiot prince's face. Vladimir turns away from the tsar, as does Euphrosyne. His face thrust forward in hatred, Ivan declares, "From now on I will be just what you say I am! I will be Terrible." With the last words, a calculating, sinister expression comes over his features.

In the church play sequence Ivan embraces his destiny as a damned and ruthless autocrat. The Bible story recounted in the play ends with the three captives enduring the furnace flames unharmed. This proof of their faith and the power of their God converts Nebuchadnezzar. But the choirboys are silenced before they can narrate the miracle. The hymn is stopped on the lines, "Now bear witness to a miracle. The terrestrial lord will be humbled by the Lord of Hosts." Philip interrupts the hymn to chastise Ivan for his impious acts and to threaten him with God's wrath. (Philip's motives, however, are political rather than spiritual.) Within the context of Orthodox religious iconography as represented in the film, Ivan's rebellion against church authority is an act of apocalyptic destruction. The most distinct image among those in the religious murals covering the palace walls and cathedral is that of the Angel of Wrath.

A figure drawn from Revelation, the Angel of Wrath is depicted trampling the universe underfoot in judgment of mankind. This huge image occupies the mural above Ivan's throne in the Kremlin. The mural figure is an image of tsarism associated with Ivan's place on the throne as both boy and adult. Ivan defies both the nobility and the church in creating and ordaining a new order of followers: "I have no confidence in you boyars. Therefore as God created man in his own image, so I have created men in mine. They will carry out my orders and only they will enjoy my confidence. That is why I have christened them Oprichniks."

Visual connection of the throne to the Angel of Wrath is a political association of fundamental importance to the film. The visual image is one of a universe in judgment, cast down and overturned. Its motifs of inversion are consonant with other narrative functions and political images in the film. Semioticians have described Orthodoxy's reaction to the supreme power of another tsar, Peter I, in terms that illuminate *Ivan the Terrible*'s iconography. Peter's state ceremonies and self-proclaimed titles, notably "Father of the Fatherland," struck many Russian church officials as a usurpation of holy authority. In analyzing the cultural implications of the tsar's politics, Boris Uspensky concludes: "Peter's contemporaries could not help but perceive pretensions to divine prerogatives in his behavior, which thus accorded precisely with their notion of the behavior of the Antichrist."[23]

The prophecy of a mighty ruler who will appear at the end of time, and whose essence is hatred of God, is a strong tradition in the Eastern church. From the church's point of view as represented in the film, Ivan's reign is like that of Antichrist as the Lord's wrath engulfs mankind. Eisenstein made *Ivan the Terrible* in a period when the state initiated rapprochement with the church as part of the Soviet war effort. In this context, depiction of Ivan as an Antichrist figure would be considered objectionable by Soviet authorities.

Specular Drama and Color Spectacle

In *Ivan the Terrible* the play of characters' eyes forms a basis for what can be termed a specular drama. The characters' regards or looks range from Ivan's farsighted gaze to exchanges of meaningful glances and acts of disregard. There are specular motifs in the decor as well, with eyes represented in bold relief on the murals.[24] The Russian religious icon gives cardinal importance to the eye as the organ of knowledge and spiritual insight. In a drama thick with palace intrigue, looks exchanged between the ruler and other individuals are political actions. No less oppressive than other forms of totalitarianism, autocracy is distinct in that absolute power has a human face. The autocrat's supreme power is wielded to a significant degree through personality.

During the years of production on *Ivan the Terrible*, Eisenstein returned often in his writings to the topic of the close-up, finding equivalents in the other arts. His most extended examples in literature are taken from Pushkin and Dickens, and in painting from Degas and Japanese woodblock artists. Eisenstein is careful to distinguish his own uses of the close-up from its use by early masters of cinema, particularly D. W. Griffith. Within the traditions of American cinema established by Griffith, in Eisenstein's estimation, close compositions function to isolate a determining or key detail in the scene. Such a shot is close-up in terms of the camera's scenic proximity and dramatic emphasis on material particulars.

Eisenstein believed American practices of the close-up serve mainly the capacities of "viewpoint" and "a means of showing." In reference to his own practices of montage, Eisenstein thinks the term *large-scale shot* is more properly applied. The large-scale shot, distinct from the American close-up, stresses "the *qualitative* side of the phenomenon, linked with its meaning." Its purpose is less to show or to present than "to *signify*, to *give meaning*, to *designate*" (*FF* 238). Its function is to create signification rather than simply to isolate significance. In his silent films, large-scale compositions serve as montage units for a variety of juxtapositions. While the content of these juxtapositions is very often dramatic in *Strike* and *Battleship Potemkin*, in *October* and *Old and New* it is as often conceptual. In *Ivan the Terrible* the dramatic and conceptual codes are far more integrated than in the silent films.

Large-scale shot compositions in *Ivan the Terrible* are the principal means through which the power of personality is conveyed for all the main characters. Euphrosyne's role as conspirator and assassin is conveyed through her fierce, darting eyes. Her furtiveness is signified by the shadows into which her face merges. Her role as an ambitious, manipulative mother is most evident in the lullaby scenes. After meeting with Pimen to plot Ivan's assassination, Euphrosyne is shown reassuring her frightened son, Vladimir. The black shawl she normally wears is removed to reveal a white headdress. She comforts Vladimir, stroking his head as it rests on her lap, and improvises a lullaby from Russian folk lyrics. Her song tells of the hunt of a black beaver, whose fur is to adorn "Tsar Vladimir." As she sings, her eyes look furiously about the darkened room and then down upon her son. Euphrosyne's voice becomes vigorous and agitated, alarming Vladimir. With a scream of horror, he recoils from her lap. In a later scene, Euphrosyne sings the lyrics a second time, over the dead body of her son. The lullaby is now a song of mourning, which she continues after the body has been dragged from her lap. Her eyes are glazed and vacant.

Anastasia's complete faith in Ivan and his cause is as evident as the bright, clear, and innocent look in her eyes. When she raises the poisoned wine to drink, the goblet's lip rises toward her eyes and then is lowered. A close-up of Euphrosyne's head, shrouded in black, is inserted between two shots of Anastasia drinking. The old woman's eyes, placed compositionally near the bottom frame, look up over a balustrade and in the tsarina's direction. In the next shot the goblet is raised gradually until Anastasia's eyes are blocked. A completely frontal composition, the shot

prolongs the gesture and then fades into black. The next scene fades in
with an overhead shot of Anastasia in her coffin.

The guileless and victimized Vladimir is characterized through the vacant, unfocused look of his eyes. Fear is the only emotion that distinctly
registers on his face. The admiration and devotion Ivan inspires among
oprichniki is made plain in the expressions of the Basmanovs. On the
battlefield and later in the palace, they regard Ivan with a radiant look.
These compositions, both within the frame and among shots of the montage unit, are flamboyant and rayonnant in style. An influence evident in
such compositions is the painter El Greco, whose distinctive attenuation
and modeling of limbs and hands is echoed throughout the film.

Ivan's personality is marked by drastic change from his unblinking,
clairvoyant gaze upon coronation to a heavylidded, manic stare as he in-
stigates terror. Where *October* opens with the symbolic dismantling of
tsardom as the masses dismember the Alexander III statue, *Ivan the Terrible* opens with a ceremony that constructs the tsar's image and his symbols of power. The coronation scene is a complex, extended specular
drama. After the opening credits, but before any conventional establishing shot, there is a montage of large-scale shots. The first is of a crown,
followed by one of the scepter, royal orb, and other regalia. Prokofiev's
stylized rendition of pealing church bells accompanies the compositions
and thus provides a sense of place. The third shot establishes the location
as the Kremlin cathedral.

In subsequent long shots during the coronation, the church setting
dwarfs the human figures. Even in closer shots of clusters of boyars and
foreign diplomats, the scale diminishes the stature of characters. The coronation platform remains empty of characters for the first part of the
scene. It is subsequently filled when the robed Ivan is seen from behind
in medium and close shots. Only after completion of the ceremony, with
placement of the crown, does Ivan turn around to face the coronation
audience. But he does not regard the people gathered. His sight is fixed
on a horizon above their heads and beyond the cathedral walls.

Skeptical and conspiratorial glances are exchanged among the international diplomats in attendance. The Livonian ambassador's tinted spectacles mark him as a crafty politician. The ambassador draws near Kurbsky,
insinuates his head over the prince's shoulder, and arouses his political
jealousy. Moments later, during the shower of gold to baptize Ivan as tsar,
Kurbsky makes known his divided loyalty in an exchange of glances with
Fyodor Kolychev, who has already decided to renounce the court and
pursue a religious career. The attention of Kolychev and Kurbsky is exclusively directed toward one another and toward the seated Ivan. At this
point, Ivan has still not exchanged glances with anyone.

Through the curtain of falling gold coins, an action reprised and dilated through montage, Ivan continues to stare into the distance. Where *October* and the *Capital* project intended to demystify monetary luxury, in the present context the shower of gold is mythic, even godly. A suggestion of demystification, left undeveloped, comes at the start of the Kazan sequence, when each soldier going into battle drops a coin into a large dish. The number of unclaimed coins at the end of battle will indicate the number of lives lost in the tsar's army.

Graphically, the regards Kolychev and Kurbsky exchange and the ones they cast downward during the coronation form a triangle whose apex is Ivan. The tsar's regard projects entirely away from this graphic plane. The three-dimensional graphics of the compositions and montage sequence depict Ivan's other-sightedness. An idealized intelligence in the coronation scene, Ivan is depicted as removed from the realm of politics and respondent to the call of history. The political reality of tsarist history will be disclosed as the narrative unfolds from the coronation scene. Ivan's farsighted gaze returns at moments in the subsequent drama, but his look becomes for the most part inward and morbid.

During the wedding feast Euphrosyne, after directing a glance toward Pimen, lifts her goblet to lead a toast to the royal couple. Over the top of the raised goblet she looks slyly toward Ivan; the gesture foreshadows the poisoning scene. Malyuta, the tsar's chief of political intelligence, typically emerges from the periphery of a scene to overhear or interrupt confidential meetings among Ivan's opponents. His prying eye is practically ubiquitous. With Ivan seriously ill, Euphrosyne presses Kurbsky to swear loyalty to her son; they hear approaching footsteps. A medium shot of an empty staircase shows a vast shadow moving slowly downward, then Malyuta emerges into view. In a subsequent large-scale shot, Malyuta's eyebrows rise suspiciously as he directs a penetrating stare toward the plotters. Turning in Malyuta's direction, Euphrosyne and Kurbsky are momentarily frozen in his stare, then they visibly recoil. In shadowing conspirators against the tsar, Malyuta focuses on them with one cocked eye. In one large-scale composition he uses two fingers to prop his eye fully open.

Malyuta is present in the royal bedchamber when Anastasia is poisoned, but he does not detect the murder plot. When the scene opens, the tsarina, in high fever, is confined to her bed. Seated by the bedside is Euphrosyne, who holds Anastasia in her fixed stare. Upon hearing the approach of Ivan, she rises and leaves the bedside. Ivan passes Euphrosyne then suddenly pauses and turns toward her. He puts an arm around the woman and gazes intently into her eyes. Without a word he holds her in his eyes for a few moments, then turns to approach Anastasia. Within the sequence's montage of physical movement, the action is pointedly unexpected and awkward. In terms of later plot development, the encounter establishes Ivan's knowledge of Euphrosyne's presence at the death scene. But the regard Ivan directs to Euphrosyne is unsuspecting and curiously intimate. At this moment the two are strikingly similar in appearance. In his commentary, Eisenstein notes Euphrosyne's "resemblance to the look and face of the Tsar, 'transposed' into the face of the Tsar's aunt." One draft of the script contains the notation, "His aunt's eye, resembling Ivan's, looked at Ivan's eye" (*NN* 325). The correlation suggests that villain and victim are counterparts to one another, much as in Dostoevsky's fiction.

In the scene's subsequent action, Ivan does not see Euphrosyne, who remains in the room hidden by a wall along the stairway leading down from the bedchamber. With sinister concentration she peers over the wall to look upon Ivan at his wife's side. After Anastasia faints, Ivan quickly approaches the side of the room where Euphrosyne hides. She crouches, in the immediate foreground, as Ivan reaches for the wine goblet Euphrosyne has a moment earlier placed on the stone ledge above the stairway. To reach that spot Ivan passes Malyuta, who stares ahead grimly, but in the opposite direction. In returning to Anastasia's bedside Ivan passes Malyuta a second time. And for a second time Malyuta does not register the movement with his eyes, which remain fixed and distant. With Ivan's gaze distracted and Malyuta's preoccupied, Euphrosyne's presence goes undetected. As yet, the tsar and his watchdog are powerless against boyar cunning. Autocratic power has yet to perfect its own abilities in subterfuge and surveillance.

The large-scale, open eye in palace and church murals is an emphatic feature. It is prominent, for instance, when Kurbsky proposes to Anastasia that they rule together in the event of Ivan's death. The wall behind Ivan's throne in the Kremlin is dominated by two huge, open eyes. While the "great eye" is a common religious symbol, any reference in the film to the all-seeing presence of God is ironic. Ivan's political world is a godless autocracy. The specular regard most commonly cast among the film's characters is the evil eye. The atmosphere of both church and palace is dark, confining, and oppressive. The buildings' low, vaulted ceilings, thick walls, and heavy arches create an oppressive atmosphere. Russia under Ivan's rule is like a prison. Passageways are so restricted that an individual must stoop awkwardly to enter and exit the palace chambers. Perspective in interior shots is often limited severely. The effect of decor and lighting is to make the dramatic space abruptly divided and discontinuous. The shots' depth of field is rarely unobstructed or continuous.

Autocracy, instituted through personal and absolute rule, is embodied in Ivan's fanatical behavior and frenzied assertions of power. His historic decision to found the oprichnina is made in a moment of hysteria over the death of Anastasia. Eisenstein describes the dramatic action as "an inner

struggle 'for a soul' " represented through two voices. Ivan does not speak
for several minutes. As he sprawls prostrate before Anastasia's bier, Pimen is heard reading from the Psalms. Pimen is visible in the near background as Malyuta approaches Ivan in the foreground. In dialogue that
overlaps Pimen's voice, Malyuta recites in the tsar's ear names of boyars
who have fled to the West. The two voices summon the tsar in opposing
directions. The Psalms, Eisenstein indicates, "drags the Tsar's soul toward despair, darkness and ruin" (NN 312). Affirmation of life, according
to Eisenstein, is developed through the dramatic line of Malyuta and continued through the Basmanovs.

The conflict is rendered in montage through two sets of images. Despair and resignation are developed through shots of the slain Anastasia,
her facial expression fixed in death, of Ivan paralyzed with grief, of Pimen
intoning the Psalms, and of the assassin Euphrosyne watching the ceremony with a stony expression. Affirmation is visualized through the gazes
of Malyuta and the Basmanovs upward toward Ivan in expectation of guidance and decisiveness. In the context of the executions of adherents in
part 3, any "affirmation of life" through the Basmanovs in the scene of
Anastasia's funeral is brutally ironic.

In assessing the possibilities for color in cinema while at work on *Ivan
the Terrible,* Eisenstein reasoned much as he had in the 1928 manifesto
on sound: "the creaking of a boot seen on the screen is not art. Art begins
the moment when the creaking of a boot on the soundtrack is related to a
different visual image and thereby stimulates corresponding associations.
The same is true for color: color begins when it no longer corresponds to
natural coloring."[25] He argues for a cinema of color images rather than a
cinema representing colored objects and contemplates subjects in color
for which entire ranges in the spectrum are eliminated to achieve thematic effect. These themes would require the director to "intensify the
group of chosen color elements [and] bind them into a genuine system of
color values." Color in cinema would thus not be "just coloring, but an
inner necessary dramatic quality."[26]

The idea of directing a color film was first proposed to Eisenstein in
1940 by the State Directorate for Cinema, which had in mind a lavish
historical costume drama. Eisenstein fully understood that authorities
considered the genre "ideologically interesting and acceptable." For
GUK, "the colorful past was inevitably sought on the border between the
Middle Ages and the Renaissance." Paradoxically, the director thought of
doing a color film on the theme of darkness. He envisioned a story set
during the Black Death with "the spreading plague engulfing everything
in *blackness.*"[27] A key scene was to depict a banquet in full celebration as
it is overtaken by the darkening plague. Eisenstein's proposed treatment
of the historical transition from Middle Ages to Renaissance developed a

dark vision instead of conforming to an ideologically safe perspective on Russia's "colorful past," and his proposal was refused.

Eisenstein carefully devised the coloration of decor and costumes for the banquet and dance scene of *Ivan the Terrible* in order to intensify a select range. Limitations in Soviet processing techniques, which for color film were still in the experimental stage, fortuitously contributed to the harsh luster and clash of colors in the sequence. Its tonality was intended as the sharpest possible contrast to the black and white sequences that precede and follow: "The feast must burst like an explosion between the dark scene of the conspiracy against the Tsar and the gloomy scene of the attempt to kill him."[28] With a feverish combination of red, orange, gilt, and black—set awhirl in the frenzied oprichnik dance—the effect is achieved.

Eisenstein's ideas on color as sign and psychological symbol also involve tonality within black and white cinematography. His production design for part 2 designates the three closing master sequences as "gray—color—black and white." The modulated gray tones in the scene of boyar conspiracy against Ivan are distinct from the high contrast in the scene of Vladimir's death. Eisenstein describes the latter as "totally executed in black (pierced by a scintillating streak of the brocade robes of the doomed prince and by moving dots of candle lights in the hands of the *Oprichniks'* choir)" (*NN* 58). Though designed and processed in black and white, the cathedral scene was apparently shot on color film stock. The resulting texture of contrasts compounds the scene's melodrama and terror.

Three major color themes emerge during the last scenes to part 2. The first, gold, is associated with imperial majesty and the royal prerogative. When Vladimir is clad in the tsar's regal garments his behavior is influenced by such associations. As the banquet becomes turbulent, colors in the range of red and orange begin to dominate. In commentary on the sequence, Eisenstein relates this coloration to "the theme of fatality and . . . the role of blood." Close-ups of Ivan and the elder Basmanov are taken against the hall's crimson-hued ceiling as they argue. Ivan proclaims that "ties of blood" are stronger than those between the tsar and his oprichniki. Basmanov protests that "blood which has been shed" creates a stronger bond. The theme is intensified by the red tint cast upon their faces by torch flames and the ceiling. The third color theme is black, with associations to terror and murder. A signal that the banquet is to be stopped is Ivan's change from a red blouse to a black monk's robe. Similar robes replace the bright blouses and brocade caftans worn by his men for feasting. Eisenstein describes the transformation as "gold devoured by black."[29]

With the production of *Ivan the Terrible*, Eisenstein extends his theory and practice of audiovisual montage. In contrast to the primarily homophonic structure of *Alexander Nevsky*, the relationship between image, dialogue, music, and sound effects in his last film is polyphonic, as in the scene of Anastasia's funeral. Sound and image portray Ivan's grief and self-doubt in multiple, contrasting modes: the tsar's groans; the harmonious murmur of Pimen reading from Psalms; the clatter of a crucifix Ivan wears; the white patch of his face half-swallowed by shadows; the fully lit, frozen expression on Anastasia's face; the tsar's head bent back, almost inverted (he rises alongside the catafalque and asks weakly, "Have I done wrong?," then collapses against the coffin); the soft hymn of a church choir; and Malyuta's report of boyar treachery, delivered in a hoarse whisper. Pimen's recitation continues, "I have sought consolation but without finding it." Ivan suddenly thrusts his face forward and shouts, "You lie!" Hurling aside two large candelabras, which make a great clatter, he proclaims firmly: "The Tsar of Moscow has not yet been brought to heel." Pimen stops the church service and knocks over the lectern and Bible. As Pimen hurries angrily out of the cathedral, Ivan stands firmly over the coffin, now speaking with authority.

In *Nonindifferent Nature* Eisenstein analyzes the funeral scene as an audiovisual structure that employs five major modes: Nikolai Cherkasov's performance in the role of Ivan; the screen image of Ivan; the Prokofiev music; compositional variations in camera angle, shot scale, lighting, and depth of field; and the thematic spectrum of the scene's constituent elements. The combination of elements on the soundtrack alone (diegetic sound effects, dialogue, orchestral music, choral music, the hymn's lyrics, the Psalm verses, characters' dialogue) is polyphonic. Furthermore, these elements in combination are not always synchronized with each image in the montage. Eisenstein writes that "an even articulation in the music can contrast with an unevenly accented articulation within the visual depiction" (*NN* 350).

There are incongruities and excesses in audiovisual structure as a result. For instance, an unmelodious peal of bells concludes the royal wedding song. The sound does not fit the sequence's dramatic key. Minutes later, when rioters rush into the palace, the clanging is again heard. The people protest that Moscow is bewitched, that church bells are mysteriously falling from steeples. Ivan gains the people's confidence with the quip, "A head which believes in witchcraft is itself like a bell . . . empty." As the crowd laughs, Ivan makes a sudden chopping motion and speaks of cutting off heads. At that moment furious, sinister music rises on the soundtrack. The orchestral score features the agitated rhythm of string instruments and the frantic pitch of woodwinds.

Eisenstein outlined the guiding concept of montage for *Ivan the Terrible* as follows: "With the transition to audiovisual montage, the basic support of the montage of its visual components moves *into* the passage, *into the elements within the visual depiction itself.* And the basic center of support is no longer the element between the shots, the juncture, but the element within the shot, the *accent within the piece,* that is, the constructive support of the actual structure of visual depiction." The director acknowledges that these principles contradict some tenets of montage in the silent period, when "this support . . . was, although often excessively 'aestheticized,' the *juncture between pieces,* that is, the element lying *outside* of the depiction" (*NN* 349).

Some synchronous audiovisual combinations in the film create an excess of congruity. Dialogue is used to recapitulate or intensify information made evident already in the visuals. After Ivan becomes convinced in part 2 that Euphrosyne poisoned Anastasia, he sends her a wine goblet covered by a cloth. She removes the cover to reveal the cup used to poison the tsarina. The high-angle close-up shows it to be empty. Looking up suspiciously but not yet recognizing the cup, Euphrosyne mutters with puzzlement: "Empty." The next shot, which concludes the sequence, is a composition showing the goblet in large scale and in the same position as it was on the balustrade in the bedchamber. With a sudden clash of cymbals, the image fades out. Later, as the feast and mock coronation proceed, Ivan notices that Vladimir enjoys the role of tsar. Startled by the discovery, Ivan exclaims, "He likes it." The lines Euphrosyne and Ivan deliver in these two scenes appear in the original scenario simply as commentary on the action. In the film studio, Eisenstein decided to intensify the dramatic moment by reflexively compounding the visual and audio elements.

Prokofiev's orchestral and choral score to *Ivan the Terrible* is far more ambitious and innovative than his music for *Alexander Nevsky* and Eisenstein considered it a complete success: "antiquity resounds so beautifully in Prokofiev's music, expressed not by archaic or stylized means, but by the most extreme and hazardous twists of ultra-modern musical idiom." He singled out for praise the composer's juxtapositions of medievalism and modernism: "we find in Prokofiev the same paradoxical synchronization we get when we juxtapose an icon with a cubist painting, Picasso with the frescoes of the Spaso-Nereditsa" (*N* 165).

A primary basis for contrast in the film score is the traditional music of the Orthodox liturgy. The polyphonic effect of Anastasia's funeral, with Pimen reading from Psalms and Ivan speaking aloud his thoughts, resembles a *toni versiculorum,* a recitation form for Psalm verses with responding words or sentences. The liturgy is a source for one of the score's most memorable passages. As Pimen concludes the coronation, an archdeacon raises a ceremonial scarf. The archdeacon blesses the scarf with the chant "To the Tsar, the Lord's anointed, Ivan Vassilievich" delivered in resounding bass voice. Then Kurbsky and Kolychev anoint Ivan with gold coins.

The ringing sound of coins mingles with the choir that has burst into song with "Long life to the Tsar!"

Prokofiev elaborates the drama through music rather than merely accompanying it. The film action, particularly in part 2, is like opera in the slow tempo of scenes and the dilation of dramatic events. There are alternating episodes of repose and action with transitions that are sudden and sensational. Perhaps the most expressly operatic scene in the film is Euphrosyne's lullaby to Vladimir, "A black beaver was bathing." In form, the lullaby shifts between aria and recitative. Before Euphrosyne sings, the melody is established orchestrally on the soundtrack. When she first sings, the lyrics are strictly synchronized with the melody, which is accompanied by a choir's low humming. As she progresses the lyrics are more loosely delivered against the music. At one point the lyrics change from melody to speech; Euphrosyne's manner becomes declamatory and rhetorical. After she resumes singing, the choir begins to voice the lyrics. The lullaby builds in musical effects and the volume rises until Euphrosyne sings at the top of her voice the words "Tsar Vladimir." On the last syllable of his name, Vladimir lets out a shriek of terror. There is a sudden, brief silence, then Vladimir flees from his mother in horror. His flight is accompanied by a crescendo passage for strings.

A psychological subtext to the lullaby is created through its musical arrangement. With the lines "He didn't wash himself cleaner / He only got blacker," Euphrosyne shifts from song to speech. The orchestral music continues, but it strikes a new theme, in darker tones. When Euphrosyne resumes singing, the orchestra returns to the lullaby melody yet retains the darker mode. The musical theme and Euphrosyne's voice become agitated and severe with the lines "The hunters whistle / Searching out the black beaver." In dramatic context, the lines allude to the assassination plot in which Euphrosyne has just joined with Pimen. The lullaby theme rises in pitch until it is broken off by Vladimir's cry of horror, delivered at a still higher pitch. In the scene there is a progressive contrast between the form of a lullaby, with its simple harmony and gentle melody, and the unconventional modernist treatment of the lyrics.

Referring to *Ivan the Terrible*, Eisenstein wrote that "in audiovisual cinema music begins at the moment when the ordinary coexistence of sound and image surrenders its place to an arbitrary association of sound and image, that is, when natural synchronism ceases to exist."[30] The process entails dissociation of musical themes and visual images that are traditionally linked. The lullaby scene, for instance, is performed with Euphrosyne singing to Vladimir as he rests in her lap, but the score departs from the musical traditions of the form. In the closing cathedral scene, Euphrosyne cradles the head of her dead son and begins to sing the lullaby. Unaccompanied by music and delivered in an exhausted voice, the melody resembles a dirge. Elsewhere in the soundtrack, orchestral passages written to represent the sound of church bells include elements of atonality and dissonance that dissociate the music from conventional sound.

Elements of incongruity and dissociation in audiovisual structure reinscribe the patterns of inversion in the film's dramaturgy and historiography. Among the central figures from the narrative's opening, Ivan alone survives at the close. Allies and adversaries alike have all died through assassination and execution. The executions of Metropolitans Philip and Pimen are reported in part 3 in the list of victims Ivan orders a monk to read as a royal act of penance. (Philip was in fact murdered on Ivan IV's orders in 1569; Pimen was removed from religious office in 1570 and sent to end his life in a monastery.) Prince Kurbsky, now an ally of the Polish court, falls in battle against the tsar's army. (Kurbsky actually died after a short illness in 1583 while still in Livonia.) In *Ivan the Terrible* only the secret police agent Malyuta dies heroically.

Over the course of *Ivan the Terrible*'s two completed parts, depiction of character becomes grotesque, the action is steadily confined, and dramatic space becomes lurid (the color sequence) and dark (the closing cathedral scene). A ruler with absolute power, Ivan becomes in many respects increasingly impotent. From its initial tone as a historical epic, the film becomes progressively an interior spectacle, a drama of interiority. An early scene in part 3 planned to depict Ivan as a tormented old man. By the close of part 3, the tsar was to appear as the fiery-eyed conqueror of Livonia. One imagines that Ivan's expression, though triumphant, is also haunted.

Conclusion

Structures of inversion and the grotesque in *Ivan the Terrible* figure a vision of history in which triumph of the state is an inhuman victory. *Ivan*'s historical perspective cannot be considered communist, particularly in comparison to Eisenstein's silent films. The proletarian history in his early cinema projects a revolutionary future, while the autocratic history of *Ivan the Terrible* restores a grotesque past given form through devices of exaggeration, caricature, deformation, physical absurdities, and compositional incongruities. In Eisenstein's silent cinema these same devices are the dominant means for representation of the historical forces of reaction. The utopian spirit of *October* and *Old and New* exemplifies the Marxist promise and confidence that "communism is the riddle of history solved, and it knows itself to be this solution." Accordingly, these films construct and project a transitive, generative, visionary history. No equivalent historical confidence is evident in *Ivan the Terrible*. As a Marxist configuration, *Ivan*'s perspective is closer to history's nightmare and tragicomedy of the restoration of autocracy. The trajectory of *Ivan*'s representational forms is toward an anthropology of partriarchal power and an archaeology of the autocrat's psyche.

In Eisenstein's cinema, *Ivan the Terrible* is unique in the extremes to which it develops character psychology and an individual tragedy. In identifying his previous "tragedies of individualism," Eisenstein lists the projects on *An American Tragedy, Sutter's Gold*, and *The Black Consul*, whose Emperor Christophe "fell because of his individualistic isolation from his people" (*IM* 260). Eisenstein stated that the fundamental theme in *Ivan the Terrible* is "Ivan's despair," which is symptomatic of a consciousness divided historically: "In spite of the fact that Ivan is a progressive man of the sixteenth century, looking far ahead, he is still a man tied to his own time—to the beliefs and prejudices, to the superstitions accompanying the religious fanaticism of the epoch" (*NN* 310). To understand the effect of such characterization, one need only compare Alexander Nevsky, a screen character of undivided consciousness. *Alexander Nevsky* represents Nevsky's era as one without internal contradiction. The film defines that era through his leadership of Russia's resistance to external threat. The extremes and contradictions in Ivan's personality, on the other hand, are representative of divided political consciousness in Russia's history. Russia is at times the tsar's enemy. The terms of such division have their counterpart in the divided world-historical consciousness represented in the twentieth-century phenomena of mass, totalitarian leaders. In the case of the Soviet Union under Stalin, the progressive aspect of the leader's consciousness—modern socialism—is captive of an unreconstructed world-historical idea: autocracy.

Eisenstein's inspiration for the scenic design for palace intrigue in *Ivan the Terrible* came largely from the Piranesi series of etchings *Prisons*. A chapter in *Nonindifferent Nature* is devoted to analysis of Piranesi's "frenzied architecture" and of production design in *Ivan*, Eisenstein's most extensive studio work. The director treats architecture as indicative of an era's ideology: "the architecture in different epochs is expressed in different ways, and, besides, it expresses a definite thought or idea in the most concrete sense of the word. And this is why the 'image' is always socially and historically conditioned and expresses a definite ideological content of a certain epoch" (*NN* 138). As a historical example, Eisenstein refers to the official style of nineteenth-century tsardom: "The image of absolutism frozen in the invincibility of its principles—is the structure of buildings of the Nicholas epoch. The terrestrial emperor—the concrete 'Tsar and God,' leaning on the bureaucrat and policeman" (*NN* 139).

With the silent films, the drama of social history is rendered in terms of collective heroism, even in the presence of historical leaders like Lenin and individual types like Marfa. In *Potemkin* the death of Vakulinchuk is a tragic moment whose pathos is expressed dynamically and collectively through the activities of the gathering mourners. Subsequent mass actions entirely surpass this tragic loss to convey the collective pathos of a humanism gained through political action itself. In *Ivan the Terrible*, however, social history is displaced by an individual's self-dramatization. Pathos and tragedy are contorted through the turmoil of an isolated character in often static, intimate visual compositions.

The mass of humanity in *Ivan the Terrible* is merely an accessory to the tsar's personal drama. At the conclusion to part 1 a sequence of extraordinary shot compositions in depth depicts the populace's appeal for Ivan's return to Moscow from Alexandrov. The procession forms a long, dark serpentine curve against a flat expanse of snow. Its members bear religious icons and sacred banners; a choir sings "Have mercy, O Lord! . . . O return! O return! . . . The father of us all." Along the procession's length, people fall to their knees when Ivan appears in an archway high on the palace walls. From that position, Ivan looks out and down upon his humble petitioners. In a progression of closer shots, Ivan's profile dominates the foreground while, to the other side of the screen, the procession

extends in the background to the horizon. The sequence brings foreground, background, and the two sides of screen space into closer graphic
relationships, making the procession seem like an extension of Ivan's facial geometry. In the closest shot, the thin, sinuous line of petitioners
reiterates the curvature of Ivan's beard. The graphics make the Russian
people prominent only as an extension, an appendage of the autocrat. The
fate of Russia lies exclusively with Ivan, whois identified in the accompanying choral lyrics as the absolute paternal authority.

In a 1945 essay written to preface a proposed volume in celebration of
the twentieth anniversary of *Potemkin*, Eisenstein contemplated the differences between the silent film and *Ivan the Terrible:*

> What could be more strikingly dissimilar than the themes and de-
> velopment of two such works, separated one from the other in time
> by some twenty years?
> The collective and the mass are there.
> The autocratic individual is here.
> The likeness of a chorus, merging into a collective personage and
> artistic image is there.
> A sharply defined character is here.
> A desperate struggle against Tsarism is there.
> The initial establishment of Tsarist power is here.

He remarks further that the films represent two extremes that "seem to
have polarized themselves into mutually exclusive opposites."[1] The essay
attempts, with little success, to prove there is unity among these extremes. The differences Eisenstein writes of extend well beyond cinematic themes and styles. The comparisons above trace a historical reversal
that separates not only two films and two Russian eras, but two periods in
Soviet politics and culture as well.

Much of Soviet literature and cinema on contemporary themes in the
1940s presents Stalin as the genius of world history. *The Vow* (1946), for
example, is an adulatory portrait of Stalin framed by the spectacle of Lenin's death. The film title refers to the speech Stalin made to the Congress
of Soviets five days after Lenin's death, in which he enumerated Lenin's
"commandments" and swore to each one of them. Historians have noted
its liturgical phrasing and repetitions.[2] The film's director, Mikhail Chiaureli, and co-scenarist, Pyotr Pavlenko, treat Stalin's oath as an act of sol-
emn religiosity. Alone and in profound thought Stalin (portrayed by Mikhail Gelovani) grieves the loss of Lenin. Wandering in a snow-covered and
empty Red Square, Stalin suddenly stops to receive inspiration, which an
inner voice conveys. The leader raises his eyes as a ray of light, passing
through the branches of trees, illuminates him.

Commenting on *The Vow*, André Bazin identifies the components of the Stalin myth: "In terms of History, he is omniscient, infallible, irresistible, his destiny is irreversible. In terms of humanity, his psychology typifies qualities that conform with allegory: equanimity . . . , reflection or rather conscience, the spirit of decision and goodness."[3] As historical drama, *The Vow* makes Stalin the incarnation of revolution, the entelechy of Marxism. To Stalin's mind in this period, the origins of the history fulfilled in him were to be traced to autocrats like Ivan IV and Peter I. *Ivan the Terrible* employs some of the same mythic iconography on the level of history but none of it on the level of personality.

On the level of history, the royal look in *Ivan the Terrible* conveys the same infallibility and omniscience found in Stalinist iconography. There is also a pronounced Byzantine dimension to the film's iconography, particularly in the coronation scene. With the coronation platform centered like an altar in the Kremlin's Uspensky Cathedral, young Ivan is the focal point for light rays streaming into the church. In this light, the image of the crowned Ivan replicates that of Christ Pantocrator ("Ruler of the World"), familiar in Byzantine church art.

On the level of personality, however, there is in Ivan no equanimity, decisiveness, or benevolence equivalent to the Stalin cult of personality. The political drama of instituting tsarism centers on Ivan's doubts and dread. *Ivan the Terrible* parallels Renaissance tragedies of blood in examining the effects of revenge upon the avenging hero. These effects involve psychological and political symptoms equally. In terms of the film's imagery, in autocracy the ruler alone constitutes the body politic. And, as the embodiment of Russia, Ivan is grotesque. Absolutism is represented as the historical condition of one man's absolute subjectivity. In its critique of power, *Ivan the Terrible* reasons that for the formation of Europe's ruling class there was a political necessity for evil geniuses like Ivan Grozny, Bloody Mary, and Catherine de Medici, rulers remembered in history for massive terror.

Visual figures for the body politic appear in Eisenstein's cinema from the outset, starting with the literalized analogy in *Strike* between disorganized masses and slaughtered livestock. In *Potemkin* the procession of mourners lines a narrow breakwater that curves beyond view, creating an image of stark grandeur. Its human geometry, determined by the jetty, is dynamically linked to the revolutionary cause through a gradual camera pan that moves from the dense and animate crowd around Vakulinchuk's corpse to the advancing arc of new mourners. In *October* mass movement represents human dynamism as the global signifier in both art and politics.

A major element in these dynamic images of the body politic is the carnivalesque spirit Bakhtin has associated with the popular mind and unofficial social groups. In medieval folk culture, the carnival served as a suspension of law and a collective experience of utopian freedom. The carnival spirit became "at the Renaissance stage of its development the expression of a new free and critical *historical* consciousness."[4] Eisenstein's silent cinema renders modern equivalents to this spirit. In *Potemkin* the scenes of fraternization between battleship and shore evoke a sense of newly gained freedom and consciousness. A similar effect is suggested in *October* through the dance marking the alliance of Cossacks and Bolsheviks, the storming of the Winter Palace, and the bacchanal of destruction in the wine cellars and the tsarina's private chambers. *Old and New* evokes imagery of social ecstasy in episodes celebrating the cream separator, the bull's wedding, animal husbandry, and cultivation of the soil.

Eisenstein's most direct and extensive use of carnival motifs is in *Que Viva Mexico!* The Catholic festivals featuring Indian celebrants expressly combine the sacred and the profane. The most *popular* festival portrayed is the Day of the Dead, which concludes the film with an expression of contemporary Mexico's revolutionary promise. These four earlier films offer essentially a comic plot to history in which the pathos of class conflict—as in the deaths of Vakulinchuk and Sebastian—is sublated in communist revolution. In *Que Viva Mexico!* that revolution exists in a potential state through the carnival's vitalist rebellion against death.

Bakhtin has argued that the grotesque style and inverted forms of the sixteenth-century carnival are manifested in the historical Ivan IV's destruction of boyar power and traditions. Their breakdown reflects, in his opinion, "the influence of popular forms of mockery and derision: travesties and masquerades that turned the hierarchy 'inside out,' uncrownings and debasements."[5] In cultural terms, the oprichnina functioned to overturn the nobility's ideography and to install that of tsardom. No utopian spirit comparable to the carnivalesque in Eisenstein's silent films gives form, however, to the inversions and mock rituals in *Ivan the Terrible*.

With a degree of the grotesque unrelieved by carnivalesque humor, caricature and typage are used extensively in *Ivan the Terrible*'s characterizations. Euphrosyne's beaked face, often shown in profile, suggests a bird of prey; in the script she is described as "a sable-hued bird." Malyuta, as Ivan's loyal companion, is presented in some compositions as the tsar's shaggy watchdog. As humors or types, Anastasia is a doe-eyed innocent and Ivan a guileful fox or wolf. Ivan and Malyuta, when shown in conspiratorial intimacy, suggest two ravening beasts.

Two prevalent compositional aspects of the film's grotesqueness are gigantism and deformation, which are linked directly to its political imagery. The astrolabe in the palace library, for instance, casts a huge, distorted shadow above the tsar's head and thus suggests the nature of his ambitions. The deep horizontal space, low ceilings, and unusual contours of the film's indoor settings are exaggerated further with the use of a wide-angle lens to embody, as Eisenstein noted, states of exaltation and obsession. These states of mind are given form as well in the makeup and postures Eisenstein imposed upon the actor Nikolai Cherkasov in the role of Ivan. For part 3, Eisenstein imagined Ivan's face in transformation: "the tortured old man, lamenting with tears of blood the unavoidable massacre of Novgorod—to the conqueror of Livonia, whose passionate, eagle regard subdues the Baltic's waves."

The actor Cherkasov described Eisenstein's method of direction on *Ivan the Terrible* as an effort "to make every take a finished tableau," which required him to assume exaggerated postures.[6] Expressionist lighting effects contribute to the film shots' painterly appearance. Equal attention was paid to the cut and draping of costumes in the varying postures. It is in this period that Eisenstein writes of cinema as "the *highest stage of painting*" which, as such, necessarily involves the "original stages of painting: as if again reproducing the form of the early picture scroll on the screen" (*NN* 248). A primitivism in the film's imagery is evident. Among its sources are the medieval Russian religious icon and later folk arts (especially the *lubok*). When onscreen dialogue is delivered, the film's compositions are often static like paintings or operatic tableaux. Some compositions are vertiginous in their effect. Facial features are magnified and slightly misshapen. The body is situated obliquely in relation to the screen frame. Conventions of perspective are violated. In a number of shots where the camera is moved, the emphasis remains on Ivan's crooked posture and frozen features.

Acting style in *Ivan the Terrible* approaches grotesque extremes and Ivan's behavior is strongly ritualized. The major confrontations in Ivan's drive toward autocracy take place in the church and the palace. These are the state's only public centers, opened selectively to the rest of the world. Church and palace are also the sites of the autocrat's most profound personal experiences. In public, Ivan is most often represented in situations that require of him a display of position and power. This is so even on the verge of death. Seriously ill, Ivan receives last rites from Metropolitan Pimen, his political adversary. As part of extreme unction, an open, ornate Bible is lowered to cover Ivan's face. He struggles to raise his head as the oversized Bible slowly descends but only has time to glance rapidly about the room, to ascertain who is present and how he is being regarded. The sequence ends with Ivan's head collapsing on a pillow and the Bible lowered to block the tsar from view. In the next scene Ivan hysterically demeans himself before the boyars in petitioning them to swear loyalty to the infant Dmitri, the tsar's first son. Even through suffering and abasement the tsar responds with grandiloquent gestures.

In commenting on the film's acting style, Eisenstein said of its elevated manner: "The grandeur of our subject called for monumental means of presentation. . . . This was how the style of the film was determined, a style that ran counter to many of the traditional methods to which we have grown accustomed. . . . The general custom is to try to make the historical personage 'accessible,' to portray him as an ordinary person sharing the ordinary, human traits of all other people. . . . But with Ivan we wanted a different tone. In him we wished chiefly to convey a sense of majesty, and this led us to adopt majestic forms."[7] Eisenstein's departure from convention is in the direction of histrionics and obsessional rituals.

Ivan's behavior is not stable or predictable. Dramatic situations border on extremes of solemnity or frenzy, of abnegation or ostentation. Eisenstein continued to reject the conventions of naturalist theater, but for reasons different from those offered during the silent period. With *Ivan* he aimed to develop a dramaturgy that would surpass techniques of the Moscow Art Theater in evoking the individual's pathos. In defining the theater of pathos, Eisenstein contrasts the flamboyant, presentational style of the famous nineteenth-century stage performer Frederick Lemaître with the nuance, understatement, and balance of emotions in Stanislavsky's realist ensemble effects. In the pathetic tradition of Lemaître's acting, according to Eisenstein, "the character is cut into opposites, in a flight of *pathos* uniting its opposites in the unity of an ardent, vivid image" (*NN* 106).

It is in the section from *Nonindifferent Nature* on pathos entitled "The Cream Separator and the Grail" that Eisenstein delineates two modes of ecstasy and two forms of representation in the religious procession and cream separator sequences of *Old and New*. In the procession for rain, there is a paroxysm of faith and fanaticism, a sterile spasm of prayer that goes unrewarded by the heavens. Demonstration of the separator is the consummation of a social bond, one between the individual, the collective, and the machine. Two different methods of direction and montage govern the sequences. The procession and prayer for rain, Eisenstein writes, are centered on "playacting—or, better said, 'theatrical'—means of influence through human behavior." The separator's production of cream is presented by "pure cinematographic means, impossible on such scale and form in the other arts" (*NN* 51). Rapid, often objectivist montage is the principal means of creating an image of collective ecstasy in the cream separator sequence. The overtone to the acting and visuals of *Ivan the Terrible*, in these terms, is most like that of the procession sequence in *Old and New*, where the ecstasy sought is unfulfilled and futile.

In an examination of the interpenetration of genres made in *Nonindifferent Nature*, Eisenstein expounds a unique idea of tragicomedy:

"through a comic structure there operates the same basic generalization of the law that underlies serious structures" (*NN* 195). In arguing that both tragedy and comedy are structured through a unity of opposites, Eisenstein applies Engels's universal theory of dialectics. He also revives the Formalist principles of writers and critics like Tynyanov, whose fiction achieves "generalized unification of deeds mighty and deeds insignificant, as if they were of equal and identical significance" (*NN* 91n). Eisenstein describes the form of signification in both cases as "a complete doubling, a complete rupture between essence and sign, and ultimately a brutal, arbitrary shock." The combined effect of pathos and comedy is structured as an inversion Eisenstein terms the *antipathos.* The inversion of pathos is "not just a 'mild humor' or 'a good-natured grin,' but rather a phenomenon that is comic in appearance and profoundly significant (perhaps even tragic) in essence" (*NN* 56).

Analyzing film comedy in 1945, Eisenstein identifies an unexpected analogue to the system of signification in *Ivan the Terrible.* He praises Chaplin's two most recent films—*Modern Times* and *The Great Dictator*—as a radical departure from previous comedy. To describe Chaplin's artistic advance, Eisenstein applies categories of the grotesque and the specular. The two Chaplin films represent "a break in the style of things: in thematic treatment, to the monstrous and distorted; in the inner aspect of Chaplin himself, to a complete revelation of the secret of his eyes" (*FE* 123). The secret is revealed through both Chaplin's direction and his dramatization of perception as a screen character. The regard or look of the Chaplin persona becomes ideational in content: "The sudden immediacy of his look gives birth to a comic perception. This perception becomes transformed into a conception" (*FE* 124). Eisenstein advises Soviet audiences that Chaplin's later comedy presents "socially tragic phenomena" (*FE* 125). The fairy-tale situations, childlike innocence, and infantile behavior of the Chaplin persona do not indicate any flight from reality. The horror of modern, totalitarian life represented in the two Chaplin features is conveyed through imagery "where an array of tortures, killings, fears and terrors are inevitable" (*FE* 129). Eisenstein finds the effect of "terrible actuality" to be Chaplin's most politicized perception in cinema (*FE* 138).

The atavism of a supreme individual's power, caricatured in *October's* portrayal of Kerensky and his Provisional Government, is conveyed in *Ivan the Terrible* through tragicomic attributes. The mock coronation of Vladimir in part 2 suggests many counterparts in cultural history and anthropology. It closely resembles ceremonies of the scapegoat James Frazer describes in *The Golden Bough,* a work Eisenstein prized. In one common typology the king, in order to prolong his own reign, crowns a son as his royal substitute and then has him sacrificed to appease the gods.

Similarly, in the Roman saturnalia a condemned man is placed for a brief time on the throne in robes and afforded royal pleasures, then he is dethroned and executed. In terms of the first typology, Vladimir assumes the role of the tsar's son once the actual son, Dmitri, disappears from the plot after only one scene.

In some respects, *Ivan the Terrible* implies that anthropology and ancient cultures, rather than revolutionary history, are the most immediate contexts for understanding Ivan's era. In regard to the Soviet context, Eisenstein specified: "The *oath of the oprichnina* grows through the drama . . . in the direction of a sacred oath of faith to the Tsar (which as a theme is good in and of itself for the present). . . . It is good that namely *the spy and traitor* Staden quotes the 'sacred' text of the oath. This directly calls into play the same bloody irony as when this bastard writes in his notes: 'Those who were in the oprichnina in service to the Grand Prince pledged to their ruler in the name of God and the Holy Cross. And for this God punished them, not their ruler.' "[8] For *Ivan the Terrible*, anthropology and history intersect in these kinds of inversion.

Within a Soviet intellectual environment of authoritarian totality, Eisenstein's cultural investigations of the 1940s seek to establish timeless universals in cultural experience. Where Eisenstein's efforts at theoretical synthesis in the 1920s had centered on questions of material, dialectical, and historical approaches to form, his final effort in *Nonindifferent Nature* focuses on suprahistorical issues. His operative premise in these writings is that "the structure of the *emotional behavior of the human being*" underlies perception and cultural representation equally (*NN* 4). Pathos stands as a timeless universal of emotional behavior and its primary affect in the individual is ecstasy. Eisenstein characterizes ecstasy here as "a transport out of understanding—a transport out of conceptualization— a transport out of imagery—a transport out of the sphere of any rudiments of consciousness whatever" (*NN* 178–79). The collective, utopian understanding of ecstasy as an extension of history, central to *Old and New* and *Que Viva Mexico!*, is absent from this definition.

Nonindifferent Nature concludes that the "dynamic generality of 'the formula of ecstasy' " constitutes universal laws "according to which the very movement and origin of natural phenomena occur [and should] be taken as structural prototype of the construction of pathos." Eisenstein further asserts that these laws "have endured from the beginning of the vital functioning of our planet's system until this very day as penetrating and unchanging" (*NN* 183). This formulation appears under the heading "On the Question of Suprahistory." With this term Eisenstein intends the sense of earlier than history, or *prehistoric*, yet it also stands as a sign of thought conducted beyond questions of history.

In proposing that culture and nature are unmediated structural equivalents, *Nonindifferent Nature* adheres to Engels's organicism in *Dialectics of Nature*, the authority Eisenstein cites frequently in the 1940s for his aesthetic premises. Engels's treatise on natural laws had been undertaken intermittently in the years 1875–95 and Marx in his own lifetime had reserved judgment upon it. *Dialectics of Nature* investigates nature largely in the abstract and outside the realm of history, which was for Marx the final determinant in dialectical analysis. Herbert Marcuse has remarked that in Engels's treatise "the dialectical concepts appear as mere analogies, figurative and superimposed upon the content—strikingly empty or commonplace compared with the exact concreteness of the dialectical concepts in the economic and socio-historical writings" of Marx and Engels.[9]

Emphasis on the dialectics of nature is a distinguishing feature of the Stalin period, during which any genuine Marxist critique of history was suppressed. Soviet Marxism became a set of prescriptions institutionalized in the *History of the Communist Party of the Soviet Union*, first published in 1938 and often revised as the state's versions of political orthodoxy and history shifted. The *History* presented the official rationale for the revolution from above that had already been in progress for nearly a decade. Stalin authored the section "Dialectical and Historical Materialism" in the *History*, and in later years the entire book was credited to him. The official version of Soviet Marxism Stalin establishes in the *History* is founded on Engels's *Dialectics of Nature*. Instead of the method for discovery of the truth about historical reality and the structure of society, dialectics itself is exalted in the Stalin period as universal truth and reality. Though in Eisenstein's later writings history often yields to ahistorical anthropology, speculative psychology, and the organic unity of opposites that prevails in Engels's *Dialectics of Nature*, *Ivan the Terrible* remains a profound historical critique.

In André Bazin's account of film history, from the beginnings of motion-picture photography inventors foresaw a complete mechanical reproduction of reality: "The guiding myth, then, inspiring the invention of cinema is the accomplishment of that which dominated in a more or less vague fashion all the techniques of the mechanical reproduction of reality in the nineteenth century, from photography to the phonograph, namely an integral realism, a recreation of the world in its own image unburdened by the freedom of interpretation of the artist or the irreversibility of time."[10] In the 1940s Eisenstein welcomed cinema's expanding technical capacity to render dimensions in depth, color, and sound, but he argued vigorously against any absolute correspondence between the sensorial image and external reality. Such correspondence, he asserted, was to be found in the deep structure of sensuous thought.

In Eisenstein's view, moreover, relations between image, color, and sound are specific to the art work and often achieve an effect through antinaturalism, disjunction, and noncongruence among the elements. Cinema is potentially a totalization for Eisenstein—not of reality but of traditional arts and cultural practices and their systems of representation. He finds in stereoscopic film, for example, possibilities for representing space and volume superior to the properties of sculpture and architecture: "no other art has ever furnished an example of so dynamic and perfect a transition of volume into space, space into volume, of their splicing and coexisting, and all that in the process of real motion" (*N* 133–34). Eisenstein's interests in the tonality, valuation, and semiotics of color, and his principles of denatured coloration, find their fulfillment later in the work of directors like Michelangelo Antonioni, Ingmar Bergman, Federico Fellini, Akira Kurosawa, Nagisa Oshima, and Luchino Visconti.

Among directors in the medium's first fifty years, Eisenstein stands alone as the maker of a fully historical cinema. History enters cinema as both subject and structuring form within Eisenstein's film work. Eisenstein is unique in his treatment of personality, social class, political event, and national heritage as a drama of history making. Spanning twenty-five years, his cinema explores two central movements within the history and consciousness of modern socialism, the Bolshevik Revolution and the Stalinist state. With the example of Eisenstein, international cinema since World War II has become richly historical in imagination in film works by directors such as Kurosawa, Visconti, Roberto Rossellini, Bernardo Bertolucci, Alain Resnais, Marcel Ophuls, Gillo Pontecorvo, Miklos Jancso, Andrzej Wajda, Ousmane Sembene, Patricio Guzman, Humberto Solas, and Fernando Solanas. The relatively small body of Eisenstein's finished work comprises a great legacy of historical art and Marxist perspectives for the future of cinema.

Notes

Introduction

1. Hayden White, *The Content of the Form: Narrative Discourse and Historical Representation* (Baltimore: Johns Hopkins University Press, 1987), 4.

2. Marc Ferro, "The Fiction Film and Historical Analysis," in *The Historian and Film*, ed. Paul Smith (New York: Cambridge University Press, 1976), 80.

3. Karl Marx and Friedrich Engels, *The Holy Family*, trans. Richard Dixon and Clemens Dutt (Moscow: Progress Publishers, 1975), 110.

4. *The Marx-Engels Reader*, ed. Robert C. Tucker (New York: Norton, 1972), 4. My understanding of Marxism is indebted to many sources; in relation to these introductory remarks I wish to cite specifically: Isaiah Berlin, *Karl Marx: His Life and Environment* (New York: Oxford University Press, 1978); *A Dictionary of Marxist Thought*, ed. Tom Bottomore (Cambridge, Mass.: Harvard University Press, 1983); Ernest Mandel, *Marxist Economic Theory*, 2 vols., trans. Brian Pearce (New York: Monthly Review Press, 1968); Karl Korsh, *Karl Marx* (New York: Russell and Russell, 1963); and Hayden White, *Metahistory: The Historical Imagination in Nineteenth-Century Europe* (Baltimore: Johns Hopkins University Press, 1973).

5. Karl Marx, *Capital*, trans. Samuel Moore and Edward Aveling (New York: International, 1967), 1:20.

6. *Marx-Engels Reader*, 8. In response to a parlor game, Marx once listed his favorite motto as *De omnibus dubitandum*.

7. Karl Marx and Friedrich Engels, *The German Ideology* (Moscow: Progress Publishers, 1976), 42. Valuable sources for the discussion of ideology in film study are: Bill Nichols, *Ideology and the Image* (Bloomington: Indiana University Press, 1981), and Philip Rosen, ed., *Narrative, Apparatus, Ideology* (New York: Columbia University Press, 1986). While the concern in these two books is primarily with ideology as a system of unconscious values latent in the apparatus and narrative codes of cinema, my discussion mainly concerns the critique and construction of ideology in the development of historical consciousness.

8. Marx and Engels, *The German Ideology*, 42.

9. From a letter to Franz Mehring dated July 14, 1893; *Marx-Engels Reader*, 648, 650.

10. *Marx-Engels Reader*, 5.

11. Vladimir I. Lenin, *Selected Works* (New York: International, 1971), 622.

12. Fredric Jameson, *Marxism and Form* (Princeton: Princeton University Press, 1971), 297.

13. Quoted in Klaus Völker, *Brecht Chronicle*, trans. Fred Wieck (New York: Seabury, 1975), 79.

14. Marie Seton, *Sergei M. Eisenstein* (New York: Wyn, 1952).

15. Yon Barna, *Eisenstein*, trans. Lise Hunter (Bloomington: Indiana University Press, 1973).

16. The biography is the second in Fernandez's two-volume work entitled collectively *L'arbre jusqu'aux racines*. The first volume bears the individual title *Psychanalyse et création* (Paris: Grasset, 1972); the second is entitled *Eisenstein* (Paris: Grasset, 1975). Another psychosexual approach is provided by filmmaker Stan Brakhage in an impressionistic biographical sketch in *Film Biographies* (Berkeley, Calif.: Turtle Island, 1977).

17. Jean Mitry, *Eisenstein* (Paris: Editions Universitaires, 1956). A revised and enlarged edition was published by Editions Universitaires in 1978.

18. Léon Moussinac, *Sergei Eisenstein*, trans. D. Sandy Petrey (New York: Crown, 1970).

19. Barthélemy Amengual, *Serguei Mikailovitch Eisenstein* (Lyon: Premier Plan, 1962).

20. Barthélemy Amengual, *Que Viva Eisenstein!* (Lausanne: Editions l'Age d'Homme, 1980).

21. J. Dudley Andrew, *The Major Film Theories* (New York: Oxford University Press, 1970).

22. Brian Henderson, *A Critique of Film Theory* (New York: Dutton, 1980), 3–31. Dana Polan examines Eisenstein's theory for its Marxist redefinition of realism in *The Political Language of Film and the Avant-Garde* (Ann Arbor: UMI Research Press, 1985), 33–52.

23. David Bordwell, "Eisenstein's Epistemological Shift," *Screen* 15, no. 4 (Winter 1974–75): 29–46. Bordwell examines the second period from another perspective in "Narration and Scenography in the Later Eisenstein," *Millennium Film Journal*, no. 13 (Fall-Winter 1983–84): 62–80.

24. François Albera, *Notes sur l'esthétique d'Eisenstein* (Lyon: Université Lyon, 1973).

25. Peter Wollen, *Signs and Meaning in the Cinema* (Bloomington: Indiana University Press, 1969), 7–70.

26. Vyacheslav Ivanov, "Eisenstein et la linguistique structurale moderne," trans. Andrée Robel, *Cahiers du Cinéma*, no. 220–21 (May-June 1970): 47–50. Other discussions of Eisenstein's theory from linguistic and semiotic points of view are: Herbert Eagle, "Eisenstein as a Semiotician of the Cinema," in *The Sign: Semiotics around the World*, ed. R. W. Bailey, L. Matejka, and P. Steiner (Ann Arbor: Michigan Slavic Publications, 1978), 173–93; Herbert Eagle, "Russian Formalist Film Theory: An Introduction," in his collection *Russian Formalist Film Theory* (Ann Arbor: Michigan Slavic Publications, 1981), 1–54; Alexander K. Zolkovsky, "Generative Poetics in the Writings of Eisenstein," trans. L. M. O'Toole, *Russian Poetics in Translation* 8 (1981): 40–61; and Alexander K. Zolkovsky and J. K. Sceglov, "Structural Poetics Is a Generative Poetics," in *Soviet Semiotics: An Anthology*, ed. and trans. Daniel P. Lucid (Baltimore: Johns Hopkins University Press, 1977), 175–92.

27. Christian Metz, *Langage et cinéma* (Paris: Larousse, 1971), 20–28.

28. Jacques Aumont, *Montage Eisenstein* (Paris: Editions Albatros, 1979).

29. Marie-Claire Ropars-Wuilleumier and Pierre Sorlin, *Octobre: écriture et idéologie* (Paris: Editions Albatros, 1976); Michèle Lagny, Marie-Claire Ropars-Wuilleumier, and Pierre Sorlin, *La révolution figurée: film, histoire, politique* (Paris: Editions Albatros, 1979). For a fuller discussion of these two volumes and the Aumont book, see my article "Plusiers Eisensteins: Recent Criticism," *Quarterly Review of Film Studies* 6, no. 4 (Fall 1981): 391–412.

30. Kristin Thompson, *Eisenstein's Ivan the Terrible* (Princeton: Princeton University Press, 1981).

31. Kristen Thompson, *Breaking the Glass Armor: Neoformalist Film Analysis* (Princeton: Princeton University Press, 1988), 21.

32. For discussion of this period of film studies, see Sylvia Harvey, *May '68 and Film Culture* (London: BFI, 1978), and *Screen Reader 1: Cinema/Ideology/Politics* (London: Society for Education in Film and Television, 1977).

33. Guido Aristarco, *Marx, le cinéma et la critique de film*, trans. Barthélemy Amengual (Paris: Minard, 1972).

34. Jean-Patrick Lebel, *Cinéma et idéologie* (Paris: Editions Sociales, 1971).

35. Gilles Deleuze, *Cinema 1: l'image-mouvement* (Paris: Minuit, 1983) and *Cinema 2: l'image-temps* (Paris: Minuit, 1985). I am particularly indebted to the first book's insightful comparisons of Eisenstein to Griffith in matters of montage and the close-up.

Chapter 1: Revolutionary Beginnings

1. Vladimir Lenin, *What Is to Be Done?*, in *The Lenin Anthology*, ed. Robert C. Tucker (New York: Norton, 1975), 48.

2. Sergei Eisenstein, *Immoral Memories*, trans. Herbert Marshall (Boston: Houghton, 1983), 39. All subsequent references to this volume will be noted in the text with the abbreviation *IM*. Reproductions of Eisenstein's graphic art are available in *Drawings* (Moscow, 1961); *Esquisses et dessins* (Paris: Cahiers du Cinéma, 1978); *Unpublished Mexican Drawings* (Mexico City: Cinteca Nacional, 1978); and Jay Leyda and Zina Voynow, *Eisenstein at Work* (New York: Pantheon, 1982). Discussions of his graphic sensibility from other perspectives are contained in François Albera, "Eisenstein et la question graphique," *Cahiers du Cinéma*, no. 295 (December 1978): 11–16; Naum Kleiman, "Eisenstein's Graphic Work," in *Eisenstein at 90*, ed. Ian Christie and David Elliott (Oxford: Museum of Modern Art, Oxford, 1988), 11–17; and Kleiman's introduction to the *Esquisses et dessins* volume. *Eisenstein at 90* contains a translation of the Albera essay.

3. Sergei Eisenstein, *Selected Works*, vol. 1, ed. and trans. Richard Taylor (Bloomington: Indiana University Press, 1988), 243. All subsequent references to this volume will be noted in the text with the abbreviation *W*.

4. Eisenstein's statement is recalled by Ilya Ehrenburg, as cited in *Meyerhold at Work*, ed. Paul Schmidt (Austin: University of Texas Press, 1980), 66.

5. The production is described in Nick Worrall, "Meyerhold's Production of *The Magnificent Cuckold*," *The Drama Review* 17, no. 1 (March 1973): 14–34. Worrall examines the artistic relationship between the two directors in "Meyerhold and Eisenstein," in *Performance and Politics in Popular Drama*, ed. David

Bradby, Louis James, and Bernard Sharratt (New York: Cambridge University Press, 1980), 173–87.

6. Translated by John Bowlt in *The Tradition of Constructivism*, ed. Stephen Bann (New York: Viking, 1974), 38, 40.

7. Vsevolod Meyerhold, "Biomechanics," in *Meyerhold on Theatre*, ed. and trans. Edward Braun (New York: Hill and Wang, 1969), 198–99. For an assessment of the Meyerhold system, see Mel Gordon, "Meyerhold's Biomechanics," *The Drama Review* 18, no. 3 (September 1974): 73–88.

8. The source for this quotation as well as the one in the paragraph above is Anatoli Lunacharsky, "Revolution and Art," in *Russian Art of the Avant-Garde*, ed. and trans. John Bowlt (New York: Viking, 1976), 191–92.

9. Description of this production is contained in Huntly Carter, *The New Spirit in the Russian Theater, 1917–1928* (New York: Brentano's, 1929); Daniel Gerould, "Eisenstein's *Wiseman*," *The Drama Review* 18, no. 1 (March 1974): 71–76; and Tadeusz Szczepanski, "*The Wise Man* Reconsidered," trans. Eva Forian and Eva Kziazek, in *Eisenstein Revisited: A Collection of Essays*, ed. Lars Kleberg and Håken Lövgren (Stockholm: Almqvist and Wiksell, 1987), 11–24.

10. From Gan's *Constructivism* (1922), translated in part in Camilla Gray, *The Great Experiment: Russian Art 1863–1922* (London: Thames and Hudson, 1962), 285.

11. The collaboration with Tretyakov is described in Mel Gordon, "Eisenstein's Later Work at the Proletkult," *The Drama Review* 22, no. 3 (September 1978): 107–12.

12. Sergei Eisenstein, *Film Form: Essays in Film Theory*, ed. and trans. Jay Leyda (New York: Harcourt, 1949), 15. All subsequent references to this volume will be noted in the text with the abbreviation *FF.*

13. Sergei Eisenstein and Sergei Tretyakov, "Expressive Movement," trans. Alma Law, *Millennium Film Journal*, no. 3 (Winter-Spring 1979): 30–38. The translation is prefaced by an article by Mel Gordon and Alma Law, "Eisenstein's Early Work in Expressive Behavior" (25–29).

14. Lev Kuleshov, "The Tasks of the Artist in Cinema," in *The Film Factory: Russian and Soviet Cinema in Documents*, ed. Richard Taylor and Ian Christie, trans. Richard Taylor (Cambridge, Mass.: Harvard University Press, 1988), 41.

15. See the biographical survey and interview with Kuleshov in Steven P. Hill, "Kuleshov—Prophet without Honor?" *Film Culture*, no. 44 (Spring 1967): 1–41. Kuleshov also describes the filmmaking workshop in "The Origins of Montage," an interview conducted in 1965 that appears in *Cinema in Revolution*, ed. Luda and Jean Schnitzer and Marcel Martin, trans. David Robinson (New York: Hill and Wang, 1973), 67–76. The special issue "L'Effet Koulechov" of *Iris* 4, no. 1 (1986), is particularly useful, especially the articles by Vance Kepley, Jr., "The Kuleshov Workshop," and Yuri Tsivian, "Notes historiques en marge de l'expérience de Koulechov."

16. Vsevolod I. Pudovkin, *Film Technique and Film Acting*, ed. and trans. Ivor Montagu (New York: Grove, 1970), 168–69.

17. Lev Kuleshov, "Art of the Cinema" (1929), in *Kuleshov on Film*, ed. and trans. Ronald Levaco (Berkeley: University of California Press, 1974), 52–53.

18. Noel Burch, "Film's Institutional Mode of Representation and the Soviet Response," *October*, no. 11 (Winter 1979): 77–96.

Chapter 2: *Strike*

1. Vladimir Lenin, "Lecture on the 1905 Revolution," *Lenin Anthology*, 281.
2. Leyda and Voynow, *Eisenstein at Work*, 16.
3. Friedrich Engels, *The Condition of the Working Class in England* (1845) (New York: Penguin, 1987), 233.
4. Rosa Luxemburg, *The Mass Strike*, trans. Patrick Lavin (New York: Harper, 1971), 30.
5. Sheila Fitzpatrick, *The Russian Revolution 1917–1932* (New York: Oxford University Press, 1982) 15, 31.
6. Marx, *Capital*, 1:384–85, 388.
7. Roberta Reeder, "Agit-Prop Art: Posters, Puppets, Propaganda and Eisenstein's *Strike*," *Russian Literature Triquarterly*, no. 22 (1989): 255–78.
8. Roland Barthes, "The Third Meaning," in *The Responsibility of Forms*, trans. Richard Howard (New York: Hill and Wang, 1985), 57. Further discussion of this "third meaning" in relation to Eisenstein is provided in Kristin Thompson, "The Concept of Cinematic Excess," *Ciné-Tracts* 1, no. 2 (Summer 1977): 54–63.
9. See Margaret Betz, "The Icon and Russian Modernism," *Artforum* 16, no. 1 (Summer 1977): 38–45.
10. *Marx-Engels Reader*, 344.
11. Sergei Eisenstein, *Film Essays*, ed. and trans. Jay Leyda (New York: Praeger, 1970), 18. All subsequent references to this volume will be noted in the text with the abbreviation *FE*.
12. Georges Sorel, *Reflections on Violence*, trans. T. E. Hulme (New York: Collier, 1950), 78.
13. Vladimir Lenin, "The Immediate Tasks of the Soviet Government," *Lenin Anthology*, 459.
14. Marc Ferro takes an opposite view of *Strike* in *Cinéma et histoire* (Paris: Denoel/Gonthier, 1977), 127–34, arguing that the film promotes spontaneity above organization.
15. Bertolt Brecht, "A Short Organum for the Theatre," in *Brecht on Theatre*, ed. and trans. John Willett (New York: Hill and Wang, 1964), 185, 193, 192.
16. Walter Benjamin, "Conversations with Brecht," in *Reflections*, ed. Peter Demetz, trans. Edmund Jephcott (New York: Harcourt, 1978), 216.
17. Jean-Luc Godard, "Montage, mon beau souci," in *Godard on Godard*, ed. Jean Narboni and Tom Milne, trans. Milne (New York: Viking, 1972), 40.
18. Yuri Tynyanov, "La notion de construction," in *Théorie de la littérature*, ed. and trans. Tzvetan Todorov (Paris: Seuil, 1965), 114–15, 118.
19. Taylor and Christie, *Film Factory*, 133.
20. Dziga Vertov, *Kino-Eye*, ed. Annette Michelson, trans. Kevin O'Brien (Berkeley: University of California Press, 1984), 47, 45. For further comparison of the two directors, see Vlada Petric, *Constructivism in Film: The Man with the Movie Camera* (New York: Cambridge University Press, 1987), 48–50, and my

essay "The Object(ive)s of Cinema: Vertov (Factography) and Eisenstein (Ideography)," *Praxis*, no. 4 (1978): 223–30.

21. Quoted in Walter Benjamin, "A Short History of Photography," trans. Stanley Mitchell, *Screen* 13, no. 1 (Spring 1972): 24.

Chapter 3: *Battleship Potemkin*

1. An extract from the *1905* scenario and the director's shooting script for *Potemkin* are included in Sergei Eisenstein, *Three Films*, ed. Jay Leyda, trans. Diana Matias (New York: Harper, 1974). Two shot descriptions of the film are available in English: David Mayer, ed., *Sergei M. Eisenstein's Potemkin* (New York: Grossman, 1972); and *Potemkin*, trans. Gillon R. Aitken (New York: Simon and Schuster, 1968), which is based on a Soviet shot transcription made in the 1930s. Mayer's book is based on the best print in United States circulation; my references to the film's titles follow the translations in his volume. A valuable collection in English on the film's production and reception is Herbert Marshall, ed., *The Battleship Potemkin* (New York: Avon, 1978), which translates much material collected originally in Naum Kleiman and K. Levina, eds., *Bronenosets Potemkin* (Moscow: Iskusstvo, 1969).

2. *Lenin Anthology*, 555–56.

3. For a detailed though popularized account of these events see Richard Hough, *The Potemkin Mutiny* (London: Hamilton, 1969). Some comparisons of the film's events to the available historical record are made in D. J. Wenden, "*Battleship Potemkin*—Film and Reality," in *Feature Films as History*, ed. K. R. M. Short (Knoxville: University of Tennessee Press, 1981), 37–61.

4. The historical record is examined in an article by Daniel Gerould, "Historical Simulation and Popular Entertainment: The *Potemkin* Mutiny from Reconstructed Newsreel to Black Sea Stunt Men," *The Drama Review* 33, no. 2 (Summer 1989): 161–84.

5. *Lenin Anthology*, 285.

6. Nicholas V. Riasanovsky, *A History of Russia*, 2d ed. (New York: Oxford University Press, 1969), 452.

7. Sergei Eisenstein, *Notes of a Film Director*, trans. X. Danko (New York: Dover, 1970), 18. All subsequent references to this volume will be noted in the text with the abbreviation *N*.

8. *Lenin Anthology*, 24.

9. Karl Marx, *Economic and Philosophical Manuscripts of 1844*, ed. Dirk Struik, trans. Martin Milligan (New York: International, 1964), 187. Eisenstein could not have known the *Manuscripts* at this date since its first publication came in 1927, but Marx's definitions of communism as humanism are prominent as well in *The Holy Family* (1845) and the *Communist Manifesto* (1848).

10. Stanley Kauffmann, *Living Images* (New York: Harper, 1975), 293. An informative reading of the film's figures of vision is contained in Daniel Selden, "Vision and Violence: The Rhetoric of *Potemkin*," *Quarterly Review of Film Studies* 7, no. 4 (Fall 1982): 309–29.

11. My summary of these events is based on William Henry Chamberlin, *The*

Russian Revolution, 2 vols. (1935; rpt. Princeton: Princeton University Press, 1987), 2:430–50.

12. Pudovkin, *Film Technique*, 134–35.

13. Rudolf Arnheim, *Visual Thinking* (Berkeley: University of California Press, 1969), 174.

14. E. H. Gombrich, *Art and Illusion* (New York: Pantheon, 1960), 343, 345.

15. Béla Balázs, *Theory of the Film*, trans. Edith Bone (New York: Dover, 1970), 82–83.

16. Georg Lukács, *The Meaning of Contemporary Realism*, trans. John and Necke Mander (London: Merlin, 1963), 123.

17. Georg Lukács, *Writer and Critic*, ed. and trans. Arthur D. Kahn (New York: Grosset, 1971), 107, 97–98.

18. Georg Lukács, *Studies in European Realism* (New York: Grosset, 1964), 6. A helpful explication of typicality is contained in Jameson, *Marxism and Form*, 191–95.

19. The quotation is contained in Béla Kiralyfalvi, *The Aesthetics of Gyorgy Lukács* (Princeton: Princeton University Press, 1975), 106.

20. Taylor and Christie, *Film Factory*, 109.

21. Ibid., 199.

22. Walter Benjamin, *Illuminations*, ed. Hannah Arendt, trans. Harry Zohn (New York: Schocken, 1969), 155.

23. The article, first published in *Literarische Welt* on March 11, 1927, is contained in Walter Benjamin, *Gesammelte Schriften*, ed. Rolf Tiedemann and Herman Schweppenhäuser (Frankfurt: Suhrkamp Verlag, 1980), 2:752, 753–54.

24. Benjamin, *Reflections*, 235.

25. Edgar Morin, *Le cinéma, ou l'homme imaginaire* (Paris: Minuit, 1958), 154.

Chapter 4: *October*

1. *Marx-Engels Reader*, 5.

2. Ernst Bloch, *The Utopian Function of Art and Literature*, trans. Jack Zipes and Frank Mecklenburg (Cambridge, Mass.: MIT Press, 1988), 125–26.

3. Marx, *Manuscripts of 1844*, 135.

4. For a description of these mass dramas, see Frantisek Deak, "Russian Mass Spectacles," *The Drama Review* 19, no. 2 (June 1975): 7–22.

5. See Steven P. Hill, "The Strange Case of the Vanishing Epigraphs," in Marshall, *Potemkin*, 74–85.

6. Moussinac, *Eisenstein*, 149, 152.

7. Eisenstein, *Three Films*, 181. A detailed description of *October*'s visuals, accompanied by some frame enlargements, is available in *Octobre: découpage intégral* (Paris: Seuil, 1971). Frame enlargements from each of the film's shots are available in *Octobre: continuité photogrammatique intégrale* (Paris: Cinémathèque Universitaire, 1981).

8. Moussinac, *Eisenstein*, 27–29.

9. *Lenin Anthology*, 611.

10. Alexander Rabinowitch, *The Bolsheviks Come to Power* (New York: Norton,

1976), 206. For the historical record of events of the October Revolution, I have relied on the work of William Henry Chamberlin, Sheila Fitzpatrick, and Rabinowitch, and on John Reed, *Ten Days That Shook the World* (New York: International, 1967).

11. The verbal-visual pun is explained in Yuri Lotman, *Semiotics of Cinema*, trans. Mark E. Suino (Ann Arbor: University of Michigan, 1976), 39–40 and translator's note.

12. *Marx-Engels Reader*, 553.

13. Rabinowitch, *Bolsheviks*, xxi.

14. Sergei Eisenstein, *The Film Sense*, ed. and trans. Jay Leyda (New York: Harcourt, 1947), 22. All subsequent references to this volume will be noted in the text with the abbreviation *FS*.

15. Marie-Claire Ropars-Wuilleumier, *L'écran de la mémoire* (Paris: Seuil, 1970), 202.

16. Sergei Eisenstein, *Izbrannye proizvedeniya* (Moscow: Iskusstvo, 1964), 1:140.

17. Boris Eikhenbaum, "Problems of Cine-Stylistics," trans. Richard Sherwood, in Boris Eikhenbaum, ed., *The Poetics of Cinema, Russian Poetics in Translation* 9 (1982): 12.

18. Mitry, *Eisenstein*, 46.

19. André Bazin, *What Is Cinema?*, ed. and trans. Hugh Gray (Berkeley: University of California Press, 1967), 25.

20. Julia Kristeva, *Semeiotike* (Paris: Seuil, 1969), 96.

21. *Brecht on Theatre*, 143–44.

22. The quotation is taken from George Ivask, "Russian Modernist Poets and the Mystic Sectarians," in *Russian Modernism*, ed. George Gibian and H. W. Tjalsma (Ithaca: Cornell University Press, 1976), 100.

23. Taylor and Christie, *Film Factory*, 231, 230.

24. Ibid., 217, 174.

25. Ibid., 183.

26. Ibid., 246.

27. Louis Hjelmslev, *Essais linguistiques* (Copenhagen: Nordisk Sprog, 1959), 93.

28. M. M. Bakhtin and P. M. Medvedev, *The Formal Method in Literary Scholarship*, trans. Albert J. Wehrle (Cambridge, Mass.: Harvard University Press, 1985).

29. V. N. Volosinov, *Marxism and the Philosophy of Language*, trans. Ladislav Matejka and I. R. Titunik (Cambridge, Mass.: Harvard University Press, 1986), 10, 11. Recent scholarship credits authorship of this book solely to Bakhtin and that of the *Formalist Method* book principally to him; see Katerina Clark and Michael Holquist, *Mikhail Bakhtin* (Cambridge, Mass.: Harvard University Press, 1984), 146–70.

30. Volosinov, *Marxism and the Philosophy of Language*, 92.

Chapter 5: *Old and New*

1. Mitry, *Eisenstein*, 115; the translation is taken from Moussinac, *Eisenstein*, 32–33.

2. *Lenin Anthology,* 106–7.

3. Nikolai Bukharin and Evgeni Preobrazhensky, *The ABC of Communism,* trans. Eden and Cedar Paul (Baltimore: Penguin, 1969), 57, 121.

4. Richard Stites, *Revolutionary Dreams: Utopian Vision and Experimental Life in the Russian Revolution* (New York: Oxford University Press, 1989).

5. *Lenin Anthology,* 709, 712.

6. The principal sources for my account of Soviet rural policy are: Robert Conquest, *The Harvest of Sorrow: Soviet Collectivization and the Terror-Famine* (London: Hutchinson, 1986); V. P. Danilov, *Rural Russia under the New Regime,* trans. Orlando Figes (Bloomington: Indiana University Press, 1988); R. W. Davies, *The Soviet Collective Farm, 1929–1930* (Cambridge, Mass.: Harvard University Press, 1980); Moshe Lewin, *Russian Peasants and Soviet Power: A Study of Collectivization,* trans. Irene Nove (New York: Norton, 1968); and Zhores A. Medvedev, *Soviet Agriculture* (New York: Norton, 1987).

7. A detailed account of the film's production history and script revisions is provided in Vance Kepley, Jr., "The Evolution of Eisenstein's *Old and New,*" *Cinema Journal* 14, no. 1 (Fall 1974): 34–50. Arguments that the film attempts to conform to Stalin's emerging policy on collectivization are made in Jean Narboni, "Le hors-cadre décide de tout," *Cahiers du Cinéma,* no. 271 (November 1976): 14–21; and Paul E. Burns, "Cultural Revolution, Collectivization, and Soviet Cinema: Eisenstein's *Old and New* and Dovzhenko's *Earth,*" *Film and History* 11, no. 4 (December 1981): 84–96.

8. Moshe Lewin, "Collectivization: The Reasons," in *The Stalin Revolution,* 3d ed., ed. Robert V. Daniels (Toronto: Heath, 1990), 103.

9. Three versions of the scenario have been published. The earliest draft, dated June 22, 1926, appears in *Iz istorii kino* 7 (1968): 157–82. A draft dated April 1928 is contained in Eisenstein, *Izbrannye proizvedeniya,* 6:89–104. A translation from German by Erwin Honig of a 1929 scenario published in Berlin, the one that most closely approximates the released film, is included in *Film Writing Forms,* ed. Lewis Jacobs (New York: Gotham, 1934), 24–38, 61. I am grateful to Corinne Blackmer for a complete literary translation from the Russian of the 1926 and 1928 draft scenarios.

10. Boris Arvatov, "Materialized Utopia," trans. Richard Sherwood, in *Screen Reader 1,* 271.

11. Ernst Bloch, *A Philosophy of the Future,* trans. John Cumming (New York: Herder, 1970), 95.

12. Eisenstein, *Izbrannye proizvedeniya,* 1:141.

13. Quoted in Moussinac, *Eisenstein,* 33–34.

14. Marx, *Capital,* 1:74.

15. Marfa's dream is closely analyzed in Jacques Aumont, "Un rêve soviétique," *Cahiers du Cinéma,* no. 271 (November 1976): 26–44. Aumont has adapted this essay in *Montage Eisenstein,* 91–119 (in the English translation, 73–107), where he reaches the conclusion that much in *Old and New* promotes Stalinist ideology.

16. Bloch, *Utopian Function,* 41, 108.

17. Vance Kepley argues in similar fashion that *Earth* proposes to "naturalize

the collectivization process;" see Kepley, *In the Service of the State: The Cinema of Alexander Dovzhenko* (Madison: University of Wisconsin Press, 1986), 84.

18. Taylor and Christie, *Film Factory*, 278.

19. See Robert C. Tucker, *Stalin as Revolutionary, 1879–1929* (New York: Norton, 1973), 279–88, 467–72, 481–84.

20. Quoted in Wiktor Woroszylski, *The Life of Mayakovsky*, trans. Boleslaw Taborski (New York: Orion, 1970), 283.

21. The statement, taken from Tynyanov's *Archaists and Innovators* (1929), is translated in Ladislav Matejka, "The Formal Method and Linguistics," in *Readings in Russian Poetics*, ed. Matejka and Krystyna Pomorska (Cambridge, Mass.: MIT Press, 1971), 288–89.

22. Vladimir Nilsen, *The Cinema as a Graphic Art*, trans. Stephen Garry (New York: Hill and Wang, 1941), 190–96.

23. Ernest Fenollosa, *The Chinese Written Character as a Medium for Poetry*, ed. Ezra Pound (San Francisco: City Lights, 1936), 22–23.

24. *Marx-Engels Reader*, 107.

Chapter 6: Dislocation

1. Karl Marx, *Class Struggles in France* (New York: International, 1964), 33.

2. Sergei Eisenstein, "Notes for a Film of *Capital*," trans. Maciej Sliwowski, Jay Leyda, and Annette Michelson, *October*, no. 2 (Summer 1976): 3–26. Unless otherwise specified, all quotations regarding the *Capital* project are taken from this source.

3. Leyda and Voynow, *Eisenstein at Work*, 37.

4. Marx, *Capital* 1:72, 76.

5. Benjamin, *Reflections*, 202.

6. *Lenin Anthology*, 649.

7. Cited in Jay Leyda, *Kino: A History of the Russian and Soviet Film* (New York: Collier, 1973), 246.

8. Richard T. De George, *Patterns of Soviet Thought* (Ann Arbor: University of Michigan Press, 1966), 184.

9. Cited in Barna, *Eisenstein*, 141.

10. Ivor Montagu, *With Eisenstein in Hollywood* (New York: International, 1969), 102. This book contains both the *Sutter's Gold* and *An American Tragedy* scripts, from which all quotations are taken without further citation.

11. Leyda and Voynow, *Eisenstein at Work*, 58.

12. Quoted in Woroszylski, *Mayakovsky*, 365.

13. "Eisenstein Says 'Adios,' " *Los Angeles Times*, December 7, 1930, sec. 3, p. 1.

14. The contract is reprinted in Harry M. Geduld and Ronald Gottesman, eds., *Sergei Eisenstein and Upton Sinclair: The Making and Unmaking of Que Viva Mexico!* (Bloomington: Indiana University Press, 1970), 22. The personal and professional details of this period in Eisenstein's career are fully documented in this book, which is the source (unless otherwise specified) for my citations from correspondence about the Mexico project.

15. Sinclair arranged for editing and postproduction in Hollywood on the Mex-

ico footage and in 1933 released the feature *Thunder Over Mexico*, based largely on the original "Maguey" episode; two short subjects also appeared, one from the Day of the Dead footage and the other from location shots and stills of Eisenstein at work. In 1939 Marie Seton released *Time in the Sun*, a dramatic feature based on other footage purchased from Upton Sinclair. The Bell and Howell Company also acquired material from Sinclair, which was edited into educational shorts; in 1941 five of these shorts were compiled under the title *Mexican Symphony*. In 1954 Sinclair donated the remaining footage, measuring over 100,000 feet, to the Museum of Modern Art, which sponsored Jay Leyda's work of annotation and compilation for *Eisenstein's Mexican Film: Episodes for Study* (1958). More recently, the museum arranged to duplicate the footage for Grigori Alexandrov, who edited the material following in broad outline the published scenario but altering the sequence of episodes. Alexandrov's version was released in the United States in 1979 as *Sergei Eisenstein's Que Viva Mexico!*

16. Letter to Seymour Stern, dated April 2, 1932; this quotation appears in Seton, *Eisenstein*, 238.

17. Cited in Moussinac, *Eisenstein*, 170, 171.

18. Leyda and Voynow, *Eisenstein at Work*, 37.

19. From the letter to Stern in Seton, *Eisenstein*, 238.

20. The script was originally published in *Experimental Cinema*, no. 5 (1934): 5–13, 52, and is reprinted in Sergei Eisenstein, *Que Viva Mexico!* (London: Vision Press, 1951), my source for the quotations made in the text. The other sources for script drafts and notes are: *FS* 251–55; Jay Leyda, "Eisenstein's Mexican Tragedy," *Sight and Sound* 27, no. 6 (Autumn 1958): 305–8, 329; Leyda and Voynow, *Eisenstein at Work*, 60–73; Marie Seton, "Jottings for *Que Viva Mexico*," *Film Art*, no. 4 (Summer 1934): 79–80; and an introduction Eisenstein wrote in 1947 for a prospective French translation, contained in Seton, *Eisenstein*, 504–12. Graphic, photographic, and script materials for *Que Viva Mexico!* are reproduced in Inga Karetnikova with Leon Steinmetz, *Mexico According to Eisenstein* (Albuquerque: University of New Mexico Press, 1991).

21. Ernest Gruening, *Mexico and Its Heritage* (New York: Appleton-Century, 1928), 631.

22. Sergei Eisenstein, "Prometheus," trans. François Albera et al., *Cahiers du Cinéma*, no. 307 (January 1980): 6–9.

23. Octavio Paz, *The Labyrinth of Solitude*, trans. Lysander Kemp (New York: Grove, 1961), 52–53.

24. The article is excerpted in Seton, *Eisenstein*, 494–503.

25. The letter is contained in Sergei Eisenstein, *Eisenstein 2*, ed. Jay Leyda, trans. Alan Upchurch et al. (New York: Methuen, 1988), 48–49.

26. The telegram is reprinted in Geduld and Gottesman, *Eisenstein and Sinclair*, 212.

Chapter 7: Disjunction

1. Quoted in Leyda, *Kino*, 319.

2. Taylor and Christie, *Film Factory*, 384.

3. Roy A. Medvedev, *Let History Judge*, ed. David Joravsky and Georges Haupt, trans. Colleen Taylor (New York: Knopf, 1971), 309.

4. The principal sources for my account of the cultural revolution are John Barber, "The Establishment of Intellectual Orthodoxy in the U.S.S.R. 1928–1934," *Past and Present*, no. 83 (May 1979): 141–64; Herman Ermolaev, *Soviet Literary Theories, 1917–1934* (Berkeley: University of California Press, 1963); Sheila Fitzpatrick, "Cultural Revolution in Russia, 1928–1932," *Journal of Contemporary History* 9, no. 1 (January 1974): 33–52; and Sheila Fitzpatrick, ed., *Cultural Revolution in Russia, 1928–1931* (Bloomington: Indiana University Press, 1978).

5. This discussion of the Stalin letter and its aftermath is based on John Barber, "Stalin's Letter to the Editors of *Proletarskaya revolyutsiya*," *Soviet Studies* 28, no. 1 (January 1976): 21–41; and George M. Enteen, "Marxist Historians during the Cultural Revolution," in Fitzpatrick, *Cultural Revolution*, 154–68.

6. Katerina Clark, *The Soviet Novel: History as Ritual*, 2d ed. (Chicago: University of Chicago Press, 1985), 3–24.

7. Eisenstein, "Notes for a Film of *Capital*," 21.

8. The quotation is taken from Rufus Mathewson, "The First Writers' Congress: A Second Look," in *Literature and Revolution in Soviet Russia, 1917–1962*, ed. Max Hayward and Leopold Labedz (New York: Oxford University Press, 1963), 71.

9. Sergei Eisenstein, "Lecture on James Joyce at the State Institute of Cinematography" (November 1, 1934), trans. Emily Tall, *James Joyce Quarterly* 24, no. 2 (Winter 1987): 135.

10. Volosinov, *Marxism and the Philosophy of Language*, 38.

11. Lev S. Vygotsky, *Thought and Language*, ed. and trans. Eugenia Hanfmann and Gertrude Vakar (Cambridge, Mass.: MIT Press, 1962), 71–75, 144–50.

12. Sergei Eisenstein, "Letters from Mexico," trans. Tanaquil Taubes, *October*, no. 14 (Fall 1980): 56.

13. Cited in Youngblood, *Soviet Cinema*, 117. For this section my principal sources are the film histories by Leyda, Taylor, and Youngblood; Taylor's essays "Boris Shumyatsky and the Soviet Cinema in the 1930s," *Historical Journal of Film, Radio and Television* 6, no. 1 (1986): 43–64, and "A 'Cinema for the Millions': Soviet Socialist Realism and the Problem of Film Comedy," *Journal of Contemporary History* 18, no. 3 (July 1983): 439–61; Steven P. Hill, "A Quantitative View of Soviet Cinema," *Cinema Journal* 11, no. 2 (Spring 1972): 18–25; and Ian Christie, "Soviet Cinema: Making Sense of Sound," *Screen* 23, no. 2 (July-August 1982): 34–49.

14. Taylor and Christie, *Film Factory*, 291.

15. Ibid., 368.

16. Ibid., 358–59.

17. Roland Barthes, *Mythologies*, trans. Annette Lavers (New York: Hill and Wang, 1972), 150.

18. Eisenstein, *Izbrannye proizvedeniya* 1:91–92.

19. Vance Kepley, Jr., "Building a National Cinema: Soviet Film Education, 1918–1934," *Wide Angle* 9, no. 3 (1987): 16–17.

20. The curriculum appears in English translation in Vladimir Nizhny, *Lessons*

with Eisenstein, trans. and ed. Ivor Montagu and Jay Leyda (New York: Hill and Wang, 1962), 143–64. The translation is based on a 1936 publication of the curriculum, which was the revised version of an earlier draft published in 1933.

21. Ivan Turgenev, "Bezhin Lea," in *Sketches from a Hunter's Album,* trans. Richard Freeborn (Baltimore: Penguin, 1967), 50–75.

22. Jay Leyda, "Eisenstein's *Bezhin Meadow,*" *Sight and Sound* 28, no. 2 (Spring 1959): 74–77, 105; Leyda, *Kino,* 327–34.

23. The script dialogue for both versions is taken from David Robinson, "The Two *Bezhin Meadows,*" *Sight and Sound* 37, no. 1 (Winter 1967–68): 33–37.

24. Quoted in Edward J. Brown, *The Proletarian Episode in Russian Literature, 1928–1932* (New York: Columbia University Press, 1953), 134.

25. Leyda, *Kino,* 331.

26. Taylor and Christie, *Film Factory,* 379.

27. Eisenstein, "The Mistakes of *Bezhin Lug,*" *International Literature,* no. 8 (1937); reprinted in Seton, *Eisenstein,* 372–77.

28. Eisenstein describes the Moscow performances in an article translated as "The Theatre of Mei Lan-fang," *Theatre Arts Monthly* 19, no. 10 (October 1935): 761–70.

29. *Brecht on Theatre,* 104–5, 86.

Chapter 8: *Alexander Nevsky*

1. Romm's account of the conversation appears in Norman Swallow, *Eisenstein: A Documentary Portrait* (New York: Dutton, 1977), 123.

2. M. N. Pokrovsky, *Brief History of Russia,* trans. D. S. Mirsky (2 vols., 1933; rpt. Orono, Maine: University Prints, 1968), 1:241.

3. This section draws from the accounts of Soviet historiography in Paul H. Aron, "M. N. Pokrovsky and the Impact of the First Five-Year Plan on Soviet Historiography," in *Essays in Russian and Soviet History,* ed. John Shelton Curtiss (New York: Columbia University Press, 1962), 283–302; and Enteen, "Marxist Historians," in Fitzpatrick, *Cultural Revolution,* 154–68.

4. Nadezhda Mandelstam, *Hope Against Hope: A Memoir,* trans. Max Hayward (New York: Atheneum, 1970), 84–85.

5. See the history published originally in Petrograd in 1918, A. E. Presniakov, *The Formation of the Great Russian State,* trans. A. E. Moorhouse (Chicago: Quadrangle, 1970), 69–70, 74.

6. The report is included in *The Essential Stalin,* ed. Bruce Franklin (New York: Doubleday, 1972), 224–99; the relevant section appears on pages 275–87.

7. Katerina Clark, "Utopian Anthropology as a Context for Stalinist Literature," in *Stalinism: Essays in Historical Interpretation,* ed. Robert C. Tucker (New York: Norton, 1977), 180–98. Clark provides further discussion of the myths of family and heroism in *The Soviet Novel,* 114–55.

8. Translated in Gleb Struve, *Russian Literature under Lenin and Stalin, 1917–1953* (Norman: University of Oklahoma Press, 1971), 281–82.

9. Quoted in Marc Slonim, *Soviet Russian Literature,* 2d ed., rev. (New York: Oxford University Press, 1977), 240.

10. In later years this film, like others that contributed to the personality cult,

had been re-edited by Soviet authorities to diminish the historical role attributed to Stalin. A descriptive account of the original *Lenin in October* is contained in Dwight Macdonald, *Dwight Macdonald on Movies* (Englewood Cliffs, N.J.: Prentice-Hall, 1969), 226–28.

11. Milovan Djilas, *Conversations with Stalin*, trans. Michael B. Petrovich (New York: Harcourt, 1962), 103.

12. Viktor Shklovsky, *Zhili-byli* (Moscow: Sovetsky Pisatel, 1964), 429; and Viktor Shklovsky, *Eisenstein* (Moscow: Iskusstvo, 1973), 249.

13. Translation from the fifteenth-century text is included in *Medieval Russia's Epics, Chronicles, and Tales*, ed. and trans. Serge A. Zenkovsky, rev. ed. (New York: Dutton, 1974), 224–36.

14. All quotations of translated dialogue are based on the film print in American distribution. In most instances the subtitled dialogue conforms exactly to the transcript in Eisenstein, *Three Films*, 89–143; citations from the Pavlenko-Eisenstein script are also taken from this text. Where significant differences in translation between the film's dialogue and the published transcription occur, my citations follow the subtitles in the American print.

15. See K. R. M. Short and Richard Taylor, "Soviet Cinema and the International Menace, 1928–1939," *Historical Journal of Film, Radio and Television* 6, no. 2 (1986): 131–59.

16. The letter is translated in Ronald Levaco, "The Eisenstein-Prokofiev Correspondence," *Cinema Journal* 13, no. 1 (Fall 1973): 1–16. Analysis of the Prokofiev score is available in Philip D. Roberts, "Prokofiev's Score and Cantata for Eisenstein's *Alexander Nevsky*," *Semiotica* 21, no. 1–2 (1977): 151–66; and Douglas W. Gallez, "The Prokofiev-Eisenstein Collaboration," *Cinema Journal* 17, no. 2 (Spring 1978): 13–35.

17. Quoted in Israel V. Nestyev, *Sergei Prokofiev*, trans. Rose Prokofieva (New York: Knopf, 1946), 124. For a discussion of socialist realist standards in Soviet music, see Malcolm H. Brown, "The Soviet Russian Concepts of 'Intonazia' and 'Musical Imagery,' " *Musical Quarterly* 60, no. 4 (October 1974): 557–67.

18. Hans Eisler, *Composing for the Films* (London: Dobson, 1951), 153. See also Roy M. Prendergast, *Film Music* (New York: Norton, 1977), 211–14.

19. Sergei Eisenstein, "Patriotism Is Our Theme," *International Literature*, no. 2 (1939): 91–94.

Chapter 9: *Ivan the Terrible*

1. See Sergei Eisenstein, "Shot Montage of a Monologue from Pushkin's Drama *Boris Godunov*," ed. Herbert Marshall and trans. B. P. Pockney, *Quarterly Review of Film Studies* 3, no. 2 (Spring 1978): 137–68.

2. Sergei Eisenstein, "Problems of Soviet Historical Films," trans. J. Burke, P. Micciche, and L. Wagner, *Film Criticism* 3, no. 1 (Fall 1978): 6–7.

3. Leonid Kozlov, "A Hypothetical Dedication," trans. Håkan Lövgren, in Kleberg and Lövgren, *Eisenstein Revisited*, 65–92.

4. Sergei Eisenstein, *Ivan the Terrible*, ed. and trans. Ivor Montagu and Herbert Marshall (New York: Simon and Schuster, 1962). A shot description is available in Sergei Eisenstein, *Ivan the Terrible: A Film by Sergei Eisenstein*, trans.

A. E. Ellis (New York: Simon and Schuster, 1970). All citations from the script and of film dialogue (checked against the print in American distribution) are based on these two sources.

5. The quotation is taken from the transcript of the interview published in Sergei Eisenstein and Nikolai Cherkasov, "A Conversation in the Kremlin," *Encounter* 72, no. 2 (February 1989): 3.

6. Eisenstein, "Problems of Soviet Historical Films," 4.

7. Sergei Eisenstein, *Mémoires*, ed. and trans. Jacques Aumont (Paris: 10/18, 1978), 51–52.

8. *Marx-Engels Reader*, 70, 436–39.

9. Pokrovsky, *Brief History*, 241.

10. The quotations are taken from *Le film muet sovietique* (Brussels: Musée du Cinema, 1965), 25.

11. See Robert C. Tucker, *The Soviet Political Mind*, rev. ed. (New York: Norton, 1971), 174–75, 180–82. Tucker's summation of the comparisons with Ivan cultivated by Stalin appears in his book *Stalin in Power: The Revolution from Above, 1928–1941* (New York: Norton, 1990), 17–20, 276–82, 482–86. Some parallels between Stalin and Ivan are discussed in Kristin Thompson, "*Ivan the Terrible* and Stalinist Russia: A Reexamination," *Cinema Journal* 17, no. 1 (Fall 1977): 30–43.

12. Eisenstein, *Izbrannye proizvedeniya*, 1:191.

13. For a discussion of patriarchy in the Ford and Eisenstein films, see Marsha Kinder, "The Image of Patriarchal Power in *Young Mr. Lincoln* (1939) and *Ivan the Terrible*, Part 1 (1945)," *Film Quarterly* 39, no. 2 (Winter 1985–86): 29–49.

14. Eisenstein, *Izbrannye proizvedeniya*, 1:193–94, 199.

15. The official criticism is contained in the Central Committee directive on the film *A Great Life* (1946). A translation is published in Paul Babitsky and John Rimberg, *The Soviet Film Industry* (New York: Praeger, 1955), 298–304; the censure cited appears on page 302.

16. Sergei Eisenstein, "Lettre à Tynyanov," *Change*, no. 2 (1969): 63; the letter was written in late 1943.

17. Sergei Eisenstein, *Nonindifferent Nature*, trans. Herbert Marshall (New York: Cambridge University Press, 1987), 104. All subsequent references to this volume will be noted in the text with the abbreviation *NN*.

18. Grigori Kozintsev, *King Lear: The Space of Tragedy*, trans. Mary Mackintosh (Berkeley: University of California Press, 1977), 31.

19. *Marx-Engels Reader*, 347.

20. The principal biographical sources I have consulted are: Ian Grey, *Ivan the Terrible* (London: Hodder and Stoughton, 1964); Robert Payne and Nikita Romanoff, *Ivan the Terrible* (New York: Crowell, 1975); and Sergei F. Platonov, *Ivan the Terrible*, ed. and trans. Josephy L. Wieczynski (Gulf Breeze, Fla.: Academic International Press, 1974).

21. The phrase is cited in Platonov, *Ivan*, 103.

22. Sergei Eisenstein, "*Ivan Grozny*," *VOKS Bulletin*, no. 7–8 (1942): 60.

23. Boris Uspensky, "*Historia sub specie semioticae*," in *Soviet Semiotics: An Anthology*, ed. and trans. Daniel P. Lucid (Baltimore: Johns Hopkins University Press, 1977), 111.

24. Other critics to comment on specular motifs in *Ivan the Terrible* are Roland Barthes, "The Third Meaning"; Jean-Pierre Oudart, "Sur *Ivan le Terrible*," *Cahiers du Cinéma*, no. 218 (March 1970): 15–22; and Kristin Thompson, "Non-Classical Spatial Structures in *Ivan the Terrible*: A Sample Analysis," *1977 Film Studies Annual* (Part 1): 57–64. Oudart's analysis is ingenious and suggestive throughout, but his conclusion that the character Ivan "assumes various positions in the Oedipal triangle" and "occupies the place of the dead, the Absent, the subject" illuminates the Oudart thesis of "la suture" more than it does the Eisenstein film.

25. Ilya Veissfeld, "Mon dernier entretien avec Eisenstein," *Cahiers du Cinéma*, no. 208 (January 1969): 21.

26. Sergei Eisenstein, "First Letter about Color," trans. Herbert Marshall, *Film Reader*, no. 2 (1977): 184.

27. Sergei Eisenstein, "One Path to Color," trans. Jay Leyda, *Sight and Sound* 30, no. 2 (Spring 1961): 84.

28. Ibid., 86.

29. Eisenstein, *Izbrannye proizvedeniya*, 3:600–601.

30. Ibid., 597.

Conclusion

1. Marshall, *Potemkin*, 28.

2. Tucker, *Stalin as Revolutionary*, 281.

3. André Bazin, "Le mythe de Staline dans le cinéma sovietique," *Qu'est-ce que le cinéma?* (Paris: Editions du Cerf, 1958), 1:86.

4. Mikhail Bakhtin, *Rabelais and His World*, trans. Helene Iswolsky (Cambridge, Mass.: MIT Press, 1968), 73.

5. Ibid., 270.

6. Nikolai Cherkasov, *Notes of a Soviet Actor*, excerpted in Moussinac, *Eisenstein*, 190.

7. Sergei Eisenstein, "How We Filmed *Ivan the Terrible*," *Cinema Chronicle*, February 1945; excerpted in Leyda, *Kino*, 384.

8. Eisenstein, *Izbrannye proizvedeniya*, 6:505.

9. Herbert Marcuse, *Soviet Marxism: A Critical Analysis* (New York: Columbia University Press, 1958), 144.

10. Bazin, *What Is Cinema?*, 21.

Filmography

Strike [*Stachka*]; general release: April 28, 1925
Produced by Goskino and Moscow Proletkult
Director: Sergei Eisenstein
Script: Grigori Alexandrov, Sergei Eisenstein, Ilya Kravchunovsky, Valeri Pletnyov
Cinematography: Eduard Tisse
Camera assistants: Vasili Khvatov, Vladimir Popov
Art direction: Vasili Rakhals
Assistants to the director: Grigori Alexandrov, Ilya Kravchunovsky, Alexander Levshin
Cast

Activist	Ivan Klyukvin
Member, strike committee	Alexander Antonov
Factory foreman	Grigori Alexandrov
Worker	Mikhail Gomorov
Police spy	Maxim Strauch
Chief of Police	I. Ivanov
King of Thieves	Boris Yurtsev
Queen of Thieves	Judith Glizer

Battleship Potemkin [*Bronenosets 'Potemkin'*]; general release: January 18, 1926
Produced by Goskino
Director: Sergei Eisenstein
Script: Nina Agadzhanova-Shutko and Sergei Eisenstein
Cinematography: Eduard Tisse
Camera assistant: Vladimir Popov
Art direction: Vasili Rakhals
Music: Edmund Miesel (for exhibition in Western Europe)
Assistants to the director: Grigori Alexandrov, Alexander Antonov, Mikhail Gomorov, Alexander Levshin, Maxim Strauch
Cast

Vakulinchuk	Alexander Antonov
Chief Officer Gilyarovsky	Grigori Alexandrov
Petty Officer	Alexander Levshin
Captain Golikov	Vladimir Barsky
Sailor	Mikhail Gomorov

Sailor	I. Bobrov
Woman with baby carriage on the Odessa steps	Beatrice Vitoldi
Woman with pince-nez on the Odessa steps	N. Poltavtseva
Odessa citizen	Julia Eisenstein

October [*Oktaybr*]; general release: March 14, 1928
Produced by Sovkino
Direction and script: Sergei Eisenstein and Grigori Alexandrov
Cinematography: Eduard Tisse
Camera assistants: Vladimir Nilsen, Vladimir Popov
Art direction: Vasili Kovrigin
Music: Edmund Miesel (for exhibition in Western Europe)
Assistants to the director: Mikhail Gomorov, Maxim Strauch, Ilya Trauberg
Cast

Lenin	Vasili Nikandrov
Kerensky	Nikolai Popov
Minister	Boris Livanov
Minister	Lyaschenko
German soldier	Eduard Tisse

Old and New [*Staroe i novoe*]; general release: October 7, 1929
Produced by Sovkino
Direction and script: Sergei Eisenstein and Grigori Alexandrov
Cinematography: Eduard Tisse
Camera assistant: Vladimir Popov
Art direction: Andrei Burov, Vasili Kovrigin, Vasili Rakhals
Assistants to the director: Mikhail Gomorov, Maxim Strauch
Cast

Marfa	Marfa Lapkina
Her son	M. Ivanin
Secretary of the cooperative	Vasili Buzenkov
Peasant	Mikhail Gomorov
Tractor driver	Kostya Vasiliev
Priest	G. Matvei
The Kulak	Chukhmarev

Que Viva Mexico!; filmed on location from December 1930 to January 1932
Produced by the Mexican Picture Trust, formed by Upton and Mary Sinclair
Direction and script: Sergei Eisenstein and Grigori Alexandrov
Cinematography: Eduard Tisse
Camera assistant: Gabriel Figueroa
Assistants to the director: Adolfo Best-Maugard, Augustin Aragon Leiva

Cast

Hacendado	Julio Saldivara
Matador	David Liceaga
Maria	Isabel Villasenor
Sebastian	Martin Hernandez

A significant portion of the Mexico footage was compiled by Jay Leyda into *Eisenstein's Mexico Project* (1958), a study film available through the Museum of Modern Art, New York. Grigori Alexandrov edited a version of *Que Viva Mexico!* that was released in 1979.

Bezhin Meadow [*Bezhin Lug*]; scripted, filmed, and edited from March 1935 to
   March 1937
Produced by Mosfilm
Director: Sergei Eisenstein
Script: Alexander Rzheshevsky
Revised script: Isaac Babel and Sergei Eisenstein
Cinematography: Eduard Tisse
Camera assistant: Vladimir Nilsen
Music: Gavril Popov
Assistants to the director: Pera Atasheva, Fyodor Filipov, Mikhail Gomorov, Jay
   Leyda
Cast

Stepok	Vitya Karashov
His father	Boris Zakhava
President of Kolkhoz	Elena Telesheva
Arsonist	Nikolai Maslov
Peasant	Nikolai Okhlopkov

For second version:

Stepok's father	Nikolai Khmelyov
Political commissar	Pavel Ardzhanov

The *Bezhin Meadow* film footage was apparently destroyed by an accident to the Mosfilm archives during World War II. Frames from many shots had been clipped by Pera Atasheva, however, in the original process of printing them. These still images remained in the Eisenstein archive until Naum Kleiman compiled them and, with the assistance of Sergei Yutkevich, prepared a film presentation of *Bezhin Meadow* frame enlargements, released in 1967.

Alexander Nevsky [*Aleksandr Nevsky*]; general release: December 1, 1938
Produced by Mosfilm
Director: Sergei Eisenstein
Script: Sergei Eisenstein and Pyotr Pavlenko
Cinematography: Eduard Tisse
Camera assistants: A. Astafiev, N. Bolshakov, S. Uralov
Art direction and costumes: Konstantin Eliseyev, Iosif Shpinel, Nikolai Soloviev
Music: Sergei Prokofiev
Assistants to the director: Boris Ivanov, Nikolai Maslov, Dmitri Vasiliev

Cast

Prince Alexander Nevsky	Nikolai Cherkasov
Vasili Buslai	Nikolai Okhlopkov
Gavrilo Oleksich	Andrei Abrikosov
Ignat, master armorer	Dmitri Orlov
Mother of Buslai	Varvara Massalitinova
Olga	Vera Ivasheva
Vasilisa	Anna Danilova
Governor of Pskov	Vasili Novikov
Domash Tverdislavich	Nikolai Arsky
Von Balk, Master of the Teuton Knights	Vladimir Yershov
Tverdilo, treasonous mayor of Pskov	Sergei Blinnikov
Ananias	Ivan Lagutin
Bishop	Lev Fenin
Monk in black robes	Naum Rogozhin

Ivan the Terrible [Ivan Grozny]

Part 1, produced by Alma-Ata Studio; general release: January 16, 1945
Part 2, produced by Mosfilm; general release: September 1, 1958
Direction and script: Sergei Eisenstein
Cinematography: Eduard Tisse, Andrei Moskvin
Camera assistants: V. Dombrovsky, F. Soluyanov
Art direction and costumes: Iosif Shpinel, Leonida Naumova
Music: Sergei Prokofiev
Assistants to the director: Boris Sveshnikov, Lev Indenbom, Vera Kuznetsova, I. Bir, B. Bunayev

Cast

Tsar Ivan IV	Nikolai Cherkasov
Anastasia, the tsarina	Ludmila Tselikovskaya
Malyuta Skuratov	Mikhail Zharov
Alexei Basmanov	Ambrosi Buchma
Fyodor Basmanov, his son	Mikhail Kuznetsov
Euphrosyne Staritsky, the tsar's aunt	Serafima Birman
Vladimir Staritsky, her son	Pavel Kadochnikov
Prince Andrei Kurbsky	Mikhail Nazvanov
Boyar Fyodor Kolychev, later Metropolitan Philip	Andrei Abrikosov
Metropolitan Pimen	Alexander Mgebrov
Peter Volynets, Pimen's acolyte	Vladimir Balachov
Kaspar von Oldenbock, Livonian ambassador	S. Timoshenko
Nikola, a beggar simpleton	Vsevolod Pudovkin
The Archdeacon	Maxim Mikhailov

Additional cast, for part 2:
Ivan as a youth   Eric Pyriev
King Sigismund of Poland   Pavel Massalsky
A Polish gentlewoman   Anna Golshansky

Bibliography

Albera, François. "Eisenstein en Suisse." *Travelling*, no. 48 (Winter 1976): 89–119.

———. "Eisenstein et la question graphique." *Cahiers du Cinéma*, no. 295 (December 1978): 11–16.

———. *Notes sur l'esthétique d'Eisenstein*. Lyon: Université Lyon, 1973.

Alexandrov, Grigori. "Mexico Revisited." *Soviet Film*, no. 250 (1970): 17–19.

Altman, Rick, ed. *Cinema/Sound. Yale French Studies*, no. 60 (1980).

Amengual, Barthélemy. *Que Viva Eisenstein!* Lausanne: Editions l'Age d'Homme, 1980.

———. *Serguei Mikailovitch Eisenstein*. Lyon: Premier Plan, 1962.

Andrew, J. Dudley. *The Major Film Theories*. New York: Oxford University Press, 1970.

Aristarco, Guido. *Marx, le cinéma et la critique de film*. Trans. Barthélemy Amengual. Paris: Minard, 1972.

Arnheim, Rudolf. *Visual Thinking*. Berkeley: University of California Press, 1969.

Art in Revolution. London: Arts Council, 1971.

Aumont, Jacques. *Montage Eisenstein*. Paris: Editions Albatros, 1979.

———. *Montage Eisenstein*. Trans. Lee Hildreth, Constance Penley, and Andrew Ross. Bloomington: Indiana University Press, 1987.

———. "Un rêve soviétique." *Cahiers du Cinéma*, no. 271 (November 1976): 26–44.

Babitsky, Paul, and John Rimberg. *The Soviet Film Industry*. New York: Praeger, 1955.

Bakhtin, Mikhail. *Rabelais and His World*. Trans. Helene Iswolsky. Cambridge, Mass.: MIT Press, 1968.

Bakhtin, Mikhail, and P. M. Medvedev. *The Formal Method in Literary Scholarship*. Trans. Albert J. Wehrle. Cambridge, Mass.: Harvard University Press, 1985.

Balázs, Béla. *Theory of the Film*. Trans. Edith Bone. New York: Dover, 1970.

Balter, Leon. "*Alexander Nevsky*." *Film Culture*, no. 70–71 (1983): 43–87.

Bann, Stephen, ed. *The Tradition of Constructivism*. New York: Viking, 1974.

Barber, John. "The Establishment of Intellectual Orthodoxy in the U.S.S.R. 1928–1934." *Past and Present*, no. 83 (May 1979): 141–64.

———. "Stalin's Letter to the Editors of *Proletarskaya revolyutsiya*." *Soviet Studies* 28, no. 1 (January 1976): 21–41.

Barna, Yon. *Eisenstein*. Trans. Lise Hunter. Bloomington: Indiana University Press, 1973.

Barthes, Roland. *Image—Music—Text*. Ed. and trans. Stephen Heath. New York: Hill and Wang, 1977.

———. *Mythologies*. Trans. Annette Lavers. New York: Hill and Wang, 1972.

———. *The Responsibility of Forms*. Trans. Richard Howard. New York: Hill and Wang, 1985.

Bazin, André. *Qu'est-ce que le cinéma?* Vol. 1. Paris: Editions du Cerf, 1958.

———. *What Is Cinema?* Ed. and trans. Hugh Gray. Berkeley: University of California Press, 1967.

Benjamin, Walter. *Gesammelte Schriften*. Vol. 2. Ed. Rolf Tiedemann and Herman Schweppenhäuser. Frankfurt: Suhrkamp Verlag, 1980.

———. *Illuminations*. Ed. Hannah Arendt. Trans. Harry Zohn. New York: Schocken, 1969.

———. *Moscow Diary*. Ed. Gary Smith. Trans. Richard Sieburth. Cambridge, Mass.: Harvard University Press, 1986.

———. *Reflections*. Ed. Peter Demetz. Trans. Edmund Jephcott. New York: Harcourt, 1978.

———. "A Short History of Photography." Trans. Stanley Mitchell. *Screen* 13, no. 1 (Spring 1972): 5–26.

Bennett, Tony. *Formalism and Marxism*. London: Methuen, 1979.

Berlin, Isaiah. *Karl Marx: His Life and Environment*. New York: Oxford University Press, 1978.

Betz, Margaret. "The Icon and Russian Modernism." *Artforum* 16, no. 1 (Summer 1977): 38–45.

Bloch, Ernst. *A Philosophy of the Future*. Trans. John Cumming. New York: Herder, 1970.

———. *The Utopian Function of Art and Literature*. Trans. Jack Zipes and Frank Mecklenburg. Cambridge, Mass.: MIT Press, 1988.

Bonitzer, Pascal. "Le notion de plan et le sujet du cinéma." *Cahiers du Cinéma*, no. 273 (January–February 1977): 5–18.

———. "Le système de *La Grève*." *Cahiers du Cinéma*, no. 226–27 (January–February 1971): 42–45.

Bonnet, Jean-Claude. "Fonctions du gros plan chez Eisenstein." *Cinématographe*, no. 24 (February 1977): 11–15.

Bordwell, David. "Eisenstein's Epistemological Shift." *Screen* 15, no. 4 (Winter 1974–75): 29–46.

———. "The Idea of Montage in Soviet Art and Film." *Cinema Journal* 11, no. 2 (Spring 1972): 9–17.

———. "Narration and Scenography in the Later Eisenstein." *Millennium Film Journal*, no. 13 (Fall–Winter 1983–84): 62–80.

Bottomore, Tom, ed. *A Dictionary of Marxist Thought*. Cambridge, Mass.: Harvard University Press, 1983.

Bowlt, John, ed. and trans. *Russian Art of the Avant-Garde*. New York: Viking, 1976.

Brakhage, Stan. *Film Biographies*. Berkeley, Calif.: Turtle Island, 1977.

Brecht, Bertolt. *Brecht on Theatre*. Ed. and trans. John Willett. New York: Hill and Wang, 1964.

Brewster, Ben, and Richard Sherwood, eds. "Documents from *Lef* and *Novy Lef*."

In *Screen Reader 1*. London: Society for Education in Film and Television, 1977.

Britton, Andrew. "Sexuality and Power." Parts 1, 2. *Framework*, no. 6 (Autumn 1977): 7–11, 39; no. 7–8 (Spring 1978): 4–11.

Brown, Edward J. *The Proletarian Episode in Russian Literature, 1928–1932*. New York: Columbia University Press, 1953.

Brown, Malcolm H. "The Soviet Russian Concepts of 'Intonazia' and 'Musical Imagery.' " *Musical Quarterly* 60, no. 4 (October 1974): 557–67.

Bukharin, Nikolai, and Evgeni Preobrazhensky. *The ABC of Communism*. Trans. Eden and Cedar Paul. Baltimore: Penguin, 1969.

Burch, Noel. "Film's Institutional Mode of Representation and the Soviet Response." *October*, no. 11 (Winter 1979): 77–96.

Burns, Paul E. "Cultural Revolution, Collectivization, and Soviet Cinema: Eisenstein's *Old and New* and Dovzhenko's *Earth*." *Film and History* 11, no. 4 (December 1981): 84–96.

Calandra, Denis. "Karl Valentin and Bertolt Brecht." *The Drama Review* 18, no. 1 (March 1974): 86–98.

Carr, E. H. *The October Revolution*. New York: Vintage, 1969.

Carroll, Noel. "For God and Country." *Artforum* 11, no. 5 (January 1973): 56–60.

Carter, Huntly. *The New Spirit in the Russian Theater, 1917–1928*. New York: Brentano's, 1929.

Chamberlin, William Henry. *The Russian Revolution*. 2 vols. 1935. Reprint. Princeton: Princeton University Press, 1987.

Christie, Ian. "Soviet Cinema: Making Sense of Sound." *Screen* 23, no. 2 (July–August 1982): 34–49.

Christie, Ian, and David Elliott, eds. *Eisenstein at 90*. Oxford: Museum of Modern Art, Oxford, 1988.

Clark, Katerina. *The Soviet Novel: History as Ritual*. 2d ed. Chicago: University of Chicago Press, 1985.

Clark, Katerina, and Michael Holquist. *Mikhail Bakhtin*. Cambridge, Mass.: Harvard University Press, 1984.

Cohen, Stephen F. *Bukharin and the Bolshevik Revolution*. New York: Knopf, 1973.

Conquest, Robert. *The Great Terror: Stalin's Purge of the Thirties*. London: Macmillan, 1968.

———. *The Harvest of Sorrow: Soviet Collectivization and the Terror-Famine*. London: Hutchinson, 1986.

Crofts, Stephen. "Eisenstein and Ideology." *Framework*, no. 7–8 (Spring 1978): 12–16.

Crummey, Robert O. *The Formation of Muscovy, 1304–1613*. New York: Longman, 1987.

Curtiss, John Shelton, ed. *Essays in Russian and Soviet History*. New York: Columbia University Press, 1962.

Daniels, Robert V., ed. *The Stalin Revolution*. 3d ed. Toronto: Heath, 1990.

Danilov, V. P. *Rural Russia under the New Regime*. Trans. Orlando Figes. Bloomington: Indiana University Press, 1988.

Davies, R. W. *The Soviet Collective Farm, 1929–1930*. Cambridge, Mass.: Harvard University Press, 1980.

Deak, Frantisek. "Russian Mass Spectacles." *The Drama Review* 19, no. 2 (June 1975): 7–22.

———. "Two Manifestos: The Influence of Italian Futurism in Russia." *The Drama Review* 19, no. 4 (December 1975): 88–110.

De George, Richard T. *Patterns of Soviet Thought*. Ann Arbor: University of Michigan Press, 1966.

Deleuze, Gilles. *Cinéma 1: l'image-mouvement*. Paris: Minuit, 1983.

———. *Cinéma 2: l'image-temps*. Paris: Minuit, 1985.

Denkin, Harvey. "Linguistic Models in Early Soviet Cinema." *Cinema Journal* 17, no. 1 (Fall 1977): 1–13.

Djilas, Milovan. *Conversations with Stalin*. Trans. Michael B. Petrovich. New York: Harcourt, 1962.

Eagle, Herbert. "Eisenstein as a Semiotician of the Cinema." In *The Sign: Semiotics around the World*, ed. R. W. Bailey, L. Matejka, and P. Steiner. Ann Arbor: Michigan Slavic Publications, 1978.

———. "Visual Patterning and Meaning in Eisenstein's Early Films." In *Russian Literature and American Critics*, ed. Kenneth N. Brown. Ann Arbor: University of Michigan Press, 1984.

———, ed. *Russian Formalist Film Theory*. Ann Arbor: Michigan Slavic Publications, 1981.

"L'Effet Koulechov." *Iris* 4, no. 1 (1986).

Eikhenbaum, Boris, ed. *The Poetics of Cinema* (1929). *Russian Poetics in Translation* 9 (1982).

Eisenstein, Sergei. "L'art de la mise en scène." Trans. Luda and Jean Schnitzer. *Cahiers du Cinéma*, no. 225 (November–December 1970): 29–43.

———. *Au-delà des étoiles*. Ed. Jacques Aumont. Trans. Aumont et al. Paris: 10/18, 1974.

———. *Cinématisme: peinture et cinéma*. Ed. François Albera. Trans. Anne Zouboff. Brussels: Editions Complexe, 1980.

———. *Drawings*. Moscow, 1961.

———. *Eisenstein on Disney*. Ed. Jay Leyda. Trans. Alan Upchurch. New York: Methuen, 1988.

———. *Eisenstein 2*. Ed. Jay Leyda. Trans. Alan Upchurch et al. New York: Methuen, 1988.

———. "The Enchanter from the Pear Garden." *Theatre Arts Monthly* 19, no. 10 (October 1935): 761–70.

———. *Esquisses et dessins*. Paris: Cahiers du Cinéma, 1978.

———. *Film Essays*. Ed. and trans. Jay Leyda. New York: Praeger, 1970.

———. *Film Form: Essays in Film Theory*. Ed. and trans. Jay Leyda. New York: Harcourt, 1949.

———. *The Film Sense*. Ed. and trans. Jay Leyda. New York: Harcourt, 1947.

———. "First Letter about Color." Trans. Herbert Marshall. *Film Reader*, no. 2 (1977): 180–84.

———. "Generalnaya liniya." *Iz istorii kino* 7 (1968): 157–82.

———. *Immoral Memories*. Trans. Herbert Marshall. Boston: Houghton, 1983.

———. "*Ivan Grozny.*" *VOKS Bulletin*, nos. 7–8 (1942): 60–62.

———. *Ivan the Terrible*. Ed. and trans. Ivor Montagu and Herbert Marshall. New York: Simon and Schuster, 1962.

———. *Ivan the Terrible: A Film by Sergei Eisenstein*. Trans. A. E. Ellis. New York: Simon and Schuster, 1970.

———. *Izbrannye proizvedeniya*. 6 vols. Moscow: Iskusstvo, 1964–71.

———. "Lecture on James Joyce at the State Institute of Cinematography" (November 1, 1934). Trans. Emily Tall. *James Joyce Quarterly* 24, no. 2 (Winter 1987): 133–42.

———. "Letters from Mexico." Trans. Tanaquil Taubes. *October*, no. 14 (Fall 1980): 55–64.

———. "Lettre à Tynyanov." *Change*, no. 2 (1969): 61–66.

———. *Mémoires*. Ed. and trans. Jacques Aumont. Paris: 10/18, 1978.

———. "Montage of Attractions." Trans. Daniel Gerould. *The Drama Review* 18, no. 1 (March 1974): 77–84.

———. *Nonindifferent Nature*. Trans. Herbert Marshall. New York: Cambridge University Press, 1987.

———. "Notes for a Film of *Capital.*" Trans. Maciej Sliwowski, Jay Leyda, and Annette Michelson. *October*, no. 2 (Summer 1976): 3–26.

———. *Notes of a Film Director*. Trans. X. Danko. New York: Dover, 1970.

———. *Octobre: continuité photogrammatique intégrale*. Paris: Cinémathèque Universitaire, 1981.

———. *Octobre: découpage intégral*. Paris: Seuil, 1971.

———. "*Old and New.*" Trans. Erwin Honig. In *Film Writing Forms*, ed. Lewis Jacobs. New York: Gotham, 1934.

———. "One Path to Color." Trans. Jay Leyda. *Sight and Sound* 30, no. 2 (Spring 1961): 84–86, 102.

———. "Patriotism Is Our Theme." *International Literature*, no. 2 (1939): 91–94.

———. *Potemkin*. Trans. Gillon R. Aitken. New York: Simon and Schuster, 1968.

———. "Problems of Soviet Historical Films." Trans. J. Burke, P. Micciche, and L. Wagner. *Film Criticism* 3, no. 1 (Fall 1978): 1–16.

———. "Prometheus." Trans. François Albera et al. *Cahiers du Cinéma*, no. 307 (January 1980): 6–9.

———. *The Psychology of Composition*. Ed. and trans. Alan Upchurch. New York: Methuen, 1988.

———. *Que Viva Mexico!* London: Vision Press, 1951.

———. *Selected Works*. Vol. 1. Ed. and trans. Richard Taylor. Bloomington: Indiana University Press, 1988.

———. *Sergei M. Eisenstein's Potemkin*. Ed. David Mayer. New York: Grossman, 1972.

———. *The Short Fiction Scenario*. Trans. Alan Upchurch. New York: Methuen, 1988.

———. "Shot Montage of a Monologue from Pushkin's Drama *Boris Godunov.*" Ed. Herbert Marshall. Trans. B. P. Pockney. *Quarterly Review of Film Studies* 3, no. 2 (Spring 1978): 137–68.

————. "The Theatre of Mei Lan-fang." *Theatre Arts Monthly* 19, no. 10 (October 1935): 761–70.

————. *Three Films.* Ed. Jay Leyda. Trans. Diana Matias. New York: Harper, 1974.

————. *Unpublished Mexican Drawings.* Mexico City: Cinteca Nacional, 1978.

Eisenstein, Sergei, and Nikolai Cherkasov. "A Conversation in the Kremlin." *Encounter* 72, no. 2 (February 1989): 3–6.

Eisenstein, Sergei, and Sergei Tretyakov. "Expressive Movement." Trans. Alma Law. *Millennium Film Journal*, no. 3 (Winter–Spring 1979): 30–38.

"Eisenstein Says 'Adios.' " *Los Angeles Times*, December 7, 1930.

Eisler, Hans. *Composing for the Films.* London: Dobson, 1951.

Engels, Friedrich. *The Condition of the Working Class in England.* New York: Penguin, 1987.

Erlich, Victor. *Russian Formalism.* 2d ed., rev. The Hague: Mouton, 1965.

Ermolaev, Herman. *Soviet Literary Theories, 1917–1934.* Berkeley: University of California Press, 1963.

Fenollosa, Ernest. *The Chinese Written Character as a Medium for Poetry.* Ed. Ezra Pound. San Francisco: City Lights, 1936.

Fernandez, Dominique. *Eisenstein.* Paris: Grasset, 1975.

Ferro, Marc. *Cinéma et histoire.* Paris: Denoel/Gonthier, 1977.

————. "Le paradoxe du *Potemkin.*" *Cahiers du monde russe et soviétique* 30, no. 3–4 (July–December 1989): 293–95.

Le film muet soviétique. Brussels: Musée du Cinéma, 1965.

Fitzpatrick, Sheila. *The Commissariat of Enlightenment: Soviet Organization of Education and the Arts under Lunacharsky.* New York: Cambridge University Press, 1970.

————. "Cultural Revolution in Russia, 1928–1932." *Journal of Contemporary History* 9, no. 1 (January 1974): 33–52.

————. "Culture and Politics under Stalin: A Reappraisal." *Slavic Review* 35, no. 2 (June 1976): 211–31.

————. "The Emergence of Glaviskusstvo." *Soviet Studies* 23, no. 2 (October 1971): 236–53.

————. *The Russian Revolution 1917–1932.* New York: Oxford University Press, 1982.

————. "The 'Soft' Line on Culture and Its Enemies: Soviet Cultural Policy, 1922–1927." *Slavic Review* 33, no. 2 (June 1974): 267–87.

————, ed. *Cultural Revolution in Russia, 1928–1931.* Bloomington: Indiana University Press, 1978.

Gallez, Douglas W. "The Prokofiev-Eisenstein Collaboration." *Cinema Journal* 17, no. 2 (Spring 1978): 13–35.

Geduld, Harry M., and Ronald Gottesman, eds. *Sergei Eisenstein and Upton Sinclair: The Making and Unmaking of Que Viva Mexico!* Bloomington: Indiana University Press, 1970.

Gerould, Daniel. "Eisenstein's *Wiseman.*" *The Drama Review* 18, no. 1 (March 1974): 71–76.

————. "Historical Simulation and Popular Entertainment: The *Potemkin* Mutiny from Reconstructed Newsreel to Black Sea Stunt Men." *The Drama Review* 33, no. 2 (Summer 1989): 161–84.

Getty, J. Arch. *Origins of the Great Purges.* New York: Cambridge University Press, 1985.

Gibian, George, and H. W. Tjalsma, eds. *Russian Modernism.* Ithaca: Cornell University Press, 1976.

Gleason, Abbott, Peter Kenez, and Richard Stites, eds. *Bolshevik Culture.* Bloomington: Indiana University Press, 1985.

Godard, Jean-Luc. *Godard on Godard.* Ed. Jean Narboni and Tom Milne. Trans. Tom Milne. New York: Viking, 1972.

Gombrich, E. H. *Art and Illusion.* New York: Pantheon, 1960.

Goodwin, James. "Eisenstein: Ideology and Intellectual Cinema." *Quarterly Review of Film Studies* 3, no. 2 (Spring 1978): 169–92.

———. "The Object(ive)s of Cinema: Vertov (Factography) and Eisenstein (Ideography)." *Praxis*, no. 4 (1978): 223–30.

———. "Plusiers Eisensteins: Recent Criticism." *Quarterly Review of Film Studies* 6, no. 4 (Fall 1981): 391–412.

Gordon, Mel. "Eisenstein's Later Work at the Proletkult." *The Drama Review* 22, no. 3 (September 1978): 107–12.

———. "Meyerhold's Biomechanics." *The Drama Review* 18, no. 3 (September 1974): 73–88.

Gordon, Mel, and Alma Law. "Eisenstein's Early Work in Expressive Behavior." *Millennium Film Journal*, no. 3 (Winter/Spring 1979): 25–29.

Granet, Marcel. *La pensée chinoise.* Paris: Editions Albin Michel, 1950.

Gray, Camilla. *The Great Experiment: Russian Art 1863–1922.* London: Thames and Hudson, 1962.

Grey, Ian. *Ivan the Terrible.* London: Hodder and Stoughton, 1964.

Gruening, Ernest. *Mexico and Its Heritage.* New York: Appleton-Century, 1928.

Harvey, Sylvia. *May '68 and Film Culture.* London: BFI, 1978.

Henderson, Brian. *A Critique of Film Theory.* New York: Dutton, 1980.

Hill, Steven P. "Kuleshov — Prophet without Honor?" *Film Culture*, no. 44 (Spring 1967): 1–41.

———. "A Quantitative View of Soviet Cinema." *Cinema Journal* 11, no. 2 (Spring 1972): 18–25.

Hjelmslev, Louis. *Essais linguistiques.* Copenhagen: Nordisk Sprog, 1959.

Holthof, Marc, and Luk De Vos. "Dialectics as Ideology, and the Construction of Reality." In *Semiotics and Dialectics: Ideology and the Text*, ed. Peter V. Zima. Amsterdam: John Benjamins, 1981.

Hough, Richard. *The Potemkin Mutiny.* London: Hamilton, 1969.

Ivanov, Vyacheslav. "Eisenstein et la linguistique structurale moderne." Trans. Andrée Robel. *Cahiers du Cinéma*, no. 220–21 (May–June 1970): 47–50.

———. "Functions and Categories of Film Language." Trans. Stephen Rudy. *Russian Poetics in Translation* 8 (1981): 1–35.

Jacobs, Lewis, ed. *Film Writing Forms.* New York: Gotham, 1934.

Jameson, Fredric. *Marxism and Form.* Princeton: Princeton University Press, 1971.

————. *The Prison-House of Language*. Princeton: Princeton University Press, 1972.

Karetnikova, Inga, with Leon Steinmetz. *Mexico According to Eisenstein*. Albuquerque: University of New Mexico Press, 1991.

Kauffmann, Stanley. *Living Images*. New York: Harper, 1975.

Kenez, Peter. *The Birth of the Propaganda State: Soviet Methods of Mass Mobilization, 1917–1929*. New York: Cambridge University Press, 1985.

Kepley, Vance, Jr. "Building a National Cinema: Soviet Film Education, 1918–1934." *Wide Angle* 9, no. 3 (1987): 4–20.

————. "The Evolution of Eisenstein's *Old and New*." *Cinema Journal* 14, no. 1 (Fall 1974): 34–50.

————. *In the Service of the State: The Cinema of Alexander Dovzhenko*. Madison: University of Wisconsin Press, 1986.

————. "The Origins of Soviet Cinema: A Study in Industry Development." *Quarterly Review of Film Studies* 10, no. 1 (Winter 1975): 22–38.

Kepley, Vance, Jr., and Betty Kepley. "Foreign Films on Soviet Screens, 1922–1931." *Quarterly Review of Film Studies* 4, no. 4 (Fall 1979): 429–42.

Kinder, Marsha. "The Image of Patriarchal Power in *Young Mr. Lincoln* (1939) and *Ivan the Terrible*, Part 1 (1945)." *Film Quarterly* 39, no. 2 (Winter 1985–86): 29–49.

Kiralyfalvi, Béla. *The Aesthetics of Gyorgy Lukács*. Princeton: Princeton University Press, 1975.

Kleberg, Lars, and Håkan Lövgren, eds. *Eisenstein Revisited: A Collection of Essays*. Stockholm: Almqvist and Wiksell, 1987.

Kleiman, Naum, and K. Levina, eds. *Bronenosets Potemkin*. Moscow: Iskusstvo, 1969.

Kolchevska, Natasha. "The *Faktoviki* at the Movies." *Russian Language Journal* 41, no. 138–39 (1987): 139–51.

Korsh, Karl. *Karl Marx*. New York: Russell and Russell, 1963.

Kozintsev, Grigori. *King Lear: The Space of Tragedy*. Trans. Mary Mackintosh. Berkeley: University of California Press, 1977.

Kristeva, Julia. *Semeiotike*. Paris: Seuil, 1969.

Kuleshov, Lev. *Kuleshov on Film*. Ed. and trans. Ronald Levaco. Berkeley: University of California Press, 1974.

Kurbsky, Andrei. *The Correspondence between Prince A. M. Kurbsky and Tsar Ivan IV of Russia, 1564–1579*. Ed. and trans. J. L. Fennell. Cambridge: Cambridge University Press, 1955.

————. *Prince A. M. Kurbsky's History of Ivan IV*. Ed. and trans. J. L. Fennell. Cambridge: Cambridge University Press, 1965.

Lagny, Michèle, Marie-Claire Ropars-Wuilleumier, and Pierre Sorlin. *La révolution figurée: film, histoire, politique*. Paris: Editions Albatros, 1979.

Lary, Nikita. *Dostoevsky and Soviet Film*. Ithaca: Cornell University Press, 1986.

————. "Eisenstein's (Anti-)Theatrical Art, from Kino-Fist to Kino-Tragedy." *Slavic and East European Arts* 6, no. 2 (Winter 1990): 88–123.

Lebel, Jean-Patrick. *Cinéma et idéologie*. Paris: Editions Sociales, 1971.

Lenin, Vladimir I. *The Lenin Anthology*. Ed. Robert C. Tucker. New York: Norton, 1975.

———. *Selected Works*. New York: International, 1971.

Levaco, Ronald. "The Eisenstein-Prokofiev Correspondence." *Cinema Journal* 13, no. 1 (Fall 1973): 1–16.

Levine, Norma. "The Influence of the Kabuki Theater on the Films of Eisenstein." *Modern Drama* 12, no. 1 (May 1969): 18–29.

Lewin, Moshe. *Russian Peasants and Soviet Power: A Study of Collectivization*. Trans. Irene Nove. New York: Norton, 1975.

Leyda, Jay. "Between Explosions." *Film Quarterly* 23, no. 4 (Summer 1970): 33–38.

———. "Eisenstein's *Bezhin Meadow*." *Sight and Sound* 28, no. 2 (Spring 1959): 74–77, 105.

———. "Eisenstein's Mexican Tragedy." *Sight and Sound* 27, no. 6 (Autumn 1958): 305–8, 329.

———. *Kino: A History of the Russian and Soviet Film*. New York: Collier, 1973.

Leyda, Jay, and Zina Voynow. *Eisenstein at Work*. New York: Pantheon, 1982.

Lotman, Yuri. *Semiotics of Cinema*. Trans. Mark E. Suino. Ann Arbor: University of Michigan, 1976.

Lukács, Georg. *The Meaning of Contemporary Realism*. Trans. John and Necke Mander. London: Merlin, 1963.

———. *Studies in European Realism*. New York: Grosset, 1964.

———. *Writer and Critic*. Ed. and trans. Arthur D. Kahn. New York: Grosset, 1971.

Luxemburg, Rosa. *The Mass Strike*. Trans. Patrick Lavin. New York: Harper, 1971.

Macdonald, Dwight. *Dwight Macdonald on Movies*. Englewood Cliffs, N.J.: Prentice-Hall, 1969.

Maguire, Robert A. *Red Virgin Soil: Soviet Literature in the 1920s*. Princeton: Princeton University Press, 1968.

Mandel, Ernest. *Marxist Economic Theory*. 2 vols. Trans. Brian Pearce. New York: Monthly Review Press, 1968.

Mandelstam, Nadezhda. *Hope Abandoned*. Trans. Max Hayward. New York: Atheneum, 1974.

———. *Hope Against Hope: A Memoir*. Trans. Max Hayward. New York: Atheneum, 1970.

Marcuse, Herbert. *The Aesthetic Dimension: Toward a Critique of Marxist Aesthetics*. Boston: Beacon, 1978.

———. *Soviet Marxism: A Critical Analysis*. New York: Columbia University Press, 1958.

Marshall, Herbert, ed. *The Battleship Potemkin*. New York: Avon, 1978.

Marx, Karl. *Capital*. 3 vols. Trans. Samuel Moore and Edward Aveling. New York: International, 1967.

———. *Class Struggles in France*. New York: International, 1964.

———. *Economic and Philosophical Manuscripts of 1844*. Ed. Dirk Struik. Trans. Martin Milligan. New York: International, 1964.

Marx, Karl, and Friedrich Engels. *The German Ideology*. Moscow: Progress Publishers, 1976.

———. *The Holy Family*. Trans. Richard Dixon and Clemens Dutt. Moscow: Progress Publishers, 1975.

———. *The Marx-Engels Reader*. Ed. Robert C. Tucker. New York: Norton, 1972.

Matejka, Ladislav, and Krystyna Pomorska, eds. *Readings in Russian Poetics*. Cambridge, Mass.: MIT Press, 1971.

Mathewson, Rufus. "The First Writers' Congress: A Second Look." In *Literature and Revolution in Soviet Russia, 1917–1962*, ed. Max Hayward and Leopold Labedz. New York: Oxford University Press, 1963.

Mayne, Judith. *Kino and the Woman Question: Feminism and Soviet Silent Film*. Columbus: Ohio State University Press, 1989.

Medvedev, Roy A. *Let History Judge*. Ed. David Joravsky and George Haupt. Trans. Colleen Taylor. New York: Knopf, 1971.

Medvedev, Zhores A. *Soviet Agriculture*. New York: Norton, 1987.

Metz, Christian. *The Imaginary Signifier: Psychoanalysis and the Cinema*. Trans. Celia Britton et al. Bloomington: Indiana University Press, 1982.

———. *Langage et cinéma*. Paris: Larousse, 1971.

Meyerhold, Vsevolod. *Meyerhold on Theatre*. Ed. and trans. Edward Braun. New York: Hill and Wang, 1969.

Mitry, Jean. *Eisenstein*. Rev. and enl. Paris: Editions Universitaires, 1978.

Montagu, Ivor. *With Eisenstein in Hollywood*. New York: International, 1969.

Morin, Edgar. *Le cinéma, ou l'homme imaginaire*. Paris: Minuit, 1958.

Moussinac, Léon. *Sergei Eisenstein*. Trans. D. Sandy Petrey. New York: Crown, 1970.

Narboni, Jean. "Le hors-cadre décide de tout." *Cahiers du Cinéma*, no. 271 (November 1976): 14–21.

Nestyev, Israel V. *Sergei Prokofiev*. Trans. Rose Prokofieva. New York: Knopf, 1946.

Nichols, Bill. *Ideology and the Image*. Bloomington: Indiana University Press, 1981.

Nilsen, Vladimir. *The Cinema as a Graphic Art*. Trans. Stephen Garry. New York: Hill and Wang, 1941.

Nizhny, Vladimir. *Lessons with Eisenstein*. Trans. and ed. Ivor Montagu and Jay Leyda. New York: Hill and Wang, 1962.

Oudart, Jean-Pierre. "Sur *Ivan le Terrible*." *Cahiers du Cinéma*, no. 218 (March 1970): 15–22.

Payne, Robert, and Nikita Romanoff. *Ivan the Terrible*. New York: Crowell, 1975.

Paz, Octavio. *The Labyrinth of Solitude*. Trans. Lysander Kemp. New York: Grove, 1961.

Petric, Vlada. *Constructivism in Film: The Man with the Movie Camera*. New York: Cambridge University Press, 1987.

Pirog, Gerald. "Iconicity and Narrative: The Vertov-Eisenstein Controversy." *Semiotica* 39, no. 3–4 (1982): 297–313.

Platonov, Sergei F. *Ivan the Terrible*. Ed. and trans. Josephy L. Wieczynski. Gulf Breeze, Fla.: Academic International Press, 1974.

Pokrovsky, M. N. *Brief History of Russia*. Trans. D. S. Mirsky. 2 vols. 1933. Reprint. Orono, Maine: University Prints, 1968.

Polan, Dana B. *The Political Language of Film and the Avant-Garde*. Ann Arbor: UMI Research Press, 1985.

Prendergast, Roy M. *Film Music*. New York: Norton, 1977.

Presniakov, A. E. *The Formation of the Great Russian State*. Trans. A. E. Moorhouse. Chicago: Quadrangle, 1970.

Pudovkin, Vsevolod I. *Film Technique and Film Acting*. Ed. and trans. Ivor Montagu. New York: Grove, 1970.

Rabinowitch, Alexander. *The Bolsheviks Come to Power*. New York: Norton, 1976.

Reed, John. *Ten Days That Shook the World*. New York: International, 1967.

Reeder, Roberta. "Agit-Prop Art: Posters, Puppets, Propaganda and Eisenstein's *Strike*." *Russian Literature Triquarterly*, no. 22 (1989): 255–78.

Riasanovsky, Nicholas V. *A History of Russia*. 2d ed. New York: Oxford University Press, 1969.

Roberts, Philip D. "Prokofiev's Score and Cantata for Eisenstein's *Alexander Nevsky*." *Semiotica* 21, no. 1–2 (1977): 151–66.

Robinson, David. "The Two *Bezhin Meadows*." *Sight and Sound* 37, no. 1 (Winter 1967–68): 33–37.

Ropars-Wuilleumier, Marie-Claire. *L'écran de la mémoire*. Paris: Seuil, 1970.

Ropars-Wuilleumier, Marie-Claire, and Pierre Sorlin. *Octobre: écriture et idéologie*. Paris: Editions Albatros, 1976.

Rosen, Philip, ed. *Narrative, Apparatus, Ideology*. New York: Columbia University Press, 1986.

Rosenberg, William G., ed. *Bolshevik Visions*. 2d ed. Ann Arbor: University of Michigan Press, 1990.

Schmidt, Paul, ed. *Meyerhold at Work*. Austin: University of Texas Press, 1980.

Schnitzer, Luda and Jean, and Marcel Martin, eds., *Cinema in Revolution*. Trans. David Robinson. New York: Hill and Wang, 1973.

Schwarz, Solomon. *The Russian Revolution of 1905*. Trans. Gertrude Vakar. Chicago: University of Chicago Press, 1967.

Screen Reader 1: Cinema/Ideology/Politics. London: Society for Education in Film and Television, 1977.

Selden, Daniel. "Vision and Violence: The Rhetoric of *Potemkin*." *Quarterly Review of Film Studies* 7, no. 4 (Fall 1982): 309–29.

Seton, Marie. "Eisenstein's Images and Mexican Art." *Sight and Sound* 23, no. 1 (July–September 1958): 8–13.

———. "Jottings for *Que Viva Mexico*." *Film Art*, no. 4 (Summer 1934): 79–80.

———. *Sergei M. Eisenstein*. New York: Wyn, 1952.

———. "Treasure Trove." *Sight and Sound* 8, no. 31 (Autumn 1939): 89–92.

Shklovsky, Viktor. *Eisenstein*. Moscow: Iskusstvo, 1973.

———. *Zhili-byli*. Moscow: Sovetsky Pisatel, 1964.

Short, K. R. M., ed. *Feature Films as History*. Knoxville: University of Tennessee Press, 1981.

Short, K. R. M., and Richard Taylor. "Soviet Cinema and the International Menace, 1928–1939." *Historical Journal of Film, Radio and Television* 6, no. 2 (1986): 131–59.

Slonim, Marc. *Soviet Russian Literature*. 2d ed., rev. New York: Oxford University Press, 1977.

Smith, Paul, ed. *The Historian and Film*. New York: Cambridge University Press, 1976.

Sorel, Georges. *Reflections on Violence*. Trans. T. E. Hulme. New York: Collier, 1950.

Sorlin, Pierre. *The Soviet People and Their Society*. Trans. Daniel Weissbort. New York: Praeger, 1969.

Stalin, Joseph. *The Essential Stalin*. Ed. Bruce Franklin. New York: Doubleday, 1972.

Stites, Richard. *Revolutionary Dreams: Utopian Vision and Experimental Life in the Russian Revolution*. New York: Oxford University Press, 1989.

Struve, Gleb. *Russian Literature under Lenin and Stalin, 1917–1953*. Norman: University of Oklahoma Press, 1971.

Swallow, Norman. *Eisenstein: A Documentary Portrait*. New York: Dutton, 1977.

Taylor, Richard. "Boris Shumyatsky and the Soviet Cinema in the 1930s." *Historical Journal of Film, Radio and Television* 6, no. 1 (1986): 43–64.

———. "A 'Cinema for the Millions': Soviet Socialist Realism and the Problem of Film Comedy." *Journal of Contemporary History* 18, no. 3 (July 1983): 439–61.

———. *The Politics of the Soviet Cinema, 1917–1929*. New York: Cambridge University Press, 1979.

Taylor, Richard, and Ian Christie, eds. *The Film Factory: Russian and Soviet Cinema in Documents*. Trans. Richard Taylor. Cambridge, Mass.: Harvard University Press, 1988.

Thompson, Kristen. *Breaking the Glass Armor: Neoformalist Film Analysis*. Princeton: Princeton University Press, 1988.

———. "The Concept of Cinematic Excess." *Ciné-Tracts* 1, no. 2 (Summer 1977): 54–63.

———. *Eisenstein's Ivan the Terrible*. Princeton: Princeton University Press, 1981.

———. "*Ivan the Terrible* and Stalinist Russia: A Reexamination." *Cinema Journal* 17, no. 1 (Fall 1977): 30–43.

———. "Non-Classical Spatial Structures in *Ivan the Terrible*: A Sample Analysis." *1977 Film Studies Annual* (Part 1): 57–64.

Todorov, Tzvetan, ed. and trans. *Théorie de la littérature*. Paris: Seuil, 1965.

Trotsky, Leon. *On Literature and Art*. Ed. Paul N. Siegel. New York: Pathfinder, 1970.

Tucker, Robert C. *The Soviet Political Mind*. Rev. ed. New York: Norton, 1971.

———. *Stalin as Revolutionary, 1879–1929*. New York: Norton, 1973.

———. *Stalin in Power: The Revolution from Above, 1928–1941*. New York: Norton, 1990.

———, ed. *Stalinism: Essays in Historical Interpretation*. New York: Norton, 1977.

Turgenev, Ivan. "Bezhin Lea." In *Sketches from a Hunter's Album*, trans. Richard Freeborn. Baltimore: Penguin, 1967.

Tynyanov, Yuri. "Plot and Story-line in the Cinema" (1926). Trans. Ann Shukman. *Russian Poetics in Translation* 5 (1978): 20–21.

Ulmer, Gregory L. *Applied Grammatology*. Baltimore: Johns Hopkins University Press, 1985.

Uspensky, Boris. *"Historia sub specie semioticae."* In *Soviet Semiotics: An Anthology*, ed. and trans. Daniel P. Lucid. Baltimore: Johns Hopkins University Press, 1977.

Van Wert, William F. "Eisenstein and Kabuki." *Criticism* 20, no. 4 (Fall 1978): 403–20.

———. "Intertitles." *Sight and Sound* 49, no. 2 (Spring 1980): 98–105.

Veissfeld, Ilya. "Mon dernier entretien avec Eisenstein." *Cahiers du Cinéma*, no. 208 (January 1969): 18–21.

Vertov, Dziga. *Articles, journaux, projets*. Ed. and trans. Sylviane Mossé and Andrée Robel. Paris: 10/18, 1972.

———. *Kino-Eye*. Ed. Annette Michelson. Trans. Kevin O'Brien. Berkeley: University of California Press, 1984.

Völker, Klaus. *Brecht Chronicle*. Trans. Fred Wieck. New York: Seabury, 1975.

Volosinov, V. N. *Marxism and the Philosophy of Language*. Trans. Ladislav Matejka and I. R. Titunik. Cambridge, Mass.: Harvard University Press, 1986.

Vygotsky, Lev S. *Thought and Language*. Ed. and trans. Eugenia Hanfmann and Gertrude Vakar. Cambridge, Mass.: MIT Press, 1962.

White, Hayden. *The Content of the Form: Narrative Discourse and Historical Representation*. Baltimore: Johns Hopkins University Press, 1987.

———. *Metahistory: The Historical Imagination in Nineteenth-Century Europe*. Baltimore: Johns Hopkins University Press, 1973.

Wollen, Peter. *Readings and Writings*. London: NLB, 1982.

———. *Signs and Meaning in the Cinema*. Bloomington: Indiana University Press, 1969.

Woroszylski, Wiktor. *The Life of Mayakovsky*. Trans. Boleslaw Taborski. New York: Orion, 1970.

Worrall, Nick. "Meyerhold and Eisenstein." In *Performance and Politics in Popular Drama*, ed. David Bradby, Louis James, and Bernard Sharratt. New York: Cambridge University Press, 1980.

———. "Meyerhold's Production of *The Magnificent Cuckold*." *The Drama Review* 17, no. 1 (March 1973): 14–34.

Youngblood, Denise J. *Soviet Cinema in the Silent Era, 1918–1935*. Ann Arbor: UMI Research Press, 1985.

Zenkovsky, Serge A., ed. and trans. *Medieval Russia's Epics, Chronicles, and Tales*. Rev. ed. New York: Dutton, 1974.

Zolkovsky, Alexander K. "Generative Poetics in the Writings of Eisenstein." Trans. L. M. O'Toole. *Russian Poetics in Translation* 8 (1981): 40–61.

Zolkovsky, Alexander K., and J. K. Sceglov. "Structural Poetics Is a Generative Poetics." In *Soviet Semiotics: An Anthology*, ed. and trans. Daniel P. Lucid. Baltimore: Johns Hopkins University Press, 1977.

Index

ABC of Communism, The (Bukharin and Preobrazhensky), 99, 101
Agadzhanova-Shutko, Nina, 57
Albera, François, 12
Alexander Nevsky, 2, 135; analyzed, 162–78, 210–11; and historical record, 157–60, 163; production of, 156, 159–60, 162, 171–72, 174; withdrawn from distribution, 177–78
Alexandrov, Grigori, 20, 34, 81, 102, 114, 120, 139, 174; *The Circus*, 147; *The Happy Guys*, 147
Amengual, Barthélemy, 11
American Tragedy, An, project, 2, 127–29, 143
Andrew, Dudley, 11–12
Anisimov, Ivan, 138
Annenkov, Yuri: *The First Distiller*, 22
Aristarco, Guido, 14
Aristotle, 55, 61–62
Arnheim, Rudolf, 71
Arvatov, Boris, 104
Audiovisual montage, 114, 117, 121–22, 126–29, 131, 153, 174–76, 204, 205–9
Aumont, Jacques, 13

Babel, Isaac, 139, 153–54, 162
Bakhtin, Mikhail, 46, 96–97, 213–14, 228–29n.29; *The Formal Method in Literary Scholarship*, 96
Balázs, Béla, 33, 55, 72
Barna, Yon, 10
Barthes, Roland, 43, 148
Battleship Potemkin, 30–31, 38, 40, 51, 103, 211, 213, 214; analyzed, 58–70, 74–77; criticism on, 43, 67, 145, 177, 212; and historical record, 57–59, 65; production of, 57–60, 70
Baudelaire, Charles, 76
Bazin, André, 12, 33, 92–93, 106, 213, 219

Benjamin, Walter, 124; art production, 8, 43, 50, 51, 53; shock effect, 8, 76–77
Benveniste, Emile, 3
Bergman, Ingmar, 136
Bezhin Meadow, 2; analyzed, 150–55; banned, 148–49, 153–54; production of, 150–51, 153
Biomechanics, 23–24, 28, 30
Black Consul, The, script, 149, 210
Bloch, Ernst, 143; the principle of hope, 8, 104, 109; the utopian projection, 8, 79, 104
Bogatyr, 157
Bolshakov, Ivan, 149
Bordwell, David, 12
Boris Godunov (Pushkin), 179–80, 190
Brecht, Bertolt, 26, 139, 143, 154; construction in art, 54–55; distantiation, 8, 51, 94, 117, 155; *The Rise and Fall of the City of Mahagonny*, 26, 124–25; social gest, 8
Brief History of Russia (Pokrovsky), 157–58, 183
Brik, Osip, 94, 95
Bukharin, Nikolai, 99, 100, 101, 140
Buñuel, Luis, 135; *Un chien andalou*, 74
Burch, Noel, 35–36
Burov, Andrei, 103–4

Capital project, 4, 10, 102, 119, 120–26, 143, 202
Cendrars, Blaise, 126
Championship of the Universal Class Struggle, The (Mayakovsky), 22
Chapayev (film, the Vasilievs), 140, 148, 164, 166
Chapayev (novel, Furmanov), 148
Chaplin, Charlie: *The Great Dictator*, 173, 217; *Modern Times*, 217
Charlot, Jean, 132

Cherkasov, Nikolai, 206, 215
Chiaureli, Mikhail, 212; *The Vow*, 212–13
Cinefication, 31–32, 34, 36
Cinema for the Millions, A (Shumyatsky), 147, 148
Cinema speech, 92–96
Clark, Katerina, 143, 161
Color cinema, 204–5, 219–20
Constructivism, 22–23, 28–29, 35, 52, 103–4
Cultural revolution, 82, 94–95, 97, 140–43, 145–46
Crommelynck, Fernand, 21

Dali, Salvador: *Un chien andalou*, 74
Danton, 33
Death of Tarelkin, The (Meyerhold), 21
De George, Richard T., 125
Deleuze, Gilles, 15
Dialectical materialism, 3–4, 5, 145
Dinamov, Sergei, 148
Discourse, 3, 36; in *Strike*, 43, 47–48, 51; in *Potemkin*, 67–70; in *October*, 108, 109; in *Capital* project, 121–22
Djilas, Milovan, 161–62
Dr. Mabuse der Spieler (Lang), 33
Donskoy, Dmitri, 158, 159–60
Dovzhenko, Alexander, 139, 140; *Earth*, 110, 152
Do You Hear, Moscow? (Proletkult production), 29, 31–32, 70
Dreiser, Theodore, 127, 129
Dukelsky, Semyon, 149
Duncan, Isadora, 23

Earth (Dovzhenko), 110, 152
Eccentrism, 22, 27–28, 29, 41
Ecstasy, 218; in *Old and New*, 99, 103, 107, 115, 117; in *Bezhin Meadow*, 153–54; in *Alexander Nevsky*, 176–77; in *Ivan the Terrible*, 193
Eikhenbaum, Boris, 92, 144
Eisenstein, Sergei: army service, 20; career, 1–2, 8, 9, 10, 16–17, 120, 125–26, 129, 138–40, 144–45, 150, 181; compared with Brecht, 8–9, 54–55; compared with Vertov, 53–56; criticism on, 9–15; family, 17; graphic art, 17–19, 40, 41, 45, 71–73, 137–38, 155; and homosexuality, 10, 11, 135; theater work, 19–32; and the utopian dimension, 43–44,

210. Writings: "A Dialectic Approach to Film Form," 76; "Expressive Movement," 30–31, 34; *Nonindifferent Nature*, 186, 206–7, 211, 216–19; "The Problem of the Materialist Approach to Form," 4, 50–56; "Problems of Soviet Historical Films," 179–80; "The Structure of the Film," 176–77; "Vertical Montage," 175–76
Eisler, Hans, 175
El Greco, 201
El Lissitzky, 116
Engels, Friedrich, 6–7, 37, 144–45, 217; *Anti-Dühring*, 152–53; *Dialectics of Nature*, 145, 219. See also dialectical materialism
Ensor, James, 155
Enthusiasm (Vertov), 127
Extraordinary Adventures of Mr. West in the Land of The Bolsheviks, The (Kuleshov), 146

Fantômas (Feuillade), 33
Faust (Murnau), 60
Feinzimmer, Alexander: *Lieutenant Kije*, 160, 171
Fenollosa, Ernest, 116
Ferghana Canal project, 170, 188
Fernandez, Dominique, 11
Ferro, Marc, 3
Feuillade, Louis: *Fantômas*, 33
Fitzgerald, Sheila, 38
Ford, John: *Young Mr. Lincoln*, 185
Foregger, Nikolai, 21
Formalism, 11, 14, 27, 29, 52–53, 92, 96, 114, 217; condemned, 95, 139
Frazer, Sir James, 137, 217
Freud, Sigmund: *Jokes and Their Relation to the Unconscious*, 123; *Totem and Taboo*, 144
Furmanov, Dmitri, 164; *Chapayev* (novel), 148
Futurism, 20, 21, 25, 31, 44, 94

Gan, Alexei, 23, 29
Gas Masks (Proletkult production), 29–30, 31–32, 70
Gelovani, Mikhail, 161, 167, 212
General Line, The. See Old and New
Genette, Gerard, 3
Gerasimov, Sergei, 178

Gilded Rot, 33
Glass House, The, project, 122–23, 126, 130
Godard, Jean-Luc, 51–52, 136
Gombrich, E. H., 71–72
Gorky, Maxim, 142
Goya, Francisco de, 134, 155
Great Dictator, The (Chaplin), 173, 217
Griffith, D. W., 35, 63, 127, 199–200
Grosz, Georg, 28, 72, 123

Henderson, Brian, 12
Henry V (Olivier), 178
Hill, Steven, 102
Historiography. *See* Lenin; Marx; Stalin
History: as Eisenstein's subject matter, 1–3, 15, 177–80, 183–85, 210–20; of Russia 16, 18, 37–38; Soviet, 2, 69–70
History of the Communist Party of the Soviet Union, 219
History of the Russian State (Karamzin), 195
Hitchcock, Alfred: *Murder!*, 127
Hjelmslev, Louis, 95
Humboldt, Wilhelm von, 137

Ideology, 5–7, 28, 95–97, 221n.7; in *Strike*, 48–50; in *Potemkin*, 60–70, 78; in *October*, 82–83; in *Old and New*, 106–8, 111–14, 117–19; in *Capital* project, 122–23
In Favor of a World Commune, 80
Intellectual cinema, 4, 50, 111–19, 120–23
Intellectual montage. *See* Intellectual cinema
Ivanov, Vyacheslav, 12
Ivan the Terrible, 2, 4, 120–21, 167, 174; analyzed, 181–82, 184–218; ban on part 2, 184, 185–86; criticism on, 13, 14, 43; and historical record, 181–82, 186–90, 192–93, 195, 197–98, 209; production of, 181

Jakobson, Roman, 53
Jameson, Fredric, 7
Joyce, James: *Ulysses*, 102, 122, 143

Kabuki theater, 116–17
Karamzin, Nikolai: *History of the Russian State*, 195
Kauffmann, Stanley, 67

Kepley, Vance, 102
Kerensky, Alexander, 18, 81; represented in *October*, 85–87
Khan, Aga, 121
Khlebnikov, Velimir, 94
Kinonedelya (Vertov), 33
Kinopravda (Vertov), 32–33
Kleiman, Naum, 151
Kornilov, General Lavr, 18, 88, 89; represented in *October*, 86–87
Kostylyov, Valentin, 184
Kozintsev, Grigori, 22, 181, 186
Kozlov, Leonid, 180
Kracauer, Siegfried, 3
Kristeva, Julia, 93
Kronstadt, 70
Kuleshov, Lev, 28, 33–35; *The Extraordinary Adventures of Mr. West in the Land of the Bolsheviks*, 146
Kurth, Julius, 116

Lagny, Michèle, 13
Lang, Fritz, 40; *Dr. Mabuse der Spieler*, 33; *Metropolis*, 60
Large-scale shot, 75, 199–200
Last Laugh, The (Murnau), 60
Lawrence, D. H.: *The Plumed Serpent*, 152
Lawrence of Arabia, 155
Lazarenko, Vitali, 22
Lebel, Jean-Patrick, 14
Lemaître, Frederick, 216
Lenin, 2, 4, 7, 25, 92, 113; on dialectics, 117–18; historiography, 83, 86, 157; iconography, in *Old and New*, 112–14; policy on peasants, 99, 101; represented in *October*, 83–84, 90–91, 95; on revolution, 37, 49, 57, 58; *What Is to Be Done?*, 16, 98–99
Lenin in 1918 (Romm), 161
Lenin in October (Romm), 161
Lévy-Bruhl, Lucien, 137
Lewin, Moshe, 102
Leyda, Jay, 130, 150, 153
Lieutenant Kije (Feinzimmer), 160, 171
London, Jack, 25
Love of a Poet, The, project, 179–81
Lubitsch, Ernst, 127; *To Be or Not To Be*, 173–74
Lukács, Georg, 143; the epic, 8; typicality, 8, 73–74
Lunacharsky, Anatoli, 24, 75, 84, 95, 146
Luxemburg, Rosa, 37

Machiavelli, Niccolo: *The Prince*, 183
Magnificent Cuckold, The (Meyerhold), 21–22, 23
Malevich, Kazimir, 41
Mandelstam, Nadezhda, 159
Mandelstam, Osip, 159, 162
Marcuse, Herbert, 104
Marx, Karl: historiography, 3, 4–8, 73, 79–80, 99, 120–21, 182–83, 186, 195. Writings: *Capital*, 6, 7, 38, 108, 120, 123–24; *Class Struggles in France*, 120; *A Contribution to the Critique of Political Economy*, 7; *1844 Manuscripts*, 79–80, 109; *The 18th Brumaire of Louis Bonaparte*, 4, 87, 182–83; *The Holy Family*, 4
Marx, Karl, and Friedrich Engels: *Communist Manifesto*, 7, 45, 79, 186; *The German Ideology*, 6, 145
Marxism: critique in, 5, 8; development of, 3–4, 7–9, 118, 144–45, 219; within Eisenstein's cinema, 1, 8, 9–15, 43, 61, 80–82, 96–97; utopian dimension of, 98–99. *See also* Bloch; *Capital* project
Mayakovsky, Vladimir, 41, 80, 84, 95, 113, 129; *The Championship of the Universal Class Struggle*, 22; *Mystery-Bouffe*, 20
Medvedev, Pavel: *The Formal Method in Literary Scholarship*, 96
Medvedev, Roy A., 140
Mei Lan-fang, 154–55
Méliès, Georges, 32
Melville, Herman: *Moby-Dick*, 168
Merkourov, 178
Metropolis (Lang), 60
Metz, Christian, 12
Mexican, The (Proletkult production), 25, 41
Meyerhold, Vsevolod, 19, 20–21, 24, 27, 31, 36, 139, 144, 155, 162, 180; *The Death of Tarelkin*, 21; *The Magnificent Cuckold*, 21–22, 23. *See also* Biomechanics
Minikh, O., 152
Minin and Pozharsky (Pudovkin), 160
Mitry, Jean, 11, 92, 98, 108
MMM script, 149
Moby-Dick (Melville), 168
Modern Times (Chaplin), 217
Molotov, Vyacheslav, 181
Montage, 4, 7, 11, 12–14, 28–29, 32, 51–

52. *See also* Audiovisual montage; Intellectual cinema; Kuleshov; Montage of attractions; Pudovkin; Vertical montage
Montage of attractions: in theater, 27–28; in film, 47–50, 55–56, 63, 67, 75–77
Morin, Edgar, 78
Moscow script, 149–50, 155
Moskvin, Andrei, 181
Moussinac, Léon, 11, 81, 82–83
Murder! (Hitchcock), 127
Murnau, F. W.: *Faust*, 60; *The Last Laugh*, 60
Mussorgsky, Modest, 171, 190
Mystery-Bouffe (Mayakovsky), 20
Mystery of Freed Labor, The, 80
Myth, 137, 148, 219; in *Bezhin Meadow*, 151, 152–53, 154; in *Alexander Nevsky*, 165–70; in *Ivan the Terrible*, 213

Narrative, 3, 35–36; in *Strike*, 43, 45, 47–48, 51, 71; in *Potemkin*, 58–59, 62–64, 66–67, 74; in *Old and New*, 104–5, 118; in *Capital* project, 121–23; in *Ivan the Terrible*, 182, 186–95
Neoformalism, 14
Nikandrov, Vasili, 95, 113
Nilsen, Vladimir, 114
1905 Revolution, 17, 37–38, 49, 57–59

October, 17, 31, 38, 51, 105, 183, 201, 202, 213, 214; analyzed, 83–95; censorship, 81; criticism on, 13–14, 91, 92–95, 145; and historical record, 83–85; production of, 81–82
October Revolution, 18, 83–85, 90
Old and New, 17, 38, 51, 156, 214; analyzed, 102–15, 216; censorship (*The General Line*), 81–82, 102; criticism on, 13, 145; production of (*The General Line*), 80–82, 101–4
Olivier, Laurence: *Henry V*, 178
Orozco, José, 133
Ostrovsky, Alexander, 25

Panofsky, Erwin, 53
Paramount Studios, 120, 127, 129
Pathos, 82, 85, 92, 98, 103, 114, 123; in *Strike*, 49, 59; in *Potemkin*, 60–70, 74–78; in *Alexander Nevsky*, 171; in *Ivan the Terrible*, 211, 214, 216–18
Pavlenko, Pyotr, 159, 162, 212

Paz, Octavio, 136–37
Pertsov, Viktor, 94
Peter I, 160–61, 199
Piotrovsky, Adrian, 95
Piranesi, Giambattista, 155, 211
Pisarev, D. I., 98
Piscator, Erwin, 154
Plumed Serpent, The (Lawrence), 152
Podvoisky, Nikolai, 92
Pokrovsky, M. N., 158; *Brief History of
    Russia*, 157–58, 183
Posada, José Guadalupe, 19, 136
Potemkin. See Battleship Potemkin
Preobrazhensky, Evgeni, 99, 101
Prokofiev, Sergei, 160, 170; *Alexander Nev-
    sky*, 171–73; *Ivan the Terrible*, 199,
    206–9; *Semyon Kotko*, 170
Proletkult 20, 24–30, 36, 52
Propaganda, 24
Pudovkin, Vsevolod, 33, 35, 71, 76, 114,
    116, 189; *Minin and Pozharsky*, 160
Pushkin, Alexander, 179; *Boris Godunov*,
    179–80, 190

Que Viva Mexico!, 2, 40, 129–37, 149, 162–
    63, 214

Rabinowitch, Alexander, 83, 90
Radek, Karl, 143
Reed, John, 129, 135; *Ten Days That Shook
    the World*, 81
Reeder, Roberta, 41
Revolutionary history, 1, 158; in *Strike*, 37–
    38; in *Potemkin*, 57–60; in *October*, 82–
    85, 88–91; in *Old and New*, 98–99,
    118–19. *See also* Lenin
Rivera, Diego, 129
Rivette, Jacques, 130
Robeson, Paul, 149
Rodchenko, Alexander, 28
Romanov, Mikhail, 156
Romm, Mikhail, 156, 178; *Lenin in 1918*,
    161; *Lenin in October*, 161
Ropars-Wuilleumier, Marie-Claire, 13–14,
    91
Rzheshevsky, Alexander, 150–51

Selznick, David O., 129
Seton, Marie, 10
Sharaku, 116

Shklovsky, Viktor, 52–53, 76, 95, 160, 162
Shostakovich, Dmitri, 160, 171
Shub, Esther, 33, 94–95, 138
Shumyatsky, Boris, 146, 149, 154; *A Cin-
    ema for the Millions*, 147, 148
Sinclair, Mary, 129–30
Sinclair, Upton, 129–30, 138
Siqueiros, David, 132
Socialist realism, 112, 139, 142–45, 147–
    49, 156–57
Solovyov, Vladimir, 184
Sorel, Georges, 49
Sorlin, Pierre, 13–14
Specular motifs: in *Strike*, 40, 48; in *Potem-
    kin*, 65–66, 74–76; in *Ivan the Terrible*,
    195, 199–204
Stakhanov, Alexei, 157, 162
Stakhanovite, 157, 165
Stalin, 2, 4, 92, 112, 140; and cult of lead-
    ership, 157–62, 165, 166–67, 177, 184,
    195, 213; and dialectical materialism,
    125–26; historiography, 141–42, 158–
    62, 184, 195, 219; involvement in Ei-
    senstein's career, 82, 138, 156, 181; pol-
    icy on peasants, 100–101; and the
    purges, 197–98; and revolution from
    above, 145, 195–96, 211
Stanislavsky, Constantin, 24, 26, 27, 144
Sternberg, Josef von, 129
Stites, Richard, 99
Strike, 4, 59, 63, 65; analyzed, 38–50; pro-
    duction of, 36–37
Susanin, Ivan, 156
Sutter's Gold project, 2, 126–27, 138

Tarich, Yuri: *Wings of a Serf*, 183
Tatlin, Vladimir, 80, 104
Ten Days That Shook the World (Reed), 81
Textuality, 12–14
Thompson, Kristin, 14
Tisse, Eduard, 32, 60, 114, 120, 139, 181
To Be or Not To Be (Lubitsch), 173–74
Tolstoy, Alexei, 184
Trauberg, Leonid, 22, 148, 181
Tretyakov, Sergei, 26, 29–30, 54, 139, 154,
    162
Trotsky, Leon, 2, 81–82, 84, 91, 141
Turgenev, Ivan, 150
Tynyanov, Yuri, 52, 76, 114, 160, 185, 217
Typage, 70–74, 76–77

Uccello, Paolo, 169
Udarniki, 157
Ulysses (Joyce), 102, 122, 143
Un chien andalou (Dali and Buñuel), 74
Uspensky, Boris, 199

Vasiliev, Georgi: *Chapayev*, 140, 148, 164, 166
Vasiliev, Sergei: *Chapayev*, 140, 148, 164, 166
Vertical montage, 175–76
Vertov, Dziga, 32–33, 35, 36; *Enthusiasm*, 127; factography in cinema, 53–56, 71–72; *Kinonedelya*, 33; *Kinopravda*, 32–33
Volosinov, V. N.: *Marxism and the Philosophy of Language*, 96–97, 117, 144
Vow, The (Chiaureli), 212–13
Vygotsky, Lev: *Thought and Language*, 144

Wagner, Richard, 176; *Die Walküre*, 170, 179
Walküre, Die (the Eisenstein production), 170, 179, 180
Weill, Kurt, 124
White, Hayden, 3
Wings of a Serf (Tarich), 183
Wise Man, The (Proletkult production), 25–28, 32
Wollen, Peter, 12

Yagoda, Genrikh, 198
Yezhov, Nikolai, 198
Young Mr. Lincoln (Ford), 185
Yutkevitch, Sergei, 22, 27, 151

Zhdanov, Andrei, 142, 181
Zola, Emile, 102, 118, 149